THE NATURE OF
MATHEMATICAL THINKING

Edited by:

Robert J. Sternberg
Talia Ben-Zeev
Yale University

LAWRENCE ERLBAUM ASSOCIATES, PUBLISHERS
1996   Mahwah, NJ

Lawrence Erlbaum Associates, Inc., Publishers
10 Industrial Avenue
Mahwah, NJ 07430

Cover design by Mairav Salomon-Dekel

Library of Congress Cataloging-in-Publication Data

The nature of mathematical thinking / edited by Robert J. Sternberg and
Talia Ben-Zeev
p. cm.
Includes bibilographical references and index.
ISBN 0-8058-1798-0 (cloth : alk. paper). —ISBN 0-8058-
1799-9 (pbk. : alk. paper)
1. Mathematical ability. 2. Mathematical ability—Cross cultural
studies. 3. Number concept in children. 4. Number concept in children—Cross-cultural studies. 5. Human information processing. 6.
—Cognitive psychology. I. Sternberg, Robert J. II. Ben-Zeev, Talia.
BF456.N7N35 1996
153.4'2—dc20
96-12023
CIP

Books published by Lawrence Erlbaum Associates are printed on acid-free
paper, and their bindings are chosen for strength and durability.

Printed in the United States of America
10 9 8 7 6 5 4 3 2 1

Contents

Preface

Why do some children seem to learn mathematics easily and others slave away at it, learning it only with great effort and apparent pain? Why do some of the shining lights of elementary school, high school, and even college mathematics dazzle people at one stage of mathematics learning and performance, and then fizzle out ignominiously at the next stage? Why are some people good at algebra but terrible at geometry, or vice versa? How can people who successfully run a business have failed math earlier, and conversely, how come some professional mathematicians can balance a checkbook only with difficulty? Why do school children in the United States perform so dismally on international comparisons?

These are the kinds of real and important questions we set out to answer, or at least address, when we decided to edit this book on mathematical thinking. Our goal was to seek a diversity of contributors representing multiple points of view whose expertise might converge on the answers to these and other pressing and, we believe, interesting questions regarding mathematical thinking.

This book is addressed to a varied audience: psychologists interested in the nature of mathematical thinking and mathematical abilities, computer scientists interested in simulating mathematical thinking, educators interested in how to teach and test mathematical thinking, philosophers who want to understand the quantitative aspects of logical thinking, anthropologists and others interested in how and why mathematical thinking seems to differ in quality across cultures, and laypeople and anyone else who has to think mathematically and who wants to understand how he or she is going about it. Authors were asked to write chapters that would be readable to this diverse group of potential readers, and we believe that, for the most part, they have succeeded.

Authors were asked to focus on their own approach to mathematical thinking, but also to address a common core of issues, such as the nature of mathematical thinking, how mathematical thinking is similar to and different from other kinds of thinking, what makes some people or some groups better than others in mathematical thinking, and how mathematical thinking can be assessed and taught. Therefore, although the chapter authors represent a diversity of approaches and points of view, they converge in addressing a common set of issues about mathematical thinking.

Of course, we are not the first nor will we be the last to provide a book that considers issues of mathematical thinking. What do we hope might make our book different and even special? Some of these things we have already mentioned— the common core of issues, the diversity of viewpoints, the internationally recognized expertise of the authors, and the readability of their chapters. Few books, for example, bring together psychologists with a cognitive focus, psychologists with a cultural focus, educators, and mathematicians all into one volume. However, we also hope that this book will provide a depth of understanding that renders it unparalleled among those books that deal with a concept as difficult as that of mathematical thinking.

We have tried to produce a book that is diverse but manageable. Its 11 chapters cover a great deal of ground, but, of course, there is ground they leave out, and uncharted terrain that the field has yet to address. The book is divided into six parts, roughly corresponding to psychometric, cognitive information processing, cognitive–cultural, cognitive–educational, and mathematical (i.e., mathematicians') approaches to mathematical thinking, as well as a conclusion.

Part I comprises a single chapter, by John B. Carroll, which takes the psychometric approach to mathematical thinking. In chapter 1, "Mathematical Abilities: Some Results From Factor Analysis," Carroll shows how his three-stratum theory of cognitive abilities can be applied to the understanding of mathematical thinking. Carroll starts off by defining abilities, proceeds to describe the factor-analytic techniques he has used to study abilities, and then suggests abilities within the theory that are likely to be relevant to mathematical thinking. These abilities include general ability at the highest stratum, as well as fluid intelligence, crystallized intelligence, general memory ability, general visual perception, and possibly other abilities at the second stratum. Some more specific, third-stratum abilities are described as well.

Part II, dealing with the cognitive information-processing approach to mathematical thinking, opens with chapter 2, "The Process of Understanding Mathematical Problems," by Richard E. Mayer and Mary Hegarty. Mayer and Hegarty open with a description of the nature of mathematical problem solving and of mathematics problems, and then suggest critical cognitive processes involved in mathematical thinking; in particular, translating, integrating, planning, and executing. Mayer and Hegarty then go on to present their theory of mathematical understanding, according to which there are two paths to such understanding, which they refer to as a *direct translation strategy*—selecting numbers from the problem and then preparing to perform arithmetic operations on them—and a *problem model strategy*—trying to understand the situation being described in the problem and devising a solution plan based on the ensuing representation of the situation. Mayer and Hegarty then derive six predictions from their theory—such as that students make more errors in remembering relational statements than in remembering assignment statements—and review data testing these predictions.

In chapter 3, Talia Ben-Zeev summarizes a model of mathematical thinking, called REASON, according to which mathematical thinking represents an attempt on the part of the thinker rationally to solve a quantitative problem. Even when the thinker makes errors, the errors are often rational errors, meaning that they have a certain logic to them, even if the logic is incorrect. According to her view, the very mechanisms that allow people to solve mathematical problems correctly are also often responsible for the errors these people make. These errors come about when people either overgeneralize or overspecialize partial knowledge—they err in their understanding of the domain of problems to which the procedures apply. Ben-Zeev reviews four mechanisms of mathematical thinking—inductive, analogical, schema-based, and correlational thinking—showing how they work, and how they can lead both to correct solutions and to rational errors.

Part III, on cognitive–cultural approaches to mathematical thinking, opens with chapter 4, by Kevin F. Miller and David R. Paredes. Miller and Paredes show that the verbalizations of the symbols used to express mathematical concepts have an effect on the way people think with these concepts. In other words, children in various cultures appear to learn numerical concepts differentially depending on how numbers are expressed verbally in their languages. On the whole, children learn systems of numeration more easily the more regular the verbal expressions of these systems of numeration are. For example, the verbal expressions for the numbers 11–19 (eleven, twelve, . . .) are rather irregular in comparison with the same symbols as expressed in certain other languages, causing children who learn to count in English some difficulty.

Chapter 5, by Geoffrey B. Saxe, Venus Dawson, Randy Fall, and Sharon Howard, is entitled "Culture and Children's Mathematical Thinking." Saxe and his coauthors are particularly interested in the interrelation of culture and individuals' developing mathematical understandings. They open their chapter with a brief review of Piagetian constructivism, in which they describe the approach, and consider both its contributions and its limitations. The authors are particularly critical of Piaget's failure to take cultural aspects of understanding into account, which leads to the presentation of their own sociocultural approach, according to which people construct mathematical understandings through a self-regulated process that is situated in a cultural context. The authors focus particularly on the emergent goals that people set for themselves as they learn to think mathematically. They give specific examples across cultures of how their framework can be used to understand such thinking.

In chapter 6, David C. Geary presents a sweeping view of "Biology, Culture, and Cross-National Differences in Mathematical Ability." Geary's approach is notable, as well as unusual, in combining biological and cultural considerations. He suggests that abilities, including mathematical ones, can be characterized as being either biologically primary or biologically secondary. The former kind of ability is species-typical and emerges in all cultures, whereas the latter kind is culturally specific, and thus biologically secondary. Biologically primary mathematical abilities are hypothesized to include numerosity, ordinality, counting, and simple arithmetic. Biologically secondary mathematical abilities include skills and knowledge taught by parents, concepts that children induce doing the act of counting, and skills that are formally taught in school. Geary considers cross-national differences in mathematical performance in terms of his theory, and concludes that they are a result of biologically secondary rather than primary abilities. Moreover, in other countries, such as Japan, mathematical thinking is more highly valued and children spend much more time doing it, leading to greater success in mathematical learning and problem solving.

Part IV, on cognitive–educational approaches to mathematical thinking, opens with chapter 7, by Herbert Ginsburg, entitled "Toby's Math." This chapter represents a detailed case-study analysis of a single child, Toby, a 6-year-old girl learning and thinking about math. Ginsburg shows that mathematical thinking has a number of properties that go beyond mere learning achieved in a school setting. According to Ginsburg, mathematical thinking in children is (a) in part a relationship with an adult; (b) in part a private activity only partly transparent to adults; (c) informal, employing intuitive ideas of more and less; (d) trying to get right answers quickly without thinking and feeling miserable about getting wrong answers; (e) a somewhat bizarre language game that first demands memorization of meaningless material and then involves identification of patterns; (f) trying to make sense out of material that often is not very sensibly presented; (g) engaging in what, to the children, seem to be arbitrary activities with obstacles designed to deceive and trick them; and (h) thinking about one's own thinking and taking great pride in describing it to others.

In chapter 8, "Fostering Mathematical Thinking in Middle School Students: Lessons From Research," John Bransford takes an approach that is quite different from that of Ginsburg. He describes work he and his colleagues have done over a period of 7 years to develop a program for teaching large numbers of middle school children to think mathematically. The program, which uses high-tech techniques developed at the Learning and Technology Center of Vanderbilt University, teaches children actively and reflectively to think mathematically in interesting and lively real-world contexts of the kinds they are likely to encounter, sooner or later, in their own lives. The project has gone through a number of stages, described in the chapter. The project is ongoing, and has yielded impressive results in terms of improving children's mathematical thinking skills.

Part V, describing mathematical approaches to understanding mathematical thinking, shows that psychologists and mathematicians, despite the differences in background knowledge and methodologies, have many common concerns as well as conclusions. This part opens with chapter 9, by Tommy Dreyfus and Theodore Eisenberg, "On Different Facets of Mathematical Thinking." The chapter is organized around key issues in mathematical thinking. The first is aesthetics—the mathematician's drive for elegance in their thinking about mathematics. The second key issue is self-confidence—to think well mathematically, people have to believe in their own ability to succeed. The third issue is reasoning by analogy, which involves seeing relations between different mathematical problems, some of which may not appear very related on the surface. Fourth is structure—the relationships between facts, relationships between relationships, and other related issues. Fifth is representation, or how a problem is translated into a visual or other form that will help solve it. Sixth is the visual reasoning that acts on representations. Seventh is reversal of thinking, which involves working backward from the end to the beginning—asking why something happened in the first place, or why it may occur in the way it does. Finally, eighth is flexibility of thought—the need not to get locked into any particular and rigid way of thinking about a mathematical problem.

In chapter 10, "Structuralism and Mathematical Thinking," Charles Rickart focuses on the role of structure in mathematical thinking. Rickart opens with a definition of structure as a set of objects along with certain relations among those objects. He then goes on to show how structures are key to mathematics and to mathematical thinking, such as its abstractness and its use of language, and also describes how mathematical thinking differs from ordinary thinking; for example, the lack of encouragement children often feel for learning mathematics as opposed, say, to learning language. Rickart further stresses the importance of creativity as a central element in mathematical thinking.

Part IV, the concluding section of our book, contains just a single chapter, "What is Mathematical Thinking?" The chapter attempts to sort out those things that we may know and those things that we have yet fully to comprehend in our search for understanding of the nature of mathematical thinking.

As always, a number of people have contributed to the realization of this book. We are especially grateful to Henry Kaufman for his support in all aspects of this project, to our editors and support staff at Lawrence Erlbaum Associates, to Benoit Mandelbrot for the time he spent talking to one of us about his views on mathematical thinking, and to our various mathematical teachers along the way who have helped us to come to a greater appreciation of mathematical thinking, in all its simplicity and complexity.

Robert J. Sternberg
Talia Ben-Zeev

List of Contributors

Brigid Barror. Learning Technology Center, Peabody College, Vanderbilt University, Nashville, Tennessee.

Talia Ben-Zeev. Department of Psychology, Yale University, New Haven, Connecticut.

John D. Bransford. Learning Technology Center, Peabody College, Vanderbilt University, Nashville, Tennessee.

John B. Carroll. Psychology Department, University of North Carolina at Chapel Hill, Chapel Hill, North Carolina.

The Cognition and Technology Group at Vanderbilt University. Learning Technology Center, Peabody College, Vanderbilt University, Nashville, Tennessee.

Venus Dawson. Graduate School of Education and Information Studies, University of California at Los Angeles, Los Angeles, California.

Tommy Dreyfus. Center for Technological Education, Holon, Israel.

Theodore Eisenberg. Department of Mathematics and Computer Science, Ben-Gurion University of the Negev, Beer Sheva, Israel.

Randy Fall. Graduate School of Education and Information Studies, University of California at Los Angeles, Los Angeles, California.

David C. Geary. Department of Psychology, University of Missouri, Columbia, Missouri.

Herbert P. Ginsburg. Department of Developmental and Educational Psychology, Teachers College, Colombia University, New York, New York.

Mary Hegarty. Department of Psychology, University of California at Santa Barbara, Santa Barbara, California.

Sharon Howard. Graduate School of Education and Information Studies, University of California at Los Angeles, Los Angeles, California.

Richard E. Mayer. Department of Psychology, University of California at Santa Barbara, Santa Barbara, California.

Kevin F. Miller. Department of Psychology, University of Illinois at Urbana-Champaign, Champaign, Illinois.

David R. Paredes. Department of Psychology, Texas A&M University, College Station, Texas.

Charles Rickart. Department of Mathematics, Yale University, New Haven, Connecticut.

Geoffrey B. Saxe. Graduate School of Education and Information Studies, University of California at Los Angeles, Los Angeles, California.

Daniel Schwartz. Learning Technology Center, Peabody College, Vanderbilt University, Nashville, Tennessee.

Robert J. Sternberg. Department of Psychology, Yale University, New Haven, Connecticut.

Nancy Vye. Learning Technology Center, Peabody College, Vanderbilt University, Nashville, Tennessee.

Linda Zech. Learning Technology Center, Peabody College, Vanderbilt University, Nashville, Tennessee.

This book is dedicated to Julian C. Stanley,
a psychologist who has ceaselessly dedicated himself
to understanding and promoting mathematical thinking
in the youth of tomorrow.

A PSYCHOMETRIC
APPROACH

1

▼▼▼▼▼▼▼

Mathematical Abilities: Some Results From Factor Analysis

John B. Carroll
University of North Carolina at Chapel Hill

The purpose of this chapter is to offer information on what the analysis of cognitive abilities can say about the nature of mathematical thinking. Mathematical thinking takes numerous forms, depending on the nature of the mathematical task. Mathematical tasks differ over the various branches of mathematics—arithmetic, algebra, geometry, calculus, symbolic logic, topology, number theory, and so on. Even within one of these branches, however, like arithmetic, tasks (problems) can differ in their structure and their difficulty. For example, some tasks posed in arithmetic are purely formal, such as adding, subtracting, multiplying, or dividing given numbers, whereas others are presented as "word problems," stating real-world situations in which the respondent must determine how the given numbers are correctly handled to yield an answer. Presumably, the analysis of any mathematical task, in any branch of mathematics, should yield some insight into the nature of the mathematical thinking required to perform it. This chapter, however, is not immediately concerned with such analyses; doubtless they are addressed in other chapters of this volume.

Mathematical tasks represent only a subset of the practical infinity of cognitive tasks that might exist or be imagined. If it is assumed that the satisfactory performance of a cognitive task by an individual involves the possession by that individual of adequate levels of the cognitive abilities required in performing that task, a theory of cognitive abilities may help in the identification of aspects of mathematical thinking. Such a theory would specify the nature of an ability and its relation to the performance of tasks, and lead to the enumeration and differentiation of abilities, including those presumably involved in the performance of mathematical tasks.

First, this chapter describes a theory of cognitive abilities and its empirical basis, chiefly in terms of results from studies employing psychological tests and the statistical technique of factor analysis. The factors identified by this technique are conceived as being basic latent traits or abilities that function as determining, at least in part, success or failure in performing cognitive tasks.

Next, the chapter summarizes evidence concerning which of these cognitive abilities appear to participate in affecting success or failure in learning and performing various types of mathematical tasks. Possible conclusions are drawn about the nature of mathematical thinking.

Finally, I briefly discuss various issues concerning the sources, meaning, and relevance of cognitive abilities in mathematical performances.

THE THREE-STRATUM THEORY OF COGNITIVE ABILITIES

The meaning of the term *ability* is often taken for granted. Loosely, it can be used to state the capability of anything (even a nonliving object) to do something. For the present purposes, however, it needs to be defined more precisely, as referring to *the possible variations over individuals in their threshold levels of difficulty in successfully performing some defined class of tasks.* Suppose, for the moment, that we define the class of tasks as being *mathematical*, and that these tasks vary in difficulty, from the easiest (such as adding a pair of whole numbers) to the more difficult (such as simplifying a complex algebraic equation, finding a derivative, or proving a theorem). Then an individual would be characterized as having superior mathematical ability if the individual could successfully perform all or nearly all of the tasks in this class. Likewise, an individual would be characterized as having poor mathematical ability if the individual were found to be able to perform only the easiest tasks, if any at all. The exact amount of ability the individual possesses (θ) could be estimated from test data with a model that is popular among psychometricians; that is, the three-parameter logistic item response theory (IRT) model that is specified by the following equation:

$$p = c + \frac{1 - c}{1 + \exp(-1.7a(\theta - b))},$$

where p refers to the probability that an individual can successfully perform a given task, a is a parameter for the slope of the function, b is a parameter for the difficulty of a task (or item), c is a parameter giving the probability of successfully performing the item by chance guessing, and θ is a parameter for the individual's threshold level of ability. The parameters b and θ are scaled in terms of standard scores in an assumed distribution of ability. The parameter *a* generally takes values between about .5 and 3.0, whereas the parameter *c* generally takes values between 0 and .5 (the latter value being that estimated a priori for two-choice, true–false items).

Figure 1.1 shows typical item-response curves for several patterns of parameter values. Easy items, with low values of *b*, have response curves at the left of the figure, while the response curves for more difficult items are toward the right of the figure. Items with low values of *a* have relatively flat response curves and are generally unreliable or imperfect measures of the ability, whereas items with high values of *a* have steeper response curves and yield much more reliable information on an individual's ability. Generally, tests of an ability are designed to be composed of items with a range of values of difficulty (in terms of the parameter *b*) and items that have relatively high values of *a*, so that the total number-correct scores yield good estimates of the true ability levels (θ) of the individuals tested. For further information on the design of tests according to item response theory (IRT), see, for example, Lord (1980) or Hambleton (1983).

Item-response theory assumes that all the items of a test are homogeneous in the sense that they all measure the same ability or cluster of abilities. Indeed, one of the major problems of IRT is how to determine the homogeneity of the items. In practice, homogeneity is initially judged subjectively;

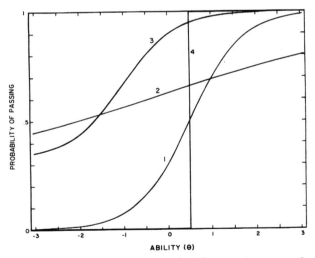

FIG. 1.1.   Item-response curves (hypothetical) for several patterns of values of parameters *a*, *b*, and *c*. The metric of the baseline is θ, individual ability, and of the ordinate, *p*, the probability of success. Parameters are: item 1: $a = 1$, $b = .5$, $c = 0$; item 2: $a = .2$, $b = 0$, $c = .25$; item 3: $a = 1$, $b = -1$, $c = .333$; item 4: $a = \infty$, $b = .5$, $c = 0$. From Carroll, J. B. (1988). Individual differences in cognitive functioning. In R. C. Anderson, R. J. Herrnstein, G. Lindzey, & R. D. Luce (Eds.), *Stevens' Handbook of Experimental Psychology, Vol. 2*, p. 822. Copyright © 1988, John Wiley & Sons, Inc. Reprinted by permission.

that is, the test constructor aspires to develop a test that will contain items or tasks that all appear to measure the same ability. Ordinarily this is done by constructing a series of items or tasks that are highly similar in format and content, although possibly differing in apparent difficulty. For example, a test of arithmetical computation ability might contain a series of tasks requiring checking the accuracy of sums of whole numbers. Various IRT procedures are available to assess whether all items measure the same ability, or whether it would be wise to eliminate or try to modify items that do not measure the same ability as the remainder of the items. Unfortunately, these procedures are not always employed. In particular, they have generally not been employed in connection with ability tests constructed at various times over the past 50 or more years. Nevertheless, many of these tests are generally acceptable in defining particular kinds of abilities, even when subjected to IRT procedures, and such tests have been widely used in studying the nature of mathematical and other abilities.

It needs to be emphasized at this point that the term *ability* is, or should be thought of, as entirely neutral with respect to whether the level of an individual's ability is a result of inherited characteristics, of learning and experience, or of some combination of them. An estimate of an individual's level of ability with respect to some class of tasks is only a statement of that individual's capability, at some given time, of performing those tasks; it says nothing about how that level of ability came about, or how that ability might change over time or with further learning and experience.

Over the years of the present century, a statistical technique known as *factor analysis* has been developed and refined to identify and classify the abilities measured by psychological and educational tests. For most of its history, the procedures favored in factor analysis have been *exploratory* (Carroll, 1985). Exploratory factor analysis examines the intercorrelations among a set of variables to determine the number of factors (basic abilities) needed to account satisfactorily for those correlations, and then, usually, to rotate the coordinates of the factors in such a way as to exhibit the best "simple structure" for interpreting the factors—a structure such that most variables have zero or near-zero weights or "loadings" on all but one (or a small number) of the factors. If the simple structure factors are found to be significantly correlated, a further analysis is made to find the simple structure for those "second-order" factors, and so on until the complete factor structure for the variables is shown, using a procedure known as a Schmid–Leiman hierarchical orthogonalization (Schmid & Leiman, 1957). Factor analysis can be applied to numerous datasets, using partially overlapping sets of variables, to identify and give substantive interpretations to factors that appear to replicate themselves over the different datasets.

In contrast, the last several decades have seen the development of procedures of what has become known as *confirmatory factor analysis*, which can be applied to different datasets to test hypotheses about factor structures, often to "confirm" or disconfirm structures revealed by exploratory factor analysis. Confirmatory factor analysis (Jöreskog & Sörbom, 1979) has a more rigorous basis than exploratory factor analysis, in that the statistical significance of findings can be better evaluated.

Both exploratory and confirmatory factor analysis can address questions about the identification and classification of abilities and aptitudes, in terms of the extent to which different kinds of psychological measurements do or do not correlate with each other in samples of individuals that may be more or less representative of the population. For use in studies employing factor analysis, psychometricians have developed tests that focus on particular hypothesized abilities, skills, or processes. In 1993, I published a report (Carroll, 1993) of my reanalyses, using exploratory factor analysis, of more than 480 datasets that had appeared in the psychometric literature of cognitive abilities over the past 60 or 70 years. Many of the datasets contained correlational information on various psychological tests that could be regarded as relevant to the analysis of mathematical abilities and achievements, although this was not the central purpose of my survey. My results tended to confirm the kind of hierarchical structure of cognitive abilities that had been proposed, in different forms, by previous investigators, such as Vernon (1961), Cattell (1971), and Cattell and Horn (1978). I attempted to integrate or synthesize the results by suggesting a three-stratum theory whereby cognitive abilities can be hierarchically classified in terms of their generality into general, broad, and narrow factors. At the top of the hierarchy, at the third or highest stratum (see Fig. 1.2) is a single general factor that is found, in varying degrees, in all or nearly all tests of cognitive ability. At a second stratum are a relatively small number of "broad" abilities, named fluid intelligence, crystallized intelligence, general memory and learning, broad visual perception, broad auditory perception, broad retrieval ability, broad cognitive speediness, and processing speed. Finally, at a first or lowest stratum are found a fairly large number of narrow factors (to date, about 65) representing quite specific abilities in various domains. The three-stratum structure shown in Fig. 1.2 is in many respects provisional; not all the factors are well demonstrated or differentiated in factorial studies, but the structure represents my best estimate from the available empirical data. Further studies are needed, using both exploratory and confirmatory factor analysis, better to define the structure of abilities.

Factorial studies tell little about the sources of the factors (e.g., to what extent they are influenced by genetic characteristics or by learning), about their stability, or about the extent to which they remain the same over the life span. It may be said at this point, however, that most factors appear to exist at most stages of the life span, even though the levels of abilities they represent may increase or decrease at various stages.

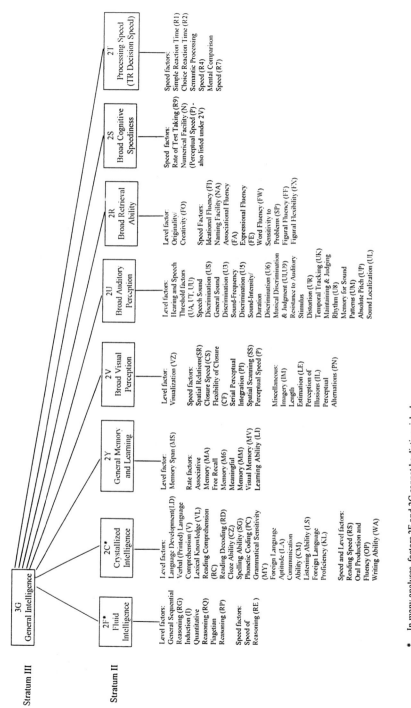

FIG. 1.2. The structure of cognitive abilities. From Carroll (1993). © 1993, Cambridge University Press. Reproduced by permission.

* In many analyses, factors 2F and 2C cannot be distinguished: they are represented, however, by a factor designated 2H, a combination of 2F and 2C.

Stratum III

Stratum II

3G General Intelligence

2F* Fluid Intelligence

Level factors:
General Sequential Reasoning (RG)
Induction (I)
Quantitative Reasoning (RQ)
Piagetian Reasoning (RP)

Speed factors:
Speed of Reasoning (RE)

2C* Crystallized Intelligence

Level factors:
Language Development(LD)
Verbal (Printed) Language Comprehension (V)
Lexical Knowledge (VL)
Reading Comprehension (RC)
Reading Decoding (RD)
Cloze Ability (CZ)
Spelling Ability (SG)
Phonetic Coding (PC)
Grammatical Sensitivity (MY)

Foreign Language Aptitude (LA)
Communication Ability (CM)
Listening Ability (LS)
Foreign Language Proficiency (KL)

Speed and Level factors:
Reading Speed (RS)
Oral Production and Fluency (OP)
Writing Ability (WA)

2Y General Memory and Learning

Level factor:
Memory Span (MS)

Rate factors:
Associative Memory (MA)
Free Recall Memory (M6)
Meaningful Memory (MM)
Visual Memory (MV)
Learning Ability (L1)

2V Broad Visual Perception

Level factor:
Visualization (VZ)

Speed factors:
Spatial Relations(SR)
Closure Speed (CS)
Flexibility of Closure (CF)
Serial Perceptual Integration (PI)
Spatial Scanning (SS)
Perceptual Speed (P)

Miscellaneous:
Imagery (IM)
Length Estimation (LE)
Perception of Illusions (IL)
Perceptual Alternations (PN)

2U Broad Auditory Perception

Level factors:
Hearing and Speech Threshold factors (UA, UT, UU)
Speech Sound Discrimination (US)
General Sound Discrimination (U3)
Sound-Frequency Discrimination (U5)
Sound-Intensity/ Duration Discrimination (U6)
Musical Discrimination & Judgment (U1,U9)
Resistance to Auditory Stimulus Distortion (UR)
Temporal Tracking (UK)
Maintaining & Judging Rhythm (U8)
Memory for Sound Patterns (UM)
Absolute Pitch (UP)
Sound Localization (UL)

2R Broad Retrieval Ability

Level factor:
Originality/ Creativity (FO)

Speed Factors:
Ideational Fluency (FI)
Naming Facility (NA)
Associational Fluency (FA)
Expressional Fluency (FE)
Word Fluency (FW)
Sensitivity to Problems (SP)
Figural Fluency (FF)
Figural Flexibility (FX)

2S Broad Cognitive Speediness

Speed factors:
Rate of Test Taking (R9)
Numerical Facility (N)
(Perceptual Speed (P) - also listed under 2V)

2T Processing Speed (TR Decision Speed)

Speed factors:
Simple Reaction Time (R1)
Choice Reaction Time (R2)
Semantic Processing Speed (R4)
Mental Comparison Speed (R7)

8

ABILITIES POSSIBLY RELEVANT
TO MATHEMATICAL THINKING

With two possible exceptions, there are no uniquely mathematical abilities. In what follows, I offer thoughts or speculations about which of the various factors identified in Fig. 1.2 may be relevant to mathematical thinking, or "doing mathematics" in the general sense of performing tasks or solving problems of a mathematical nature. At times I cite references backing up my statements, but it would consume too much space to provide extensive references to the available scientific literature on this subject (see Kilpatrick & Wagner, 1983).

The General Factor, g

In exploratory factor analysis, the general factor arises from a finding that lower order factors or variables are substantially correlated in such a way that a single factor best accounts for the correlations among them. In confirmatory factor analysis, a general factor can be postulated independently of other factors and confirmed by the analysis (Gustafsson, 1988), with loadings of variables on it estimated to afford best fit to the data. By either type of analysis, a general factor is very frequently found in cognitive ability datasets. Such a factor was postulated by Spearman (1904, 1927), and called g in his early studies of intelligence tests.

There has been much speculation and writing on the nature of g. Spearman believed that g was involved in cognitive operations whenever the individual was required to (a) apprehend experience and think about it, (b) educe or find relations among stimuli, and (c) educe or find correlates. Currently, the general factor is often interpreted as representing the maximal complexity or general difficulty of the tasks that an individual with a given level of g can perform, and hence the amount of conscious mental manipulation required by those tasks (Jensen, 1980, p. 231; Marshalek, Lohman, & Snow, 1983). This is probably not the whole story, however. For one thing, exceptional persons able to perform highly complex arithmetical tasks, such as finding the 23rd root of a 201-digit number, do not always appear to possess particularly high levels of general ability (e.g., Jensen, 1990, with reference to the case of the calculating prodigy Shakuntala Devi). Perhaps this implies that the "complexity" of a task is only in the eye of the beholder. In addition, people with obvious brilliance of intellect do not always make exceptionally high scores on tests of g or IQ. According to his biographer, in high school the brilliant mathematician Richard Feynman's score on the school's IQ test was "a merely respectable 125" (Gleick, 1992, p. 30). It was probably a paper-and-pencil test that had a ceiling, and an IQ of 125 under these circumstances is hardly to be shrugged off, because it is about 1.6 standard deviations above the mean of 100. The general experience of psychologists in applying tests would lead them to expect that Feynman would have made a much higher IQ if he had been properly tested.

It is difficult, however, to draw conclusions about the nature of g from individual cases. The matter can be better considered by analyzing the characteristics of tests that are highly loaded with g. Most such tests involve detailed and complex thinking about similarities, comparisons, the meanings of difficult words and sentences, logical relations and implications, quantitative problems, and the like. Some tests of g also involve background knowledge of a wide variety of relevant principles or facts, as well as the ability to apply those principles or facts to a variety of problems, regardless of their complexity. This could mean that g represents general ability to learn and to apply knowledge. Successful performance of tests of g may also require a large and capable working memory (Carpenter, Just, & Shell, 1990; Kyllonen & Christal, 1989), and ability to choose adequate strategies for solving problems.

The practical relevance of the g factor to mathematical work is well illustrated by several features of Stanley's (1974) Study of Mathematically Precocious Youth (SMPY). This is a program whereby selected students in grade 7 or 8 are given the opportunity of taking the Preliminary Scholastic Aptitude Test (PSAT)—essentially, or for the most part, a test of g. As Stanley characterized it, this is "out-of-level" testing because the PSAT is not normally thought of as being appropriate for grade 7–8 students. Those in the grade 7–8 group who make relatively high scores on the test, particularly on the "mathematical" section, are then offered the opportunity to receive college-level training in mathematics. Most of them succeed in this quite well, in contrast to what might be expected for students with much lower scores. Further, longitudinal studies (Lubinski & Benbow, 1994) have tended to show that students selected and trained by this program often continue in mathematical and "hard science" programs through their college and graduate years, and enter occupations requiring high-level thinking. It would appear, therefore, that the mathematically precocious students selected by the SMPY program are characterized by high levels of g, however acquired. At the opposite extreme, it is found that students with low levels of IQ (generally a good indicator of g) have considerable difficulty even in learning elementary arithmetic; even if they can learn elementary mathematical operations, they take much more than average time to do so. (See Geary, 1993, 1994, for discussions of cognitive, neuropsychological, and genetic components of mathematical disabilities.)

All these findings must be evaluated in terms of the fact that g, like most other cognitive abilities, has a strong developmental aspect. That is, the absolute level of g ability tends to increase (initially with slight positive acceleration, then with negative acceleration) during the childhood years, up to early adulthood, but the rates of increase differ over individuals. In fact, the

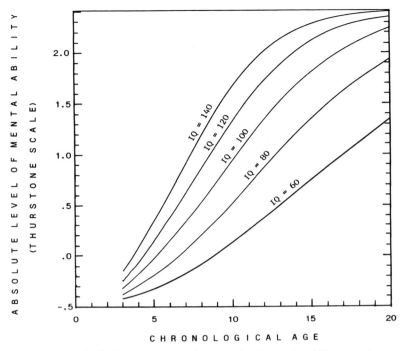

FIG. 1.3.   Idealized curves representing growth of general *g* ability over the first 20 years of life, for individuals with selected values of IQ. The ordinate uses the absolute scale of mental ability established by Thurstone and Ackerson (1929). The curves are plotted with an equation adapted from Sagiv's (1979) generalized growth function.

increases for different individuals can be thought of as forming a family of curves (Fig. 1.3). If we transform the absolute level of *g* to a "general mental age," we can divide this mental age by chronological age (and multiply by 100) to form a "general IQ" with which IQs assigned by psychological tests will be highly correlated; the general IQ is in effect a measure of the overall height of the person's curve of intellectual progress over the years of childhood to adulthood. Recent studies (Conley, 1984) have indicated that the stability of *g* over the childhood years is high, and Schaie and Hertzog (1986) found that the factor is also highly stable over the adult years. It is clear that *g* measures an important characteristic of the individual that tends to persist throughout the individual's life. It may be concluded that this characteristic is likely to affect the individual's ability to learn to perform mathematical tasks, and actually to perform them, at any time during the life span. Tests of achievement in mathematics are consistently correlated with *g* to a substantial extent at all points of individuals' courses of development.

Second-Stratum Abilities
and the Narrow Abilities They Comprise

It is convenient to discuss each of the "broad" second-stratum abilities together with the "narrow" first-stratum abilities with which they are most closely associated.

Fluid Intelligence (G_f, or 2C in my notation). A number of first-stratum abilities, notably Induction, Sequential Reasoning, and Quantitative Reasoning, tend to be highly correlated, but according to the model described here, their correlations can be accounted for not only by *g* but also, independently, by a second-stratum ability called *fluid intelligence* by Cattell (1971). It represents a general ability to perform thinking tasks that involve induction (finding rules or generalizations that account for or govern given stimulus configurations), deductive sequential reasoning (logical reasoning carried out correctly over one or more steps), and quantitative reasoning (any reasoning that involves quantitative concepts). Fluid intelligence is highly correlated with *g*, and in fact, some authorities propose that fluid intelligence is identical to *g* (Gustafsson, 1988; Undheim & Gustafsson, 1987). Nevertheless, the fact that fluid intelligence is not always found to be perfectly correlated with g has led me to conclude that it can be regarded as separate from *g*, and can be estimated independently of it. If this is the case, fluid intelligence represents an ability that refers specifically to thinking activities associated with logical and quantitative concepts.

It is interesting that such thinking activities can be sorted out into those involving inductive processes, deductive processes, and processes involving quantitative concepts, by virtue of the factor-analytic separability of the "narrow" factors called Induction (I), General Sequential Reasoning (RG), and Quantitative Reasoning (RQ). In addition, there is some evidence that a further narrow factor called Piagetian Reasoning (RP) can be identified in tasks such as seriation and "conservation" as studied by Piaget (Flavell, 1977); the relation of such a factor to fluid intelligence and to factors I, RG, and RQ has not been adequately studied. The factors found under fluid intelligence appear to characterize the major aspects of mathematical thinking. Indeed, authorities who have discussed mathematical thinking (Nesher & Kilpatrick, 1990) point out that solving mathematical problems frequently involves separate processes of induction, deduction, and mathematical conceptualization. Some authorities claim that expert mathematicians can be classified according to whether they are inclined to use induction and "intuition" more than deduction and reasoning, or vice versa (Hadamard, 1954).

Tests of inductive abilities are those that:

> require subjects to inspect a class of stimulus materials (nearly always with
> more than one instance) and infer (induce, educe) a common characteristic

underlying these materials—a concept, a class membership, a rule, a process, a trend, or a causal relation, for example. (Carroll, 1993, p. 238)

One such test, for example, is Number Series, a sample item of which is the following:

Fill in the blanks in the following series:

4　8　6　__　10　__　18　36　__

To perform this task, the student must detect rules governing the sequence: the fact that every other number is a member of a certain numerical series, and that each such number is followed by its double. Another frequently used test of factor I is Raven's Progressive Matrices test (Raven, 1962). Figure 1.4 shows a problem to illustrate the format of Raven test items. (To protect the security of the test, it is not an actual item in any of Raven's tests, but an "isomorph" of them.) The examinee has to inspect the entries in the rows and columns of the figure to induce rules that, in combination, predict which of the eight given answers correctly fits in the box in the lowest right position. In a conceptual and experimental analysis of such tasks, Carpenter et al. (1990) concluded that these tasks measure "the common ability to decompose problems into manageable segments and iterate through

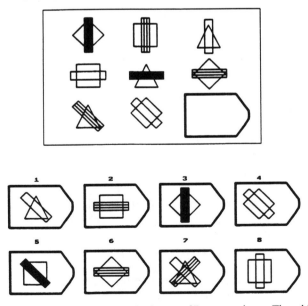

FIG. 1.4. A problem to illustrate the format of Raven test items. The subject's task is to determine which of the 8 figures at the bottom correctly fits in the position in the third row and third column of the matrix above. The correct answer is 5. From Carpenter, Just, and Shell (1990). © 1990 by American Psychological Association. Reprinted with permission.

them, the differential ability to manage the hierarchy of goals and subgoals generated by this problem decomposition, and the differential ability to form higher level abstractions" (p. 429). It can be argued that many mathematical problems require precisely such abilities.

There is a great variety of psychological tests measuring the Sequential Reasoning (RG) factor. They emphasize:

> the ability to reason and draw conclusions from given conditions or premises, often in a series of two or more sequential steps. The stimulus or test material can be of almost any type—literal, verbal (semantic), numerical, pictorial, or figural. The operations in the reasoning process can be of many types, involving comparisons of stimuli in terms of continuous attributes or class memberships, or perceptions of relations of causality, implication, etc. Above all, the processes are deductive, in the sense that there is very little load of induction or rule finding. The best tests of this factor impose little requirement on the subject to induce (educe) relationships or class memberships, since these relationships and class memberships are stated or otherwise immediately apparent to most subjects. (Carroll, 1993, p. 234)

One example of a Sequential Reasoning test is False Premises (Thurstone, 1938), illustrated by the following item that the subject is to judge as either "good reasoning" or "bad reasoning":

> Most horses live on carpet tacks; and most rabbits are horses; therefore some rabbits must live on carpet tacks if there are more rabbits than horses.

A further example is an item from a linear syllogism test (Thurstone, 1938), in which the subject must evaluate the correctness of the conclusion:

> Brown is younger than Smith.
> Brown is older than Jones.
> Therefore Jones is younger than Smith.

There is evidence that many people (but not all) solve such syllogisms by placing the concepts being compared on a number line (Sternberg & Weil, 1980). Linear syllogism tests therefore often have loadings not only on Sequential Reasoning but also on Quantitative Reasoning (factor RQ), which we now consider.

Quantitative Reasoning requires reasoning based on mathematical properties and relations. It is one of the uniquely mathematical abilities. As I have stated:

> Tests characteristically having high loadings on this factor are usually titled Arithmetic, Arithmetical Reasoning, Mathematical Aptitude, and the like.

> Typically these tests present a variety of mathematical reasoning problems
> such as word problems (solving verbally stated mathematical problems), num-
> ber series, and problems requiring selection of appropriate arithmetical opera-
> tions. Generally, the amount of actual numerical computation required is small.
> While tests are often given with a time limit, the scores are expected to depend
> mainly on the level of difficulty in the problems that can be performed. (Carroll,
> 1993, p. 241)

Further, scores generally depend on the level of mathematical understanding
that the student has attained with respect to such matters as distance and
rate of motion, total cost versus cost of items per unit, work performed per
unit of time, and so on. Some tests of Quantitative Reasoning may include
items that require inductive or deductive reasoning, but such items are only
incidental. It is most characteristic of Quantitative Reasoning tests to require
understanding of quantitative and mathematical concepts.

Also classified under Fluid Intelligence is a factor tentatively identified
as *Speed of Reasoning*, representing rate of solving reasoning problems, in
contrast to level of ability in solving them in unlimited time. There is, to be
sure, some correlation between level and speed in this case, in that people
with high-level reasoning abilities tend to solve mathematical problems faster
than people with lower levels of ability, but the correlation is far from perfect.
As a consequence, reasoning tests given with a time limit often do not correctly assess people's ability to solve problems when they are given unlimited
time to solve them.

It should be emphasized that it is difficult to judge the factorial composition of a psychological test merely by examining it. The examples of reasoning tests offered earlier must not be taken as adequately representing the
factors they are said to measure, because depending on their format, content,
and other aspects, they may measure more than one factor, or a different
factor from what might otherwise be thought. Tests titled Number Series,
for example, can be found to emphasize either Induction, Deduction, or
Quantitative Reasoning, depending on the kinds of problems they offer. Similarly, tests called Verbal Analogies are expected to measure Induction only
when the analogies they present relatively difficult problems of relating concepts; otherwise they may only measure vocabulary knowledge. Factor analysis is able to sort and identify the factors separately only when the test battery
contains an adequate sample of measures of each factor. For example, a
factor-analytic battery desirable for demonstrating the separability of Induction, Deduction, and Quantitative Reasoning should contain at least three
or four tests that typically measure or emphasize each of these factors.

Crystallized Intelligence (G_c, or 2C). A further broad second-stratum
ability is what has been called Crystallized Intelligence (Cattell, 1971). It
embraces a number of narrow, first-stratum abilities, most of them concerned

with language, both oral and written, and both receptive (listening and reading) and productive (speaking and writing) (see Fig. 1.2). Indeed, the factor might well be characterized as General Language Ability, except that it also sometimes embraces various narrow abilities that are learned through general experience or schooling, such as Number Facility, which is discussed later. For this reason, Crystallized Intelligence is often characterized as representing those aspects of general intelligence that are acquired through general experience, learning, and schooling; through "investment" of general intelligence in such learning activities.

A number of narrow verbal abilities that appear to be relevant for mathematical thinking may be mentioned. Language Development (LD) refers to the individual's general level of language ability, particularly in the early years of life; that is, the extent to which, at any given time, the person has acquired the basic phonology, vocabulary, and grammar (syntax, etc.) of the person's native language. (In the case of bilingual or multilingual individuals, there can be a separate LD factor for each language involved.) It is notable that in performing mathematical thinking, people tend to use number names in a particular language, usually the native language, but sometimes in another language (Cohen, 1994). More generally, the individual's language development plays some role in mathematical problem solving, and mathematics teachers must consider students' degrees of general language development in assessing those students' likelihoods of succeeding in mathematics.

The Verbal or Printed Language Comprehension Ability (factor V) is highly similar to, and usually highly correlated with, Language Development, except that it refers to the degree to which individuals have acquired the ability to read language in its written or printed form. Therefore, the ability of the student to solve mathematical problems presented in written language (as in what are often called "word problems") will depend on the student's level of ability on factor V. This ability may be relevant even in the performance of mathematical problems presented in purely symbolic form, in that some students may not be able to distinguish the symbols adequately. (We have in mind here innate or acquired dyslexia that is a problem for some students; see DeFries & Gillis, 1993.)

There is evidence (Carroll, 1993, pp. 159–190) that a number of other narrow language ability factors can be identified and differentiated, such as Lexical Knowledge (VL), Reading Comprehension (RC), Reading Decoding (RD), Reading Speed (RS), Spelling Ability (SG), Phonetic Coding (PC), Listening Ability (LS), and Oral Production (OP). Although some of these factors may be relevant to the learning and performance of mathematics either in classroom situations or in studying mathematics from textbooks, they are not specific to mathematics learning and thus will not be considered here in detail.

One of the most frequently found ability factors is what is often called Number (N) or Numerical Facility, measured by tests in which individuals are required to perform simple numerical operations (adding, subtracting, multiplying, and dividing numbers, usually integers). Because of its content, this is possibly a uniquely mathematical ability, although there have been attempts (Coombs, 1941) to show that it generalizes to the learning and manipulation of any simple rule system. Because a number-ability factor is frequently found to correlate substantially with other narrow factors classified under Crystallized Intelligence, this factor N is considered here, although it can also be considered under speed factors (see later discussion). As I have described it (Carroll, 1993):

> Factor N refers simply to the degree to which the individual has developed skills in dealing with numbers, from the most elementary skills of counting objects and recognizing written numbers and their order, to the more advanced skills of correctly adding, subtracting, multiplying, and dividing numbers with an increasing number of digits, or with fractions and decimals. These are skills that are learned through experiences in the home, school, or even in the workplace. In the early years, skills deal with simple numbers and operations, and the important object is to be able to deal with number problems correctly, at whatever speed. In later years, practice is aimed at handling computations with greater speed as well as accuracy. More complex problems can be dealt with effectively and efficiently only if skills with simple problems are increasingly automatized. (p. 469)

Most tests of factor N that have been used in factorial studies have emphasized speed, in that they are usually given with a severe time limit, although scored for accuracy. They would be more informative if they were designed to distinguish level (accuracy) and speed aspects of skill, which logically could be quite independent. Indeed, Kyllonen (1985) has found evidence for separate numerical speed and level factors.

Individual differences in numerical facility undoubtedly play a role in mathematical thinking whenever rapid and accurate handling of numerical quantities is involved. At advanced levels of mental mathematics, it appears that success is associated with having memorized many properties of numbers, such as their squares and square roots, their logarithms, and so on (Smith, 1983).

General Memory Ability (G$_y$, or 2Y). A number of types of memory ability are sufficiently correlated with each other to define what may be called General Memory Ability. Narrow factors that are covered by it include Memory Span (MS), Associative Memory (MA), and Meaningful Memory (MM). Memory Span is often tested by giving the subject a series of digits (or letters) to repeat exactly in the order in which they are spoken. Several such series are given, increasing the number of digits or letters, with the object of determining the largest number of elements that the subject can consistently repeat correctly. The fact that Memory Span is often correlated substantially with g may perhaps be interpreted as showing that this factor is a measure of the size of working memory; that is, the memory in which a person stores and calls on new information that must be used in solving a problem. Therefore, Memory Span can be involved if the person is required to solve a mathematical problem, especially if it must be solved "mentally," taking account of several different numerical values. On the other hand, Kyllonen and Christal (1989) claimed that "what is required in span tests seems contrived and not typical of what people actually do when engaged in realistic learning" (p. 156). They have proposed more realistic measures of working memory.

Associative Memory (MA) is usually tested by giving the subject a series of arbitrarily paired stimuli to study in a relatively limited time, and then asking the subject to demonstrate learning by responding to each stimulus with the element with which it was paired in the learning series. An obvious instance in which Associative Memory may be involved is the learning of a foreign language vocabulary, but this factor could also be involved in the rate at which a subject could learn any series of elements, such as the number facts involved in elementary arithmetic, the squares or logarithms of a series of numbers, or even a mathematical formula or equation. The factor appears to concern the *rate* at which learning occurs, not the way in which it occurs or the maximal amount that can be learned. Individual differences in learning rates are often very striking, both in children and adults.

One other factor that might be involved in mathematical learning and thinking is Meaningful Memory (MM), as observed in tests that require the subject to memorize or remember "meaningful" ideas (as opposed to seemingly arbitrary pairings or sequences of elements). Success in such tests seems to depend not only on the ability of the subject to comprehend or understand the ideas to be remembered, but also on the rate at which these ideas can be learned. Because the tests rarely involve mathematical ideas, it is not clear whether this Meaningful Memory factor would show up as a determinant of success in learning mathematics, but I would speculate that it might. This question would possibly be fruitful for future research.

General Visual Perception (G_v, or 2V). It is highly likely that the second-stratum factor called General Visual Perception is involved in many types of mathematical thinking. It could also be called General Spatial Ability; spatial ability has often been cited (e.g., Werdelin, 1961) as possibly being involved in mathematical work. Actually, General Visual Perception seems to represent a common element in a variety of tests measuring narrow factors, such as Visualization (VZ), Spatial Relations (SR), Mechanical Knowledge (MK), Perceptual Speed (P), Closure Speed (CS), and Closure Flexibility (CF). Exactly which of these factors, along with General Visual Perception, is actually relevant to mathematical thinking, if at all, is a question that as yet has not been adequately answered by research. Gustafsson and Balke (1993) did not find any significant relation between grade 9 mathematics grades and a General Visual Perception factor measured at grade 6. Similarly, Lubinski and Humphreys (1990) found that measures of Visualization were not useful as predictors of success in general mathematics, although measures of g were excellent predictors. On the other hand, Humphreys, Lubinski, and Yao (1993) found that high spatial visualization abilities seemed to function in influencing people to become engineers or physical scientists, that is, to choose occupations involving mathematics.

Visualization tests appear to require the examinee to apprehend a visual form and form an image of it that can be manipulated to help solve a problem in visual space. For example, in paper-formboard tasks, "subjects combine imaginatively the various parts of a figure to complete a whole figure" (Eliot & Smith, 1983, p. 147). In paper-folding tasks, subjects are shown drawings that illustrate successive foldings of a piece of paper; the final drawing shows a hole in a given place. The subject has to imagine and predict the pattern of holes in the paper when it is unfolded. In surface-development tasks, subjects are presented with a drawing depicting a form in three-dimensional space, and are then asked to relate it to a two-dimensional drawing showing the form opened up. (See Fig. 1.5 for an example taken from one of Thurstone's, 1938, tests, where the subject has to identify parts of the "diagram" that are identical to parts of the "picture.") To the extent that a test measures the Visualization factor, it measures the level of difficulty and complexity of visual forms that the individual can handle, not necessarily the speed with which they can be handled.

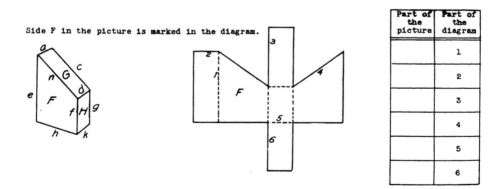

FIG. 1.5. A sample item from Thurstone's (1938) Surface Development test. The subject's task is to match elements in the "picture" at the left with the "diagram" at the right. © 1938 by University of Chicago Press. Reprinted with permission.

In contrast, tests of Spatial Relations present simple problems, such as matching letters in different rotations, and measure the individual's speed in performing them correctly. Tests of Closure Speed, also given in a time limit, require the subject to recognize what is pictured by drawings that are partially obscured in that they omit many of the lines and parts of the original picture. Tests of Closure Flexibility present a form or geometric drawing; the subject must then detect whether a further drawing contains the original drawing. Tests of Perceptual Speed require the subject to remember a given spatial configuration and search through a series of such configurations to find those that are exactly identical to the one remembered.

None of these tasks is identical to any of the perceptual operations required in mathematical work, such as in geometry or the analysis of functions, but it would be expected that persons who have difficulty with tests of visual perception or spatial ability might also have difficulty with similar operations in mathematical thinking, unless they could circumvent these difficulties with nonperceptual strategies, such as logical analysis.

Other Second-Stratum Cognitive Abilities. Factor-analytic studies have identified several other broad abilities, such as Auditory Perception, Broad Retrieval Ability, Broad Cognitive Speediness, and Information-Processing Speed, but I would not expect any of these abilities to be particularly relevant to mathematical thinking. Auditory Reception, for example, has to do with abilities in perceiving speech, music, and other types of sound stimuli. Although it has sometimes been stated that mathematicians tend to be particularly fond of music, I know of no evidence that this, if true, indicates something about their thinking. Broad Retrieval Ability involves individuals' abilities to produce different types of responses facilely, drawing on the contents of long-term memory, including the ability to be creative in cognitive domains. Whether such abilities relate to mathematical creativity—the production of new mathematical ideas—is not known.

The two broad speed factors, Broad Cognitive Speediness and Information-Processing Speed, are possibly relevant to mathematical thinking in that they might correlate with individuals' speeds in performing mathematical operations. I have already mentioned Numerical Facility as one aspect of Crystallized Intelligence to the degree that it represents an effect of school learning. One of the narrow factors under Broad Cognitive Speediness is Rate of Test Taking, which might show up in students' rates of performing mathematical achievement tests. Narrow factors under Information-Processing Speed include Simple Reaction Time (R1), Choice Reaction Time (R2), Semantic Processing Speed (R4), and Mental Comparison Speed (R7), but I know of no evidence to indicate that these are specifically relevant to mathematical activities.

ISSUES ABOUT THE SOURCES, MEANING, AND RELEVANCE OF FACTOR-ANALYTICALLY DERIVED COGNITIVE ABILITIES

In offering the foregoing account of a theory of cognitive abilities as it might apply to mathematical thinking, I must admit to a degree of hesitancy and uncertainty. Despite six or seven decades of work in the psychometric tradition, relations between factor-analytically derived abilities and actual performances in various real-world domains, such as mathematics, have remained unclear. There is no doubt that relations exist, but exactly what they are and how they operate is not known as well as might be desired. We also know that mathematics ability is not unitary. That is, one may say that there are at least several types of abilities that appear to underlie mathematical performances, but we cannot easily predict which abilities are most relevant for particular performances.

A number of serious researchers (e.g., Ceci, 1990; Winch, 1990) have called into question some of the basic assumptions of the psychometric tradition—for example, the assumption that cognitive abilities identified by factor-analytic and related procedures truly represent important and enduring characteristics of individuals, and the assumption that scores on psychological tests are or can be reliable and valid measures of such characteristics. In the space assigned to this chapter, I can only give hints of the arguments that have been brought forth.

One argument is that psychological tests are typically "decontextualized"; that is, that they present tasks that are not embedded in contexts like those in which persons perform tasks in the "real world." Examples are cited in which some people are found to be able to perform complex and involved thinking despite attaining only mediocre scores on tests that presumably present tasks calling for such thinking. For instance, Ceci and Liker (1986) told us that experienced racetrack gamblers, despite making only average scores on IQ tests, are able to perform complex thought manipulations in successfully predicting, from numerical and other data that they can get, the odds that a horse will win a race.

Another argument is that the generally positive correlations of psychological tests (often called "positive manifold") are mainly the result of the fact that people differ in the quantity, diversity, and complexity of their experiences and learnings, partly because of differences in the social environments in which they were nurtured. This argument calls into some question the notion that *g* or "general intelligence," derived from the positive manifold in test correlations, is something much more than a mathematical artifact. It is argued, furthermore, that the lower order factors found in factor analysis (such as the second- and first-stratum factors mentioned earlier) simply reflect classes of experiences that tend to occur and be learned together, like word meanings, number facts, or spatial forms. It is pointed out that specialization of abilities frequently results from long-lasting devoted practice (Ericsson & Charness, 1994), not necessarily from superiority in any innately laid down cognitive abilities.

Finally, it is argued that the apparently high heritability coefficients often cited for mental abilities can possibly be reinterpreted in terms of complex interactions between hereditary and environmental forces such that there are no direct biological constraints on the development of cognitive abilities.

Although some of these arguments may have merit, in my view they go too far. There is abundant evidence for the existence of mental abilities that can be measured by psychological tests and that show at least substantial relations to the learning and performance of mathematical tasks. Even if the tasks presented in psychological tests are "decontextualized," there are strong similarities between those tasks and those encountered in the real world. Even if learning is dependent to a large extent on environmental conditions and opportunities, there is evidence that the degree to which people can and do take advantage of those opportunities is at least partly dependent on their biological constitution.

Further, none of these arguments has any immediate bearing on whether the factor-analytic results cited in this chapter are relevant to the analysis of mathematical thinking, because, as I have stressed, the ability measures used in these studies pertain only to performances of individuals at given points of time and do not imply anything about the sources of these abilities—genetic or environmental—or about their future development. For example, none of these arguments goes against the conclusion that inductive, deductive, and quantitative conceptual processes are aspects of mathematical thinking. What would be questionable, however, is any prediction that persons showing low levels of ability on such processes would thereby be unlikely to profit from specific training in them. The possibility of training cognitive processes involved in mathematics presents empirical questions that as yet have not been resolved. It would go beyond the scope of this chapter to review efforts along these lines, but the reader may refer to Geary (1994) for discussions on the improvement of mathematical abilities and the possible influences of heredity on the limits to which mathematical abilities can be enhanced by educational interventions.

To illustrate how the abilities discussed in this chapter may apply to mathematical thinking in the solution of tasks presented in mathematics teaching, let us consider several such tasks.

According to Carpenter, Corbitt, Kepner, Lindquist, and Reys (1980), only 9% of the 17-year-olds tested in the 1977–1978 National Assessment of Education Progress could solve the following exercise:

> How many cubic feet of concrete would be needed to pave an area 30 feet long and 20 feet wide with a layer four inches thick? (p. 237)

First, verbal comprehension and reading ability would be required to solve this. Beyond this, knowledge of the quantitative concepts of *area* and *cubic foot*, as well as knowledge of how to compute areas and volume, would be required. Also, the student would have to notice that "a layer four inches thick," for a single cubic foot, would be one-third of a cubic foot, and therefore, for the area computed as 600 square feet, the amount of concrete needed would be one-third of that, or 200 cubic feet. (At least, this would be one way of approaching the problem.) Presumably, this would require some degree of general intellectual ability, quantitative reasoning ability, or both, or perhaps more specifically, the ability to deduce the answer from the information given and the rules for computing areas and cubic dimensions.

A more difficult problem illustrating the use of inductive and deductive reasoning comes from an example for grades 5–8 provided in the *Curriculum and Evaluation Standards for School Mathematics* (National Council of Teachers of Mathematics, 1989):

> Students can be asked to explore the numbers that occur between twin primes for primes greater than 3. They might first look for twin primes to find examples and then make, test, and validate conjectures.
>
> 5 *6* 7; 11 *12* 13; 17 *18* 19; 29 *30* 31
>
> What do 6, 12, 18, and 30 have in common? Is this true for all twin primes? Why or why not? (p. 82)

It might be found that students high in inductive ability are more likely to notice that 6, 12, 18, and 30 are multiples of the first four prime numbers (1, 2, 3, 5) and thus to investigate whether further examples of twin primes would exhibit this property. The source cited here contains many more examples of the use of inductive and deductive reasoning in solving mathematical problems.

It would be a useful project to investigate the relations between various abilities mentioned here and the actual probabilities that students with different levels of ability could perform mathematical tasks of different degrees of difficulty. Such an investigation, or a series of them, would more clearly establish the role of these abilities in mathematics learning and achievement.

REFERENCES

Carpenter, P. A., Just, M. A., & Shell, P. (1990). What one intelligence test measures: A theoretical account of the processing in the Raven Matrices Test. *Psychological Review, 97*, 404–431.

Carpenter, T. P., Corbitt, M. K., Kepner, H. S., Jr., Lindquist, M. M., & Reys, R. E. (1980). National assessment: A perspective of students' mastery of basic mathematics skills. In M. M. Lindquist (Ed.), *Selected issues in mathematics education* (pp. 215–257). Berkeley, CA: McCutchan.

Carroll, J. B. (1985). Exploratory factor analysis: A tutorial. In D. K. Detterman (Ed.), *Current topics in human intelligence, Vol. 1: Research methodology* (pp. 25–58). Norwood, NJ: Ablex.

Carroll, J. B. (1988). Individual differences in cognitive functioning. In R. C. Anderson, R. J. Herrnstein, G. Lindzey, & R. D. Luce (Eds.), *Stevens' Handbook of Experimental Psychology, Vol. 2*, p. 822.

Carroll, J. B. (1993). *Human cognitive abilities: A survey of factor-analytic studies.* New York: Cambridge University Press.

Cattell, R. B. (1971). *Abilities: Their structure, growth, and action.* Boston: Houghton Mifflin.

Cattell, R. B., & Horn, J. L. (1978). A check on the theory of fluid and crystallized intelligence with description of new subtest designs. *Journal of Educational Measurement, 15*, 139–164.

Ceci, S. J. (1990). *On intelligence . . . more or less: A bioecological treatise on intellectual development.* Englewood Cliffs, NJ: Prentice-Hall.

Ceci, S. J., & Liker, J. K. (1986). A day at the races: A study of IQ, expertise, and cognitive complexity. *Journal of Experimental Psychology: General, 115*, 255–266.

Cohen, A. D. (1994). The language used to perform cognitive operations during full-immersion maths tasks. *Language Testing, 11*, 171–195.

Conley, J. J. (1984). The hierarchy of consistency: A review and model of longitudinal findings on adult individual differences in intelligence, personality, and self-opinion. *Personality and Individual Differences, 5*, 11–25.

Coombs, C. H. (1941). A factorial study of number ability. *Psychometrika, 6*, 161–189.

DeFries, J. C., & Gillis, J. J. (1993). Genetics of reading difficulty. In R. Plomin & G. E. McClearn (Eds.), *Nature, nurture, and psychology* (pp. 121–145). Washington, DC: American Psychological Association.

Eliot, J., & Smith, I. M. (1983). *An international directory of spatial tests.* Windsor, England: NFER-Nelson.

Ericsson, K. A., & Charness, N. (1994). Expert performance: Its structure and acquisition. *American Psychologist, 49*, 725–747.

Flavell, J. H. (1977). *Cognitive development.* Englewood Cliffs, NJ: Prentice-Hall.

Geary, D. C. (1993). Mathematical disabilities: Cognitive, neuropsychological, and genetic components. *Psychological Bulletin, 114*, 345–362.

Geary, D. C. (1994). *Children's mathematical development: Research and practical applications.* Washington, DC: American Psychological Association.

Gleick, J. (1992). *Genius: The life and science of Richard Feynman.* New York: Pantheon.

Gustafsson, J.-E. (1988). Hierarchical models of individual differences in cognitive abilities. In R. J. Sternberg (Ed.), *Advances in the psychology of human intelligence* (Vol. 4; pp. 35–71). Hillsdale, NJ: Lawrence Erlbaum Associates.

Gustafsson, J.-E., & Balke, G. (1993). General and specific abilities as predictors of school achievement. *Multivariate Behavioral Research, 28*, 407–434.

Hadamard, J. (1954). *An essay on the psychology of invention in the mathematical field.* New York: Dover.

Hambleton, R. K. (Ed.). (1983). *Applications of item response theory.* Vancouver, BC: Educational Research Institute of British Columbia.

Humphreys, L. G., Lubinski, D., & Yao, G. (1993). Utility of predicting group membership: Exemplified by the roles of spatial visualization in becoming an engineer, physical scientist, or artist. *Journal of Applied Psychology, 78*, 250–261.

Jensen, A. R. (1980). *Bias in mental testing.* New York: The Free Press.

Jensen, A. R. (1990). Speed of information processing in a calculating prodigy. *Intelligence, 14*, 259–274.

Jöreskog, K. G., & Sörbom, D. (1979). *Advances in factor analysis and structural equation models.* Cambridge, MA: Abt.

Kilpatrick, J., & Wagner, S. (1983). *Bibliography on mathematical abilities.* Athens, GA: Mathematical Abilities Project, University of Georgia.

Kyllonen, P. C. (1985). *Dimensions of information-processing speed.* Brooks Air Force Base, TX: Air Force Systems Command, AFHRL–TP–84–56.

Kyllonen, P. C., & Christal, R. E. (1989). Cognitive modeling of learning abilities: A status report of LAMP. In R. F. Dillon & J. W. Pellegrino (Eds.), *Testing: Theoretical and applied perspectives* (pp. 146–173). New York: Praeger.

Lord, F. M. (1980). *Applications of item response theory to practical testing problems.* Hillsdale, NJ: Lawrence Erlbaum Associates.

Lubinski, D., & Benbow, C. P. (1994). The Study of Mathematically Precocious Youth: The first three decades of a planned 50-year study of intellectual talent. In R. F. Subotnik & K. D. Arnold (Eds.), *Beyond Terman: Contemporary longitudinal studies of giftedness and talent* (pp. 255–281). Norwood, NJ: Ablex.

Lubinski, D., & Humphreys, L. G. (1990). A broadly based analysis of mathematical giftedness. *Intelligence, 14,* 327–355.

Marshalek, B., Lohman, D. F., & Snow, R. E. (1983). The complexity continuum in the radex and hierarchical models of intelligence. *Intelligence, 7,* 107–127.

National Council of Teachers of Mathematics. (1989). *Curriculum and evaluation standards for school mathematics.* Reston, VA: Author.

Nesher, P., & Kilpatrick, J. (Eds.). (1990). *Mathematics and cognition: A research synthesis by the International Group for the Psychology of Mathematics Education.* Cambridge, England: Cambridge University Press.

Raven, J. C. (1962). *Advanced progressive matrices, Set II.* London, England: H. K. Lewis. (Distributed in the United States by The Psychological Corporation, San Antonio, TX)

Sagiv, A. (1979). General growth model for evaluation of an individual's progress in learning. *Journal of Educational Psychology, 71,* 866–881.

Schaie, K. W., & Hertzog, C. (1986). Toward a comprehensive model of adult intellectual development: Contributions of the Seattle Longitudinal Study. In R. J. Sternberg (Ed.), *Advances in the psychology of human intelligence* (Vol. 3; pp. 79–118). Hillsdale, NJ: Lawrence Erlbaum Associates.

Schmid, J., & Leiman, J. M. (1957). The development of hierarchical factor solutions. *Psychometrika, 22,* 53–61.

Smith, S. B. (1983). *The great mental calculators: The psychology, methods, and lives of calculating prodigies.* New York: Columbia University Press.

Spearman, C. (1904). "General intelligence", objectively determined and measured. *American Journal of Psychology, 15,* 201–293.

Spearman, C. (1927). *The abilities of man: Their nature and measurement.* New York: Macmillan.

Stanley, J. C. (1974). Intellectual precocity. In J. C. Stanley, D. P. Keating, & L. H. Fox (Eds.), *Mathematical talent: Discovery, description, and development* (pp. 1–22). Baltimore: Johns Hopkins University Press.

Sternberg, R. J., & Weil, E. M. (1980). An aptitude × strategy interaction in linear syllogistic reasoning. *Journal of Educational Psychology, 72,* 226–238.

Thurstone, L. L. (1938). Primary mental abilities. *Psychometric Monographs, 1.* (With supplement containing the experimental psychological tests that were used in the factorial analysis described in the monograph)

Thurstone, L. L., & Ackerson, L. (1929). The mental growth curve for the Binet tests. *Journal of Educational Psychology, 20,* 569–583.

Undheim, J. O., & Gustafsson, J.-E. (1987). The hierarchical organization of cognitive abilities: Restoring general intelligence through the use of linear structural relations (LISREL). *Multivariate Behavioral Research, 22,* 149–171.

Vernon, P. E. (1961). *The structure of human abilities* (2nd ed.). London: Methuen.

Werdelin, I. (1961). *Geometrical ability and the space factor in boys and girls.* Lund, Sweden: Gleerups.

Winch, C. (1990). *Language, ability, and educational achievement.* New York: Routledge, Chapman & Hall.

II

COGNITIVE/INFORMATION-PROCESSING APPROACHES

2

▼▼▼▼▼▼▼

The Process of Understanding
Mathematical Problems

Richard E. Mayer
Mary Hegarty
University of California, Santa Barbara

INTRODUCTION TO MATHEMATICAL UNDERSTANDING

Anyone who has reviewed the recent outpouring of national and international assessments of mathematics achievement (e.g., Dossey, Mullis, Lindquist, & Chambers, 1988; LaPointe, Mead, & Phillips, 1989; Robitaille & Garden, 1989; Stevenson & Stigler, 1992; Stigler, Lee, & Stevenson, 1990) is confronted with an inescapable fact concerning the mathematics achievement of students in the United States: Although many students eventually learn to perform well on tests of low-level skills such as arithmetic computation, they tend to perform poorly on tests of high-level skills such as mathematical problem solving. For example, the 1986 National Assessment of Educational Progress found that nearly all tested 17-year-olds could solve basic arithmetic problems such as the one shown in the top of Fig. 2.1, but nearly all failed to solve multistep word problems such as the one shown in the bottom of the figure (Dossey et al., 1988). On average, many students may know how to carry out basic mathematical procedures when problems are presented in symbolic form but may not be able to apply these procedures to solve problems presented in words. In short, these assessments suggest that the difficulty for students lies in understanding problems rather than executing procedures.

In light of such performance, a call has gone out in the United States for the teaching of mathematical problem solving. For example, the *Curriculum*

Problem that Requires Computation

$604 - 207 = $ ___

Problem that Requires Understanding and Computation

Christine borrowed $850 for one year from the Friendly Finance Company. If she paid 12% simple interest on the loan, what was the total amount she repaid?

FIG. 2.1. Two types of mathematics problems. From Dossey et al. (1988). © 1988 by Educational Testing Service. Reprinted with permission.

and Evaluation Standards for School Mathematics (National Council of Teachers of Mathematics, 1989) calls for "a shift in emphasis from a curriculum dominated by memorization of isolated facts and procedures to one that emphasizes conceptual understandings, multiple representation and connection, mathematical modeling, and mathematical problem solving" (p. 125). The call is being heard. Around the nation, educators are busily revising mathematics curricula to emphasize higher order mathematical thinking—as exemplified in the *Mathematics Framework for California Public Schools* (California Department of Education, 1992).

The reform movement in American mathematics education provides an appropriate backdrop for cognitive psychologists who are interested in mathematical problem solving. Although the reforms continue, cognitive psychologists may be reminded of the unanswered theoretical questions whose answers could and, in my opinion, should, contribute to changes in mathematics education. Why are some students able to successfully compute answers for arithmetic problems, although they are unable to solve word problems that require using the same basic arithmetic computations? Which cognitive processes underlie mathematical problems solving? What do successful mathematical problem solvers know? These are the questions that motivate this chapter.

The domain of mathematical problem solving is becoming an exciting venue for cognitive science (Campbell, 1992; Mayer, 1989, 1992; Schoenfeld, 1985, 1987). Although the creation of a general theory of problem solving—based on general problem-solving strategies—was a major goal in the 1970s (Newell & Simon, 1972), current trends in the study of expertise point to the crucial role of domain specific knowledge in any complete account of problem solving (Chi, Glaser, & Farr, 1988; Ericsson & Smith, 1991; Smith, 1991; Sternberg & Frensch, 1991). By virtue of its long research history (Grouws, 1992; Resnick & Ford, 1981), its status as a premier "psychology of subject matter" (Mayer, 1989), and its affordances for cognitive modeling, the study of mathematical problem solving offers an important context for studying questions about cognition.

In constructing cognitive theories of problem solving, researchers have tended to focus on the procedures that problem solvers use in problem solution rather than the processes they use for representing problems (Mayer, 1985, 1992). Similarly, cognitive research in mathematics sometimes emphasizes the acquisition of mathematical skills such as computational procedures and strategies (Siegler & Jenkins, 1989; Singley & Anderson, 1989), whereas an equally important goal is to develop an account of the ways in which problem solvers understand problems (Kintsch & Greeno, 1985). By focusing on comprehension processes, we in no way wish to diminish the crucial role of basic cognitive skills such as computational procedures. Our motivation for studying problem comprehension processes derives from growing evidence that most problem solvers have more difficulty in constructing a useful problem representation than in executing a problem solution (Cardelle-Elawar, 1992; Cummins, Kintsch, Reisser & Weimer, 1988; De Corte, Verschaffel, & DeWinn, 1985).

What Is Mathematical Problem Solving?

A good place to start is with a workable definition of what is meant by basic terms such as problem, problem solving, mathematical problem, and mathematical problem solving. A problem exists when a problem solver "has a goal but does not know how this goal is to be reached" (Duncker, 1945, p. 1). In short, you have a problem when a situation is in a given state, you want the situation to be in a goal state, and there is no obvious way of moving from the given to the goal state. There are three elements in a description of a problem—the given state, the goal state, and the allowable operations. For example, if the problem is to reform the K–12 mathematics curriculum in the United States to foster problem solving, then the given state is the current curriculum, the goal state is a revised curriculum, and the allowable operators involve changing what happens in classrooms.

Problem solving (or thinking) occurs as a problem solver figures out how to solve a problem; that is, as the problem solver understands how to get from the given state to the goal state. Duncker (1945) eloquently stated: "Whenever one cannot go from the given situation to the desired situation simply by action, then there has to be recourse to thinking. Such thinking has the task of devising some action which will mediate between the existing and desired situations" (p. 1). In sum, problem solving (or thinking) refers to the cognitive processes enabling a problem solver to move from a state of not knowing how to solve a problem to a state of knowing how to solve it.

A problem can be categorized as a mathematics problem whenever a mathematical procedure, such as an arithmetic or algebraic procedure, is needed to solve the problem. For example, the foregoing word problem about Christine (shown in the bottom of Fig. 2.1) is a mathematics problem because the solution requires executing arithmetic computations. Similarly, mathematical problem solving (or thinking) occurs when a problem solver wishes to solve a mathematics problem but does not know how to do so. In summary, mathematical problem solving is the cognitive process of figuring out how to solve a mathematics problem that one does not already know how to solve.

What Are the Types of Mathematics Problems?

It is useful to further analyze mathematics problems into those that are routine and those that are not routine. A routine problem exists when a problem solver knows how to carry out the correct solution procedure and recognizes that the solution procedure is appropriate for the problem. For example, consider the problem: $(70 - 60) + (90 - 80) = $ ___. This is a routine problem for most educated adults because what to do is obvious and most adults know how to compute. The problem solver knows how to represent the problem—namely, carry out two subtractions and add the results—and the problem solver knows how to carry out the required operations—namely, how to subtract and add. According to a strict definition, routine problems are not really problems at all because the problem solver knows what to do and how to do it. For this reason, such problems are often referred to as *exercises*.

A nonroutine problem exists when a problem solver has a problem but does not immediately see how to solve it. For example, consider the horse-trading problem:

> A man bought a horse for $60 and sold it later for $70. Then he bought it back for $80 and sold it for $90. How much did he make in the horse-trading business? (Maier & Burke, 1967, p. 307)

This is a nonroutine problem because what to do is not obvious. When Maier and Burke gave this problem to students, they found that many students subtracted 60 from 70, subtracted 80 from 70, subtracted 80 from 90, and added the three results to yield an answer of 10. Although they carried out the computations correctly, these students had misunderstood the problem. They correctly carried out computations based on an incorrect representation of the problem. If the students were told that the first transaction involved a white horse and the second transaction involved a black horse, they were more likely to represent the problem correctly and carry out the correct solution plan (subtract 60 from 70 for the first transaction, subtract 80 from 90 for the second transaction, and add the results).

Some word problems may be routine for a problem solver, whereas other word problems are nonroutine. For example, if a student knows how to use the formula *distance = rate × time*, and is familiar with distance–rate–time problems, then the following problem is routine:

> A car travels for 2 hours at a rate of 40 miles per hour.
> How far does it go?

In this case, the problem is routine because the problem solver knows what to do (i.e., multiply 2 times 40) and how to do it (i.e., $2 \times 40 = 80$).

In contrast, consider the following problem which on the surface also seems like a distance–rate–time problem:

> A car in Philadelphia starts toward New York at 40 miles per hour. Fifteen minutes later, a car in New York starts toward Philadelphia, 90 miles away, at 55 miles per hour. Which car is nearest Philadelphia when they meet?

Although this problem may appear to be routine, Davidson (1995) found that most students failed to give the correct answer. It is really a nonroutine problem for most students because they fail to recognize what they are being asked to find. Once students understand the importance of the phrase "when they meet," it becomes clear that computation is not needed. Both cars are equally distant from Philadelphia when they meet.

As another example, consider the following word problem, which is routine for most high school students:

> Water lilies double in area every 24 hours. At the beginning of the week, there is one water lily on a lake. How many are there after 7 days?

This is a routine problem for someone who has solved many problems involving series sums because what to do is obvious—multiply $1 \times 2 \times 2 \times 2 \times 2 \times 2 \times 2 \times 2$—and the problem solver knows how to multiply.

In contrast, the following version of the water lily problem is nonroutine for most students:

> Water lilies double in area every 24 hours. At the beginning of the summer, there is one water lily on the lake. It takes 60 days for the lake to be completely covered with water lilies. On what day is the lake half covered?

When Sternberg and Davidson (1982) gave this problem to students, a common answer was to divide 60 by 2, and give 30 as the answer. In this case, the computation was correctly carried out but was based on an incorrect representation of the problem. Instead of trying to carry out computations, the problem solver needs to realize that on day 59 the lake must be half covered. This problem is nonroutine because the way to solve the problem is not immediately obvious. In this chapter, we focus on nonroutine rather than routine problems in order to better understand the process of how students represent mathematics problems.

What Are the Cognitive Processes in Mathematical Problem Solving?

It is customary in the problem solving literature to distinguish between two major kinds of problem-solving processes—representation and solution. Representation occurs when a problem solver seeks to understand the problem and solution occurs when a problem solver actually carries out actions needed to solve the problem.

For example, suppose a student who knows how to read English sentences and who knows how to compute answers to arithmetic problems is asked to solve the butter problem shown in Fig. 2.2. This problem requires two computations, so we call it a two-step problem. When we asked high school and college students to solve this problem, a common incorrect approach was to subtract 2 from 65 and multiple the result by 4, whereas the correct solution is to add 2 to 65 and multiply by 4 (Hegarty, Mayer, & Green, 1992; Hegarty, Mayer, & Monk, 1995; Lewis & Mayer, 1987). However, when we asked these same students to solve two-step computation problems, such as $4(65 + 2) =$ ___, they performed flawlessly.

Although all of the students in our study could solve computation problems such as $4(65 + 2) =$ ___, many generated the wrong answer for word problems requiring the identical computations. In these cases, the problem solver knows how to correctly execute the solution procedure—that is, knows how to carry out two-step arithmetic computations—but applies the procedure to an incorrect representation of the problem. In short, problem execution is routine but problem representation is nonroutine. This pattern suggests that students have difficulty in representation—that is, understanding the problem—but not in solution—that is, carrying out the computations in a solution plan.

Mayer (1985, 1992, 1994) has proposed four main component processes in mathematical problem solving—translating, integrating, planning, and executing. Translating involves constructing a mental representation of each statement in the problem, such as recognizing that the first statements means that the cost (in cents) of a stick of butter at Lucky is 65. Integrating involves constructing a mental representation of the situation described in the problem, including the recognition that butter costs more at Vons than at Lucky. Planning involves devising a plan for how to solve the problem, such as first computing the cost of a stick of butter at Vons by adding 2 to 65 and then finding the total cost by multiplying the result by 4. Executing involves carrying out the plan, including computations such as $65 + 2 = 67$ and $67 \times 4 = 268$.

In this chapter we focus on the processes involved in problem representation; namely, translating and integrating, as well as the natural product of problem representation; namely, planning. We focus on the process of

At Lucky, butter costs 65 cents per stick.
This is 2 cents less per stick than butter at Vons.
If you need to buy 4 sticks of butter,
how much will you pay at Vons?

FIG. 2.2.   The butter problem.

problem representation because students often correctly devise and carry out computational plans based on an incorrect representation of the problem. In short, we base our approach on the premise that an important key to mathematical problem solving rests in the processes by which students seek to understand mathematics problems. Consistent with classic theories of problem solving (Duncker, 1945; Mayer, 1992; Wertheimer, 1959), we contend that the major creative work in solving word problems rests in understanding what the problem means. According to this view, carrying out a solution plan naturally follows from the problem solver's representation of the problem.

THEORY OF MATHEMATICAL UNDERSTANDING

Two Paths to Mathematical Understanding

When confronted with a mathematical story problem, some people begin by selecting numbers from the problem and preparing to perform arithmetic operations on them—a procedure we call the *direct translation strategy*—whereas other people begin by trying to understand the situation being described in the problem and devising a solution plan based on their representation of the situation—a procedure we call the *problem model strategy*. The direct translation strategy is a short-cut heuristic approach that emphasizes computation, whereas the problem model approach is an in-depth rational approach based on problem understanding. The direct translation strategy emphasizes quantitative reasoning—that is, computing a numerical answer—whereas the problem model strategy emphasizes qualitative reasoning—that is, understanding the relations among the variables in the problem.

Direct Translation Strategy. For example, in the Christine problem presented in Fig. 2.1, a problem solver using the direct translation strategy would select at least some of the key numbers in the problem (such as 850 and 12) and perform an arithmetic operation that is most strongly primed by the keywords in the problem (such as "interest"). In this case, a problem solver might multiply 850 by .12, yielding the answer 102. This short-cut approach can be summarized as "compute first and think later" (Stigler et al., 1990, p. 15) because the problem solver engages in quantitative reasoning prior to qualitative reasoning (Mayer, Lewis, & Hegarty, 1992).

The direct translation strategy is a familiar character in several research literatures, as the method of choice for less successful problem solvers. For example, cross-national research on mathematical problem solving reveals that American children are more likely than Japanese children to engage in short-cut approaches to story problems, and that instruction in U.S. schools is more likely than instruction in Japanese schools to emphasize computing correct numerical answers at the expense of understanding the problem

(Stevenson & Stigler, 1992; Stigler et al., 1990). Similarly, research on expert/novice differences also reveals that novices are more likely to focus on computing a quantitative answer to a story problem (such as in physics), whereas experts are more likely initially to rely on a qualitative understanding of the problem before seeking a solution in quantitative terms (Chi et al., 1988; Smith, 1991; Sternberg & Frensch, 1991).

An advantage of the direct translation strategy is that it makes minimal demands on memory, and it does not depend on extensive knowledge of problem types. An important disadvantage is that it frequently leads to incorrect answers (Hegarty et al., 1992; Lewis & Mayer, 1987; Mayer et al., 1992; Verschaffel, De Corte, & Pauwels, 1992).

Problem Model Strategy. In contrast, the problem model strategy consists of constructing a qualitative understanding of the problem situation before attempting to carry out arithmetic computations. In the case of the Christine problem, for example, the problem solver begins by seeking to construct an internal representation of the individual statements in the problem—such as that the amount borrowed is a specified amount, the interest rate is a specified amount, and the amount owed is unknown. Also, the problem solver seeks to understand the general situation described in the problem—a person borrowed a certain amount of money (i.e., BORROWED AMOUNT), incurs a certain amount of interest (i.e., INTEREST AMOUNT), and must repay a total (i.e., TOTAL AMOUNT) consisting of the sum of the borrowed amount and the interest amount. Then the problem solver constructs a plan for solving the problem, such as first determining the interest amount (i.e., by multiplying .12 and 850) and then determining the total amount (i.e., by adding this product and 850). These three components—local understanding of problem statements, global understanding of the problem situation, and construction of a solution plan—constitute three major components in the process of mathematical problem solving (Mayer, 1985, 1992).

A Closer Look at the Comprehension Process

When a problem solver is confronted with a mathematical problem, how does the problem solver figure out what to do? In this section, we examine in more detail each of the three core components in the comprehension process—translation, integration, and planning. The role of these component processes in each of the two kinds of comprehension strategies is summarized in Fig. 2.3.

Construction of the Text Base. The first step is to represent each statement in the problem—a translation process that we assume is identical for both direct translation and problem model strategies. As in most theories of text comprehension (Just & Carpenter, 1987; Perrig & Kintsch, 1985; van Dijk & Kintsch, 1983; Weaver & Kintsch, 1992), we assume that the text in a

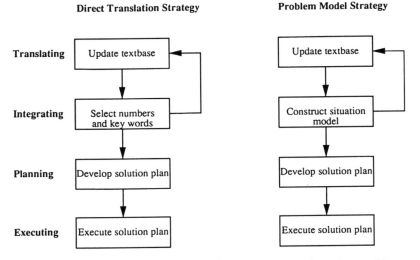

FIG. 2.3.   Cognitive processes in the direct translation and problem model strategies.

mathematics problem is processed in increments. At each increment, we assume that the problem solver reads a statement; that is, a clause or sentence expressing a piece of information about one of the variables or values in the problem. In constructing a text base, the problem solver must represent the propositional content of this statement and connect it with other information in his or her current representation of the problem.

In the process of representing each statement, the problem solver may use knowledge of types of statements that occur in mathematics problems, which have been analyzed formally by Mayer (1981). These include assignments, which express a value for a certain variable; relations, which express the quantitative relation between two variables; and questions, which express that the value of a certain variable is unknown. For example, the butter problem cited in Fig. 2.2 can be analyzed into two assignments, one relation, and a question:

((equals) BUTTER AT LUCKY, .65)
((equals) BUTTER AT LUCKY ((minus) BUTTER AT VONS, .02)
((equals) NUMBER OF BUTTER STICKS, 4)
((equals) TOTAL COST, unknown)

Units of measure and scale conversion must also be encoded as part of each statement.

As the problem solver reads over each new statement, he or she connects it with the current text base by making referential connections. This process depends on computing coreference as specified in general models of text comprehension (Clark, 1969; Ehrlich & Rayner, 1983). For example, in the butter problem, the problem solver must recognize that "this" in the second sentence refers to the same object as "butter at Lucky" in the first sentence, and that "sticks of butter" in the third sentence refers to "stick" in the first and second sentences. In summary, the primary task of the problem solver is to translate each statement from the problem into an internal propositional representation and to connect the propositions on basis on coreference into a semantic network representation.

Construction of the Problem Representation. The second step is the construction of a coherent representation of the problem—an integration process that we assume is quite different in the direct translation and problem model strategies. We propose that the problem solver cycles between this process and the process of constructing a text base several times while reading a problem. That is, we propose that as a problem solver reads each new statement of the problem, he or she first updates the text base and then updates the problem representation (Kintsch & Greeno, 1985; van Dijk & Kintsch, 1983). In the direct translation strategy, the integration process involves processing each proposition in the text base to determine whether or not it contains a key fact—that is, a number or a keyword such as "more," "less," or "altogether." We propose problem solvers delete nonessential information, so that after several cycles this representation contains much less information than the original text base—that is, only propositions that contain numbers and keywords. For example, in the butter problem, the problem solver abstracts 65 cents, 2 cents, less, how much, 4 sticks.

In contrast, consider the problem model strategy. We propose that problem solvers using this approach construct a mental model of the situation described in the problem using an object-centered representation. As each proposition is processed, the problem solver must determine whether it refers to a new object or an object that is already represented in his or her model. The problem model has been conceptualized as a collection of objects arranged in sets (Riley & Greeno, 1988; Riley, Greeno, & Heller, 1983) or as an array of objects along a number line where the position of an object represents its value (Case & Okamoto, in press; Lewis, 1989; Lewis & Nathan, 1991). We use the number line format here because it is more appropriate for the large quantities described in our example problems.

For example, in the butter problem, the first statement mentions one quantity—the price of a stick of butter at Lucky. When this is read, the problem solver might construct a representation of a number line with a symbol for Lucky at 65 on the number line. The second statement adds a second quantity—the price of a stick of butter at Vons, which is 2 cents more than the price at Lucky, so the problem solver must add a symbol for Vons 2 units to the right of Lucky on the number line. Therefore, the problem model consists of two objects, Lucky and Vons (representing the price of a stick of butter at these stores), with their relation represented by their relative positions on the number line. When the third sentence is processed, the problem solver must note that object in question is the cost of 4 sticks at Vons—so the symbol for Vons on the number line is so marked.

In summary, people who construct a problem model change the format of their representation from a proposition-based to an object-based representation and elaborate their representation at this stage of problem comprehension. In contrast, people who use the direct translation approach construct a more impoverished representation at this stage; that is, a representation that contains less information than the initial text base.

Construction of Solution Plan. Once the problem solver has represented the information in the problem, the problem solver is ready to plan the arithmetic computations necessary to solve the problem. A problem solver using the direct translation strategy must base the plan on the numbers and keywords that have been identified in the problem statement—"65," "2," and "less" suggest that the first step of the plan is to subtract 2 from 65 because "less" primes subtraction, and "how much" and "4" suggest that the second stage is to multiply the result by 4 because "how much" primes multiplication. The plan can be expressed as: $(65 - 2) \times 4 = \_\_\_\_$.

In contrast, a problem solver using the problem model strategy has a richer representation on which to base a solution plan. For example, the relative position of Vons and Lucky on the number line indicates that to determine the value of a stick of butter at Vons one must add because Vons is to the right of Lucky. This representation allows the problem solver to develop a plan that can be expressed as $(65 + 2) \times 4 = \_\_\_\_$. Another important function of the problem model representation is that it is an aid to monitoring the solution process. For example, if the problem solver computes a value for the price at Vons that is less than 65 cents, he or she knows it is wrong because the price is greater than at Lucky.

In summary, we propose that a problem solver may use one of two types of strategies for representing a word problem—a direct translation strategy or a problem model strategy. The direct translation strategy consists of a translation process in which a problem solver mentally represents each statement in the word problem as a semantic network, and an integration process in which a problem solver extracts numbers and key words that prime arithmetic operations to be performed on them. The resulting solution plan is likely to be incorrect for problems in which the key words prime incorrect operations (e.g., when the problem contains "less" but the required operation is addition). In contrast, the problem model approach consists of the same translation process but a different integration process in which the problem solver seeks to mentally construct a model of the situation described in the problem. The resulting solution plan is likely to be correct even for problems in which the key words prime incorrect operations, such as the butter problem. We expect the direct translation strategy to be the choice of unsuccessful problem solvers and the problem model strategy to be preferred by successful problem solvers.

RESEARCH ON MATHEMATICAL UNDERSTANDING

In this section, we explore the two-strategy theory of problem representation by examining how experienced students process arithmetic word problems. In particular, we draw on a program of research carried out at the University of California, Santa Barbara, over the past 15 years that examines how people read, remember, and learn to solve word problems.

Reading Word Problems

In one strand of research (Hegarty et al., 1992; Hegarty et al., 1995), we examined the eye fixations of high school and college students as they read word problems. For example, Fig. 2.2 shows how a typical problem was presented on a computer screen. The student's task was to tell how to solve the problem—such as saying "add 2 to 65 and then multiply by 4." Therefore, this task requires the cognitive processes of translating, integrating, and planning, but does not require executing. An eye-tracking system monitored and recorded the student's eye fixations, and a video camera recorded the student's answer.

Each student saw a mixture of problems, including some consistent and some inconsistent language problems, as shown in Fig. 2.4. These are two-step problems in which the first step requires addition or subtraction and the second step involves multiplication. In consistent language problems, the required operation for the first step is primed by the key word (e.g., the required operation was subtraction when the key word was "less," or the required operation was addition when the key word was "more"). In inconsistent language problems, the required operation for the first step was the reverse of the operation primed by the key word (e.g., the required operation was addition when the key word was "less," or the required operation was subtraction when the key word was "more"). Some students (who we labeled as unsuccessful) made many errors in planning solutions to the problems, whereas others (who we labeled as successful) did not make many errors. The most common error was a reversal error in which a student used the arithmetic operation primed by the key word when the opposite operation

Consistent-Less

At Lucky, butter costs 65 cents per stick.
Butter at Vons costs 2 cents less per stick than butter at Lucky.
If you need to buy 4 sticks of butter,
how much will you pay at Vons?

Consistent-More

At Lucky, butter costs 65 cents per stick.
Butter at Vons costs 2 cents more per stick than butter at Lucky.
If you need to buy 4 sticks of butter,
how much will you pay at Vons?

Inconsistent-Less

At Lucky, butter costs 65 cents per stick.
This is 2 cents less per stick than butter at Vons.
If you need to buy 4 sticks of butter,
how much will you pay at Vons?

Inconsistent-More

At Lucky, butter costs 65 cents per stick.
This is 2 cents more per stick than butter at Vons.
If you need to buy 4 sticks of butter,
how much will you pay at Vons?

FIG. 2.4. Consistent and inconsistent language versions of the butter problem.

was required, such as saying "subtract 2 from 65 and multiply by 4" for the version of the butter problem in Fig. 2.2.

Prediction 1: Successful Problem Solvers Spend More Time Reading Inconsistent Problems Than Reading Consistent Language Problems. Research on reading allows us to examine the impact of the direct translation and problem model approaches on understanding word problems. If students use a problem model approach, then inconsistent problems will require more time to read than will consistent problems. This is so because constructing a problem model for an inconsistent problem involves mentally reversing the relational term, whereas constructing a problem model for a consistent problem does not include this extra step. For example, for the inconsistent problem in Fig. 2.2, the second quantity (denoted by "Vons") must be placed to the right of Lucky on the number line, although the key word "less" suggests placing it to the left of Lucky. In contrast, if students use a direct translation approach then inconsistent problems and consistent problems will require approximately the same amount of time to read because the process of extracting key words and numbers is equivalent for consistent and inconsistent problems. This pattern is predicted because successful problem solvers—that is, those who devise a correct solution plan—presumably use a problem model approach.

The results of a series of studies revealed that, as expected, successful problem solvers required more time to read inconsistent language problems than to read consistent language problems. We interpret this result to suggest that successful engaged in more cognitive processing for inconsistent than for consistent problems.

How was this extra time spent? To answer this question, we examined the eye-fixation data for consistent and inconsistent versions of two-step compare problems such as the butter problem presented in Fig. 2.4. We defined the translation phase as the time it took to read from the first line to the end of the fourth line—that is, the time to initially read the problem over from start to finish. We defined the integration and planning phase as the time it took from that point to when the student began to verbally state the answer—that is, the time to reread parts of the problem. Interestingly, successful students devoted approximately the same amount of time to the translation phase for both consistent and inconsistent problems—about 10 seconds; however, they went on to spend considerably more time rereading parts of inconsistent problems than rereading parts of consistent problems.

If the extra time is used to build a situation model of the problem, then the extra time should be devoted disproportionately to rereading the variable names and key terms—such as "Lucky" in line 1, "Vons" (or "Lucky") in line 2, "more" (or "less") in line 2, and "Vons" in line 4. This is the information that the reader needs in order to determine, for example, at which store butter costs more—a key component in building a situation model. If the extra time is used mainly to grab numbers, then students are more likely to reread the numbers in the problem—"65 cents" in line 1, "2 cents" in line 2, and "4 sticks" in line 3. A comparison of the number of times successful problem solvers reread each word in consistent and in inconsistent problems reveals significant differences for only four groups of words—for the variable name in line 1, the variable name in line 2, "less" (or "more") in line 2, and the variable name in line 4. Overall, problems solvers reread these items more than twice as many times when then were in inconsistent problems than when they were in consistent problems. These results suggest that successful problem solvers are sensitive to the need to devote extra time to inconsistent language problems, and that this extra time is spent constructing a qualitative rather than a quantitative representation of the problem.

Prediction 2: This Pattern of Longer Reading Time for Inconsistent Than for Consistent Problems Will Be Present for Successful Problem Solvers but not for Unsuccessful Problem Solvers. A second prediction is that this pattern of longer reading time for inconsistent than for consistent problems will be present for successful problem solvers—who presumably are more likely than unsuccessful problem solvers to use a problem model approach on both types of problems—but not for unsuccessful problem solvers—who presumably are more likely than successful problem solvers to use a direct translation approach on both types of problems. This prediction follows from the contention that students using a problem model strategy (i.e., the method of choice of successful problem solvers) must engage in more cognitive processing for inconsistent than for consistent problems, whereas students using a direct translation strategy (i.e., the method of choice of unsuccessful problem solvers) need to devote the same amount of processing to both types of problems.

In several studies, we compared the eye-fixation patterns of unsuccessful and successful problem solvers (Hegarty et al., 1992; Hegarty, Mayer, & Monk, 1995). In a typical study, we defined a successful problem solver as someone who made 0 or 1 errors on a set of 16 word problems; we defined an unsuccessful problem as someone who made 4 or more errors on a set of 16 word problems. We expected unsuccessful problem solvers to be more likely than successful problem solvers to use a direct translation approach—that is, mainly grabbing numbers and key words—whereas we expected successful problem solvers to be more likely than unsuccessful problem solvers to use a problem model approach—that is, constructing a model of the situation described in the problem statement.

The results indicated that, as predicted, successful problem solvers spent more time on inconsistent than on consistent problems whereas unsuccessful problem solvers spent about the same amount of time on both types of problems. A further analysis of the students' eye fixations revealed that, overall, unsuccessful problem solvers made more regressions (i.e., reread parts of the problem more times) than successful problem solvers, suggesting that they were struggling more to construct problem representations than were successful problem solvers. Our main focus, however, is on the type of words that successful and unsuccessful problem solvers reread as they struggled to represent problems. If unsuccessful problem solvers are using a direct translation approach, we expect them to devote proportionately more attention to numbers (e.g., 65, 2, and 4 in the butter problem). In contrast, if successful problem solvers are using a problem model approach, we expect them to devote relatively more attention to variable names (e.g., Lucky and Vons in the butter problem).

As expected, successful problem solvers devoted a significantly higher percentage of their rereadings to variable names and a lower percentage of rereadings to numbers than did unsuccessful problem solvers. It apears that unsuccessful problem solvers work hard to represent the problems, but spend their additional effort disproportionately in rereading numbers rather than in rereading variable names. This focus on numbers suggests that unsuccessful problem solvers tend to use a direct translation strategy. In contrast, successful problem solvers need to devote less extra processing to problems than do unsuccessful problem solvers, but when they are more balanced than the unsuccessful problem solvers in devoting their attention to both variable names and numbers. This more balanced focus on words and numbers is consistent with the problem model strategy.

The picture that emerges from research on reading mathematics problems is that there is more to successful problem representation than reading every word of the problem. Our research suggests that although successful and unsuccessful problem solvers both showed evidence of engaging in a translation process, only successful problem solvers followed up with an integration process resulting in the construction of a situation model. These results are consistent with the claim that successful problem solvers are model builders who seek to understand the situation being described in the problem statement. In contrast, unsuccessful problem solvers appear to be number grabbers who extract numbers and perform arithmetic operations primed by keywords in the problem statement.

Remembering Word Problems

An examination of recall protocols provides a second useful approach to the study of mathematical understanding (Hegarty et al., 1995; Mayer, 1982). In our research, we asked students to read a series of arithmetic word problems. For each problem, students were assigned to treatment groups that required them either to write down the key information, draw a picture, construct a diagram, or compute an answer. Then they were given memory tests such as cued recall and recognition.

Mayer (1981) has shown that word problems consist of assignment statements and relational statements. Assignment statements specify a numerical value for a variable, such as "At Lucky, butter costs 65 cents per stick." In this case, the value is 65 and the variable is the cost (in cents) per stick at Vons. The assignment can be expressed as $LUCKY = 65$. A relational statement expresses the quantitative relation between two variables such as "This is two cents less per stick than butter at Vons." In this case, the relation can be expressed as an equation, $LUCKY = 2 + VONS$, where LUCKY is the cost (in cents) per stick at Lucky and VONS is the cost (in cents) per stick at Vons.

Prediction 3: Students Make More Errors in Remembering Relational Statements Than in Remembering Assignment Statements. The construction of a situation model requires special attention be paid to relations among the variables, particularly as expressed in the relational statements. Therefore, if a student uses a problem model approach, then the student should remember the actual relation between the two variables described in a relational statement. For example, the crucial relation in the relational statement in the butter problem is that butter at Vons costs more than butter at Lucky. In contrast, if a student uses a direct translation strategy, a primary goal is to assign values to variables. Therefore, the student is less likely to correctly remember relational statements. It follows that when students make errors in remembering word problems, they will be more likely to make errors in remembering relations than assignments.

In order to test this prediction, we asked college students to read and later to recall a series of eight problems. The student had 2 minutes to read each problem, and was asked to draw a picture, write an equation, or summarize the main information. As predicted, students made 3 times as many errors in recalling relational statements than in recalling assignment statements that had appeared in the problems. Furthermore, an analysis of errors revealed 20 cases in which students remembered a relation as an assignment, but only one case in which an assignment was recalled as a relation. For example, one student changed the relational statement "The steamer's engine drives in still water at a rate of 12 miles per hour more than the rate the current," to an assignment statement, "its engines push the boat at 12 mph in still water." These results suggest that students have more difficulty in representing, storing, or retrieving relations (or any combination thereof) than assignments, and point to the difficulty some students may face in using a problem model approach on problems involving relational statements.

Prediction 4: Successful Problem Solvers Are More Likely to Remember the Relation Between Two Variables and Less Likely to Remember the Exact Wording of the Relational Term Than Are the Unsuccessful Problem Solvers.

We can make a more specific prediction concerning the retention performance of unsuccessful and successful problem solvers. We define successful problem solvers as those who use a correct solution plan in solving a set of word problems and unsuccessful problems as those who make errors in solving a set of word problems. If unsuccessful students use a direct translation approach, we expect them to remember the key word (e.g., "less" or "more"), but not necessarily to remember the correct relations among the variables (e.g., that butter costs more at Vons than Lucky), especially when the key word is inconsistent with the correct relation. If successful students use a problem model approach, we expect them to remember the correct relations among the variables, but not necessarily to remember the exact wording of the key word.

To test this prediction, we asked college students to solve a series of 12 word problems that contained four target problems, which were two-step problems with relational statements such as the butter problem. Then we asked students to recall the problems and to take a recognition test. In scoring the retention performance, we scored a response as a semantic error if the student remembered the key word (i.e., "less"), but not the actual relation between the variables (e.g., butter costs less at Lucky than at Vons or butter costs more at Vons than at Lucky). For example, if one of the target problems was the version of the butter problem presented at the top of Fig. 2.5, then a semantic error involves recalling or recognizing the middle problem in Fig. 2.5. In this case, the student remembers the wording of the relational term in the relational statement (i.e., "less") but changes the meaning of the problem. Similarly, we scored a response as a literal error if the student remembered the wrong keyword (e.g., "more" instead of "less") but retained the correct meaning of the problem, such in the bottom problem in Fig. 2.5. In this case, the relational statement is reworded but describes the same situation as the original.

As expected, unsuccessful problem solvers were more likely than successful problem solvers to make semantic errors in recalling and recognizing the problems, whereas successful problem solvers were more likely than unsuccessful problem solvers to make literal errors in recalling and recognizing the problems. This pattern is consistent with the idea that unsuccessful problem solvers are more likely than successful problem solvers to use a direct translation strategy—thereby focusing on wording rather than on meaning. Successful problem solvers, however, are more likely than unsuccessful problem solvers to use a problem model strategy for understanding the problems— thereby focusing on the meaning of the situation rather than on wording.

Overall, research on remembering word problems pinpoints relational statements as a major source of difficulty, with direct translation strategy users more likely than problem model strategy users to make semantic errors in remembering the relations between variables.

Original Problem
  At Lucky, butter costs 65 cents per stick.
  This is 2 cents less per stick than butter at Vons.
  If you need to buy 4 sticks of butter,
  how much will you pay at at Vons?

Semantic Error
  At Lucky, butter costs 65 cents per stick.
  Butter at Vons costs 2 cents less per stick than butter at Lucky.
  If you need to buy 4 sticks of butter,
  how much will you pay at at Vons?

Literal Error
  At Lucky, butter costs 65 cents per stick.
  Butter at Vons costs 2 cents more per stick than butter at Lucky.
  If you need to buy 4 sticks of butter,
  how much will you pay at at Vons?

FIG. 2.5. Semantic and literal errors in remembering the butter problem.

Learning to Solve Word Problems

The foregoing analyses provide evidence for two distinct strategies that students use for understanding word problems—a direct translation strategy based on a superficial analysis of the problem statement and a problem model strategy based on the construction of a situation model of the problem statement. Unfortunately, a review of mathematics textbooks shows that most of the word problems can be solved by using a direct translation strategy and that in, some cases, a direct translation strategy is explicitly taught (Briars & Larkin, 1984). For example, when a set of exercises contains problems that can all be solved using exactly the same computational procedure, students can be successful by using a direct translation strategy and do not need to use a problem model strategy. In this case, there is no need to expend the effort to understand the meaning of the problem because the problem can easily be solved by extracting the numbers in the problem statement and using key words to determine the mathematical operations that should be applied to them.

Prediction 5: Students Make More Errors on Solving Inconsistent Problems Than on Solving Consistent Problems. If many students become accustomed to using a direct translation strategy during their K–12 education in mathematics, we would expect them to perform errorlessly on problems that can be correctly solved using direct translation (i.e., consistent language problems), but to make errors on problems requiring the problem model strategy (i.e., inconsistent language problems). Therefore, we predict that college students will be more likely to make errors in solving inconsistent than on consistent problems. In particular, we predict that the type of errors students will make on inconsistent problems involves carrying out the operation primed by the key word in the problem. We refer to this as a *reversal error* because the problem solver adds when the correct operation is to subtract or subtracts when the correct operation is to add.

To test this prediction, we examined the errors that college students made as they solved a series of word problems containing both consistent and inconsistent language problems (Lewis & Mayer, 1987). Interestingly, students made errors on about 10% of the problems and the overwhelming majority of errors were reversal errors rather than computational errors. This finding helps to pinpoint the locus of difficulties for students who presumably have learned how to solve word problems: They have more difficulty in representing problems than in carrying out arithmetic procedures; that is, they are more likely to make errors in problem understanding than in solution execution. As predicted, students made almost no reversal errors on consistent language problems but produced reversal errors on many of the inconsistent language problems. Similarly, in follow-up studies, students were 5 to 10 times more likely to make reversal errors on inconsistent than on consistent language problems (Hegarty et al., 1992; Lewis, 1987).

Prediction 6: Teaching Students How to Represent Problems Reduces Problem-Solving Errors.   These results provide evidence that students who have received many years of mathematics education often fail to correctly understand word problems—as indicated by failures to understand the relations among variables in inconsistent language problems. A straightforward instructional implication of this line of research is that students should be taught how to represent word problems—particularly, relational statements in word problems. If students who make reversal errors on inconsistent problems tend to use a direct translation strategy, then instruction in how to use a problem model strategy should reduce problem-solving errors.

This prediction was tested in an instructional study by Lewis (1989). College students took a pretest containing both consistent and inconsistent language problems, and approximately one-third showed a pattern of making many errors on inconsistent but not on consistent language problems. These students, whose error pattern suggested they tended to sometimes use a direct translation strategy, were given instruction in how to represent word problems within the context of a number line diagram. A typical instructional worksheet is shown in Fig. 2.6. In this example, students first translated the first sentence by placing Megan's savings on the number line and then translated the second line by placing James to the right or left of Megan's savings. Once the student had determined the correct qualitative relation between Megan's savings and James' savings, the next step was to determine the amount of the difference and finally to determine the required arithmetic operation for finding the value of James' savings. The use of the number line was intended to help students to learn how to build a situation model of the problem.

What is the effect of training aimed at helping direct translation strategy users to become problem model strategy users? Students who received problem model strategy training showed large pretest-to-posttest reductions in problem-solving errors on word problems, whereas comparison students who did not receive problem model strategy training did not show large reductions. This result provides converging evidence that a major source of problem solving difficulty is problem representation, and that problem representation strategies can be taught.

Overall, the picture that emerges from research on learning to solve word problems is that many students fail to learn how to represent word problems during their K–12 mathematics education; that is, they seem to have learned to rely on a direct translation strategy for at least some problems. However, when unsuccessful problem solvers learn how to use a problem model strategy, their problem-solving errors are dramatically reduced, suggesting that their

Sample Problem

Megan has saved $420 for vacation. She has saved 1/5 as much as James has saved. James has been saving for his vacation for 6 months. How much has he saved each month?

Diagramming Steps

1. Draw a number line and place the variable and the value from the assignment statement in the middle of the line.

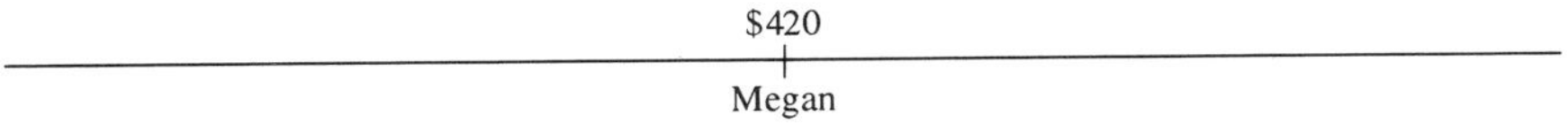

$420
|
Megan

2. Tentatively place the unknown variable (James' savings) on one side of the middle.

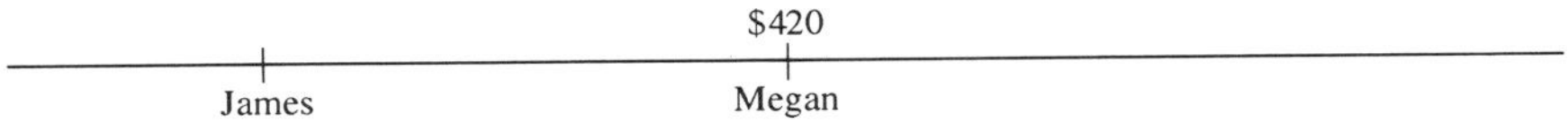

$420
| |
James Megan

3. Compare your representation with the information in the relation statement, checking to see if your representation agrees with the meaning of the relation statement. If it does, then you can continue. If not, then try again with the other side.

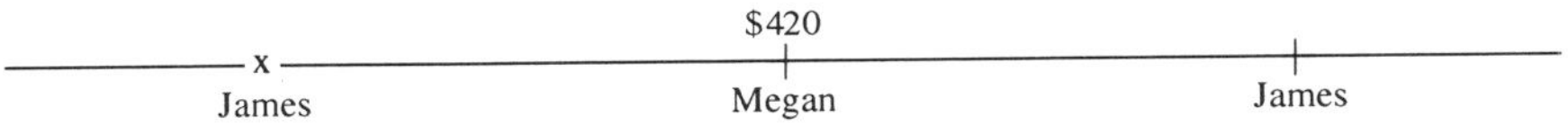

$420
——— x ———— | ————————— |
James Megan James

4. Translate your representation into an arithmetic operation. If the unknown variable is to the right of the center, then the operation is an increase, such as addition or multiplication. If the unknown variable is to the left of the center, then the operation is a decrease, such as subtraction or division.

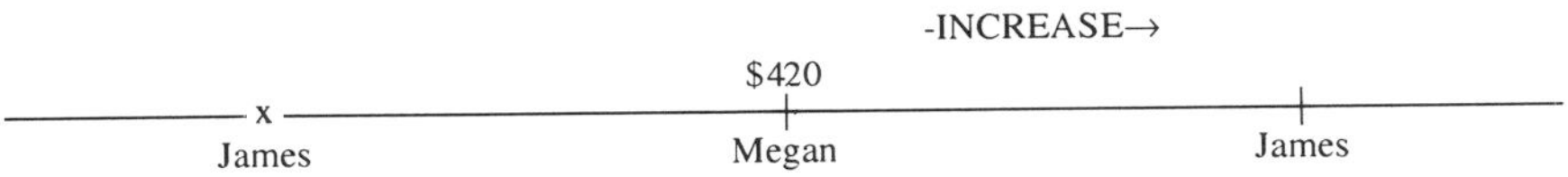

-INCREASE→
$420
——— x ———— | ————————— |
James Megan James

FIG. 2.6. A worksheet for learning to construct a number line representation of a word problem.

problem representation strategies are a major determinant of their problem-solving performance.

DISCUSSION

A review of a series of research studies on reading of word problems (Hegarty et al., 1992; Hegarty et al., 1995), remembering word problems (Hegarty et al., 1995; Mayer, 1982), and learning to solve word problems (Lewis, 1989; Lewis & Mayer, 1987) yields six major pieces of evidence concerning our two-strategy theory of problem understanding:

1. *Consistency effect in reading time for word problems.* Successful students take more time to read inconsistent problems than to read consistent prob-

lems, and spend that extra time by rereading variable names more in inconsistent than in consistent problems. This evidence supports the contention that successful students use a problem model strategy.

2. *Expertise effect in reading time for word problems.* Unsuccessful students focus a larger proportion of their rereading on numbers than do successful students, whereas successful students focus a larger proportion of their rereading on variable names than do unsuccessful students. This evidence supports the contention that unsuccessful students are more likely than successful students to use a direct translation strategy whereas successful students are more likely than unsuccessful students to use a problem model strategy.

3. *Statement type effect in remembering word problems.* In recalling word problems, students make more errors in remembering relational statements than in remembering assignment statements, and are more likely to change a relational statement into an assignment statement than to change an assignment statement into a relational statement. This evidence supports the contention that many students emerge from high school with the tendency to use a direct translation strategy rather than a problem model strategy for understanding word problems.

4. *Expertise effect in remembering word problems.* In recalling and recognizing relational statements in word problems, unsuccessful students are more likely to remember the exact wording of the relational key word and less likely to remember the correct relation between variables in the situation than are successful students. This evidence supports the contention that unsuccessful students are more likely than successful students to use a direct translation strategy, whereas successful students are more likely than unsuccessful students to use a problem model strategy.

5. *Consistency effect in learning to solve problems.* Unsuccessful students make more errors on inconsistent than on consistent problems, and most errors are reversal errors rather than computational errors. This evidence supports the contention that many students emerge from high school with the tendency to use a direct translation strategy rather than a problem model strategy for understanding word problems.

6. *Instructional effect in learning to solve problems.* Unsuccessful students can become successful students when they are given direct instruction in how to build a situation model. This evidence supports the contention that unsuccessful students are more likely than unsuccessful students to use a direct translation strategy, whereas successful students are more likely than unsuccessful students to use a problem model strategy.

Overall, our program of research provides converging evidence that students often emerge from K–12 mathematics education with adequate problem execution skills—that is, the ability to accurately carry out arithmetic and algebraic procedures—but inadequate problem representation skills—that is, the ability to understand the meaning of word problems. In particular, our research program has examined two distinct problem representation strategies—a direct translation strategy, which is based on a superficial understanding of word problems, and a problem model strategy, which requires mentally constructing a model of the situation described in the word problem. We have developed a diagnostic measure of students' problem representation strategies—namely, a pattern in which students make reversal errors on inconsistent but not on consistent problems (with no difference in solution times) indicates a direct translation strategy, whereas a pattern in which students take more time to solve inconsistent than consistent problems (with no difference in error rates) indicates a problem model strategy.

Furthermore, we have traced the source of problem-representation difficulty to relational statements—as indicated by a pattern in which students are far more likely to make errors in remembering relations, which express the quantitative relation between two variables—than in remembering assignments, which express the value of a single variable. Students using a direct translation strategy are more likely to remember the wording of the key word in a relational statement than are students using a problem model approach, but students using a problem model approach are more likely to remember the correct relation between variables in relational statement than are students using a direct translation approach.

Finally, we have identified a major difference in the problem-representation strategies of successful and unsuccessful problem solvers: Successful problem solvers tend to use a problem model strategy, whereas unsuccessful problem solvers tend to use a direct translation strategy. However, when direct translation strategy users (who are unsuccessful problem solvers) are taught how to use a problem model strategy, their problem-solving errors are largely eliminated (allowing them to become successful problem solvers).

In summary, our research on how students read, remember, and solve word problems reveals that the source of difficulty in mathematical problem solving is in problem representation rather than solution execution, the source of difficulty in problem representation is in comprehending relational statements rather than assignment statements, and the source of difficulty in understanding relational statements involves using a problem model strategy rather than a direct translation strategy.

REFERENCES

Briars, D. J., & Larkin, J. H. (1984). An integrated model of skill in solving elementary word problems. *Cognition and Instruction, 1*, 245–296.

California Department of Education. (1992). *Mathematics framework for California public schools*. Sacramento, CA: Author.

Campbell, J. I. D. (Ed.). (1992). *The nature and origins of mathematical skills.* Amsterdam: Elsevier.

Cardelle-Elawar, M. (1992). Effects of teaching metacognitive skills to students with low mathematics ability. *Teaching and Teacher Education, 8,* 109–121.

Case, R., & Okamoto, Y. (in press). The role of central conceptual structures in the development of children's numerical, literary, and spatial thought. *Monographs of the Society for Research in Child Development.*

Chi, M. T. H., Glaser, R., & Farr, M. J. (Eds.). (1988). *The nature of expertise.* Hillsdale, NJ: Lawrence Erlbaum Associates.

Clark, H. H. (1969). Linguistic processes in deductive reasoning. *Psychological Review, 76,* 387–404.

Cummins, D., Kintsch, W., Reisser, K., & Weimer, R. (1988). The role of understanding in solving word problems. *Cognitive Psychology, 20,* 439–462.

Davidson, J. E. (1995). The suddenness of insight. In R. J. Sternberg & J. E. Davidson (Eds.), *The nature of insight* (pp. 125–155). Cambridge, MA: MIT Press.

DeCorte, E., Verschaffel, L., & DeWinn, L. (1985). The influence of rewording verbal problems on children's problem representation and solutions. *Journal of Educational Psychology, 77,* 460–470.

Dossey, J. A., Mullis, I. V. S., Lindquist, M. M., & Chambers, D. L. (1988). *The mathematics report card: Are we measuring up?* Princeton, NJ: Educational Testing Service.

Duncker, K. (1945). On problem solving. *Psychological Monographs, 58* (5, Whole No. 270).

Ehrlich, K., & Rayner, K. (1983). Pronoun assignment and semantic integration during reading: Eye movements and immediacy of processing. *Journal of Verbal Learning and Verbal Behavior, 22,* 75–87.

Ericsson, K. A., & Smith, J. (Eds.). (1991). *Toward a general theory of expertise.* Cambridge, England: Cambridge University Press.

Grouws, D. A. (Ed.). (1992). *Handbook of research on mathematics teaching and learning.* New York: Macmillan.

Hegarty, M., Mayer, R. E., & Green, C. (1992). Comprehension of arithmetic word problems: Evidence from students' eye fixations. *Journal of Educational Psychology, 84,* 76–84.

Hegarty, M., Mayer, R. E., & Monk, C. A. (1995). Comprehension of arithmetic word problems. *Journal of Educational Psychology, 85,* 18–32.

Just, M., & Carpenter, P. A. (1987). *The psychology of reading and language comprehension.* Newton, MA: Allyn & Bacon.

Kintsch, W., & Greeno, J. G. (1985). Understanding and solving word problems. *Psychological Review, 92,* 109–129.

LaPointe, A. E., Mead, N. A., & Phillips, G. W. (1989). *A world of differences: An international assessment of mathematics and science.* Princeton, NJ: Educational Testing Service.

Lewis, A. B. (1989). Training students to represent arithmetic word problems. *Journal of Educational Psychology, 79,* 521–531.

Lewis, A. B., & Mayer, R. E. (1987). Students' miscomprehension of relational statements in arithmetic word problems. *Journal of Educational Psychology, 79,* 363–371.

Lewis, A. B., & Nathan, M. J. (1991). A framework for improving students' comprehension of word arithmetic and word algebra problems. In L. Birnbaum (Ed.), *Proceedings of the International Conference on the Learning Sciences* (pp. 305–314). Charlottesville, VA: Association for the Advancement of Computing in Education.

Maier, N. R. F., & Burke, R. J. (1967). Response availability as a factor in the problem-solving performance of males and females. *Journal of Personality and Social Psychology, 5,* 304–310.

Mayer, R. E. (1981). Frequency norms and structural analysis of algebra story problems. *Instructional Science, 10,* 135–175.

Mayer, R. E. (1982). Memory for algebra story problems. *Journal of Educational Psychology, 74,* 199–216.

Mayer, R. E. (1985). Mathematical ability. In R. J. Sternberg (Ed.), *Human abilities: An information-processing approach* (pp. 127–150). New York: Freeman.

Mayer, R. E. (1989). Cognition and instruction in mathematics. *Journal of Educational Psychology, 81,* 452–456.

Mayer, R. E. (1992). *Thinking, problem solving, cognition* (2nd ed.). New York: Freeman.

Mayer, R. E. (1994). Mathematical ability. In R. J. Sternberg (Ed.), *Encyclopedia of intelligence* (pp. 127–150). New York: Macmillan.

Mayer, R. E., Lewis, A. B., & Hegarty, M. (1992). Mathematical misunderstandings: Qualitative reasoning about quantitative problems. In J. I. D. Campbell (Ed.), *The nature and origins of mathematical skills* (pp. 137–153). Amsterdam: Elsevier.

National Council of Teachers of Mathematics. (1989). *Curriculum and evaluation standards for school mathematics.* Reston, VA: Author.

Newell, A., & Simon, H. A. (1972). *Human problem solving.* Englewood Cliffs, NJ: Prentice-Hall.

Perrig, W., & Kintsch, W. (1985). Propositional and situational representations of text. *Journal of Memory & Language, 24,* 503–518.

Resnick, L. B., & Ford, W. (1981). *The psychology of mathematics for instruction.* Hillsdale, NJ: Lawrence Erlbaum Associates.

Riley, M. S., & Greeno, J. G. (1988). Developmental analysis of understanding language about quantities and of solving problems. *Cognition and Instruction, 5,* 49–101.

Riley, M. S., Greeno, J. G., & Heller, J. I. (1983). Development of children's problem solving ability in arithmetic. In H. P. Ginsberg (Ed.), *The development of mathematical thinking* (pp. 153–196). San Diego: Academic Press.

Robitaille, D. F., & Garden, R. A. (1989). *The IEA study of mathematics II: Contexts and outcomes of school mathematics.* Oxford, England: Pergamon.

Schoenfeld, A. H. (1985). *Mathematical problem solving.* San Diego: Academic Press.

Schoenfeld, A. H. (Ed.). (1987). *Cognitive science and mathematics education.* Hillsdale, NJ: Lawrence Erlbaum Associates.

Siegler, R. S., & Jenkins, E. (1989). *How children discover new strategies.* Hillsdale, NJ: Lawrence Erlbaum Associates.

Singley, M. K., & Anderson, J. R. (1989). *The transfer of cognitive skill.* Cambridge, MA: Harvard University Press.

Smith, M. U. (Ed.). (1991). *Toward a unified theory of problem solving: Views from the content domains.* Hillsdale, NJ: Lawrence Erlbaum Associates.

Sternberg, R. J., & Davidson, J. E. (1982). The mind of the puzzler. *Psychology Today, 16,* 37–44.

Sternberg, R. J., & Frensch, P. A. (Eds.). (1991). *Complex problem solving: Principles and mechanisms.* Hillsdale, NJ: Lawrence Erlbaum Associates.

Stevenson, H. W., & Stigler, J. W. (1992). *The learning gap.* New York: Summit.

Stigler, J. W., Lee, S-Y., & Stevenson, H. W. (1990). *Mathematical knowledge of Japanese, Chinese, and American elementary school children.* Reston, VA: National Council of Teachers of Mathematics.

van Dijk, T. A., & Kintsch, W. (1983). *Strategies of discourse comprehension.* New York: Academic Press.

Verschaffel, L., De Corte, E., & Pauwels, A. (1992). Solving compare problems: An eye movement test of Lewis and Mayer's consistency hypothesis. *Journal of Educational Psychology, 84,* 85–94.

Weaver, C. A., III, & Kintsch, W. (1992). Enhancing students' comprehension of the conceptual structure of algebra word problems. *Journal of Educational Psychology, 84,* 419–428.

Wertheimer, M. (1959). *Productive thinking.* New York: Harper & Row.

3

▼▼▼▼▼▼▼

When Erroneous Mathematical Thinking Is Just as "Correct": The Oxymoron of Rational Errors

Talia Ben-Zeev
Yale University

Students are inventive. When they reach a problem they do not know how to solve, they create algorithms that get them unstuck. Often, these algorithms result in erroneous solutions. For example, in the process of learning subtraction, students often commit the following smaller-from-larger "bug" (VanLehn, 1983, 1986):

$$\begin{array}{r} 63 \\ -29 \\ \hline 46 \end{array}$$

Similarly, students learning addition of fractions often erroneously add the numerators and denominators of the fractions directly (Silver, 1986), as follows:

$$\frac{1}{3} + \frac{1}{2} = \frac{2}{5}$$

The intriguing aspects of these and similar erroneous algorithms is that they are often systematic and rule-based rather than random. They therefore result in solutions termed *rational errors* (Ben-Zeev, 1995a). The term *rational* has a very specific meaning. It refers to a process where a student first induces an incorrect rule and then proceeds to follow it "correctly" in a logically consistent manner.

Where do rational errors come from? Teachers do not instruct students on how to create erroneous algorithms, yet rational errors appear time and again in students' solutions to mathematics problems. One is forced to conclude that students create their own rules in the mathematical learning process. Aside from the students' own inventiveness, however, could the current form of the mathematics instructional system inadvertently encourage the production of students' rational errors as well? Could rational errors, in fact, result in part from a school reality where children are simply learning too well? In a paper entitled "When Good Teaching Leads to Bad Results: The Disasters of 'Well-Taught' Mathematics Courses," Schoenfeld (1988) made the point that instruction which teaches rote memorization leads to the formation of misconceptions.

This idea can be illustrated by the examples presented at the outset of this chapter. Specifically, the question of interest is whether these errors have been generated by students' overlearning of prior instruction. Students who exhibit the smaller-from-larger bug simply subtract the smaller from the larger digit on multicolumn subtraction problems, irrespective of the positions of the digits. This kind of error may have been motivated by prior instruction on single-digit subtraction, where the student has always been taught to subtract the smaller from the larger number (negative numbers are only introduced later on). In essence, the student who commits the smaller-from-larger bug is overgeneralizing from previous instructions.

In the addition of fractions example, students erroneously add the denominators and numerators of the fractions. Silver (1986) explained this error by saying that students may extrapolate this erroneous algorithm from traditional instruction on the representation of fractions. Teachers and textbooks often represent fractions by using pie graphs. A "½," for instance, is taught as one piece of a two-piece pie. When it comes to performing addition, a student may reason: "Well, if I have a ½ then I have one piece of a two-piece pie; I add a ⅓, which is one piece of a three-piece pie; so I get two pieces out of a total of five pieces altogether, which is ⅖." This addition error makes sense given the fact that the pie representation of fractions is often taught by rote and that the student is searching for systematic rules that would get him or her "unstuck."

There are even more extreme examples that show how students overlearn from prior knowledge. For instance, in the domain of subtraction, VanLehn (1986) showed that students who are taught how to borrow only on two-column subtraction problems may later decide that a borrowing action occurs only in the units column of a multicolumn subtraction problem. Similarly, Schoenfeld (1991) described a classroom where children learned subtraction by solving only the following kind of problems: "$n - ? = m$," where $n > m$. Students in that classroom quickly learned to solve these problems by simply subtracting m from n. Therefore, when students were presented with new types of problem, such as $7 = ? - 3$, they erroneously answered "4." Because these kinds of subtraction errors are rule-based and systematic, they are rational, even though they violate important principles of subtraction (e.g., noncommutativity).

Students construct their own algorithms in the face of and often in opposition to what the teacher intended them to do. However, students learn well what teachers instruct. Indeed, as was shown by the examples presented earlier, students may learn "too well," and thus overgeneralize from the instruction they receive. For instance, if a subtraction algorithm is taught by rote, as a symbol-pushing routine, then it makes sense for the student to subtract the smaller from the larger digit, irrespective of the digits' positions, because subtracting the smaller from larger digit was always the case in single-digit subtraction, and furthermore, it appears to work.

The main argument of this chapter, therefore, is that students' erroneous mathematical thinking is "correct" in the sense that it follows systematic rules. The erroneous rules, in turn, are based on procedures that have successfully worked in past problem-solving episodes. The procedures may have been inadvertently taught in the classroom, or be the result of the student's idiosyncratic approach, or an interaction of the two. If this argument is true, then we should see examples where the same procedures that underlie correct learning lead, under certain circumstances, to erroneous performance. This chapter therefore focuses on four mechanisms that are hypothesized to underlie the correct acquisition of mathematical thinking, and points out the conditions under which the mechanisms lead to the production of rational errors. The mechanisms are induction from examples (Anderson, 1993; Ben-Zeev, 1995a; Holland, Holyoak, Nisbett, & Thagard, 1986; Simon & Zhu, 1988; VanLehn, 1986), analogical thinking (Anderson & Thompson, 1989; Gick & Holyoak, 1980, 1983; Novick, 1988; Novick & Holyoak, 1991), schema-based thinking (Davis, 1982; Hinsley, Hayes, & Simon, 1977; Mayer, 1982, 1985; Riley, Greeno, & Heller, 1983; Ross, 1984), and, finally, correlational thinking (Lewis & Anderson, 1985).

The inductive, analogical, schema-based, and correlational reasoning mechanisms are overlapping rather than distinct. The main reason for examining each one separately is that each mechanism has been the focus of much research on cognition, in general, and mathematical thinking, in particular. For example, although learning by analogy is a special case of inductive learning, it has unique properties that make it a worthwhile topic in its own right.

Examining both the correct acquisition of mathematical thinking and the conditions under which it leads to erroneous performance are not only important from a theoretical point of view, but from an educational one as well. In order to teach students how correctly to acquire a mathematical skill, one needs access to the conditions under which students are prone to make mistakes. This chapter therefore concludes by briefly presenting a new taxonomy of rational errors in mathematical thinking called REASON (Ben-Zeev, 1995b). The new taxonomy integrates different error-production mechanisms across a wide range of mathematical domains.

THE INDUCTIVE NATURE OF MATHEMATICAL THINKING

There is agreement in the problem-solving literature that students learn inductively by studying worked-out examples (Anderson, 1993; Simon & Anzai, 1979; Simon & Zhu, 1988; VanLehn, 1986, 1990). That is, by following the steps in a worked-out example, students may generalize or abstract the correct procedure for the given skill, especially when the example is specific rather than general (Sweller & Cooper, 1985; VanLehn, 1990), and students are able to generate explanations in the learning process (Chi, Bassok, Lewis, Reimann, & Glaser, 1989; Chi & VanLehn, 1991; VanLehn, Jones, & Chi, 1992).

For instance, Simon and Zhu (1988) demonstrated that students who were given examples of the factorization of polynomials (e.g., $X^2 + 5X + 6 = (X + 2)(X + 3)$), and were then asked to solve problems on their own (e.g., $X^2 + 9X + 18 = (\quad)(\quad)$), were able to abstract the underlying rules of factorization correctly (i.e., $X^2 + aX + b = (X + c)(X + d)$, where $c * d = b$ and $c + d = a$). Simon and Zhu referred to this kind of learning process as "learning by doing."

Students' reliance on worked-out examples has been demonstrated in several studies. Specifically, when students are given a choice between using worked-out examples versus written instructions or explanations, students tend overwhelmingly to choose the former (Anderson, Farrell, & Saurers, 1984; LeFevre & Dixon, 1986; Pirolli & Anderson, 1985). Furthermore, Le-Fevre and Dixon found that when students were given a conflicting instruction set (i.e., the written instructions asked subjects to perform a different procedure than the example illustrated), the majority of students tended to follow the procedure illustrated by the worked-out example without realizing that doing so was logically problematical.

The Circumstances Under Which Inductive Thinking Leads to Rational Errors

Under particular conditions, the same inductive processes that facilitate correct learning may lead to erroneous performance as well. Indeed, evidence from students' erroneous performance supports the idea that students overgeneralize or overspecialize solutions from familiar examples in a given domain. This work has been advanced, most notably, by VanLehn (1986, 1990), and further elaborated on by Ben-Zeev (1995a).

Brown and VanLehn's (1980) repair theory argues that when students reach a new problem they do not know how to solve, they do not quit, but instead create repair algorithms that get them unstuck. Because these algorithms are oftentimes erroneous they result in "buggy" solutions (i.e., solutions that contain one or more errors).

VanLehn (1986) showed that buggy algorithms are either overspecialized or overgeneralized from worked-out examples students receive in the learning process. For example, VanLehn offered the bug N-N-Causes-Borrow (pronounced N–minus–N–Causes Borrow) as an example of overgeneralization. N-N-Causes-Borrow is illustrated as follows:

$$\begin{array}{r} \overset{5}{6}{}^{1}2 \\ -\ 3\ 2 \\ \hline 210 \end{array}$$

The student who commits the N-N-Causes-Borrow bug has correctly acquired the procedure of borrowing when T < B, but not when T > B. Problems arise, however, when the student faces a new problem where T = B. The student then overgeneralizes the rule "borrow when T < B" into the rule "borrow when T ≤ B." Overall, VanLehn discovered that only 33% of errors could by explained by induction from examples.[1]

Ben-Zeev's (1995a) empirical and computational work on rational errors in a new number system called NewAbacus provides stronger evidence for the induction-from-examples hypothesis. Specifically, subjects were first instructed on NewAbacus number representation. Then subjects were divided into different groups, where each group received an example of only a certain part of the NewAbacus addition algorithm. Finally, subjects were given a range of both new and familiar NewAbacus addition problems to solve.

Results showed that subjects who received the same kind of worked-out examples produced similar rational errors (i.e., errors that are algorithmic variations of one another). For instance, subjects who received examples of how correctly to carry the digit 6, produced a variety of illegal carries of 6 in their solutions (for a brief tutorial on NewAbacus number representation and addition, see Appendices A and B).

Computational modeling in LISP showed that subjects' rational errors were modeled best by modifying the example procedure subjects received. For

---

[1]VanLehn also conducted a more "liberal" analysis of the induction hypothesis. He showed that by modifying the correct procedure for subtraction (based on visual–numerical features of subtraction problems such as top-of, left-of, bottom-equal-0, etc.), he could explain 85% of students' subtraction errors. As he himself admitted, however, the liberal approach does not show a direct connection between the worked-out examples to which students are exposed during the learning process and the rational errors students produce.

example, illegal carries of the digit 6 were recreated computationally by modifying the example condition that illustrated how correctly to carry the digit 6. From a purely syntactic viewpoint, subjects' performance was reasonable; that is, subjects created rules based on the worked-out examples they studied, and proceeded to follow these rules. Overall, Ben-Zeev found that 67% of students' rational errors could be explained by the induction hypothesis.

The Inductive Nature of Mathematical Thinking: A Short Summary

There is strong evidence that students abstract or generalize a procedure from following the steps in a worked-out example. However, when either the student's knowledge is rote or insufficient, a generalization may turn into an overgeneralization. Therefore, the same inductive processes that lead to correct mathematical thinking may also result in erroneous performance.

A specific kind of inductive thinking—analogical thinking—has been a particular focus of study on cognition in general and on mathematical thinking in particular. Therefore, although analogical is a special case of inductive thinking (see also VanLehn, 1990), it still merits its own discussion.

THE ANALOGICAL NATURE OF MATHEMATICAL THINKING

In the process of solving a new problem (the "target") by analogy, the student retrieves a similar problem that he or she has solved successfully in the past (the "source"), and then proceeds to perform a *mapping* between the two problems in order to reach a solution (Gentner, 1983; Holyoak & Thagard, 1989b). Finding an adequate source problem, however, is not a trivial task. In order to use a problem as a source analog, one needs to recognize its relevance to the target problem. Analogical reasoning becomes a challenging task when the source and target share an underlying "deep" similarity (i.e., they operate on the same principles) but have different surface features.

For example, Gick and Holyoak (1980, 1983) gave subjects Duncker's (1945) tumor problem. This problem describes a patient with an inoperable stomach tumor. Subjects are told that there are rays that can destroy the tumor, but that a ray with sufficient intensity will destroy the healthy as well as the unhealthy tissue. Subjects are then asked to think of a way to destroy the tumor without causing damage to the healthy tissue that surrounds it.

In the experimental condition, subjects were first given a story analog that had a different content (different surface structure) but operated on the same underlying principles (same deep structure). One version of the story describes a general who is planning to conquer a fortress. The general's problem is that the roads leading to the fortress are mined such that they explode when a large group of soldiers passes over them, but do not explode if the group is small. The general then decides to solve the problem of attacking the fortress with a big enough army by sending a large number of small troops along the different roads that lead to the fortress, and having them meet at the fortress. This story provides an analogy for solving the tumor problem; namely, that one needs to emit several weaker rays that together converge on the tumor with the intensity of a single strong ray.

The results indicated that only 10% of control subjects who were given the radiation problem alone were able to solve the problem, versus 30% of experimental subjects who had read the fortress problem. An interesting point, however, is that a full 70% of experimental subjects solved the problem when given a hint to use the fortress problem as a source analog. Therefore, analogical reasoning can greatly facilitate problem solving. However, when the source and target have dissimilar surface structure one needs to make the connection between them explicit.

The literature on problem solving by analogy is extremely relevant for mathematical thinking as well. Importantly, Novick and Holyoak (1991) showed that in agreement with Holland et al. (1986) and Holyoak and Thagard (1989a), the end result of analogical mapping in the domain of mathematical word problems is the induction of a schema, or a set of more abstract rules that embodies the relationship between the source and target problems. Holyoak and Thagard suggested that the resulting schema from forming an analogy between the fortress and radiation problems is a more general principle (i.e., converging small forces onto a single object results in a force with a sufficient intensity to destroy the object without causing unnecessary harm). Similarly, Novick and Holyoak showed that the result of mapping a mathematical word problem (e.g., about a garden) onto a target problem (e.g., about a marching band) resulted in a more general procedure (e.g., the "LCM procedure").

The idea that analogical thinking results in an abstracted structure is also expressed in the work of Anderson and colleagues (Anderson, 1993; Anderson et al., 1984; Anderson & Thompson, 1989; Pirolli & Anderson, 1985). Specifically, Anderson and Thompson's (1989) theory of problem solving by analogy (PUPS) argues that if the analogy between a source and target problem proves successful, the declarative structure becomes proceduralized into a set of production rules. This kind of proceduralized knowledge enables more efficient problem solving in future episodes because it does not require rebuilding a solution path from "scratch."

The Circumstances Under Which Analogical Thinking Leads to Rational Errors

There are two primary origins of analogical failures: The first occurs when the student uses an inadequate source problem; the second results from an inadequate mapping between the source and target problems. For example, when a student tries to solve a new mathematical problem, he or she may be "reminded" of a familar problem that shares a similar surface but not deep structure. The failure adequately to find a source problem is illustrated by Ross (1984). Ross instructed college students on how to solve elementary probability problems that required different principles (e.g., permutation) by using worked-out examples. Each example was associated with a particular content (e.g., involving dice). Ross found that when subjects were given new problems to solve, they associated the given problem's content with the particular probability principle with which it had appeared in the worked-out example. In essence, subjects were reminded of the prior principle the content was associated with and therefore decided erroneously to apply that principle to the new problem.

The second kind of failure—namely, performing an inadequate mapping—is illustrated in Anderson's (1989) work on the analogical origins of errors. For instance, Anderson found that a common algebraic error that students committed on the "algebra tutor" (i.e., an intelligent tutoring system that is aimed toward teaching students a variety of algebra skills by using the computer in an interactive way) involved erroneously factoring out a common product. The tutor provided the following source problem: $factor(5 * 3X + 5 * 1) = 5(3X + 1)$. The common error on a target problem was $factor(5 * 3Z + 5) = 5(3Z + 5)$. This error lies in an incorrect mapping, where students mapped both the "5" and "1" in the source problem onto the "5" in the target problem.

What then differentiates students who are able to perform adequate mathematical analogies from those who cannot? The answer may lie in the student's level of expertise. It appears that novices, in particular, are more susceptible to making errors based on surface-structural similarities between the source and the target problems, whereas experts pay more attention to deep-structural patterns (Novick, 1988; Schoenfeld & Herrmann, 1982).

These novice–expert differences have also been demonstrated in other learning domains, such as physics and chess (Chi et al., 1981; Simon & Chase, 1973). A related source of individual differences that is suggested to facilitate analogical thinking is the ability to generate self-explanations during the problem-solving process (Chi et al., 1989; VanLehn et al., 1992).

The Analogical Nature of Mathematical Thinking: A Short Summary

In sum, analogical thinking can be characterized by (a) finding an appropriate source analog for the target problem at hand, a task which is particularly hard for novices; (b) forming a mapping between the source and target problems (although neither finding the appropriate source problem nor performing the adequate mapping is sufficient for performing an analogy, as suggested by Novick and Holyoak's (1991) discussion of "adaptation"); and finally (c) proceduralizing the mapping into a set of rules (Anderson, 1993; Anderson & Thompson, 1989), or forming an abstract schema of the mapping in order to use it in future problem-solving events (Holland et al., 1986; Novick & Holyoak, 1991).

The last characteristic of problem solving suggests that the use of schemata is central to achieving successful problem solving. The chapter thus turns to a detailed discussion of schema-based accounts of mathematical thinking.

THE SCHEMATIC NATURE OF MATHEMATICAL THINKING

In cognition and memory, schemata have been postulated as useful mental mechanisms that organize incoming information from the environment (Bartlett, 1932; Piaget, 1965; Schank & Abelson, 1977). Schemata also play a similarly important role in mathematical problem solving and thinking (Mayer, 1985).

For example, in early arithmetical thinking, students rely on schemata in order to solve word problems successfully. Greeno (1980) and Riley et al. (1983) suggested that children develop three types of models for solving arithmetic word problems. These types are *change* (Joe had some marbles. Then Tom gave him 5 marbles. Now Joe has 8 marbles. How many marbles did Joe have at the beginning?), *combination* (Joe has 3 marbles. Tom has 5 marbles. How many marbles do they have together?), and *comparison* (Joe has 3 marbles. Tom has 5 marbles more than Joe. How many marbles does Tom have?).

Riley et al. (1983) suggested that children acquire a "part–whole" schema in order to solve these kinds of arithmetic word problems successfully. For instance, in solving "change" problems such as "Joe had some marbles. Then Tom gave him 5 marbles. Now Joe has 8 marbles. How many marbles did Joe have at the beginning?", children need to distinguish the whole from its parts. The part–whole schema relates Joe's current number of marbles (the whole) to the number of marbles Tom has given him (the known part) and the number of marbles Joe had originally (the unknown part).

Furthermore, Resnick (1989) argued that the part–whole schema has origins in preschool experience. That is, she claims that preschool children develop a protoquantitative part–whole schema from dealing with everyday life events. For example, preschoolers know that two quantities added together are bigger than any one of the quantities alone. This knowledge allows children to judge part–whole relationships, such as that a whole cake is larger than any one of its slices.

Children in the first few grades experience more difficulties with comparison problems not because they lack understanding of part–whole relationships, but because comparison problems have a more complex semantic structure than do other word problems. Following Hudson's (1983) work, Riley and Greeno (1988) argued that if comparison problems are worded differently, in a language to which children can relate (i.e., "How many x's won't get a y?" instead of "How many more x's are there than y's?"), young children are able to solve these problems earlier than was thought possible. Therefore, schema construction of mathematical word problems involves more than the ability to calculate correctly, and is affected by variables such as semantics and language (see also Kintsch & Greeno, 1985).

In the domain of more advanced algebraic word problems, schemata play an important role as well. Hinsley et al. (1979) showed that college and high school students could categorize mathematics problems into different types by using information contained in the first few words of the problem. For example, problems that began with "A river steamer . . ." cued retrieval of the "river current" category of problems. In essence, particular features in the problems were cueing a more generalized solution path.

Additional evidence for schema use in solving mathematical word problems comes from Mayer (1981, 1982). Mayer conducted an analysis of algebra textbooks, and found that it was possible to categorize over 100 problem types. In a subsequent study, Mayer presented subjects with different types of word problems. The problems were either high or low frequency (where frequency refers to how commonly the problem types were found in algebraic textbooks). Mayer asked subjects to read and later to recall the problems. He found that when subjects tried to recall the low-frequency problems, they often changed these problems' forms into the more familiar high-frequency versions. This result lends support to the idea that high-frequency problems were associated with more well-formed schemata, and therefore formed the basis for the recall of less familiar problem types.

The Circumstances Under Which Schema-Based Mathematical Thinking Leads to Rational Errors

As we have seen, schema-based thinking is a useful way of organizing mathematical experiences. However, its advantages may turn into disadvantages if the schema is applied rigidly. A striking example of this phenomenon comes from Paige and Simon (1966). They gave students problems that were logically impossible. For example:

> The number of quarters a man has is seven times the number of dimes he has. The value of the dimes exceeds the value of the quarters by two dollars and fifty cents. How many has he of each coin?

Paige and Simon found that some subjects actually proceeded to solve the problem by forming the equations $Q = 7D$ and $.10D = 2.5 + .25Q$, without realizing that doing so is nonsensical. In essence, subjects invoked a correct schema and applied it in the wrong context. Note, however, that a possible critique of this study is that students are usually given "true" rather than purposefully misleading problems. Therefore, the students in the Paige and Simon study may have doubted their own understanding instead of questioning the validity of the problems themselves.

More recently, Davis (1982) showed that correct schemata (or *frames*, in his terminology) that are used in an incorrect context lead to rational errors, as well. For instance, Davis argued that students create a correct "units or label frame" for dealing with equalities such as "12 inches = 1 foot." He suggested that inappropriate uses of this frame results in errors such as the common "reversal error" (Rosnick & Clement, 1980), where students incorrectly assert that "6S = P," instead of "6P = S," on the following problem:

> In a certain college there are 6 times as many students as professors. Write an equation that formalizes the relation between the number of students (S) and the number of professors (P).

The misuses of schemata in mathematical thinking are nicely illustrated by Matz's (1982) work on students algebraic problem solving, as well. Matz proposed that students construct underspecified schemata in the learning process. For example, when students learn the distributive law of multiplication, $A(B + C) = AB + AC$, they form the schema: $\square(X \triangle Y) = \square X \triangle \square Y$. This schema is underspecified because any operator can falsely fill in the missing variable slots. Underspecification, in turn, gives rise to common errors such as $\sqrt{(A + B)} = \sqrt{A} + \sqrt{B}$.

Another area in which Matz identified misuse of schemata is in the factorization of polynomials. Students who learn how to factor polynomials are taught the following:

If: $(X - n)(X - m) = 0$
Then either: $(X - n) = 0$ or $(X - m) = 0$
Thus: $X = n$ or $X = m$

Matz argued that students may fail to recognize that the n and m are incidental to the problem, and can thus be "variabilized," but that "0" is a relevant feature which cannot be replaced by any other number. Students thus proceed to abstract the following erroneous schema:

$$(X - n)(X - m) = K$$
$(X - n) = K$ or $(X - m) = K$
$X = K + n$ or $X = K + m$

The Schematic Nature of Mathematical Thinking:
A Short Summary

Schema-based thinking is a useful way for organizing mathematical experiences. Students can correctly use cues in a word problem (e.g., a car starts a race at a certain time and with a certain speed) to predict the type of solution the problem will require (e.g., distance–rate–time). If applied rigidly or without understanding, however, schemata can lead to erroneous performance as well. For example, Hinsley et al. (1977) showed that a problem can "fool" a student if its content cues a certain schema (e.g., triangle) but is really of a different type (e.g., distance–rate–time). Therefore, a correct schema that is used in an incorrect context will lead to rational errors.

Furthermore, Schoenfeld (1988) pointed out that in learning to solve arithmetic problems that require subtraction, children are taught to look for cue words that trigger the solution, such as "left" (e.g., how many apples are left?). Therefore, many students proceed to look for cue words immediately, without even properly reading the problem.

A group of schemata that has received particular attention in the mathematical literature is one which deals with perceived correlations between a problem's features and the operator that is required for solving the problem. These schemata are known as "operator schemata" (Lewis & Anderson, 1985). I chose to devout the next section to these schemata because they (a) are an important part of the student's repertoire of strategies, and (b) illustrate well what I refer to as the rationality behind students' erroneous performance.

THE CORRELATIONAL NATURE
OF MATHEMATICAL THINKING

Lewis and Anderson (1985) claimed that mathematics textbooks often contain correlations between specific features in problems and the operators that are used for solving the problems. For instance, geometrical problems that involve triangle congruence using the SAS (side–angle–side) postulate usually have givens that involve two sides and an angle.

Because certain features in geometry problems tend to covary with a particular algorithm or operator, it is adaptive for students to rely on these feature–operator correlations in order to predict what strategy to use on a given problem. In order to test the hypothesis that students use feature–operator correlations in that manner, Lewis and Anderson (1985) conducted an experiment on geometrical problem solving that consisted of a learning phase and a test phase. In the learning phase, subjects were divided into active (i.e., generating hypotheses and receiving feedback) and passive (i.e., taking a pencil-and-paper test with no feedback) groups. Both groups received geometry problems that contained high correlations between a congruence postulate (e.g., SAS) and particular features of the problem (e.g., vertical angles). The test phase was the same for all subjects. They were shown congruence problems on a screen for a brief duration and were asked to "guess" the correct postulate for solving the problem.

Results indicated that subjects who were active in the learning phase did better than chance. That is, they were able to use the feature–operator correlations in order to guess the correct strategy for solving the problems.

The Conditions Under Which Correlational Thinking Leads to Rational Errors

If students think correlationally, then they should also pick up on spurious correlations that would lead them to commit errors. Even though the teacher or textbook may have designed an example to illustrate a particular algorithm or concept, the student may induce completely different rules than the teacher had intended. A worked-out example or set of examples may contain a spurious correlation between a particular feature and a specific algorithm, which the student abstracts into an erroneous rule.

A particularly compelling example comes from a high school geometry class where students were asked to matched polynomials to functions (Dugdale, 1993). Students in that class committed an error of confusing the y-intercept of a parabola with its vertex. Therefore, if the y-intercept was at –0.6 and the vertex was at –1, students who committed this error decided that the function was of the form $Y = X^2 - 1$. Dugdale suggested that the confusion between the y-intercept and its vertex could be explained by the fact that in previous examples students were given, the y-intercept had always coincided with the vertex of the parabola. The students thereby created a functional invariance between the y-intercept and the vertex, in an erroneous but rule-based manner.

Reliance on spurious correlations may be rational. That is, if there is a high correlation between a feature and an algorithm, then it is efficient to abstract that correlation into a rule. This approach fits in with a Gibsonian framework. Gibson (1979) has emphasized the role of detecting invariants as an important mechanism in perceptual problem solving (e.g., he suggested that people perceive depth as a function of texture gradients that contain invariant information about a particular object). Furthermore, based on the visual or syntactic patterns of mathematical examples, people may construct erroneous rules based on spurious correlations in a Bayesian manner.

The Bayesian odds formula as applied to feature–algorithm correlations is presented as follows (where "Alg" is an abbreviation of "Algorithm"):

$$\frac{P(Alg/Feature)}{P(\sim Alg/Feature)} = \frac{P(Alg) * P(Feature/Alg)}{P(\sim Alg) * P(Feature/\sim Alg)}$$

Rewritten, it can be read as follows:

$$P(Alg/Feature) = \frac{P(Alg) * P(Feature/Alg)}{P(Alg) * P(Feature/Alg) + P(\sim Alg) * P(Feature/\sim Alg)}$$

The P(Alg/Feature) is the probability that the algorithm can solve a particular problem that contains the feature. The P(Feature/Alg) is the probability that the feature exists in the problem given that the algorithm is used to solve that problem. The P(Alg) is the base rate of the algorithm, or the relative frequency with which it has been used in prior problem-solving events. The P(~A) is the base rate of an alternative algorithm, or the relative frequency with which the alternative algorithm has been used in past problem-solving episodes.

Worked-out examples are often confirmatory. That is, they illustrate how a feature correlates with a particular algorithm but do not show how the same feature can also correlate with an alternative algorithm. Therefore, given confirmatory examples, the P(F/~Alg) goes to zero as follows:

$$P(Alg/\ Feature) \approx \frac{P(Alg) * 1}{P(Alg) * 1 + 0} \rightarrow 1$$

In sum, when students abstract rules from spurious correlations, they are acting rationally from a Bayesian perspective.

Correlational Thinking: A Short Summary

Developing an operator schema is advantageous because more often than not specific features in worked-out examples (e.g., angle, side, and angle in a geometry problem) contain predictive correlations with a particular algorithm (e.g., ASA postulate). However, when there are spurious correlations between features and operators, students will abstract erroneous rules, in much the same manner as they do with the relevant correlations.

WHAT PIECES ARE STILL MISSING FROM THE MATHEMATICAL THINKING PUZZLE? A NEED FOR A MORE GENERAL ACCOUNT OF ERRORS

As we have seen, examining erroneous versus correct performance is important for understanding students' mathematical thinking. Currently, the primary contribution to the rational-errors field comes from Brown and Van-Lehn's (1980) repair theory, and VanLehn's (1986) induction hypothesis. This work, along with other accounts of error production, tends to be domain-specific (but see Davis, 1984). Although domain-specific accounts are extremely valuable, they provide a fragmented view of the origin of rational errors in mathematical thinking as a whole. Repair theory, for instance, focuses on subtraction errors, whereas other researchers have identified sources of errors in counting (Ginsburg, chapter 7, this volume), arithmetic (Ben-Zeev, 1995a; Brown & Burton, 1978; Brown & VanLehn, 1980, Young & O'Shea, 1981), algebra (Matz, 1982; Payne & Squibb, 1990; Sleeman, 1984), geometry (Anderson 1989, 1993; Dugdale, 1993; Schoenfeld, 1988), and calculus (Davis & Vinner, 1986).

There is thus a need for a more comprehensive account of rational errors that would incorporate domain-specific error-production mechanisms, but would also emphasize the commonalties between rational errors across various mathematical domains. I have attempted to reach this goal by putting forth a new taxonomy of rational errors in mathematical thinking called REASON (Rational Errors as Sources of Novelty). Because a detailed discussion of the taxonomy is provided elsewhere (Ben-Zeev, 1995b), I present it only briefly here.

REASON: A NEW TAXONOMY OF RATIONAL ERRORS IN MATHEMATICAL THINKING

REASON incorporates rational errors that result from either monitoring failures or misinduction from examples. Monitoring failures occur, for instance, when the student is not aware that he or she has just committed a violation on a particular problem state. Inductive failures occur when the student overgeneralizes or overspecializes a rule from worked-out examples. Induction can either be syntactic—that is, it may involve symbol manipulation without regard to underlying principles, or it can be semantic—meaning that it draws on the student's conceptual understanding or meaning-based representation of the problem. A more detailed account of each error-production mechanism follows (see Fig. 3.1 for the taxonomy of REASON).

Failures at the Monitoring Level: The Role of Internal Critics

In order to monitor the validity of a particular problem state correctly, one needs to develop internal *critics*, or mechanisms which signal that a number-representation or rule violation has occurred. In Artificial Intelligence (AI), a critic is defined as a procedure that monitors the current problem state and fires when a constraint is violated (Rissland, 1985). REASON elaborates on this definition by positing critics that also signal when they encounter an unfamiliar situation that the system does not know how to handle.

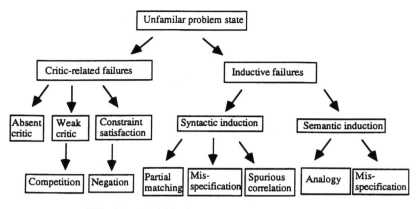

FIG. 3.1.   REASON's taxonomy of rational errors.

Rational errors result from three kinds of critic-related failures. The first occurs when the critic is absent, and results in a violation that goes unnoticed. Because this is a trivial case, it is not elaborated on in this chapter. The second failure occurs from a *competition* process between a critic and a stronger prior-knowledge rule. Even if the critic exists, it is still "inhibited" by a stronger familiar rule from a different domain. The strength of a rule is defined as how successfully the rule has performed in past problem-solving episodes (Anderson, 1993; Holland et al., 1986).

For example, during NewAbacus Addition (Ben-Zeev, 1995a), students often fail to convert illegal numbers in NewAbacus that are valid in base-10 (e.g., "65") into their valid representations, because their NewAbacus number-representation critics were only recently formed and therefore not consolidated enough to "win" the competition with the stronger base-10 number-representation rules. The fact that students had indeed developed the adequate critics but were unable to use them was determined by giving subjects a test of NewAbacus number representation (i.e., a subject is presented with a number and has to say whether it is valid or not in NewAbacus, and why). Only subjects who did well on the test, and had therefore developed the relevant number-representation critics, were retained in the study.

Finally, the third critic-related failure occurs when the student makes a problem seem valid by removing the violation in the problem that caused the critic to fire, an action that prevents the critic from refiring. This process is termed *negation*, and in essence regards a situation where the critic is "tricked." An example of negation comes from students' errors on NewAbacus addition (Ben-Zeev, 1995a). For instance, when subjects produced an illegal number in an intermediate problem-solving stage (e.g., "9"), they did not convert it to the correct NewAbacus representation (e.g., "63") but proceeded to delete it. After deletion the problem state became "valid."

In addition to critic-related failures, REASON also incorporates inductive-related failures as well. These kind of failures are discussed next.

Failures at the Inductive Level:
The Role of Syntactic and Semantic Induction

REASON breaks down inductive failures into two main components: *syntactic* and *semantic*. In performing syntactic induction, the student builds on the surface-structural features of familiar examples as a basis for generalizing or specializing an algorithm. In the process of semantic induction, performance is still erroneous but is based on the conceptual rather than the syntactic aspects of the problem. The student applies an intuitive mathematical approach by attempting conceptually to map the problem onto examples from prior mathematical or real-world experiences. Problems arise from a situation where either the experience is an inadequate source or the mapping process itself is flawed.

Syntactic Induction. Syntactic induction is a process of overgeneralizing or overspecializing a solution from the surface-structural features of familiar examples. REASON encompasses three types of syntactic failures. The first results when the student reaches an unfamiliar problem and searches for a familiar example that contains overlapping features. Once such an example is found, its corresponding solution path is implemented. This process is termed *partial matching* and is consistent with ACT* (Anderson, 1983).

The second syntactic failure takes place when the student applies a spurious rule that he or she has previously abstracted from a familiar example or set of examples. For instance, as was shown by Dugdale (1993), a student may believe that the vertex of the parabola is equivalent to its intercept if he or she was exposed only to examples of parabolas that were symmetrical around the y-axis (i.e., where the y-intercept always coincides with the vertex of the parabola).

Finally, the third syntactic failure results from a situation where students abstract an under- or overspecified schema in the problem-solving process. An example of this kind is Matz's schema for the distributive law of multiplication (i.e., $A(B + C) = AB + AC$), which results in errors such as $\sqrt{(A + B)} = \sqrt{A} + \sqrt{B}$.

Semantic Induction. Mathematical induction may be based on a student's experience with and conceptual interpretation of (a) familiar examples within the mathematical domain and (b) familiar real-world examples that lie outside the classroom. In the first case, students may overspecialize or overgeneralize solutions to new problems based on the semantic properties of examples they encountered in their previous mathematical experience (see also Resnick et al., 1989).

Semantic overspecification can be illustrated by Davis and Vinner's (1986) work on students' understanding of the concept of limit in calculus. They found that students commonly produced the following erroneous definition of limit:

> A limit is a boundary beyond which the sequence cannot go. A speed limit, like one on the highway, defines only a point beyond which you are not supposed to go. But the limit of a sequence is never reached by that sequence.

Davis and Vinner suggested that the underlying cause of this error lies in the fact that students' previous examples were of primarily monotonically increasing or decreasing functions that never reached their limit (e.g., ".01, .001, .0001, . . ."). Based on these examples, students overspecialized the concept of the limit to mean a boundary that can never be reached.

The second type of semantic induction is one that is based on examples from beyond the classroom. The primary mechanism in this case may be analogical failure. For instance, Payne and Squibb (1990) argued that the common "precedence error" in algebraic manipulation problems (i.e., $n + m$ $X \Rightarrow (n + m)X$, where $\Rightarrow$ stands for erroneous equivalence), is caused by a linguistic analogy of the form: "three apples plus four gives seven apples." In REASON's framework, when the critic signals an unfamiliar problem state, the student makes the following erroneous analogy: "three apples plus four:seven apples::$n + m$ X:$(n + m)X$."

REASON: A Short Summary

In REASON's framework, the origin of rational errors ranges from critic-related failures, through syntactic induction, to semantic induction. Therefore, it adds to repair theory which accounts for rational errors that are induced syntactically, or by a process of "symbol pushing" alone. REASON allows for error production that encompasses a variety of diverse mechanisms operating at different levels of processing. It also incorporates errors from different mathematical domains, ranging from counting to calculus, and, therefore, offers a balanced view of rational errors. (For a more detailed discussion of REASON, see Ben-Zeev, 1995b.)

WHAT HAVE WE LEARNED
ABOUT MATHEMATICAL THINKING,
AND WHERE DO WE GO FROM HERE?

The student often meets the challenge of a new mathematical problem state by creating rule-based but erroneous algorithms that lead to rational errors. Where do these erroneous algorithms come from? The answer lies in the interaction between the inherent inventiveness of the student coupled with the kind of instruction the student receives. On the one hand, the student will create his or her own rules, in the face of, and at times in opposition to, what the teacher has intended. On the other hand, the student may learn too well. That is, if the instruction teaches for rote rather than meaning, then the student will correctly learn how to follow a procedure, and will view the procedure as a symbol-pushing operation that obeys what seem to be arbitrary constraints. The student will thus overgeneralize from "bits and pieces" of prior knowledge without paying adequate attention to their underlying principles.

This chapter has demonstrated these ideas by pointing out the circumstances under which the same reasoning mechanisms that lead students to acquire mathematical knowledge correctly result in erroneous performance. For example, there is ample evidence that students abstract or generalize a mathematical procedure from following the steps in a worked-out example. However, when the student's knowledge is rote (e.g., the student holds a belief that subtraction is a process of manipulating symbols), a generalization may turn into an overgeneralization (e.g., subtract the smaller from the larger digit in multicolumn subtraction because that was the case for single-digit subtraction). Therefore, the same inductive processes that lead to correct mathematical induction from examples may also result in erroneous performance.

Similarly, in the more specific case of analogical thinking, a correct mapping may produce an erroneous result. That is, in order to perform a correct mapping from the source to the target problem, the student has to pick an appropriate source with which to begin. Novices in particular can be easily misled by a problem that shares similar surface features with the target problem but does not have a similar deep structure. As was previously shown, teachers often tell students explicitly to look for trigger words in a mathematical word problem (e.g., "left" cues a subtraction procedure). The same trigger word in a different problem type will lead to rational errors (e.g., when the word "left" refers to the left-hand side).

Research on analogical thinking suggests that its end product is a schema, or an organized set of abstract rules (Anderson, 1993; Anderson & Thompson, 1989; Holland et al., 1986; Novick & Holyoak, 1991). The use of schemata is important for organizing mathematical experiences in a more general way that allows transfer to similar problems. For example, in the radiation problem, students who correctly used the fortress problem as a source achieved a schema that was more general then either the radiation or the fortress problem alone (i.e., converge small forces onto a single target in order to achieve sufficient intensity without causing harm). As we have seen, this principle also applies in the mathematics domain, especially in the process of solving mathematical word problems (Novick & Holyoak, 1991). Schemata, however, can also lead students to create rational errors. For example, a correct schema that is used out of proper context results in erroneous performance, or a spurious correlation may be abstracted into an erroneous schema or rule.

An important question that has educational as well as theoretical importance is whether students' erroneous mathematical thinking can be predicted a priori. Repair theory has shown that it is possible to predict students rational errors on subtraction problems before students actually perform them. Similarly, REASON provides a framework in which to investigate a priori production of rational errors across a wide range of mathematical domains.

From an experimental point of view, instead of "waiting" for a student to produce an error and only then examining its origin, the researcher should "force" the student into producing predictable errors. This task is best achieved by providing subjects with new number systems such as NewAbacus, or with new operators (see Ben-Zeev, 1995a, 1995b), where one has control over what knowledge the student acquires, and can specifically predict where it will "go wrong." By investigating the conditions under which mechanisms that underlie correct acquisition of mathematical skill break down, and by using novel experimental manipulations, we may achieve a better understanding of the processes underlying mathematical thinking in general.

ACKNOWLEDGMENTS

The author wishes to thank Robert Sternberg for his extremely helpful comments on an earlier version of this chapter.

This chapter was supported by a graduate fellowship from Yale University, as well as by a grant under the Javits Act program (Grant #R206R00001) given to Robert Sternberg as administered by the Office of Educational Research and Improvement, U.S. Department of Education. The findings and opinions expressed in this chapter do not reflect the positions or policies of the Office of Educational Research and Improvement or the U.S. Department of Education.

Correspondence should be sent to Talia Ben-Zeev, Department of Psychology, Yale University, P.O. Box 208205, New Haven, CT 06520–8205. Email: Talia@yalevm.cis.yale.edu.

APPENDIX A: THE NEWABACUS SYSTEM

The NewAbacus number system can be seen in Fig. 3.2. Each familar base-10 digit is represented by two digits in NewAbacus. In the NewAbacus pair, the left digit is either 6 or 0, and the right digit can range from 0 through

0 = 00	10 = 0100	20 = 0200
1 = 01	11 = 0101	30 = 0300
2 = 02	12 = 0102	40 = 0400
3 = 03	13 = 0103	50 = 0500
4 = 04	14 = 0104	60 = 6000
5 = 05	15 = 0105	70 = 6100
6 = 60	16 = 0160	80 = 6200
7 = 61	17 = 0161	90 = 6300
8 = 62	18 = 0162	100 = 010000
9 = 63	19 = 0163	

FIG. 3.2.   A list of base-10 numbers and their representation in NewAbacus.

5. The sum of left and right digits in the NewAbacus pair produces the familiar base-10 digit. For example, 7 in base-10 is equivalent to 61 in NewAbacus (6 + 1 = 7). Although 64 and 65 in NewAbacus sum up to be 10 and 11 in base-10 respectively, they are illegal in the NewAbacus system, because 64 and 65 violate the rule that each base-10 digit must be represented by two digits in NewAbacus. The correct representation for 10 and 11 in NewAbacus is 0100 and 0101 respectively.

APPENDIX B: ADDITION IN NEWABACUS

The NewAbacus addition algorithm is divided into four main parts. They are: *no carry, carry into the 6 digit, carry from the 6 digit,* and *carry into and from the 6 digit* (see Table 3.1). In the *no-carry* example, there is no difference between the base-10 and the NewAbacus addition algorithms; that is, the addition is performed column by column. In the *carry into the 6 digit* example, adding column by column produces an intermediate solution where the right digit in a pair is equal to or greater than 6. In order to correct this violation,

TABLE 3.1
Examples of the Different Parts of the NewAbacus Addition Algorithm

Example 1 No carry	Example 2 Carry into 6		Example 3 Carry from 6		Example 4 Carry into and from 6	
	6		1		16	
0261	04		0362		63	
+0202	+03		+0161		+0205	
0463	7̶	invalid number	0523	sum columns	8̶	invalid number
	61	carry a six		carry a one		so carry a six and
		leave remainder	05̶2̶3̶	add digits		leave remainder
			0505	form valid	0322	sum columns
				number		carry a ten
					03̶2̶2̶	add digits
					0304	form valid number

one carries the 6 to the left and leaves the remainder. For example, when the right column in the intermediate solution is 9, one carries a 6 and leaves a remainder of 3.

In the *carry from the 6 digit* example, a carry of a 1 is required *between*, rather than *within* a NewAbacus pair. When two 6s are added in one column the sum is 12. Therefore, one carries a 1 to the next pair, and leaves a remainder of 2. However, because the 2 remains in the left digit, it violates the left-digit rule (it can only be 6 or 0). In order to correct the violation, one sums the 2 with the right digit, to form a valid NewAbacus pair. Finally, the *carry into and from the 6 digit* example is a combination of the latter cases. It is the most complete algorithm out of all the example types.

REFERENCES

Anderson, J. R. (1983). *The architecture of cognition.* Cambridge, MA: Harvard University Press.

Anderson, J. R. (1989). The analogical origin of errors in problem solving. In D. Klahr and K. Kotovsky (Eds.), *Complex information processing: The impact of Herbert A. Simon* (pp. 343–371). Hillsdale, NJ: Lawrence Erlbaum Associates.

Anderson, J. R. (1993). *Rules of the mind.* Hillsdale, NJ: Lawrence Erlbaum Associates.

Anderson, J. R., Farrell, R., & Saurers, R. (1984). Learning to program in LISP. *Cognitive Science, 8,* 87–129.

Anderson, J. R., & Thompson, R. (1989). Use of analogy in a production system architecture. In S. Vosniadou & A. Ortony (Eds.), *Similarity and analogical reasoning* (pp. 267–297). Cambridge, MA: Cambridge University Press.

Bartlett, F. C. (1932). *Remembering.* Cambridge, MA: Cambridge University Press.

Ben-Zeev, T. (1995a). The nature and origin of *rational errors* in arithmetic thinking: Induction from examples and prior knowledge. *Cognitive Science, 19,* 341–376.

Ben-Zeev, T. (1995b). *Rational errors and the mathematical mind.* Manuscript submitted for publication.

Brown, J. S., & Burton, R. B. (1978). Diagnostic models for procedural bugs in basic mathematical skills. *Cognitive Science, 2,* 155–192.

Brown, J. S., & VanLehn, K. (1980). Repair Theory: A generative theory of bugs in procedural skills. *Cognitive Science, 4,* 379–426.

Chi, M. T. H., Bassok, M., Lewis, M. W., Reimann, P., & Glaser, R. (1989). Self-explanations: How students study and use examples in learning to solve problems. *Cognitive Science, 13,* 145–182.

Chi, M. T. H., Feltovich, P. J., & Glaser, R. (1981). Categorization and representation of physics problems by experts and novices. *Cognitive Science, 5,* 121–152.

Chi, M. T. H., & VanLehn, K. (1991). The content of physics self-explanations. *Journal of the Learning Sciences, 1,* 69–105.

Davis, R. B. (1982). The postulation of certain specific, explicit, commonly-shared frames. *Journal of Mathematical Behavior, 3,* 167–201.

Davis, R. B. (1984). *Learning mathematics: The cognitive science approach to mathematics education.* Norwood, NJ: Ablex.

Davis, R. B., & Vinner, S. (1986). The notion of limit: Some seemingly unavoidable misconception stages. *Journal of Mathematical Behavior, 5,* 281–303.

Dugdale, S. (1993). Functions and graphs—Perspectives on student thinking. In T. A. Romberg, E. Fennema, & T. Carpenter (Eds.), *Integrating research on the graphical representation of functions* (pp. 101–130). Hillsdale, NJ: Lawrence Erlbaum Associates.

Duncker, K. (1945). On problem solving. *Psychological Monographs, 58* (Whole No. 270).

Gentner, D. (1983). Structure-mapping: A theoretical framework. *Cognitive Science, 7,* 155–170.

Gibson, J. J. (1979). *The ecological approach to visual perception.* Boston, MA: Houghton Mifflin.

Gick, M. L., & Holyoak, K. J. (1980). Analogical problem solving. *Cognitive Psychology, 12,* 306–355.

Gick, M. L., & Holyoak, K. J. (1983). Schema induction and analogical transfer. *Cognitive Psychology, 15,* 1–38.

Greeno, J. G. (1980). Some examples of cognitive task analysis with instructional implications. In R. E. Snow, P. Federico, & W. E. Montague (Eds.), *Aptitude, learning, and instruction* (Vol. 2, pp. 1–21). Hillsdale, NJ: Lawrence Erlbaum Associates.

Hinsley, D., Hayes, J. R., & Simon, H. A. (1977). From words to equations. In M. Just & P. Carpenter (Eds.), *Cognitive processes in comprehension* (pp. 89–106). Hillsdale, NJ: Lawrence Erlbaum Associates.

Holland, J. H., Holyoak, K. J., Nisbett, R. E., & Thagard, P. R. (1986). *Induction: Processes of inference, learning, and discovery.* Cambridge, MA: MIT Press.

Holyoak, K. J., & Thagard, P. R. (1989a). A computational model of analogical problem solving. In S. Vosniadou & A. Ortony (Eds.), *Similarity and analogical reasoning* (pp. 242–266). Cambridge, England: Cambridge University Press.

Holyoak, K. J., & Thagard, P. R. (1989b). Analogical mapping by constraint satisfaction. *Cognitive Science, 13,* 295–355.

Hudson, T. (1983). Correspondences and numerical differences between disjoint sets. *Child Development, 54,* 84–90.

Kintsch, W., & Greeno, J. G. (1985). Understanding and solving word arithmetic problems. *Psychological Review, 92,* 109–129.

LeFevre, J., & Dixon, P. (1986). Do written instructions need examples? *Cognition and Instruction, 3,* 1–30.

Lewis, M. W., & Anderson, J. R. (1985). Discrimination of operator schemata in problem solving: Learning from examples. *Cognitive Psychology, 17,* 26–65.

Matz, M. (1982). Towards a process model for high school algebra errors. In D. Sleeman & J. S. Brown (Eds.), *Intelligent tutoring systems* (pp. 25–49). New York: Academic Press.

Mayer, R. E. (1981). Frequency norms and structural analysis of algebraic story problems into families, categories, and templates. *Instructional Science, 10,* 135–175.

Mayer, R. E. (1982). Memory for algebra story problems. *Journal of Educational Psychology, 74,* 199–216.

Mayer, R. E. (1985). Implications of cognitive psychology for instruction in mathematical problem solving. In E. A. Silver (Ed.), *Teaching and learning mathematical problem solving: Multiple research perspectives* (pp. 123–138). Hillsdale, NJ: Lawrence Erlbaum Associates.

Novick, L. R. (1988). Analogical transfer, problem similarity, and expertise. *Journal of Experimental Psychology: Learning, Memory, and Cognition, 14,* 510–520.

Novick, L. R, & Holyoak, K. J. (1991). Mathematical problem solving by analogy. *Journal of Experimental Psychology: Learning, Memory, and Cognition, 17,* 398–415.

Paige, J. M., & Simon, H. A. (1966). Cognitive processes in solving algebra word problems. In B. Kleinmuntz (Ed.), *Problem solving: Research, method, and theory* (pp. 51–118). New York: Wiley.

Payne, S., & Squibb, H. (1990). Algebra mal-rules and cognitive accounts of error. *Cognitive Science, 14*, 445–481.

Piaget, J. (1965). *The child's conception of number*. New York: Norton.

Pirolli, P. L., & Anderson, J. R. (1985). The role of learning from examples in the acquisition of recursive programming skill. *Canadian Journal of Psychology, 39*, 240–272.

Resnick, L. B. (1989). Developing mathematical knowledge. *American Psychologist, 44*, 162–169.

Resnick, L. B., Nesher, P., Leonard, F., Magone, M., Omanson, S. F., & Peled, I. (1989). Conceptual bases of arithmetic errors: The case of decimal fractions. *Journal for Research in Mathematics Education, 20*, 8–27.

Riley, M. S., & Greeno, J. G. (1988). Developmental analysis about understanding language about quantities and solving problems. *Cognition and Instruction, 5*, 49–101.

Riley, M. S., Greeno, J. G., & Heller, J. (1983). The development of children's problem solving ability on arithmetic. In H. P. Ginsburg (Ed.), *The development of mathematical thinking* (pp. 153–196). New York: Academic Press.

Rissland, E. L. (1985). Artificial intelligence and the learning of mathematics: A tutorial sampling. In E. A. Silver (Ed.), *Teaching and learning mathematical problem solving: Multiple research perspectives* (pp. 147–176). Hillsdale, NJ: Lawrence Erlbaum Associates.

Rosnick, P., & Clement, J. (1980). Learning without understanding: The effect of tutoring strategies on algebra misconceptions. *Journal of Mathematical Behavior, 3*, 3–27.

Ross, B. (1984). Remindings and their effects in learning a cognitive skill. *Cognitive Psychology, 16*, 371–416.

Schank, R., & Abelson, R. P. (1977). *Scripts, plans, goals, and understanding: An inquiry into human knowledge structures*. Hillsdale, NJ: Lawrence Erlbaum Associates.

Schoenfeld, A. H. (1988). When good teaching leads to bad results: The disasters of "well-taught" mathematics courses. *Educational Psychologist, 23*, 145–166.

Schoenfeld, A. H. (1991). On mathematics as sense making: An informal attack on the unfortunate divorce of formal and informal mathematics. In J. F. Voss, D. N. Perkins, & J. W. Segal (Eds.), *Informal reasoning and education* (pp. 311–343). Hillsdale, NJ: Lawrence Erlbaum Associates.

Schoenfeld, A. H., & Herrmann, D. J. (1982). Problem perception and knowledge structure in expert and novice mathematical problem solvers. *Journal of Experimental Psychology: Learning, Memory, and Cognition, 8*, 484–494.

Silver, E. A. (1986). Using conceptual and procedural knowledge: A focus on relationships. In J. Hiebert (Ed.), *Conceptual and procedural knowledge: The case of mathematics* (pp. 181–198). Hillsdale, NJ: Lawrence Erlbaum Associates.

Simon, H. A., & Anzai, Y. (1979). The theory of learning by doing. *Psychological Review, 86*, 124–140.

Simon, H. A., & Chase, W. G. (1973). Skill in chess. *American Scientist, 61*, 394–403.

Simon, H. A., & Zhu, X. (1988). Learning mathematics from examples and by doing. *Cognition and Instruction, 4*, 137–166.

Sweller, J., & Cooper, G. A. (1985). The use of worked examples as a substitute for problem solving in learning algebra. *Cognition and Instruction, 2*, 59–89.

VanLehn, K. (1983). On the representation of procedures in repair theory. In H. P. Ginsburg (Ed.), *The development of mathematical thinking* (pp. 201–252). Hillsdale, NJ: Lawrence Erlbaum Associates.

VanLehn, K. (1986). Arithmetic procedures are induced from examples. In J. Hiebert (Ed.), *Conceptual and procedural knowledge: The case of mathematics* (pp. 133–179). Hillsdale, NJ: Lawrence Erlbaum Associates.

VanLehn, K. (1990). *Mind bugs: The origins of procedural misconceptions.* Cambridge, MA: MIT Press.

VanLehn, K., Jones, R. M., & Chi, M. T. H. (1992). A model of the self-explanation effect. *Journal of the Learning Sciences, 2,* 1–59.

Young, R. M., & O'Shea, T. (1981). Errors in students' subtraction. *Cognitive Science, 5,* 153–177.

COGNITIVE/CULTURAL
APPROACHES

On the Shoulders of Giants: Cultural Tools and Mathematical Development

Kevin F. Miller
University of Illinois at Urbana–Champaign

David R. Paredes
Texas A & M University

> *If I have seen further it is by standing on ye shoulders of Giants.*
> —Newton (1675/1959, p. 416)

> *Our own generation enjoys the legacy bequeathed to it by that which preceded it. We frequently know more, not because we have moved ahead by our own natural ability, but because we are supported by the [mental] strength of others, and possess riches that we have inherited from our forefathers. Bernard of Chartres used to compare us to [puny] dwarfs perched on the shoulders of giants. He pointed out that we see more and farther than our predecessors, not because we have keener vision or greater height, but because we are lifted up and borne aloft on their gigantic stature.*
> —John of Salisbury (1159/1982, p. 167)

The claim that our intellectual accomplishments depend in large measure on the unacknowledged contributions of our predecessors is usually associated with Sir Isaac Newton (1675/1759). Appropriately enough, however, that metaphor itself is part of the intellectual heritage on which Newton drew, and can be traced back to at least the 12th century (John of Salisbury, 1159/1982) and perhaps further (Merton, 1965). Mathematical thinking, like thought in other domains, rests on a set of concepts, procedures, and representational systems that constitute a major portion of each generation's intellectual inheritance. The purpose of this chapter is to explore the contribution that these cultural tools make to the development of mathematical thinking, by describing some of the variation in mathematical tools that have existed in different times and places, and reporting research on how current variations in mathematical representations are associated with variations in the development of mathematical competence. This discussion is placed in the context of a more general framework for considering how symbolic tools might affect cognitive development, which is described next.

HOW SYMBOLS MIGHT MATTER

Representational systems such as calendars, numbers, and written language have an internal structure that may serve to highlight some aspects of the underlying domains (time, mathematics, and language) they represent and obscure others. Children start learning to use symbolic systems before their concepts of number, time, and language are fully formed, and this fact raises the question of what role the structure of symbolic systems plays in the acquisition of a conceptual understanding of these domains. Not all of the difficulty children have in understanding mathematics, for example, is due to the tools their culture provides them for representing number. On the other hand, tools for representing number may facilitate or inhibit children's understanding of certain mathematical principles.

It would be simple to determine the role that symbolic systems play in cognitive development if one could compare "symbolic thought" with "nonsymbolic thought" in children of the same age. Unfortunately, the very prevalence of symbolic systems for representing number, time, and language makes the enterprise of comparing development with and without symbolic tools nearly impossible. In the case of mathematics, infants show a sensitivity to number as a feature of their world within the first few days of life (Antell & Keating, 1983), and show some limited ability to map transformations between small numerosities (Baillargeon, Miller, & Constantino, 1995; Wynn, 1992) several months later. However, children begin the process of learning the counting system by as early as the end of the first year (Durkin, Shire, Riem, Crowther, & Rutter, 1986), and from then on the task of acquiring mathematical symbol systems becomes a major component of mathematical development.

General claims about the cognitive consequences of different symbol systems have often been placed within the framework of the Sapir–Whorf hypothesis that language structure is reflected in the structure of thought. As operationalized by Brown (1956), tests of the Sapir–Whorf hypothesis have involved attempts to associate "nonlinguistic thought" with some aspect of a language's structure. Such tests have generally not produced evidence of substantial Sapir–Whorf effects (Foss & Hakes, 1978). We believe that understanding the ways in which the organization of symbols affects cognition requires a different framework that focuses more specifically on an analysis of the structure of specific symbol systems and the challenges learners face as they try to acquire, use, and understand particular symbol systems.

In general, there are at least three different ways in which the organization of symbol systems might affect cognition. First, the structure of symbols may affect the ease with which children initially acquire the system of symbols. Second, there may be continuing effects of the organization of symbol systems on the ease with which competent users exploit these symbols in online processing and problem solving. Third, the organization of symbols may facilitate or retard the development of a conceptual understanding of the domains they represent. Each of these kinds of effects will be considered separately, then used as a framework for discussing how the organization of specifically mathematical symbol systems mediate the development of mathematical reasoning.

Symbolic Structure Effects on Initial Acquisition

In order to master a system such as numbers or an alphabetic orthography, children need to learn something about how that system is organized. The manifest organization of the system provides much of the data from which learners can induce its conceptual structure, so one may expect that the structure of symbolic systems could affect even relatively early stages of acquisition. Research on very early symbol processing (e.g., Tolchinksy-Landsmann & Karmiloff-Smith, 1992) indicates that children may evince an appreciation for the structural differences between symbol systems before they master particular systems. Tolchinksy-Landsmann and Karmiloff-Smith reported that Spanish preschoolers were aware that strings of repeated digits (e.g., "2222") were valid numbers, but that strings of repeated consonants (e.g., "kkkk") were not valid words. It is likely that children's understanding of symbol systems shows a "prehistory" in which they gradually become aware of how these systems are organized. Therefore, effects of symbolic structure may begin to emerge even before children begin to really use a symbol system. The relevant structural principle of number-naming systems is the base-10 principle, and evidence will be reviewed indicating that difficulty in mastering this principle is a major obstacle to learning some components of counting, and later in learning Arabic numerals.

Symbolic Structure Effects on Symbol Processing: "Online" Effects

After children first learn a symbol system, there may be continuing effects of the structure of the system on processing by competent users. For example, the structure of the "ABC song" can be found by looking at the time subjects take to produce the next or previous letter (Klahr, Chase, & Lovelace, 1983; Miller & Meyer, 1989). To the extent that the structure of a symbol system has been incorporated into adults' computational processes, one might expect to find continuing effects of that structure on the efficiency of computation and the kinds of errors that emerge in processing. Effects of the structure of number-naming systems and of special calculation techniques such as the abacus on computational performance are discussed later.

Symbolic Structure Effects and Conceptual Representations

The final aspect of symbolic structure to be considered is the effect that such systems might have on conceptual representation, particularly the perceived relevance of meaningful relations in a domain (e.g., the base-10 principle in numbers) versus those that are merely adventitious (e.g., the fact that a "6" can be rotated into a "9"). Miller and Stigler (1991) found that novice and intermediate abacus users (but not experts) were very likely to emphasize abacus-specific features in judging similarity among numerals presented as abacus figures—even those features that had very limited mathematical significance. Developmentally, the effects of specific symbolic systems on children's access to conceptual features of domains should diminish—with increasing sophistication, adventitious characteristics of the symbol system (such as the fact that the word "bank" can represent the place one parks either one's money or one's canoe) should have diminishing effects on judgments of the conceptual structure of a domain. This was the pattern found by Miller and Stigler for abacus skill, and they termed this decrease in emphasis of representation-specific features *conceptual transparency* of skill. Effects of specific kinds of representations provided by variation in language and numerical symbols on children's judgments of number similarity are discussed later.

In understanding how the structure of mathematical symbols affects the development of mathematical thinking, it is important to consider separately effects that affect early acquisition, online computation by skilled users, and conceptual understanding of mathematics. The next section looks at the structures underlying number-naming systems in different languages that might affect mathematical development.

THE VARIETY OF NUMERICAL SYMBOL SYSTEMS

It is possible to count or at least to keep a count of things without using words at all. One could use fingers, stones, sticks, beads, or any denumerable set of things to keep track of other discrete things. If one wished to communicate how many windows there are in a room, it would be a simple matter to make a fist and then raise a finger for each window in the room. Similarly, a shepherd could drop a pebble into a bag for each sheep in the herd. The quantity of pebbles in the bag would represent the quantity of sheep in the herd, and to be sure that no sheep have been lost on the return of the flock, the shepherd could merely remove a pebble for each sheep returned. When all the pebbles have been removed, all the sheep are accounted for, and if any pebbles remain after all the sheep have been matched with a pebble, the remaining stones represent lost sheep. Homer described the ill-fated Cyclops Polyphemus using this method to keep track of his ewes as they went in and out of his cave, and it is one that has been invented in quite a variety of times and places (Menninger, 1969; Zaslavsky, 1973).

Numerical Representation and the Origins of Writing

Schmandt-Besserat (1992) argued that such object-based counting systems, used about 10,000 years ago in the Near East, gave rise to the world's first writing system. To resolve disputes over counts of other agricultural and manufactured products, it was necessary to seal the counters in a container after the count had been made. Archeological evidence indicates that this was done with small clay containers or envelopes into which clay tokens were deposited. A drawback to this system was that the opaque clay envelopes would have to be broken open each time an accounting was needed. To solve this problem, Neolithic accountants began to impress the tokens on the soft clay of the envelopes before dropping them in. Therefore, if there were 12 sheep to be counted, there would be 12 tokens in the sealed envelope and 12 marking on its surface. Only if there were a discrepancy at accounting time between the number of markings and the number of sheep would it be necessary to break open the envelope. As commerce became more complicated, the token system became more elaborate. Tokens of different sizes, shapes, and markings were used to represent different goods, and tally marks were added to the impressions of the tokens on the envelopes. If there were 30 sheep and 10 jars of oil involved in a transaction, the accompanying clay envelope would contain 30 sheep tokens and 10 jar tokens and would display on its surface an impression of a sheep token followed by 30 tally marks and an impression of an olive jar token followed by 10 tally marks. Eventually, according to Schmandt-Besserat, the tokens themselves were no longer kept in envelopes, and accounting records were made by impressions on clay tablets—the beginning of writing.

The Structure(s) of Number-Naming Systems

Although harder to find in the archeological record than tokens, the most basic symbolic tool for mathematics is the set of names a language has for numbers. After describing the organization of several number-naming systems, we describe research which demonstrates that the structure of number names has significant, specific effects on children's efforts to master these mathematical tools.

Names for numbers can be (and have been) generated according to a bewildering variety of systems (see Ifrah, 1985; Menninger, 1969). Because the base-10 system is so familiar and widespread and because we have 10 fingers, it may appear that the development of a base-10 system is somehow natural and inevitable (e.g., Lehrer, 1990/1965) and perhaps optimal for all cultures. This is certainly not the case. Flegg (1983) cited examples of people developing counting systems based on 2 (Bushmen of Botswana in Africa as well as native peoples of Australia and South America), 4 (in South America), 5 (in South America, Africa, and Asia), and 20 (the Mayan and Aztec people of South America). Babylonian astronomers used a base-60 system (Karpinski, 1925), and Menninger (1969) theorized that base-4 and base-8 systems were historically common, arising out of counting systems using the four fingers (excluding thumbs) of each hand. In addition to evidence that the base-10 number system is not the only "natural" system, there is debate over how desirable it is as a computational system. The 18th-century naturalist Buffon argued that a base-12 system would be universally preferable because it has twice as many integral divisors (four) as does the base-10 system, whereas the mathematician LaGrange argued that a prime base, such as 11, would have the advantage of producing only irreducible fractions (Dantzig, 1956). Ifrah (1985) sided with Buffon:

> It is regrettable that 12 was not chosen as the universal base, because it is mathematically superior to 10 and would not require a much greater effort of memory. But the habit of counting by tens is so deeply ingrained that the corresponding base will probably never be replaced. (p. 36)

Although 10 is perhaps not the ideal base, nearly all modern languages have number naming systems organized around base 10. In the course of learning to count, children must induce the structure of the system they are trying to learn, and the organization of number names constitutes much of the raw data for this inductive process. Therefore, careful consideration of the structure of these sequences can permit specific predictions about different patterns of acquisition for children learning to count in different languages. The structure of number names in a number of different representational systems is presented in Fig. 4.1. The spoken number names in seven modern languages (Chinese, Korean, English, German, Italian, Spanish, and French) are depicted, as well as one dead language (Latin) that had a strong influence on modern European number names. Korean was included because it employs two sets of number names. The first (based on Chinese numbers) is known as "Formal numbers" and is more widely used in mathe-

a) From one to ten

Arabic Numeral	1	2	3	4	5	6	7	8	9	10
Chinese (written)	一	二	三	四	五	六	七	八	九	十
Chinese (spoken)	yī	èr	sān	sì	wǔ	liù	qī	bā	jiǔ	shí
Korean Formal	il	i	sam	sa	o	yeuk	chil	pal	ku	sip
Korean Informal	hana	dool	set	net	dasut	yusut	ilgob	yudulb	ahob	yul
English	one	two	three	four	five	six	seven	eight	nine	ten
German	eins	zwei	drei	vier	fünf	sechs	sieben	acht	neun	zehn
Italian	uno	due	tre	quattro	cinque	sei	sette	otto	nove	dieci
Spanish	uno	dos	tres	cuatro	cinco	seis	siete	ocho	nueve	diez
French	un	deux	trois	quatre	cinq	six	sept	huit	neuf	dix
Latin	unus,-a,-um	duo,-ae,-a	tres,tria	quattuor	quinque	sex	septem	octo	novem	decem
Roman Numeral	I	II	III	IV	V	VI	VII	VIII	IX	X

b) Eleven to twenty

Arabic Numeral	11	12	13	14	15	16	17	18	19	20
Chinese (written)	十一	十二	十三	十四	十五	十六	十七	十八	十九	二十
Chinese (spoken)	shí yī	shí èr	shí sān	shí sì	shí wǔ	shí liù	shí qī	shí bā	shí jiǔ	èr shí
Korean Formal	sip il	sip i	sip sam	sip sa	sip o	sip yeuk	sip chil	sip pal	sip ku	i-sip
Korean Informal	yul hana	yul dool	yul set	yul net	yul dasut	yul yusut	yul ilgob	yul yudulb	yul ahob	sumul
English	eleven	twelve	thirteen	fourteen	fifteen	sixteen	seventeen	eighteen	nineteen	twenty
German	elf	zwölf	dreizehn	vierzehn	fünfzehn	sechzehn	siebzehn	achtzehn	neunzehn	zwanzig
Italian	undici	dodici	tredici	quattordici	quindici	sedici	diciassette	diciotto	diciannove	venti
Spanish	once	doce	trece	catorce	quince	diez y seis	diez y siete	diez y ocho	diez y nueve	veinte
French	onze	douze	treize	quatorze	quinze	seize	dix-sept	dix-huit	dix-neuf	vingt
Latin	undecim	duodecim	tredecim	quattuordecim	quindecim	sedecim	septendecim	octodecim	undeviginti	viginti
Roman Numeral	XI	XII	XIII	XIV	XV	XVI	XVII	XVIII	XIX	XX

FIG. 4.1. (Continued)

c) Twenty to ninety-nine

Language	Rule	Example
Chinese (written)	Decade unit (two,three,four,five,six,seven,eight,nine)+ten(shí)+unit	三十七
Chinese (spoken)		sān shí qī
Korean Formal	Decade unit (i,sam,sa,o,yeuk,chil,pal,ku)+ten(sip)+unit	sam sip pal
Korean Informal	Decade name (sumul, solhun,mahun,shehun,yesun,ilhun,yodun,ahun) + unit	solhun yudulb
English	Decade name (twen,thir,for,fif,six,seven,eight,nine) + "-ty" + unit	thirty seven
German	Unit + "und"+Decade name (zwan,drei, vier, fünf, sech,sieb, acht,neun)+"-zig" or "-ßig"	sieben und dreißig
Italian	Decade name (vent,trent,quarant,sinquant,sessant,settant,ottant,novant)+"-i" or "a"+unit	trentasette
Spanish	Decade name (veinte,treinta,cuarenta,cincuenta,sesenta,setenta,ochenta, noventa)+"-y" + unit	trenta y sette
French	Decade name (vingt, trente, quarante, cinquante, soixante, soixante-dix, quatre-vingts, quatre-vingt-dix)+unit	trente-sept
Latin	Decade name (vi,tri,quadra,quinqua,sexa, septua, octo, nona) + "-ginta" + unit	triginta tres (XXXIII)

d) One hundred to nine hundred ninety-nine

Language	Rule	Example
Chinese (written)	Hundreds unit + hundred + [líng if remainder < 10]+ [Name for portion < 100]	五百零八
Chinese (spoken)		wǔ bǎi líng bā
Korean Formal	Hundreds unit (optional if = 1)+ hundred (baek) + [Name for portion < 100]	o baek pal
Korean Informal	Not used for numbers > 100	
English	Hundreds unit +hundred + [Name for portion < 100]	five hundred eight
German	Hundreds unit + hundred + [Name for portion < 100]	fünf hundert und acht
Italian	Hundreds unit (optional if = 1)+ hundred + [Name for portion < 100]	cinqcentootto
Spanish	Hundreds unit (optional if = 1) + hundred + [Name for portion < 100]	cinco ciento ocho
French	Hundreds unit (optional if = 1) + cent + [Name for portion < 100	cinq cent huit
Latin	Hundreds unit +hundred term ("centi" or "genti") + [Name for portion < 100]	quingenti octo (DVIII)

FIG. 4.1. Number formation in a variety of languages and orthographies.

matics; the second, "Informal numbers," is used in counting many common objects. Three written systems are also presented (Arabic numerals, Roman numerals, Chinese characters), but are discussed further in a separate section. Each of these systems can be described to a first approximation as a base-10 system, but the variation among the systems represents the variety among systems in the clarity and consistency with which the base-10 structure is reflected in actual number representations.

In describing how number names are formed, it is useful to distinguish four ranges of numbers: 1 through 10, 11 through 19, 20 to 29, and 100 to 999.

Number Names From 1 to 10. For all the spoken languages, representations for numbers in the range 1–10 consist of an unsystematically organized list. There is no way to predict that "five" or "wǔ" come after "four" and "si," respectively, in the English and Chinese systems. Therefore, there is no rule that can be used to generate the number names in any of these sequences in this portion of the list.

From 11 to 19. Above 10, the languages diverge in interesting ways, as the second part of Fig. 4.1 demonstrates. Chinese number names in this range (as well as both Korean systems) form a strict base-10 system. The name for any number from 11–19 consists of the word for 10 plus the word for unit value of the number; thus the Chinese name for 14—"shí si"—can be literally translated as "10-4." English and German, on the other hand, have unpredictable names for "11" and "12" that bear only an historical relation to "1" and "2" (Menninger, 1969), perhaps deriving from "1 left" and "2 left" (beyond 10). Names in the other European languages for 11 and 12 incorporate at least some phonetic representation of "10," albeit heavily modified in the case of French and Spanish. Whether the boundary between 10 and 11 is marked in some way may be very significant, because this is the first potential clue to the fact that number names are organized according to a base-10 system, and such a clue is completely lacking in languages like English and German.

Beyond 12, English and German names do have an internal structure, but in the case of English this relation is obscured by phonetic modifications of many of the elements from those used in the first decade (e.g, "ten" → "teen," "three" → "thir," "five" → "fif"). Furthermore, names for some or all teens in the European languages reverse place value compared with the Hindu–Arabic and Chinese systems, naming the smaller value before the larger value. The Romance languages of Italian, Spanish, and French change the structure of teens names between 15 and 16 (Spanish) or between 16 and 17 (Italian and French); such as from "sedici" (from "6–10") to "diciassette" (from "10–7"). English, German, and Latin do not make this order reversal in number names during the teens decade, but the Latin name for 19 ("undeviginti") is derived from the name for 20 by subtraction (from "1 from 20").

It is puzzling that Latin number names did not incorporate the switch in structure that the Romance languages most closely related to Latin all employ. Menninger (1969) reported that switched forms such as "decem et septem" for 17 can be found in Latin texts, and that this was a feature of rural and lower class Latin speech that was presumably particularly prevalent among the settlers and soldiers, whose speech most directly affected modern European languages.

One can make two opposing hypotheses about the effect on acquisition of the Romance languages' structure regularizing number names somewhere in the middle of the second decade. The relatively early (compared to English) introduction of regular names based on 10 might facilitate learning the system. On the other hand, the practice of changing morphological structure somewhere in the middle of a decade might tend to diminish the importance of decade as a salient organizing rule for number names.

From 20 to 99. Above 20, all the number-naming systems except for German converge on the Chinese structure of naming the larger value before the smaller one. German continues to use the unit-decade structure that all the European languages used in the teens. Despite this convergence, the systems continue to differ in the clarity of the connection between decade names and the corresponding unit values. Chinese and Korean Formal numbers are consistent in forming decade names by combining a unit value and the base (10). Korean Informal number names include a set of decade names that cannot be easily derived from the corresponding unit names. Decade names in European languages generally can be derived from the name for the corresponding unit value, with varying degrees of phonetic modification (e.g., "five" → "fif" in English, "quattro" → "quarant" in Italian) and some notable exceptions, primarily the special name for 20 used in Latin and the Romance languages and the complex derivation of decade names for 70 ("soixant-dix," "sixty-ten"), 80 ("quatre-vingt," "four-twenty"), and 90 ("quatre-vingt-dix," "four-twenty-ten") in French.

Above 100. All the listed languages follow the same basic rule for naming hundreds, naming the unit value (2, 3, 4, etc.) followed by the word for "hundred." In all the listed languages except for Chinese and English, the "one" can be omitted in the case of 100, which Hurford (1975) has argued reflects a general transformational rule ("one-deletion") of number naming. In general, the names for the remaining (two-digit) portion of numbers above 100 are not altered by being part of a larger number. Chinese is an exception in this regard, with a special name for numbers in the first decade above

100 (101–109). In Chinese, the word "líng" is inserted in measurement situations in which there are one or more empty units between larger and smaller units (e.g., 5 years [no months] and 3 days becomes "5 years líng 3 days," or 8 dollars [no dimes] and 3 cents becomes "8 dollars líng 3 [cents]). The word líng can be variously translated as "fractional remainder," or simply "and," and is also used to represent zero.[1] Number names above 100 follow this measurement convention, and number names in the first decade are formed by interposing "líng" between the hundreds value and the unit position. Therefore, a literal translation of the Chinese name for 107 is "one hundred and (líng) seven."

As noted earlier, Korean Formal number names are modeled directly on Chinese number names. There are two important exceptions to this modeling. First, Korean Formal numbers do not mark the absence of a tens value in numbers like "107" by including any analogue to the Chinese líng. Second, Korean utilizes one deletion in naming 100, which would be called "il baek" ("one hundred") according to the Chinese model, but is instead named "baek" ("hundred").

The structure of number naming systems is well characterized by Wittgenstein's (1958/1953) metaphorical description of language in general:

> Our language can be seen as an ancient city: a maze of little streets and squares, of old and new houses, and of houses with additions from various periods; and this surrounded by a multitude of new boroughs with straight regular streets and uniform houses. (p. 8)

Languages differ in the length and complexity of the irregular portion of the system of names that must be learned, but children in general must learn quite a few number names prior to coming across data supporting the induction that they are dealing with an ordered base-10 system of names.

Written Numeral Representations

Just as any number of arbitrary sounds may be used to name a number, so any number of markings may be used to represent the number graphically. Although the earliest prehistoric numerical representations may have been as simple as notches on a counting stick, by the beginning of the 12th century A.D. two sophisticated representations of the base-10 system were competing for ascendancy (Menninger, 1969). Roman alphabetic numerals were pre-

---

[1]Hurford (1975, 1987) has asserted that the use of líng in Chinese represents the only explicit use of zero in the formation of number names among natural languages. Although líng can be translated as "zero," its use in Chinese is much more general than the term "zero" implies, and a translation as "fractional remainder" seems more accurate.

dominate in Europe, whereas Hindu–Arabic notations were used throughout the Indian subcontinent and the Arab empire.

Hindu–Arabic Numerals.   Originating in India, and refined and spread by a flourishing Arab culture, the Hindu–Arabic system is familiar today as the numerals 1, 2, 3, and so on. The arrangement of these numerals constitutes a "place-value" or positional system in which the value of the numeral is determined by where it occurs in the sequence (Menninger, 1969). The rightmost value is defined as the value of the numeral multiplied by 10^0, the next left value is the numeral $\times 10^1$, the next left is the numeral $\times 10^2$, and so on. Therefore, the number three hundred and eighty-seven is represented as "387." The notational system clearly reflects its base-10 underlying structure.

Roman Numerals.   The Roman system, in contrast, is a modified count-value system in which the total number of occurrences of an individual numeral determines the value of the numerical string. The basic Roman numerals and their Hindu–Arabic equivalents are as follows: I = 1, V = 5, X = 10, L = 50, C = 100, D = 500, M = 1000. The Roman notation for thirty-two consists of a count of three tens and two ones: XXXII. There is a basic positional rule that numerals proceed from higher to lower and from left to right, and there is a positional subtraction rule: The numeral "I" to the left of "V" or "X" indicates that one should be subtracted from the higher numeral. Therefore, IV = 4, and LIX = 59 (Ifrah, 1958).

Chinese Character Representations of Numbers

Although Chinese characters for numbers are part of the Chinese writing system rather than a form of numerical notation, we noted earlier that the structure of the Chinese number-naming system closely resembles that of the Hindu–Arabic numeral system. It is important to point out, however, that there is a subtle distinction between the two systems. Chinese number names employ a "name-value" system (Menninger, 1969): For values higher than one (10^0), the rank value (power of 10) of the number is given not by its position but by an explicit name. In the Hindu–Arabic numeral system, the value of the 4 in 41 is understood to be 4×10^1 because of its position, but in the Chinese writing of 41, the character for four is followed by the character for ten to indicate that its value is 4×10. Therefore, although the Hindu–Arabic system uses two characters to represent forty-one (41), Chinese writing uses three (corresponding to "four ten one"). As will be seen, this slight difference presents a surprising and formidable obstacle to Chinese students when they are required to use Chinese characters for doing simple computations.

Ascendancy of the Hindu–Arabic System

Consider the task of multiplying CXXXIV by XX as compared to the equivalent task of multiplying 134 by 20. Fibonacci (Leonardo of Pisa), one of the great mathematicians of the Middle Ages, was one of the first Europeans to describe the advantages of the Hindu–Arabic system over that of Roman numerals. His Book of Computations (*Liber Abaci*) proclaimed the wonders of the new system to his contemporaries in 1202:

> But all this, the agorithm and the arch of Pythagoras, I regarded as an error as compared to the methods of the Indians. . . . The nine numerals of the Indians are these: 9 8 7 6 5 4 3 2 1. With them and with this sign 0, which in Arabic is called *cephirum* [cipher], any desired number can be written. (Menninger, 1969, p. 425)

Slowly but powerfully, the new numerals spread from scholars to merchants and bankers and from Italy throughout Europe so that by the 16th century Hindu–Arabic numerals had completely supplanted Roman numerals in education and commerce.

Summary of the Separate Development of Number Names and Numeral Systems

It is clear that both number naming systems and numerical notation systems are cultural legacies that provide tremendous support for numerical cognition. It is also clear, however, that the two systems are not the same thing, nor were they produced concurrently and cooperatively by a single ancient genius nor even by a single culture. Instead, each evolved separately and both still preserve aspects of their evolutionary histories. Menninger (1969) summarized the process in his work on the cultural history of numbers:

> The writing of numerals is *not* merely the representation of the number-word sequence. . . . Our letters are not akin to our numbers. One would be inclined to suppose, in all innocence, that the human mind, when it took the trouble to record its ideas and concepts, would have devised similar systems of writing words and numbers, "seven" and "7," but this did not happen, neither in our Western culture nor anywhere else in the world. (pp. 53–54)

The Abacus

Abacus-like calculating devices have been invented the world over. The English word "abacus" derives from an ancient Greek device in which clay balls were manipulated in a series of troughs excavated in a clay tablet, or moved along parallel lines marked on a table (Pullan, 1969). The abacus has taken on a variety of forms over time, but a popular modern version is the Japanese abacus currently used through much of Asia and depicted in Fig. 4.2. Beads

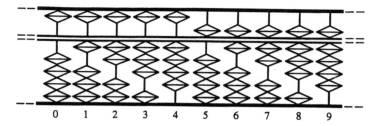

FIG. 4.2. Representation of digits on the Japanese-style abacus. Beads "count" as they are moved toward the center (horizontal) bar. The top bead represents 5, the lower beads each represent 1. Value within a column is the sum of the top bead (0 or 5) plus the number of lower beads (0-4) pushed toward the center bar.

"count" as they are pushed toward the center (horizontal) bar by the thumb (lower beads) or forefinger (upper bead). The upper bead represents 5 times the column value, whereas the lower beads represent one unit each. The value represented by a column is the sum of the top bead (0 or 5) and the lower bead (0–4), with the total multiplied by the column value (as with standard place value notation). Within a column, the abacus represents a modulo 5 number system while remaining a base-10 system between columns. Therefore, numbers such as 1 and 6 that differ by ±5 have similar abacus representations, with the same number of lower beads counted.

The abacus is of particular interest as a symbol system for representing number because of the that persons who have developed a high level of skill calculate with reference to a "mental abacus," using an image of the abacus to perform mental arithmetic (Hatano, Miyake, & Binks, 1977; Hatano & Osawa, 1983; Stigler, 1984). Data on effects of abacus experience on calculation speed and strategies, and on conceptual understanding of number are described in the appropriate parts of the next section.

PSYCHOLOGICAL EFFECTS OF THE STRUCTURE OF NUMBER NAMES

The structure of number names affect all three of the processes mentioned earlier as possibly being affected by symbol systems—in early acquisition, in the online computations of adults, and in effects on conceptual processing. Each is discussed in turn.

Acquisition Effects

Research on the development of counting has focused on the relations between procedural and conceptual knowledge in early mathematical development. Learning to count also requires mastering a new symbolic system—the number names—which presents children with another potential source of structure in mathematical development. As discussed in the last section, mathematical symbols incorporate certain regularities, some of which have broader mathematical significance (e.g., the incorporation of a base such as 10), and others that do not (e.g., the fact the English number names "seven" and "thirteen" are both two syllables long). This section discusses the contribution that these symbolic systems can make to mathematical development, primarily by describing cognitive consequences of variation between languages in the organization of numerical symbols.

Effects of Number-Naming Systems on Early Counting. When children first learn to count, they must induce the structure of the number names that they are using. Not surprisingly, many of the difficulties children have in learning to count can be related to the structure of the system they are acquiring. Research on children's acquisition of number names (Fuson, Richards, & Briars, 1982; Miller & Stigler, 1987; Siegler & Robinson, 1982) suggests that American children learn to recite the list of number names through at least the teens as essentially a rote-learning task. When first counting above 20, American preschoolers often produce idiosyncratic number names, indicating that they fail to understand the base-10 structure underlying larger number names, often counting "twenty-eight, twenty-nine, twenty-ten, twenty-eleven, twenty-twelve."

In a study comparing American and Chinese preschool children, Miller and Stigler (1987) found different patterns of errors and stopping points in early counting by children learning these two languages. Americans commonly made mistakes that indicated they were not sure whether numbers like "10," "11," or "12" could be combined freely with other numbers—for example, counting "twenty-eight, twenty-nine, twenty-ten, twenty-eleven . . ." Chinese children never made this type of mistake.

If the structure of number names accounts for the differences in early counting between American and Chinese children, then differences should only emerge where the structures of the number-naming systems differ, and should reflect the nature of those differences. As noted earlier, Chinese and English number names are equally unpredictable in the range 1 through 10, so this means that the earliest stages of number name learning should look very similar for American and Chinese children. Miller, Smith, Zhu, and Zhang (1995) looked at early mathematical development in 3–5-year-olds in China and the United States, and found a pattern of results that indicates strong and specific effects of the structure of number names on early mathematical development in these two countries. Figure 4.3 shows the median level of abstract counting (reciting number names like "1, 2, 3 . . ."). Notably, there are no significant differences at age 3, when the median level of counting in both groups is only slightly above 10. Between 3 and 4 years, however,

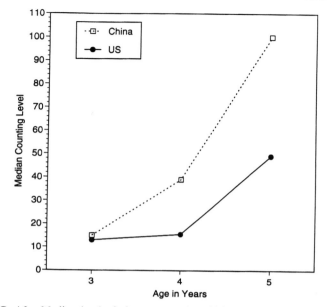

FIG. 4.3. Median level of abstract counting (highest number reached) by age and language. Significant differences favoring Chinese-speaking subjects were found at ages 4 and 5, but not at age 3, emerging as children mastered the second "teens" decade, where differences in number-name formation rules differentiate the two languages. Data from Miller et al. (1995).

a large difference emerges in counting level between the American and Chinese subjects, a gap that increases between ages 4 and 5 years.

A more precise way of looking at which portions of the number-naming sequence posed particular difficulty for children learning the two number-naming systems is presented in Fig. 4.4, which shows for each number of the counting sequence the proportion of children in each country who were able to count to that number or beyond. These profiles of counting "mortality" can be analyzed using survival analysis techniques from the biomedical statistical literature (McCullagh & Nelder, 1991), to determine whether there are steeper drops in the depicted data for one country or the other for specific parts of the number-naming sequence.

Four effects are apparent in Fig. 4.4, all of which are confirmed by survival analyses. (a) In the range from 1 to 10, there are no significant differences in counting mortality for either language. (b) In the second decade of the number-naming sequence, English-speaking children show a substantially greater dropoff in counting success than do Chinese speaking children. (c) Between 20 and 99, there are no significant differences in the counting survival profiles of children learning these two languages. (d) Finally, Chinese subjects show a much greater drop after 100 than do their American peers.

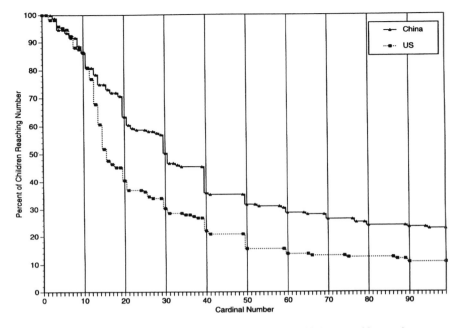

FIG. 4.4. Percentage of a group of 3–5-year-old children reaching each number in abstract counting, by country. The difficulty U.S. children have in mastering the teens portion of English number names is shown by their substantial dropoff during this region.

These effects are precisely those that were predicted based on the analysis of number-naming systems described earlier. In learning to count to 10, children in both countries must memorize a long, unstructured system of names, a task of equal difficulty in both countries. Between 10 and 20, the simpler and more consistent structure of Chinese teens names is associated with much faster acquisition of this portion of the sequence by Chinese than by American children. Above 20, the two systems converge on a common structure of number names, and children in both countries show a parallel scalloped pattern in which errors are concentrated at decade boundaries and do not differ between countries. As noted previously, Chinese introduces a new element (líng) in number names in the first decade above 100, and this transition becomes a serious stumbling block for Chinese children, with a significantly greater drop for Chinese than American subjects.

These cross-national differences between American and Chinese preschoolers' success in mastering the number-naming sequences of their native language occurred in very specific parts of the number-naming sequence, and did not extend to other aspects of early counting skill. In object counting and in simple mathematical problem solving, Miller et al. (1995) found no significant differences in the ability of children in the two countries to keep track of which objects had been counted, or to generate sets of a given numerosity (producing *n* candies to feed to a toy panda as part of a game). The effects of differences in number-name structure on early mathematical development appear to be very specific to those aspects of mathematics that require one to learn and use these symbol systems.

Finding that Chinese and American children show differences in early mathematical development in the direction and at the points that an analysis of the two symbol systems would predict lends some support to the view that these differences in symbol systems cause the associated learning difficulties. There are clearly substantial differences in the contexts in which children develop in these two countries, however, which compels caution in drawing strong causal conclusions from these cross-language comparisons. There are, for example, many anecdotal reports (e.g., Gardner, 1988) suggesting that adults in the United States use quite different teaching strategies with their preschool children compared to Asian families.

Because a true experiment, with random assignment of subjects to cultural group is clearly impossible, claims about the causal relationship between language structure and acquisition can be strengthened by proxy experiments and simulations that expose the same subjects or model to learning problems that are modeled on the actual number naming systems children must learn. An initial effort in this direction has been started in our lab. A quite simple, morphology-based connectionist model learned to count in systems modeled after Chinese and English. The simulation is a three-layer (input, hidden, output) nonrecurrent feedforward artificial neural network that learns a slightly idealized morphology-based counting system. The layers are pairwise fully connected. The models were trained under a back propagation algorithm using a modified supervised learning patterned after children's counting behavior.

Number names consisted of one element each of otherwise unordered sets corresponding to decade names, bases, and units. For English, the set of decade names consisted of twen-, thir-, fo(u)r-, fif-, six-, seven-, eight-, nine-, & {null}. The set of bases consisted of -ty, -teen, and {null}. The set of units consisted of one, two, three, four, five, six, seven, eight, nine, ten, eleven, twelve, and {null}. For Chinese, the set of decade names consisted of er-, san-, si-, wu-, liu-, qi-, ba-, jiu-, and {null}. The set of bases consisted of shi and {null}. The set of units consisted of yi, er, san, si, wu, liu, qi, ba, jiu, and {null}.

This analysis ignores several obvious semantic and morphological aspects of number names. For example, the relation between the "sixes" in "six-ty-six" is not represented; they are independent tokens.

Training used a modification of supervised learning intended to permit some model control of learning sequences. In this sequential training approach, training and testing are collapsed into the same process: the learner is presented with a stimulus (starting with "one" or "yi"), generating a response that is evaluated. If the response is correct, the learner is presented with the next stimulus in the sequence, continuing in this fashion until an error is made. On making an error, the model is adjusted via back propagation, but the model continues with the given response (not the correct response) as the stimulus for the next trial. Counting terminates either when no response is given or probabilistically after errors are made.

Figure 4.5 presents results from training this model with the Chinese and English counting sequences. The first epoch in which a number was correctly produced is depicted. A negative y-axis scale is used to facilitate comparison with the survival profiles presented in Fig. 4.4.

The model demonstrates three basic phenomena that children show. First, performance in the initial part of the sequence (1–10) does not differ between languages. Second, differences favoring the Chinese language emerge during the "teens." Third, counting beyond the teens in both countries produces a scalloped difficulty profile, with mistakes likely to occur at decade boundaries.

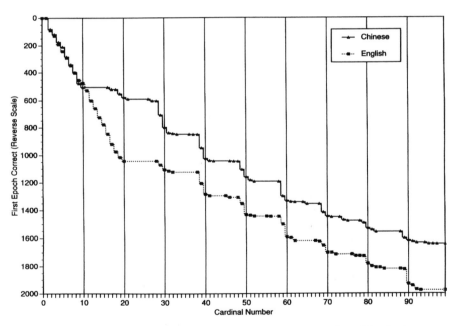

FIG. 4.5. Performance of a morphology-based neural-network model trained to count in Chinese and English. First epoch to produce a number is shown; to facilitate comparision with the previous figure, this is plotted on a reverse axis. The model reproduces the most prominent phenomena shown in children's behavior: (a) similar performance before 10, a larger dropoff for English in the teens, and a scalloped profile of difficulty at decade boundaries for both languages in the range from 20–99.

There are a number of very substantial limitations with this model. First of all, the U.S. profile for the higher numbers is distinctively less scalloped than is the corresponding curve for Chinese data; a phenomenon not observed in children's counting. Overall, the model's performance is "too scalloped." Unlike real children, the model does not catch on to the recurrent structure of number names. In fact (as one would expect from catastrophic interference analyses), learning additional decade transitions tends to become harder as training progresses. Furthermore, looking only at the first correct epoch in which a transition is made obscures a substantial amount of catastrophic interference in the previously learned parts of the model. A recently completed longitudinal study (Miller, Smith, Zhang, & Zen, in preparation) indicates that a certain amount of such interference may occur in real life, but clearly not to the extent that the model indicates. Finally, the model cannot exhibit an important limitation that young children show: the inability to randomly access number names. That is, when asked to produce the number following "5," they need to count from 1 in order to come up with "6." Nonetheless, these modeling results are encouraging as presenting evidence that differences between English and Chinese number names are sufficient to produce a number of the empirically observed differences in difficulty of acquisition of these two systems by children learning to count in their native language.

Online Computational Effects

The effects of the idiosyncratic English number system do not entirely disappear with development. Miller and Zhu (1991) explored a task that required subjects to access the names of two digit numbers in an unusual way, by reversing number names (that is, naming the number produced by reversing the tens' and unit's places, saying "24" to the stimulus "42"). In ordinary naming, the fact that the name for "14" begins with the rightmost element, whereas the name for "24" begins with the leftmost element and does not affect speed or accuracy of naming. When subjects had to reverse number names, however, the idiosyncracy of English teens names emerged in naming latencies. For Chinese, which has a consistent structure for names of two-digit numbers, no such disparity was observed. The fact that with practice even complicated structures can become automatized (e.g., Shiffrin & Dumais, 1981) suggests symbolic structure effects on symbolic computation should be most prominent in unfamiliar or complex tasks, and that automaticity or local processes that can provide computational shortcuts.

Format Effects in Children's Addition in the United States and China.
Fuson and Kwon (1991) have argued that the complexity of English number names in the teens causes difficulty for children learning to add and subtract

in early elementary school, because the fact that $12 = 10 + 2$ is not reflected in the word "twelve," adding an extra step to problems involving carrying and borrowing. In general, Hindu–Arabic numerals are used for computation, whereas language-specific number names are used almost purely for linguistic communication and Roman numerals are reserved for special uses such as indicating years and Super Bowl sequences. Indeed, it is somewhat disconcerting to see the use of number words or Roman numerals in the context of doing arithmetic. Figure 4.6 shows the same addition problem presented in four formats: Roman numerals, Arabic numerals, Chinese characters, and as words in the English-language alphabetic orthography.

Consider how one might try to add this problem using the representations in which it is presented. Both the Roman numeral and English alphabetic notations present parsing problems—determining what is to be added to what—that are absent in the other representations. Paredes (1995) asked second-, third-, and fourth-grade students in China and the United States to mentally add sets of single-digit Arabic numerals as well as two double-digit numbers displayed either as Arabic numerals (the numeral condition) and as number names written in the orthography of their native language as shown in Fig. 4.5 (the word condition). As Fig. 4.7 shows, for two-digit Arabic numerals there was no significant difference in the accuracy of U.S. and Chinese children, but Chinese students were significantly faster than U.S. students at every grade level (a finding predicted from comparative studies of arithmetic achievement—Geary, Fan, & Bow-Thomas, 1992; Stevenson, Stigler, & Lee, 1986; Travers et al., 1987).

When problems were presented in the two word orthographies (English alphabetic and Chinese character orthographies), a different pattern of results emerged, depicted in Fig. 4.8. Chinese students continued to be significantly faster than their American peers, but the accuracy results showed a significant difference at all ages favoring the U.S. subjects. An analysis of the types of errors the children made helps to explain these surprising results.

Errors were coded into three basic types: (a) *Near misses* were within two of the correct answer for each digit and contained the correct number of digits. These were believed to represent calculation errors, and were relatively constant between countries. (b) *Reversals* involved adding the units portion of one addend to the tens portion of the other. As Fig. 4.9 shows, this mistake was limited to American subjects. In the word example shown in Fig. 4.6,

```
 XXVII          27
+  XIV         + 14
```

FIG. 4.6. The same arithmetic problem presented in four formats (clockwise): Roman numerals, Arabic numerals, English alphabetic orthography, and Chinese characters.

```
 二十七
             twenty-seven
+ 十四        +    fourteen
```

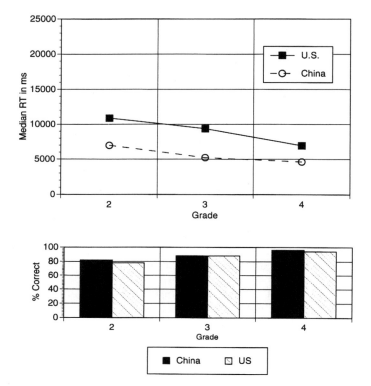

FIG. 4.7. Median RT for 2-digit addition problems presented as numerals. Top panel shows median adding time by grade and country for problems correctly solved. Bottom panel shows percent of problems answered correctly. Despite similar levels of accuracy, Chinese subjects were substantially faster than their U.S. peers.

this would typically involve adding the four in "fourteen" to the two in "twenty-seven" and the one in "fourteen" to the seven in "twenty-seven," to produce 68 as the sum of 27 + 14. The final error type was termed (c) *Expansions*, in which the answer contained the wrong *number* of digits. This problem was limited to the Chinese subjects, and accounted for their high error rate. This occured because Chinese children often treated each character of the number name as having the value corresponding to its position in the Hindu–Arabic numeral system. In the example in Fig. 4.6, for instance, the number 27 is represented by Chinese characters equivalent to 2, 10, and 7. Chinese students tended treat that string as though it were 217, failing to appreciate the distinction Menninger (1969) drew between place-value systems (like Arabic numerals) and name-value systems (like Chinese characters), in which there is an explicit representation of each place.

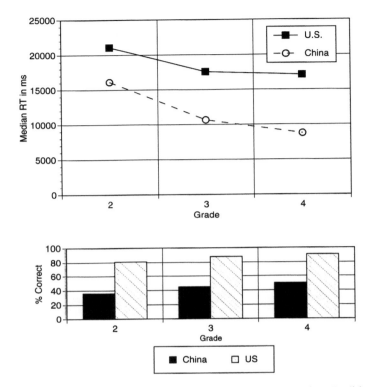

FIG. 4.8. Median RT for 2-digit addition problems presented as English words (U.S. subjects) or Chinese characters (Chinese subjects). Top panel shows median adding time by grade and country for problems correctly solved. Bottom panel shows percent of problems answered correctly. Chinese subjects were again much faster than their U.S. peers, but a large difference in accuracy favoring U.S. children was found.

Although the mapping between Chinese characters and Arabic numerals is more direct and consistent than is the mapping between English words and Arabic numerals, in this special and unusual task that similarity of representation proved to be a problem for Chinese subjects. Unless one has a deep understanding of the difference between place-value and name-value systems, one is very likely to attempt to simply carry over algorithms that work for place-value numbers and apply them to Chinese characters, with the results revealed in this study.

Abacus. Prior research has documented the impressive computational skills developed by adults and children who receive extended practice in abacus calculation (Hatano et al., 1977; Hatano & Osawa, 1983; Stigler, 1984). Perhaps the most intriguing aspect of this skill is the development of

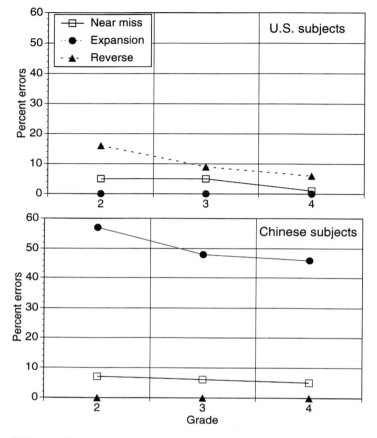

FIG. 4.9. Errors on the word/character format addition task. Errors were coded into (a) Near misses (within ±2 on both digits of answer, and correct number of digits); (b) Expansions (in which the answer contained the wrong number of digits); and (c) Reverses (in which the units portion of one addend was added to the tens portion of the other). Error profiles differed substantially across countries and reflected the nature of the orthography used.

"mental abacus calculation," in which subjects calculate with reference to an internal image of the abacus. Persons who develop a high level of skill at abacus calculation report calculating with reference to a "mental abacus," using an image of the abacus to perform mental arithmetic. Supporting this claim, studies of the mental calculation of abacus experts find several ways in which the structure of the abacus is reflected in subjects' performance. Stigler (1984) reported that for abacus-trained children the number of steps involved in an abacus calculation was associated with reaction time for mental calculation. He also reported that these abacus-trained children could distinguish true intermediate states from foils. Perhaps the strongest evidence for the abacus-like nature of the mental calculation of these children came from analysis of their errors. Abacus calculators (but not American college students) were prone to make errors that could be accounted for by misrepresenting the location of one bead on the abacus. These included leaving out the value of one column, and errors in which the answer was off by 5 in some column from the correct sum. Because the abacus represents numbers that differ by 5 in a similar way, the finding of an increased incidence of these modulo-5 errors provides a convincing demonstration of the abacus-like nature of the calculation of those who have become experts at the skill of mental abacus calculation.

The prevalence of modulo-5 errors in the mental calculation of abacus trained children is important, because it provides clear evidence that the structure of the abacus has impressed itself on the organization of calculation by these children.

Conceptual Consequences of Numerical Symbols

Building Base-10 Representations. The difficulties young children have in figuring out the base-10 structure of English are not limited to mistakes they make in counting. Miura, Kim, Chang, and Okamoto (1988) reported that first graders in China, Japan, and Korea (all speaking languages that use the basic Chinese system for forming number names) showed a substantially greater ability than did American children to use base-10 blocks (Dienes blocks) to form object representations that incorporate base-10 principles.

Abacus. Models of expertise permit two contradictory predictions about the effects of abacus expertise on experts' judgments of similarity between numbers. One view, stretching back to Bryan and Harter (1899), argues that domains of knowledge should be organized in terms of the functional expertise one has within those domains—a view Miller and Stigler (1991) called *conceptual determination by skill*. In this view, abacus experts should view numbers in terms of the relations that are important in abacus calculation (such as the modulo-5 relations prominent on the abacus). The opposite prediction, which we termed *conceptual transparency of skill* has an equally distinguished ancestry, going back to Binet (1893/1966). Binet argued that experts develop a representation which is much more abstract than the constraints of a particular expertise would imply. In this view, abacus experts should judge as salient only features that are meaningful in a larger mathematical context. The fact that 1 and 6 have similar representations on an abacus is of very limited mathematical significance. Conceptual transparency implies that, although abacus experts are prone to make abacus-specific mistakes in calculation (e.g., substituting a "1" for a "6"), abacus-specific factors should not be prominent in their judgments of similarity between numbers.

To evaluate the effect of abacus skill on number representation, we collected similarity judgments for pairs of numbers in the range 0–20 from three groups of sixth graders: Novices (U.S. children with no abacus experience); Intermediates (Chinese children with only general abacus training, who knew how numbers were represented on the abacus, but had no special training in abacus calculation beyond brief exposure in the general school curriculum); and Experts (Chinese children who had participated in special after-school abacus training and were rated at one of the top three levels of skill in the Chinese Abacus Association rating system). Children judged similarity of pairs of numbers, and each child saw stimuli presented either as Arabic numerals or as abacus figures (in a truncated display showing 2 columns).

Figures 4.10 and 4.11 present the results of a SINDSCAL (Carroll & Chang, 1970) analysis of the similarity judgments of these two kinds of numbers (Numerals vs. Abacus depictions) by these three groups of subjects (Abacus Experts, Abacus Intermediates, and complete Novices—Americans). A three-dimensional solution is described, with an overall correlation of $r =$ .638 between predicted and actual judgments. The first dimension corresponds to numerical magnitude, and is most stressed by U.S. children judging numerals and Intermediates judging the abacus. The abacus does not provide a direct representation of magnitude, as the relatively low weighting of this dimension by U.S. children judging the abacus shows. Therefore, Intermediates judging abacus stimuli are going beyond the relations explicitly encoded on the abacus when they emphasize numerical magnitude in judging the similarity of abacus figures. Figure 4.11 presents the first dimension of the SINDSCAL solution paired with the third dimension, which corresponds to the number of beads used to present a particular number. It is essentially a modulo-5 dimension; thus the numbers 0,5,10,15,20 (all of which are depicted with 0 lower beads) have a similar low value on this dimension.

Intermediates' judgments of abacus and number stimuli were quite different from each other, however, indicating that not every mathematical feature known to these children was incorporated in their abacus judgments. Intermediates judging abacus stimuli placed little emphasis on Odd versus Even, although their judgments of numerals emphasized this feature heavily. In terms of the developmental progression from magnitude to multiplicative relations described earlier, Intermediates' judgments of abacus representations were less mature than their judgments of numerals. U.S. and Intermediate subjects judging abacus figures placed a greater emphasis than did experts on the modulo-5 relations used to represent numbers on the abacus.

Expert judgments of the different types of stimuli were much more similar to each other than were those of Intermediates, and both resembled Intermediates' judgments of numerals more than Intermediates' judgments of abacus figures. This indicates that Experts' judgments tend to deemphasize aba-

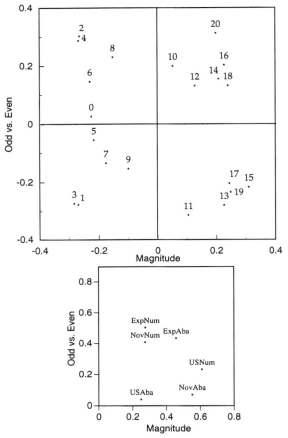

FIG. 4.10. Weighted MDS analysis of abacus–numeral similarity judgments by U.S. subjects (Novices), Abacus Intermediates, and Abacus Experts. This figure pairs the first two dimensions, which roughly correspond to Magnitude and Odd versus Even. The top panel shows weighting of stimuli in a common space derived from all subjects' judgments. The lower panel presents the subject or weight space corresponding to the dimensions presented in the upper panel. Therefore, for example, U.S. subjects judging the abacus placed very little weight on the Odd–Even dimension relative to Magnitude.

cus specific features, consistent with the conceptual transparency view of the conceptual consequences of expertise.

Judgments of numerical stimuli show a different pattern with expertise. In this case, U.S. subjects show the strongest influence of magnitude, consistent with other data (e.g., Stevenson, Lee, & Stigler, 1986) in suggesting that U.S. children are less mathematically sophisticated than their Chinese peers. Intermediate and Expert children show a correspondingly greater influence of Odd/Even parity than do U.S. children, whereas there is a small

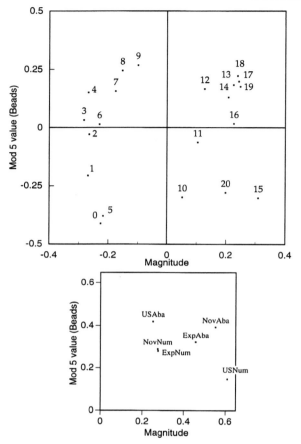

FIG. 4.11.   Weighted MDS analysis of abacus–numeral similarity judgments by U.S. subjects (Novices), Abacus Intermediates, and Abacus Experts (continued). This figure pairs the first and third dimensions, which roughly correspond to Magnitude and the number of beads that represent a given number on the abacus.

effect of modulo-5 features that does not show a consistent change with expertise.

Conceptual Consequences of Expertise

Abacus experts show some evidence of a unified representation of number across different external representations. This representation does not, however, emphasize the features that are important in the skill they have acquired. Instead, features of number that are more significant in a broader mathematical context assume prominence in the judgments of abacus experts, at the expense of those features on which abacus calculation is based. The differences between Intermediates and U.S. subjects are interesting, because even though Intermediates knew the numerical value of abacus representations, their results for abacus stimuli fell between U.S. subjects (who were perforce judging on the features of the abacus depiction) and Experts (who placed strong emphasis on non-abacus mathematical features). Intermediate subjects enriched their judgments of abacus stimuli by including the non-abacus feature of magnitude, yet their judgments of abacus figures failed to include multiplicative relations that were prominent when Intermediates judged numerals. This finding suggests that the conceptual transparency model provides a good description of the conceptual consequences of expertise, but it also indicates that simply knowing the mapping between two systems is not enough to ensure that all relations known in one will transfer to the other. The problem of accessing knowledge across different but parallel representational systems is one that extends beyond the domain of abacus calculation. The final study looks at the effects of different orthographies for writing numbers on the mathematical relations children perceive.

Orthography and Number-Similarity

Even if one doesn't learn a special calculation technique, everyone is familiar with multiple representations for numbers. The final data to be presented here report how number similarity judgments are affected by language and orthography. Chinese and American children in Grades 2, 4, and 6 judged similarity of numbers presented as either Arabic numerals or in a word orthography (English words or Chinese characters). Another group of children in the same grades in South Korea judged numbers presented in three orthographies: Arabic numerals, Korean Informal, and Korean Formal notation. Korean is particularly interesting because it uses two different number naming systems: one for mathematics and most measurement situations (Formal numbers), and another that must be used instead of Formal numbers for many common nouns (Informal numbers). Research on early counting (Song & Ginsburg, 1988) has shown that having to learn two separate systems of numbers is initially quite confusing for young children; whether both are later mapped onto some unified number concept was explored in this study.

Results for a two-dimensional SINDSCAL analysis for U.S. and Chinese subjects are presented in Fig. 4.12, with an overall correlation of $r = .76$ between predicted and actual judgments. Korean results are presented in Fig. 4.13, with an overall correlation of $r = .68$ between predicted and actual judgments. In both analyses, the two dimensions correspond generally to Magnitude and Odd versus Even. The developmental pattern within each country for Arabic numerals corresponds to that found by Miller and Gelman (1983), with increasing emphasis on Odd/Even and decreasing emphasis on Magnitude. The rate of this change differs across countries, with U.S. fourth graders looking more like second graders in the other countries in

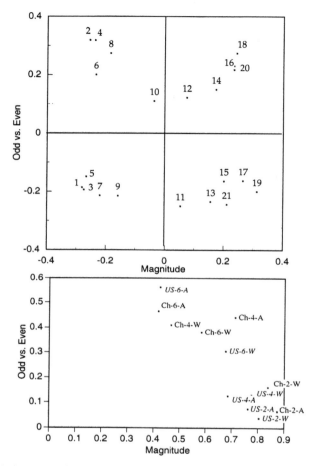

FIG. 4.12. Weighted MDS analysis of number similarity judgments by U.S. and Chinese children, judging numbers presented as Arabic numerals or as words (U.S.) or characters (Chinese). This figure pairs the first two dimensions, which roughly correspond to Magnitude and Odd versus Even. Data points in the lower panel correspond to the weighting of these two dimensions by groups of subjects. For example, U.S. second graders judging words placed very little emphasis on the odd/even dimension.

their emphasis on Magnitude, although by 6th grade all groups of subjects showed a greater emphasis on Odd–Even than on Magnitude.

Judgments of "Word" orthographies showed a smaller, later, and less consistent shift from magnitude toward multiplicative relations. Both groups of second graders and U.S. fourth graders placed much more emphasis on Magnitude than on Odd–Even. As with Arabic numeral stimuli, U.S. subjects consistently placed more of an emphasis on magnitude relative to multipli-

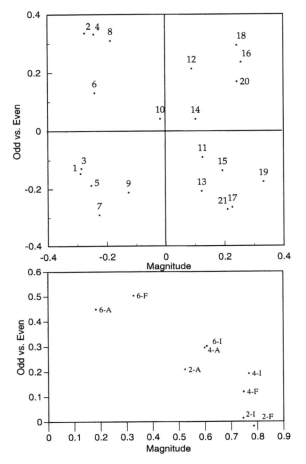

FIG. 4.13. Weighted MDS analysis of number similarity judgments by Korean children judging numbers presented in three different orthographies: Arabic numerals, and the formal and informal number systems. This figure pairs the first two dimensions, which roughly correspond to Magnitude and Odd versus Even. Data points in the lower panel correspond to the weighting of these two dimensions by groups of subjects. For example, sixth graders judging numbers presented in both the Arabic numeral and Formal systems placed relatively high emphasis on the odd/even dimension.

cative features than their Chinese peers. Results for the two Korean word orthographies are particularly interesting, with evidence by Grade 6 of much greater similarity in judgments for the Arabic and Formal notations, which are both used in school mathematics, than between either of these numbers and the Informal numbers, which are generally not used in school situations.

Although children are very familiar with the mapping between the various orthographies used to represent numbers, there are still substantial effects of orthographic variation on children's judgment of relations between numbers. Overall, it appears that Arabic numerals do have a privileged role in children's early numerical reasoning. This could be due to a number of factors, two of which are state-dependent learning (that is, this is the preferred notation used for teaching mathematics and performing arithmetic), and the consistency of Arabic numerals as a base-10 representational system. Support for the second explanation is suggested by results from the Chinese character condition, in which children were more likely to access multiplicative relations when judging an orthography that maps consistently onto the base-10 structure of Arabic numerals than does the English alphabetic orthography for writing number names.

Children also provided justifications for their judgments of a set of triads presented at the end of each packet. Children in all conditions saw the same four triads (in the appropriate orthography), and their judgments were not incorporated in the scaling results. Coding of children's justifications are consistent with results from the analyses of judgments described earlier. U.S. children were less likely to cite Odd–Even relations, prime numbers, or other multiplicative features as a basis for their judgments when stimuli were presented as Arabic numerals, although Chinese subjects showed no such effect. Judgments based on the sound or writing of numbers (e.g., picking "ten" and "thirteen" as most similar because "they both end in 'en.' ") were relatively rare (8% of U.S. children in the word orthography used this rationale at least once), and were limited to U.S. children viewing word stimuli. The alphabetic nature of English words can be a distraction from accessing mathematical relations, but as with Abacus experts judging abacus stimuli, U.S. children generally do not incorporate idiosyncratic features of English words in their judgments of relations among numbers presented in this format.

SUMMARY AND CONCLUSIONS

The symbol systems that children use in learning and performing mathematics have a number of distinct effects on the course of mathematical development. To use these systems, they must first be learned, and acquiring a new symbol system requires a massive intellectual investment. Systems differ in the extent and consistency with which they reflect a small number of generative rules (such as the base-10 principle); these differences can have a substantial impact on the time it takes children to acquire them and on the mistakes and misconceptions they show along the way. Mathematics is an area in which one often must master multiple, related symbol systems, such as Arabic numerals and the names for those numbers. Learning a new symbol system involves in part mapping previous knowledge and relations onto a new set of tools. This can be a difficult process, and differences in organization (such as that between Arabic numerals and English number names) can have an impact on the ease with which children acquire and use a new symbol system. At the same time, parallel structure between two systems can seduce children into inappropriate transferring algorithms whose use is limited to a particular system, as shown by the case of Chinese children's erroneous arithmetic with Chinese characters. Finally, the clarity and consistency with which mathematical symbols reflect an organizing principle such as a base structure can affect the ease with which children develop a conceptual access to that principle.

Mathematical tools such as numerical symbols constitute a major portion of the intellectual legacy on which we build our own mathematical competence. Understanding how the nature of these symbols affects their acquisition and use is vital to helping children overcome the difficulties that the complexity of such symbols can present to learners. For example, it is not surprising that English-speaking children should have difficulty acquiring aspects of mathematics related to the base-10 structure of numbers, but making that structure explicit early in instruction might prove to be a way to compensate for the complexity that the English language presents. More generally, the organization of mathematical symbols may provide a new key to understanding both the problems that traditional symbols present and the prospects that new representational systems may afford to future mathematical development.

ACKNOWLEDGMENTS

Preparation of this chapter and the bulk of the research discussed herein was supported by NIMH Grants K02MH01190 and R01MH50222 to the first author. Address correspondence to: Kevin F. Miller, Department of Psychology, University of Illinois at Urbana–Champaign, 603 E. Daniel Street, Champaign, IL 61820–6267 (electronic mail: kmiller@s.psych.uiuc.edu).

REFERENCES

Antell, S. R., & Keating, D. (1983). Perception of numerical invariance by neonates. *Child Development, 54,* 695–701.

Baillargeon, R., Miller, K. F., & Constantino, J. (1995). *9.5-month-old infants' intuitions about addition.* Unpublished manuscript, University of Illinois at Urbana–Champaign.

Binet, A. (1966). Mnemonic virtuosity: A study of chess players. *Genetic Psychology Monographs, 74,* 127–162. (Original work published 1893)

Brown, R. W. (1956). Language and categories [appendix]. In J. S. Bruner, J. J. Goodnow, & G. A. Austin (Eds.), *A study of thinking* (pp. 247–321). New York: Wiley.

Bryan, W. L., & Harter, N. (1899). Studies on the telegraphic language. The acquisition of a hierarchy of habits. *Psychological Review, 6,* 345–375.

Carroll, J. D., & Chang, J. J. (1970). Analysis of individual differences in multidimensional scaling via an N-way generalization of Eckart–Young decomposition. *Psychometrika, 35,* 283–319.

Dantzig, T. (1956). *Number: The language of science; a critical survey written for the cultured mathematician* (4th ed). Garden City, NY: Doubleday.

Durkin, K., Shire, B., Riem, R., Crowther, R. D., & Rutter, D. R. (1986). The social and linguistic context of early number word use. *British Journal of Developmental Psychology, 4,* 269–288.

Flegg, G. (1983). *Numbers: Their history and meaning.* London: Andre Deutsch.

Foss, D. J., & Hakes, D. T. (1978). *Psycholinguistics: An introduction to the psychology of language.* Englewood Cliffs, NJ: Prentice-Hall.

Fuson, K. C. (1988). *Children's counting and concepts of number.* New York: Springer-Verlag.

Fuson, K. C., & Kwon, Y. (1991). Systems of number words and other cultural tools: Effects on children's early computations. In J. Bideaud & C. Meljac (Eds.), *Les chemins du nombre* [Pathways to number] (pp. 283–306). Villeneuve d'Ascq, France: Presses Universitaires de Lille.

Fuson, K. C., Richards, J., & Briars, D. J. (1982). The acquisition and elaboration of the number word sequence. In C. J. Brainerd (Ed.), *Children's logical and mathematical cognition* (pp. 33–92). New York: Springer-Verlag.

Gardner, H. (1988). *To open minds: Chinese clues to the dilemma of contemporary education.* New York: Basic Books.

Geary, D. C., Fan, L., & Bow-Thomas, C. C. (1992). Numerical cognition: Locus of ability differences comparing children from China and the United States. *Psychological Science, 3,* 180–185.

Hatano, G., Miyake, Y., & Binks, M. G. (1977). Performance of expert abacus operators. *Cognition, 5,* 47–55.

Hatano, G., & Osawa, K. (1983). Digit memory of grand experts in abacus-derived mental calculation. *Cognition, 5,* 95–110.

Hurford, J. R. (1975). *The linguistic theory of numerals.* Cambridge, England: Cambridge University Press.

Hurford, J. (1987). *Language and number: The emergence of a cognitive system.* Oxford, England: Blackwell.

Ifrah, G. (1985). *From one to zero: A universal history of numbers.* New York: Viking.

John of Salisbury. (1982). *The metalogicon of John of Salisbury: A twelfth-century defense of the verbal and logical arts of the trivium* (Daniel D. McGarry, Trans.). Westport, CT: Greenwood Press. (Original work published 1159)

Karpinski, L. C. (1925). *The history of arithmetic.* New York: Rand McNally.

Klahr, D., Chase, W. G., & Lovelace, E. A. (1983). Structure and process in alphabetic retrieval. *Journal of experimental psychology: Learning, Memory, & Cognition, 9,* 462–477.

Lehrer, T. (1990). New math. On *That was the year that was* [CD]. Burbank, CA: Reprise.

McCullagh, P., & Nelder, J. A. (1991). *Generalized linear models.* New York: Chapman & Hall.

Menninger, K. (1969). *Number words and number symbols, a cultural history of numbers.* Cambridge, MA: MIT Press.

Merton, R. K. (1965). *On the shoulders of giants: A Shandean postscript.* New York: The Free Press.

Miller, K. F., & Gelman, R. (1983). The child's representation of number: A multidimensional scaling analysis. *Child Development, 54,* 1470–1479.

Miller, K. F., & Meyer, D. (1989, April). *Never on a Sunday: Developmental changes in children's processing of familiar ordered lists.* Paper presented at the biennial meeting of the Society for Research in Child Development, Kansas City, MO.

Miller, K. F., Smith, C. M., Zhu, J., & Zhang, H. (1995). Preschool origins of cross-national differences in mathematical competence: The role of number naming systems. *Psychological Science, 6,* 56–60.

Miller, K. F., Smith, C. M., Zhang, H., & Zen, H. (in preparation). A longitudinal study of the development of early mathematical ability in China and the U.S. Unpublished manuscript, University of Illinois.

Miller, K. F., & Stigler, J. W. (1987). Counting in Chinese: Cultural variation in a basic cognitive skill. *Cognitive Development, 2,* 279–305.

Miller, K. F., & Stigler, J. W. (1991). Meanings of skill: Effects of abacus expertise on number representation. *Cognition and Instruction, 8,* 29–67.

Miller, K. F., & Zhu, J. (1991). The trouble with teens: Accessing the structure of number names. *Journal of Memory and Language, 30,* 48–68.

Miura, I. T., Kim, C. C., Chang, C-M., & Okamoto, Y. (1988). Effects of language characteristics on children's cognitive representation of number: Cross-national comparisons. *Child Development, 59,* 1445–1450.

Newton, I. (1959). Newton to Hooke. In H. W. Turnbull (Ed.), *The correspondence of Isaac Newton* (pp. 416–417). Cambridge, England: Cambridge University Press. (Original letter dated 1675)

Paredes, D. R. (1995). *Sources and consequences of developing skill in mental addition: A comparison of U.S. and Chinese grade school children.* Unpublished manuscript, Texas A&M University.

Pullan, J. M. (1969). The history of the abacus. New York: Praeger.

Schmandt-Besserat, D. (1992). *Before writing.* Austin: University of Texas.

Shiffrin, R. M., & Dumais, S. T. (1981). The development of automatism. In J. R. Anderson (Ed.), *Cognitive skills and their acquisition* (pp. 111–140). Hillsdale, NJ: Lawrence Erlbaum Associates.

Siegler, R. S., & Robinson, M. (1982). The development of numerical understandings. In H. Reese & L. Lipsitt (Eds.), *Advances in child development behavior, Vol. 16* (pp. 241–310). New York: Academic Press.

Stevenson, H. W., Lee, S-Y., & Stigler, J. W. (1986). Mathematics achievement of Chinese, Japanese, and American children. *Science, 233,* 693–699.

Stigler, J. W. (1984). "Mental abacus": The effect of abacus training on Chinese children's mental calculation. *Cognitive Psychology, 16,* 145–176.

Tolchinsky-Landsmann, L. T., & Karmiloff-Smith, A. (1992). Children's understanding of notations as domains of knowledge versus referential–communicative tools. *Cognitive Development, 7,* 287–300.

Travers, K. J., Crosswhite, F. J., Dossey, J. A., Swafford, J. O., McKnight, C. C., & Cooney, T. J. (1987). *Second international mathematics study summary report for the United States.* Champaign, IL: Stipes.

Wittgenstein, L. (1958). *Philosophical investigations* (3rd ed.). New York: Macmillan.

Wynn, K. (1992). Addition and subtraction by human infants. *Nature, 358,* 749–750.

Zaslavsky, C. (1973). *Africa counts: Numbers and patterns in African culture.* Boston, MA: Prindle, Weber, & Schmidt.

Culture and Children's Mathematical Thinking

Geoffrey B. Saxe
Venus Dawson
Randy Fall
Sharon Howard
UCLA

Examination of mathematical systems across cultures reveals a remarkable diversity. Groups use different symbolic vehicles to represent numerical information and different procedures to organize the mathematical applications of these symbols. The Incas of Peru (1200 A.D.–1540 A.D.), for instance, used collections of cotton knotted cords ("quipu") to systematically record the numerical contents of their storehouses, census of geographical areas, and quantitative outputs of gold mines (Asher & Asher, 1981). The ancient Babylonians (c. 1750 B.C.–538 B.C.) used a base-60 number system to produce complex computations in diverse commercial practices (Menninger, 1969). Today's traditional Oksapmin of Papua New Guinea use a counting system consisting of 27 body parts to serve such functions as counting valuables, measuring string bags, and tallying bride price payment contributions (Saxe, 1981). Furthermore, we, in Western technological societies, use a number-word system and a number orthography organized in terms of a base-10 structure that is used to serve a wide variety of functions in our technologically complex world.

This chapter addresses a question concerning the interrelation of culture with individuals' developing mathematical understandings: How do forms of thought that have been invented, appropriated, and specialized over the course of a culture's social history come to be interwoven with individuals' developing abilities to accomplish problems in everyday life? In this chapter we begin by sketching mainstream psychological approaches that bear on this developmental question, pointing both to insights that they have yielded, and to their shortcomings, particularly with regard to the representation of culture in the developmental process. Next, we introduce Saxe's cultural practice framework as a means of elevating culture more centrally into analyses of cognition, illustrating the framework with examples drawn from Saxe's prior work with the Oksapmin of Papua New Guinea. In the final section of this chapter, we argue that clinical assessment interviews with children are a form of cultural practice, and show the way in which "culture" is interwoven with microgenetic and ontogenetic shifts in students' evolving approaches to the solution of an individual interview measurement task.

PIAGETIAN CONSTRUCTIVISM: ITS CONTRIBUTIONS AND SHORTCOMINGS FOR THE REPRESENTATION OF CULTURE IN COGNITIVE DEVELOPMENT

A fundamental assumption that dominates today's discussions of the psychological nature of mathematical thinking is that it is a construction of the human mind. Piaget (1970), who produced seminal studies on children's mathematics, pointed to this constructive aspect in a lecture at Clark University when he described a story related to him by a mathematician friend about an incident when the friend was only a young boy:

> When he was a small child, he was counting pebbles one day; he lined them up in a row, counted them from left to right, and got 10. Then, just for fun, he counted them from right to left to see what number he would get, and was astonished that he got 10 again. He put the pebbles in a circle and counted them, and once again there were 10. He went around the circle in the other way and got 10 again. And no matter how he put the pebbles down, when he counted them, the number came to 10. (pp. 16–17)

Piaget went on to question what it was that the boy discovered. Piaget argued that his friend had not discovered a property of pebbles, noting that there was no order inherent in the pebbles. Indeed, the young boy ordered those pebbles through his own activity and the boy himself had produced the sum. His friend, through counting the pebbles in various orders, had invented a new concept—that the sum was necessarily independent of order. Piaget used the example to illustrate that in a very basic sense number is not in our environment, our number system, or our language. Individuals structure their worlds into numerical ones by cognitive operations such as summing and ordering. In essence, Piaget argued that number is created by individuals through a series of constructions that occur over the course of ontogenesis—it is neither a direct reflection of our environment nor our genetic makeup. For Piaget, what was fundamental for the analysis of the constructive process was a focus on the development of abstract cognitive structures, such as systems of operations related to correspondence and order. These structures were manifest across all knowledge domains, emerging in an epigenetic and universal sequence.

The developmental concerns of Piaget—the cognitive structures that underlie our mathematical thought—are evident in the work of other investigators. Researchers have documented evidence of cognitive structures underlying counting (Fuson, 1988; Gelman & Gallistel, 1978; Gelman & Meck, 1983; Saxe, 1977), arithmetic (Klein & Starkey, 1988), fundamental numerical concepts like equivalence and conservation (Piaget & Szeminska, 1952), and a wide range of rational number concepts (e.g., Inhelder & Piaget, 1958; Kieren, 1988; Kieren, Nelson, & Smith, 1983; Lamon, 1993; Lesh, Post, & Behr, 1988). Although such structural developmental analyses have contributed to our understanding of children's mathematics, they have tended to omit the analysis of cultural aspects of children's developing understandings—the manner in which particular mathematical systems and cultural practices with which children are engaged become interwoven with the character of their mathematical thought. This chapter argues that by sidestepping an analysis of culture in children's cognitive development, we blind ourselves to core processes in individuals' developing mathematics.

A SOCIOCULTURAL APPROACH:
THE EMERGENT GOALS FRAMEWORK

Like Piaget's constructivism, the framework that we sketch is guided by the assumption that individuals *construct* mathematical understandings through a self-regulated process. Unlike the Piagetian perspective, however, a critical concern is to understand the individual's cognition as it takes form in cultural practices, whether they be practices like trade in Stone Age cultures, baseball card trade in today's urban youth, or mathematics tutorial and assessment practices involving educator and child. In cultural practices, individuals structure and accomplish practice-linked mathematical goals that are necessarily interwoven with the artifacts used (such as number and measurement systems), social interactions (with a trading partner, or a teacher), activity structures (institutionalized patterns of activity characteristic of practices), and individuals' prior knowledge (such as understandings of one-to-one correspondence or arithmetical operations). In constructing solutions to those goals, individuals create cognitions that are interwoven with everyday cultural life.

We show below that a focus on mathematical goals as situated in cultural practices serves to reorient the analytic lens through which we view individuals' developing mathematical knowledge. For instance, in Piagetian analyses, investigators focus on children's verbalizations and actions that provide evidence for the existence of general cognitive structures. The way particular cultural-bound symbolic forms are linked to the conceptualization and accomplishment of problems in practices, and the way the acquisition and use of those forms may be supported through engagement in particular practices, are understood to be largely extraneous to the analysis of cognitive structures. In contrast, by focusing on emergent practice-linked goals and the means that individuals structure to accomplish those goals, we are led to analyses of individuals' cognitive constructions as rooted in cultural practice.

The Emergent Goals framework has emerged from studies of the interplay between out-of-school and in-school mathematics of Brazilian child candy sellers and straw weavers (Saxe, 1988, 1991; Saxe & Gearhart, 1990), indigenous groups in Papua New Guinea (Saxe, 1981, 1982, 1985; Saxe & Moylan, 1982), mother–child interaction involving young children's everyday numerical practices (Saxe, Gearhart, & Guberman, 1984; Saxe, Guberman, & Gearhart, 1987), and the arithmetical understandings that emerge in inner city children's sustained play of an educational game (Saxe, 1992; Saxe & Bermudez, in press; Saxe, Gearhart, Note, & Paduano, 1993; Saxe & Guberman, in press).

To illustrate the analytic approach, we draw on prior research with the Oksapmin, a community of people who live in remote highland hamlets in Papua New Guinea (Saxe, 1982, 1991).[1] These studies provide insight into the emergence of novel mathematical understandings in a community of people engaging in new trade-related cultural practices. In the example drawn from the Oksapmin community, we focus on adults to show that fundamental developments in mathematical thinking are not restricted to children, but occur across the life span. In the latter part of the chapter, we show how the framework provides a basis for understanding children's developing cognitions in schools in the United States.

Emergent Goals Framework Applied to the Sociogenesis of Arithmetic in the Oksapmin

Oksapmin is a community emerging from the Stone Age. Historically, Oksapmin subsistence depended on hunting for small mammals and birds with bow and arrow and growing root crops using slash-and-burn methods. In traditional life, numerical problems involved use of a 27-body-part counting system to solve nonarithmetical problems in activities like determining the number of one's pigs. To count as Oksapmin do, one begins with the thumb on one hand

---

[1]The material presented on the Oksapmin was drawn from Saxe (1991). The text is abridged from the original account.

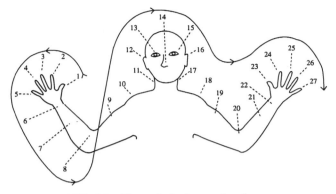

FIG. 5.1.　Oksapmin body counting figure.

and follows a trajectory around the upper periphery of the body down to the little finger on the opposite hand (see Fig. 5.1). Recent Western contact brought the introduction of novel trade-related practices involving currency for economic exchange in newly established tradestores. In the new tradestore activities, Oksapmin must use the indigenous body-part counting system to solve arithmetical problems involving currency, problems that were nonexistent in traditional life.

The Emergent Goals Framework consists of three principal components concerned with the analysis of development in relation to children's engagement with practices. The components include analyses of the *goals* that emerge in practices like economic exchanges at Oksapmin tradestores (Component 1), the *shifting relations* between the cognitive *forms* like the indigenous number system and cognitive *functions* like counting or arithmetic linked to individuals efforts to accomplish emergent goals (Component 2), and the *interplay* between cognitive developments *across practices* (Component 3). Following, we illustrate each component, pointing to the insights that it yields about practice-linked cognitive developments in Oksapmin communities.

Component 1: Practice-Linked Goals in Oksapmin Trade Stores

Specifying the character of the goals that individuals structure in practices is an analytic endeavor of some complexity. Not only do individuals shape and reshape their goals as practices take form in everyday life, but they also construct goals that vary in character as a function of the knowledge that they bring to practices.

Four principal parameters are implicated in the process of goal formation (Fig. 5.2)—the *activity structures* that often become routine phases of a practice, the *social interactions* in which goals become modified and take particular forms (through assistance, instruction, negotiation), particular *con-*

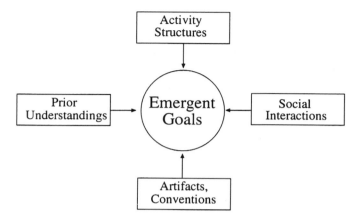

FIG. 5.2. Four parameter model.

ventions and cultural artifacts, and the *prior understandings* that individuals bring to bear on practices. We consider each briefly here to illustrate how individuals' practice-linked emerging goals are rooted both in their own sense-making activities and the cultural practices in which they participate.

The *activity structure* of a practice consists of a routine organization of participation. For instance, a purchase in Oksapmin trade stores consists of several phases, including the selection of goods and payment. A principal motive while participating in this activity may be to acquire as many desired goods as possible while sacrificing as little money as possible, and mathematical goals that emerge in item selection and payment may be guided by this economic motive. Goals that emerge in one practice may be distinct from other practices in which an individual participates. For instance, in indigenous Oksapmin practices like weaving and horticulture, we do not find individuals accomplishing tasks that require arithmetical solutions.

Social interactions between participants in practices may further influence the character of the goals that individuals address. During an exchange, an Oksapmin tradestore owner may help the customer with a computation in any number of ways, thus modifying the kinds of arithmetical goals a customer addresses. Such assistance permits customers of varying degrees of competence to participate in the practice, much like mothers' assistance to their children permit toddlers to engage in activities beyond their unassisted levels of numerical competence (Saxe et al., 1987). In the case of tradestore transactions, assistance may be in the form of helping a customer add currency, completing a subtraction problem in helping a customer check the computation of change, or helping to clarify an arithmetical problem. Regardless, practice-linked social interactions often are interwoven with the goals and subgoals that emerge, and that individuals accomplish, in the practice.

Artifacts and *conventions* are cultural forms that have been created over the course of social history which also figure into the goals that emerge in cultural practices. Examples of such cultural forms are the Oksapmin indigenous body-part counting system and cultural artifacts like a particular currency system. The use of the body-part counting system in economic exchanges leads Oksapmin to such goals as adding a biceps to a forearm, a representation of an addition problem that both constrains and supports the construction of particular kinds of subgoals for a computational solution. Similarly, the particular denominational structure of a currency system also influences the particular values addressed in activities and the subgoals that emerge in problem solving.

Finally, the *prior understandings* that individuals bring to bear on cultural practices both constrain and enable the goals they construct in practices. In the case of the Oksapmin, we find that Oksapmin with different levels of experience participating in the money economy bring to bear different arithmetical understandings on practice-linked problems, and consequently their goals differ. Therefore, an Oksapmin with little experience in the money economy typically conceptualized a purchase in terms of a multiple items-of-merchandise for multiple units of currency exchange. The goal was thus to produce an appropriate one-for-one or many-for-one correspondence. In contrast, individuals with greater expertise conceptualized problems as arithmetical ones, summing the total cost of items of merchandise.

Component 2: Form–Function Shifts in Cognitive Development

Component 2 of the approach consists of a conceptualization of cognitive developmental processes that draws on a formulation put forth by Werner and Kaplan (1962) in *Symbol Formation* and has been subsequently extended in Saxe's work on early number development and cultural practices (Saxe, 1991; Saxe & Bermudez, in press; Saxe et al., 1987). The formulation also reflects a dominant concern of Vygotsky and other Soviet writers (e.g., Leontiev, 1978, 1981; Vygotsky, 1978, 1986), to identify analytic units that preserve intrinsic relations between cognitive developmental and sociocultural processes. The model presented here focuses on the cultural forms that are linked to practice participation and the interplay between these forms and the cognitive functions which they come to serve.

Cognitive Forms. We use the term *cultural form* to refer to historically elaborated constructions like number systems, currency systems, and other artifacts and social conventions. Cultural forms vary in their specialization. For instance, with its orthography and notational system for place value, the Western numeration system is highly specialized for computation. Other number systems, like that of the Oksapmin, have been specialized for counting and certain forms of measurement, but not for arithmetical computation. Still other artifacts, such as currency systems, have been specialized for exchanges linked to the constraints of particular economies and related social institutions. Regardless of their properties, in the daily lives of individuals, these *cultural* forms become *cognitive* forms as they are acquired to accomplish various mathematical functions.

Cognitive Functions. We use *function* to refer to the purposes for which forms are used. In the domain of mathematical cognition, these purposes include the representation of cardinal and ordinal values, arithmetic, measurement, and algebra. In our use of the term, cognitive or mathematical functions are related but are not identical to mathematical operations of the sort with which Piaget was concerned. Indeed, mathematical structures like that of one-to-one correspondence have implications for the kinds of mathematical functions individuals create—such as the representation of cardinal value. For each of the aforementioned domains, we can also consider more specific mathematical functions. For instance, in the case of measurement, functions include ordinal comparison purposes (you have more rope than I do), interval level measurement purposes (you have 3 more inches of rope than I do), and purposes of ratio level measurement (you have three times as much rope as I do). Each of these measurement functions entails different structures of mathematical operation for their meaning.

Cognitive functions vary in the extent to which they are created and used by individuals in cultural practices. For example, in Oksapmin traditional life, the cardinal and ordinal representation of values was a common mathematical function in practices like horticulture or trade, but arithmetic functions like addition or subtraction were not. Mathematical development in the form–function framework can be understood as a process of appropriating forms that have been specialized to serve developmentally prior cognitive functions and respecializing them such that they take on new properties. Let us consider again the Oksapmin case.

Form–Function Shifts in the Development of Arithmetic in the Oksapmin. With increasing participation in the new practice of economic exchange brought about by the introduction of tradestores, Oksapmin people become engaged with novel mathematical goals that require the addition and subtraction of values, goals that do not emerge in traditional life. In this process, we witness the cultural form of body counting gradually shift in function over changing levels of economic participation. The shift is one in which the body system—a form that traditionally serves only an enumerative function for the Oksapmin—becomes a form that serves an arithmetical one. Consider four approaches to the solution of 9 + 7 coins that emerged with increasing participation in the money economy depicted in Fig. 5.3 (see Saxe, 1982).

Those Oksapmin people with only minimal participation in the money economy first attempt to extend the body-counting cognitive form as it is used to serve enumerative functions in traditional activities to accomplish arithmetical tasks that emerge in economic transactions. This direct extension, however, is not adequate to accomplish arithmetical solutions, and it is not even clear that Oksapmin with little experience treated the task as one that involves the cognitive function of arithmetic. In these prelimin... y efforts, Oksapmin attempt to count the sum with a prior counting strate... y linked to the body system. Figure 5.3a illustrates this "global enumeration strategy." In this strategy, an individual begins with the first term (9) of the problem— thumb (1) to bicep (9)—and then continues to count the second term (7) from the shoulder (10). Because the problem of nine coins plus seven coins seems to be understood as an enumeration rather than an addition, individuals do not recognize the need to keep track of the addition of the second term on to the first term, and they typically produce an incorrect sum.

Oksapmin with greater experience in the money economy make a clumsy and labored effort to restructure their prior global counting strategy in such a way that one term is added on to the other (the "double enumeration strategy"). In one example of this strategic form (Figure 5.3b), individuals again enumerate the first term—thumb (1) to forearm (9)—but now, as they

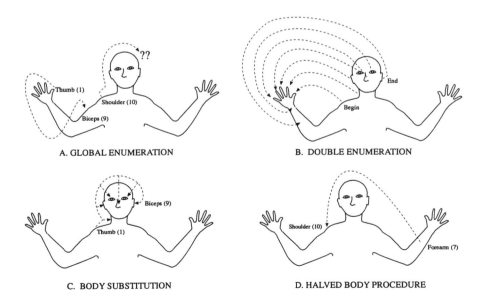

A. GLOBAL ENUMERATION

B. DOUBLE ENUMERATION

C. BODY SUBSTITUTION

D. HALVED BODY PROCEDURE

FIG. 5.3. Oksapmin body strategies: (a) Global enumeration; (b) Double enumeration; (c) Body substitution; (d) Halved body.

enumerate the second, they make efforts to keep track of their enumeration. Therefore, the shoulder (10) is paired with the thumb (1), the neck (11) is paired with the index finger (2), and so on, until the ear on the other side (16) is paired with the forearm (7), yielding the answer. Therefore, in this initial extension of the body system to accomplish the arithmetical problem, the body parts begin to take on a new function of keeping track of the addition of one term onto another.

At more advanced levels in the developmental sequence, we see the body-part-counting form progressively specialized into more sophisticated cognitive forms that serve distinctly arithmetical functions. Now, individuals, rather than establishing physical correspondences between body parts as they do previously, efficiently use the name of one body part to refer to another in a "body substitution strategy" (Fig. 5.3c). To solve 7 + 9, the shoulder (10) is called the thumb (1), the neck (11) is called the index finger (2), and so on, until the ear on the other side (16) is called the forearm (7). The result is a more rapid computational process, one in which body-part names are differentiated from the names of body parts themselves.

Cognitive forms that are distinctively specialized to serve arithmetical and not enumerative functions are more frequently displayed by trade store owners who have the most experience with problems of arithmetic that emerge in economic transactions with currency. In their strategies, some trade store owners incorporate a base-10 system linked to the currency as an aid in computation. With this strategic form (Fig. 5.3d), individuals use the shoulder as a privileged value. In their computation of 9 + 7, they may represent the 9 on one side of the body as biceps (9) and 7 on the other side of the body as forearm (7). To accomplish the problem, a trade store owner might simply "remove" the forearm from the second side (the seventh body part of 7) and transfer it to the first side where it becomes the shoulder (the 10th). He then "reads" the answer as 10 + 6, or 16.

Component 3: The Interplay Between Developments Across Contexts and Practices

Component 3 concerns the interplay between learning across practices. To illustrate an instance of the interplay between cognitive forms constructed in one practice to accomplish emergent goals in another, consider a study conducted with Oksapmin children attending a newly introduced Western-styled elementary school. Children in the first, third, and fifth grades were observed as they took an arithmetic test in their classrooms. Even though teachers were not aware of the indigenous body system and therefore had not instructed children in the body system, many Oksapmin children were observed pointing around their bodies as they solved problems on the test. Individual interviews with Oksapmin children revealed that children at more advanced grade levels progressively used strategies to keep track of the addition of one term on the other—strategies that resembled (but were not identical to) those of the adults with greater experience with the money economy (Saxe, 1985).

The study of Oksapmin school children illustrates the way that out-of-school cognitive forms may be appropriated and specialized to address problems in school, thus leading to novel cognitive developments. It may be that Oksapmin were at the same time making use of knowledge structures acquired in school, linked to the Western orthography, to address problems in out-of-school practices, although this was not investigated in the Oksapmin case.

UNDERSTANDING THE CLINICAL INTERVIEW AS A CULTURAL PRACTICE

We have noted that cultural practices are not limited to the exotic activities of remote communities of people; indeed, they characterize everyday life as lived by us all. In our technological society we are witness to a wide range of highly specialized cultural practices. One such practice well known to educators, psychologists, and many children living in technological societies is the clinical interview. The interview is used for cognitive assessments of children in psychological research and educational evaluations (for analyses of interviews as specialized practices, see Cole & Scribner, 1974; Donaldson, 1978; Siegal, 1991). Interviews may be more structured, as in the standardized administration of an IQ test, or less structured, as in a child and teacher's engagement in a tutorial interaction. Some interviews are structured by theory-driven questions, as in the case of the cognitive tasks and questioning techniques used in cognitive developmental research.

In the remainder of our chapter, we extend the Emergent Goals Framework to understand the microgenesis of children's problem solving that takes place in assessment interviews, viewing the interview as a particular form of cultural practice. As a practice, we find that the interview activity creates a setting that is just as much about a process of teaching and learning (enculturation) as it is about assessment.

Clinical Interviews on Fractions

The two fractions tasks that are our focus were conducted with fifth-grade children before and after they participated in a 2- to 3-month curriculum unit on fractions. In the unit, children were engaged with activities in which they explored fractions as areas (how can we partition this square into fourths?), as ratios (if two apples cost 50¢, how much would six apples cost?), and as parts of linear units of measure (how tall is the desk in terms of my

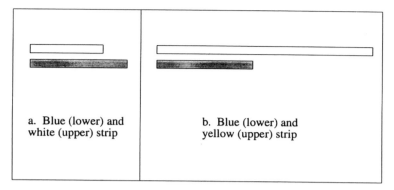

FIG. 5.4. The strips used in the Blue Strip interview. (a) The blue strip and
the white strip; (b) The blue strip and the yellow strip.

body as a unit of measurement?).[2] Our two targeted tasks involved a linear
model of fractions that were designed to circumvent children's often memorized procedures for solving school-linked fractions problems. In the first
task, depicted in Fig. 5.4a, the child is asked to measure a strip of white
paper (6 inches long) with a longer unmarked strip of blue paper (8 inches
long)—the white strip is thus ¾ of the length of the blue. In a second task,
depicted in Fig. 5.4b, the child is presented with a strip of yellow paper that
is 18 inches long, and the child is asked to measure this strip with the shorter
unmarked blue strip (8 inches long)—the yellow strip is thus 2¼ of the length
of the blue.

Component 1: Emergent Goals

As in the case of economic exchange in the Oksapmin, we represent the
mathematical goals that emerge for children in the interview practice in relation to the four parameter model. Following, we sketch each parameter
as it bears on the interview practice, pointing to the way that children's
mathematical goals are rooted in sense-making activity and sociocultural
processes.

Parameter 1. Activity Structure. The interview, like most clinical interviews used for cognitive assessment, consists of loosely defined phases of
introduction, task presentation, children's efforts at task solution supported
by questions from the interviewer, and task resolution. Associated with these
phases are norms for participation for which children may have different
degrees of familiarity, norms that also have implications for children's emer-

---

[2]The curriculum unit that is our focus was adopted by the State of California (*Seeing Fractions,*
Corwin, Russell, & Tierney, 1990).

gent goals. This activity structure constrains the character of the interactions with which interviewer and child engage and thus has implications for children's goals. For instance, the interviewer, constrained by principles of assessment, often asks questions that violate everyday conversational rules but are linked to the assessment practice (Siegal, 1991). To perform appropriately, the child in such a setting must realize that the questions are asked not because the interviewer does not know the solution; rather, they are requests for the child to offer judgments and explain reasoning. Children's participation in the activity structure as well as children's understanding of activity structure-specific norms both have implications for the child's construction of mathematical goals.

Parameter 2. Social Interactions. As we observed in the Oksapmin case, the face-to-face social interaction between participants has implications for the participants' construction of goals. In the same way, during the clinical assessment, interviewer and child engage in reciprocal social interactions that shape the construction of their emergent goals. In the introduction, the interviewer attempts to present the task in a way that is comprehensible to the child. If the measurement function of the blue strip is not clear, the child may construct goals that are not in accord with the interviewer's task definition. In turn, the interviewer may offer more explanation, restructuring the task in more accessible ways, leading children to structure new mathematical goals.

For our particular task, we created a semistandardized "hint structure" for interviewers to use—one that was contingent on children's successes and difficulties in creating a definition of the task that was similar to our intended definition.

Parameter 3. Artifacts and Conventions. The mathematical goals generated by the children as they participate in practices take form in relation to the practice-linked artifacts and conventions. In the blue strip tasks, children are presented with a new form (the blue strip), and are faced with the problem of using it as a nonstandard unit to measure another strip. The blue strip does not have an extended social history, with established uses and conventions, as do other cultural forms we have considered, such as the Oksapmin indigenous body-part counting system or our Western number system. In children's efforts to tailor the blue strip to serve a measurement function, we can observe that the physical properties of the strip both constrain and enable children's construction of mathematical measurement goals. For instance, in using the blue strip, which unlike a ruler does not consist of historically evolved standard units, some children develop their own units—creating the goal of using the difference in length between the white and the blue as a basis to partition the blue into segments that become units with which to estimate the white in terms of the blue.

Parameter 4. Prior Understandings.   In the Oksapmin example, we saw that individuals' knowledge about a Western number system, as represented in a money economy, influenced the goals that they constructed. Similarly, the prior understandings of mathematical operations like one-to-one correspondence and partitioning that children bring to bear on the interview practice have implications for their construction of mathematical goals. For instance, in approaching the task of measuring the white strip, some children are limited to forming only ordinal comparison goals, such as determining whether the white is longer than, shorter than, or the same length as the blue. Other children with an understanding of multiplicative relations may attempt to determine how many times longer the blue is than the white.

In cognitive developmental psychology, the interview setting is often treated as a neutral situation in which the child's understandings are simply recorded. In marked contrast to this view, we have argued that in their participation, children structure and accomplish cognitive goals that are interwoven with their prior understandings, the activity structure of the interview, the artifacts used, and the give and take of communicative interactions between child and interviewer. From this perspective, the child's emerging goals are often in flux, becoming articulated and then fading in a microgenetic process. We consider in more detail the characteristics of this process as we sketch shifting relations between form and function in Component 2.

Component 2: Form–Function Shifts

We noted in our introductory remarks that representational systems for number like the Oksapmin body system are cultural forms that have been specialized over social history to serve varied mathematical functions. In turning to an analysis of the blue strip interview practice, we are dealing with a cultural form (the blue strip), which, unlike the Oksapmin number system, has not been specialized over social history to serve measurement purposes. Videotaped records of children's solutions provide access to the dynamics of the interview practice, allowing us to extend our prior analyses of shifting relations between form and function in cognitive development. Further, our analyses are now linked to a practice common in educational settings in Western technological societies.

We focus on two types of cognitive development related to the interview practice. First, our concern is to understand *microgenesis*—the short-term structuring of the blue strip task in the joint activity of the interviewer and child, and the way that this structuring is interwoven with the interview practice.[3] Second,

---

[3]Some researchers have made use of "microgenesis" to refer to a methodological approach involving the intensive study of children over short periods of time to track what are assumed to be relatively stable cognitive developments (see, for example, Kuhn & Phelps, 1982; Metz, 1985; Siegler & Jenkins, 1989). Our use of the term is more consistent with earlier treatments of the construct (Langer, 1969; Werner & Kaplan, 1962), in which the process of schematization of a phenomenon, perceptually or conceptually, is understood as a short-term developmental process.

our concern is to produce a *longitudinal analysis* of microgenesis before and after the intervention. In this case, our concern is to understand differences in the microgenetic process as a result of ontogenetic changes in a child's fractional understandings that occur over the course of the 3-month instructional intervention.

Microgenesis. To accomplish a microgenetic analysis of children's solutions, we will need to sharpen our analytic lens. Not only must we understand the forms that individuals are using and the mathematical functions that these forms are serving, we must analyze with greater precision how forms and functions become situated in the individual's construction of solutions to tasks. For instance, how do mathematical forms (which may be as complex and specialized as comprehensive number systems or as undifferentiated as a strip of blue paper) become specific *means* of solution that are tailored to the situated mathematical goals that emerge in children's activities? Correlatively, how are mathematical functions transformed into situated and *emergent goals* that are interwoven with the parameters discussed under Component 1? Finally, what is the relation between the transformation of cognitive forms into solution means and cognitive functions into emergent goals? Are these independent processes? Next we offer some guided speculations about these questions, viewing the blue strip interview as a microcosm for general cognitive developmental processes.

Figure 5.5 contains our working model. The figure represents the process of microgenesis (dynamic relations between form and function that emerge over the course of the construction and accomplishment of emergent goals) embedded in the four-parameter framework. The figure depicts the child and the interviewer participating in an activity structure in which they take on

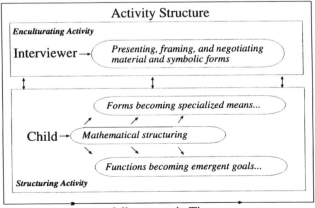

FIG. 5.5. Elaboration of the Emergent Goals Framework.

asymmetric roles. Further, through social interactional processes, the interviewer presents, frames, and reframes particular artifacts that have intended functions. These enculturating aspects of the interview practice are interwoven with a developmental trajectory of form and function that begins with the child's appropriation of mathematical forms (like the blue strip artifact) and functions (like measurement) framed by the adult in the interview practice. In the child's initial appropriation of the blue strip, neither forms nor functions are inherently mathematical entities. They take on mathematical meaning as they are *structured* in their use, through mathematical and measurement operations like one-to-one correspondence, partitioning, and displacement.

The developmental trajectories of form and function are analytically separable but interact with one another in the microgenetic process. In order for the blue strip *form* to serve as a *means* for accomplishing the task, a child must specialize the blue strip form as a mathematical object—partitionable into equivalent intervals. Indeed, such a partitioning is necessary for the blue strip to serve an interval or ratio measurement function. In order for the *function* of measurement to become realized as an *emerging goal*, the white strip—the target of measurement—must be conceptualized as a physical entity that can be partitioned in terms of equal intervals. This twofold structuring of forms becoming means and functions becoming goals occurs as a bootstrapping: The blue *form* becomes specialized as a *means* as the child transforms it into a mathematical object, but this means must be accomplished with at least a local *goal* in mind. Reciprocally, the *function* of measurement becomes manifest as a *goal* to measure the white, a goal framed with some conceptualization of a potential *means* of accomplishment in mind. Therefore, forms and goals as well as functions and means are linked in their microgenetic histories.

To illustrate more concretely the interplay between form and function in the process of microgenesis, we consider two interviews with a single child—one before the curriculum unit and the other after. In the first interview, our concern is with relations between form and function in the microgenetic process itself. In the second, our focus is on a longitudinal analysis of change across interviews.

A Microgenetic Analysis of Form–Function Relations: John's Efforts on the Blue Strip Task **Before the Unit on Fractions.** John is in the fifth grade and prior to participation in the unit, his understanding of fractions is quite limited. Table 5.1 presents excerpts from the first task in his pre-unit blue strip interview. Next we consider the development of John's understandings during the course of the interview with regard to relations between form and function as John creates and recreates means and goals tailored to the blue strip task.

In lines 1–3 of the table, we note the interviewer's efforts to frame the task for John, providing the blue strip form and implicitly indicating that

TABLE 5.1
Excerpts From John's Blue Strip Interview Prior to Instruction

---

1. *Interviewer:* I want you to tell me how long the white paper is in blues.
2. *John:* Can I measure like this? (John tries to measure the white strip with the width of the blue strip; see Fig. 5.6a.)
3. *Interviewer:* No, let's measure this way (indicating the length, see Fig. 5.6b), using this to measure how long the white strip is. And you can move the strips around to help you.
4. *John:* About four inches.
[Interviewer prompts John to think about the blue as one blue and measure the white strip with that blue. John doesn't seem to understand what the interviewer wants him to do.]
6. *John:* You want me to count the inches?
7. *Interviewer:* No, we're in a pretend country and they don't know about inches or centimeters so we're going to use blues—this is one blue long. How long is this white one in this pretend country?
8. *John:* Half a blue long.
9. *Interviewer:* How do you know it is half a blue long?
10. *John:* Because it's not to here (end of the blue), so you need to call it half.

---

the strip is to serve a measurement function. Faithful to the request, John appropriates the blue strip form apparently to serve an *interval* measurement function—to measure how many blues make a white (through operations of partitioning and displacement). The function is realized in the emergent mathematical goal—to determine the length of the white strip in blue *widths* (see Fig. 5.6a). Concomitantly, the blue strip form becomes specialized into a means—a moveable unit—to accomplish the goal. The process of solution, however, is cut short by John's apparent uncertainty that his definition of the goal and means for accomplishing it is one valued by the interviewer (in line 2, John asks, "Can I measure like this?"), a concern linked to the interview practice in which he is a participant. If he completed his initial efforts, John's construction would have allowed him to represent the length of the white in terms of the blue. However, from the interviewer's perspective John has created a solution that allows him to circumvent the construction of a fraction; for the interviewer, it is John's fractional understanding that is the principal target of the assessment interview. Therefore, in response to John's query about the use of widths, the interviewer responds, "No, let's measure this way" (Fig. 5.6b), refocusing John's efforts on the use of the length and not the width of the blue as a means to accomplish the goal of measuring the white.

In lines 3–4, we observe a second microgenetic process of solution structuring, one influenced by the constraint presented by the interviewer to use the length rather than the width of the blue to measure. In his effort to represent this contrast, John appears not to understand how to describe the shorter white using the longer blue as a unit. Perhaps as a result, John puts aside the blue strip and appropriates a nonmaterial cultural form to serve a

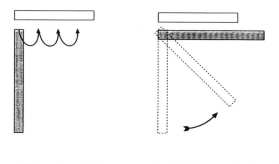

a. Using the width   b. Shifting to the length
as a unit   as a unit

FIG. 5.6.   Use of blue widths then length as a unit of measure.

measurement function, again as in his first attempt, in terms of integer values—the British system of units (i.e., inches). In his efforts we again infer a
process of transformation in which the function of interval measurement is
realized in terms of the goal of measurement in inches. At the same time,
the British system of inches becomes specialized in the process as a 4-inch
count or estimate of the white.

In lines 5–10, the interviewer makes two more efforts to redirect John
toward the intended definition of the task, both of which have consequences
for John's construction of goals. In one of these efforts, for instance, the
interviewer presents the pretend country theme (a country where no one
knows of inches) in an attempt to reorient John's efforts (lines 7–10). John
responds by using the blue strip form to accomplish a hybrid of two measurement functions, an ordinal and perhaps an incipient understanding of a
ratio level of measurement. John attempts to determine the relative length
of the white in relation to the blue and express the white's length in terms
of a fractional part of the blue. To accomplish these goals, John appropriates
the language of fractions—a form—specializing it as a means to suit his
needs with the expression of "half a blue long." In this final activity, we are
unclear as to whether John is using the expression of "one half" as a means
to indicate the white is smaller than the blue, where "one half" may be a
way John has of making an ordinal comparison, or whether John is making
an effort to express the white as a fractional part of the blue, but lacks the
formal language of fractions, partitioning operations, or both to adequately
accomplish this function.

John's Efforts on the Blue Strip Task **After** *the Unit on Fractions.*
John was reinterviewed later in the school year after participating in the
classroom practices designed to support students' developing understandings
of fractions. Table 5.2 contains excerpts from the postintervention interview

TABLE 5.2
Excerpts From John's Blue Strip Interview After Instruction

1. *Interviewer:* I want you to measure the length of this paper using the blue strip.
2. *John:* No numbers?
3. *Interviewer:* No numbers. How would you measure it—the white strip (indicating the white strip)?
4. *John:* About three-fourths.
5. *Interviewer:* Why do you say three-fourths?
6. *John:* 'Cause I measure this into four equal pieces this size so it went over and it was four.

involving the blue strip task. We focus here on the shift in the microgenesis of John's solution.

John's initial reaction to the task in lines 1–3—"No numbers?"—suggests knowledge about the interviewer's conception of the activity structure and its purpose as well as knowledge of different solution paths that could be created in efforts to address the interviewer's request. Indeed, John's query is a self-initiated effort to determine what solution avenues the interviewer values—what forms and functions are appropriate and what particular goals should be created.

In lines 4–6, John appears to have created an understanding of a ratio measurement function, and can structure it with fractional values in the blue strip task. Indeed, as he constructs a goal of measuring the white with the blue, John specializes the blue strip form as a means, using the length difference between the blue and white as a unit to partition the blue into four equal segments. Finding the white to be equivalent in length to three of the four imaginary blue segments, he concludes that the white is three-fourths of the blue.

Longitudinal Shifts Across the Pre- and Postintervention Interviews. Analyzing the continuities and discontinuities in John's performances across pre- and postintervention interviews provides insight into ontogenetic developmental change. In the preintervention interview, we observe John deploying the blue strip form to serve two principal measurement functions. First, he created an interval level of measurement, specializing the blue by turning it perpendicular to the white and counting imaginary segments of the white in terms of blue widths; he later used the blue strip to serve a similar interval function in his count of inches. In both cases, his uses of these functions was restricted to integer values. Later in the interview, he created a second measurement function, although it was not clear from the videotape whether the function was ordinal or ratio measurement: As he compared the length of the white relative to the blue, John expressed this comparison as "one half."

As in the first interview, where he used the width of the blue to partition the white and attempted to represent the white in terms of the blue, in the postinterview, John again applied the partitioning operations, and again represented the white in terms of the blue. In the postinterview, however, he applied his partitioning to both the blue and white themselves, appropriating and specializing a different aspect of the material form as a unit—the difference in length between blue and white. In this effort, unlike the preintervention interview, John created a difference unit as a means to accomplish his partitioning. In using the difference unit to serve a ratio and not simply an interval function, he created a goal of determining the relation between the number of white units to blue units, and created a solution means that led him to express this relation as "about three-fourths."

Component 3: The Interplay Between Development Across Practices

In their daily lives, children often participate in a variety of practices in which mathematical goals emerge. These include board game play, trips to the store, and participation in sports. In our focus on the microgenesis of children's solutions in a targeted practice, we find that children often appropriate forms acquired in other practices, respecializing them to serve practice-specific functions. Correlatively, children may appropriate functions created in other practices, identifying them as relevant to emergent concerns in a targeted practice. Therefore, in the microgenesis of solutions in any targeted practice, we find an interplay between forms and functions across practices. Figure 5.7 contains an elaboration of the general model that includes a representation of this interplay. Following, we discuss characteristics of this interplay with specific reference to the blue strip task.

Forms With Prior Functions in the Blue Strip Task. Various forms used in the blue strip task have been used to serve functions other than measurement. For instance, children use our lexicon of number words and fraction words, in a wide range of practices in which numerical and arithmetical problems emerge. In accomplishing the blue strip task, we find that children appropriate forms that have served prior functions, specializing them to accomplish emergent goals in the blue strip task. For example, we observed previously that John drew on his knowledge of fraction words to represent the white as "one-half" of the blue.

Functions With Prior Forms in the Blue Strip Task. The functions that children identify in the blue strip task, like ratio or interval measurement, can be accomplished by children using various forms, some of which, as we noted previously, are quite specialized with function-specific properties. For

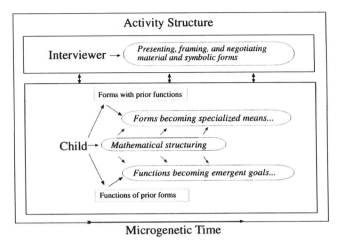

FIG. 5.7.   Further elaboration of the Emergent Goals Framework.

instance, although a ruler may be used as a straight edge or to prop open a door, it is specialized to serve the function of linear measurement and typically used to serve both interval and ratio measurement functions. One key concern for a microgenetic analysis is the way that cultural forms associated with particular functions may be drawn into the specialization of means and goals in targeted practices. In the case of John, we observed that such a process occurred as John made efforts to draw into his accomplishment of an interval measurement function, the British system of measurement. In this case, John tried to count or estimate the length of the white in terms of inches.

The Interplay Between Form and Function Across the Two Blue Strip Tasks.   The interplay between form and function across different instances of microgenesis is quite striking in the following solution of the blue strip task. In this case, we follow a single child's accomplishment of both the task of measuring the white strip and measuring the yellow strip. We find that the child appropriates the solution means that he has specialized to accomplish the task with the white strip to accomplish the task with the yellow strip, a special case of the appropriation of forms with prior functions.

1. *Measuring the white with the blue.* In Marcello's measurement of the white strip, he used his thumb and forefinger to represent the difference in length between the two strips. Holding his fingers at this length, he measured the white strip with this new unit, finding that three of the units would fit on the white strip, and four on the blue (see Figs. 5.8 and 5.9). He then gave a correct answer, three-fourths, with the rationale: "It's three-fourths because

there was four. There would be one, two, three, four" (counts off one-fourth intervals comparing number found in each strip).

2. *Measuring the yellow with the blue.* In the second task, Marcello was asked to measure the yellow using the blue strip (the yellow is 2¼ times the length of the blue). Using the unit created with the white strip (¼ of the blue) as if it were a standard unit, Marcello measured the yellow:

S: "OK. Eight. Another one. That's . . . I think . . . this is um . . . hm. Four ninths. Yeah. Four ninths."

I: "Four ninths? OK."

S: " 'Cause there's four here (the blue) and nine of those (the yellow)."

Therefore, rather than creating a new (nonstandard) unit based on the two new strips, Marcello appropriated and respecialized a solution means used in the first task to measure the yellow strip. His answer to the problem is a ratio of the two lengths, an answer which suggests that Marcello has lost sight of the blue as a measuring tool, and instead sees the fraction name ("four-ninths") as a relation of the two strips in terms of his new unit. Indeed, it appears as if he no longer thinks of his new unit as "¼ of a blue," but instead thinks of the unit as the standard of measure of both strips.

This student's invention and appropriation of a standard unit not only illustrates the particular course of microgenetic development for one individual, it also illustrates a process whereby new measurement conventions can emerge in communities. Marcello's standard unit could, if appropriated by others, serve as a basis to communicate about length independent of the specific relation between a particular artifact (e.g., the blue) and a particular

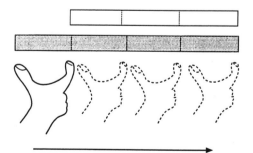

FIG. 5.8. John's use of his fingers to partition the blue and white strips.

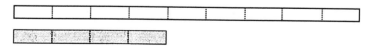

FIG. 5.9. Using the prior partitioning of the blue to partition the white.

target (e.g., the white). Therefore, in a microgenetic analysis of one student's response to two measurement tasks we see an inventive process that could contribute to shared conventions for measurement.

CONCLUDING REMARKS

This chapter began with a problem statement concerning culture and mathematical thinking. We asked how representational and conceptual forms that have emerged over the history of cultures become interwoven with the mathematical thinking of the individual. Our problem formulation echoes the concerns of earlier developmentalists like Vygotsky (1978, 1986), who argued that human thought must be understood as the product of four separate developmental lines—evolutionary, historical, ontogenetic, and microgenetic. In extending Vygotsky's analytic concern, we have targeted cultural practices—routine, socially organized activities—as a critical focus in which these separate lines of development converge.[4]

Our account of the practice of economic exchange in the Oksapmin conforms well to traditional anthropological visions of cultural studies—investigations of a remote people whose dress is extraordinarily different from our own, who use tools of stone and bone, and who employ an exotic system for numbering. Further, the study puts in clear relief the interdependence of historical and ontogenetic lines in the development of mathematical thought. We documented individuals' appropriation and specialization of sociohistorical knowledge forms (the body system) in their efforts to structure and accomplish newly emerging goals in a practice, and in this process, brought forward a cultural history in their creation of new forms of mathematical thinking.

What may seem odd in an essay on culture and mathematics, however, is the treatment of a clinical interview as a form of cultural practice. Such interviews are commonly used as a means of investigating "intellectual functioning" or "competence" of individuals and are not themselves cast as practices. To the contrary, we have argued that the interview is subject to the same kind of analysis as are practices of economic exchange in a remote group of Melanesian people. Indeed, just as Oksapmin are engaged in the construction of emergent goals, appropriating and specializing cultural artifacts as means to accomplish novel problems in structures of activity, so too are Western children (and adult interviewers) as they participate in the clinical interview. Further, because of our added ability to use videotape to

---

[4]In this chapter, we have sidestepped discussions of the evolutionary roots of mathematical cognition, although the topic is one that is currently the subject of considerable attention (e.g., Fodor, 1983; Gallistel, 1990).

record the clinical interviews, we have been able to analyze a dynamic central to the process of understanding cognition in practice—the negotiated construction of forms that become specialized as means and the concomitant process of functions becoming transformed into emergent goals in the microgenesis of solutions to the Blue Strip task. We would argue that a similar process is occurring not only in Oksapmin economic exchanges, but also in the multitude of cultural practices in which individuals participate.

Although our analytic focus differs markedly from that of Piagetian research, at the core we see the approach as commensurate with principal features of Piaget's structural developmental approach. Indeed, central to our practice-linked analyses was a focus on the mathematical structuring activities in which individuals were engaged. In the case of the Oksapmin, we focused on the shift in the structure of correspondence operations, from the traditional adults' one-to-one correspondences between body parts and objects used in their global enumeration strategies to the trade store owners' body-part-to-body-part correspondences used to mediate arithmetical problem solving with objects. In the Blue Strip task, the focus of concern was on partitioning and displacement operations as children structured means of measuring the white and yellow strips.

What we find problematic in the Piagetian focus on structures is its exclusivity, which leads to a neglect of the central role of cultural practice. In contrast, our focus on form and function in the Emergent Goals framework weds the structural and culturally adaptive aspects of cognitive activity, leading us to represent developments occurring along multiple lines, which are deeply interwoven with the diversity and complexity of practices in which individuals participate. In so doing, we mark the central status of cultural practices in the process of cognitive development.

ACKNOWLEDGMENTS

Support from the National Science Foundation (#MDR–9154512) and the Spencer Foundation (#M890224) during preparation of this manuscript is gratefully acknowledged. The opinions expressed in this article are those of the authors and not necessarily those of the funding agencies.

REFERENCES

Asher, M., & Asher, R. (1981). *Code of the Quipu.* Ann Arbor: University of Michigan.
Cole, M., & Scribner, S. (1974). *Culture and thought.* New York: Wiley.
Corwin, R. B., Russell, S. J., & Tierney, C. C. (1990). *Seeing fractions: Representations of wholes and parts: A unit for the upper elementary grades.* Sacramento: California Department of Education, Technical Education Research Center (TERC).

Donaldson, M. (1978). *Children's minds*. New York: Norton.

Fodor, J. (1983). *The modularity of mind*. Cambridge, MA: MIT Press.

Fuson, K. (1988). *Children's counting and concepts of number*. New York: Springer-Verlag.

Gallistel, R. (1990). *The organization of learning*. Cambridge, MA: MIT Press.

Gelman, R., & Gallistel, C. R. (1978). *The child's understanding of number*. Cambridge, MA: Harvard University Press.

Gelman, R., & Meck, E. (1983). Preschoolers' counting: Principles before skill. *Cognition, 13*, 343–359.

Inhelder, B., & Piaget, J. (1958). *The growth of logical thinking from childhood to adolescence*. New York: Basic Books.

Kieren, T. E. (1988). Personal knowledge of rational numbers: Its intuitive and formal development. In J. Hiebert & M. Behr (Eds.), *Number concepts and operations in the middle grades* (pp. 162–181). Reston, VA: The National Council of Teachers of Mathematics.

Kieren, T. E., Nelson, D., & Smith, G. (1983). Graphical algorithms in partitioning tasks. *Journal of Mathematical Behavior, 4*, 25–36.

Klein, A., & Starkey, P. (1988). Universals in the development of early arithmetic cognition. In G. B. Saxe & M. Gearhart (Eds.), *Children's mathematics* (pp. 5–26). San Francisco: Jossey-Bass.

Kuhn, D., & Phelps, E. (1982). The development of problem-solving strategies. In H. Reese & L. Lipsitt (Eds.), *Advances in child development and behavior* (Vol. 17, pp. 2–44). New York: Academic Press.

Lamon, S. J. (1993). Ratio and proportion: Connecting content and children's thinking. *Journal for Research in Mathematics Education, 24*(1), 41–61.

Langer, J. (1969). *Theories of development*. New York: Holt.

Leontiev, A. N. (1978). The problem of activity in psychology. In J. Wertsch (Ed.), *The concept of activity in Soviet psychology* (pp. 37–71). New York: Sharpe.

Leontiev, A. N. (1981). *Problems in the development of mind*. Moscow: Progress.

Lesh, R., Post, T., & Behr, M. (1988). Proportional reasoning. In J. Hiebert & M. Behr (Eds.), *Number concepts and operations in the middle grades* (pp. 93–118). Hillsdale, NJ: Lawrence Erlbaum Associates/Reston, VA: The National Council of Teachers of Mathematics.

Menninger, K. (1969). *Number words and number symbols*. Cambridge, MA: MIT Press.

Metz, K. E. (1985). The development of children's problem solving in a gears task: A problem space perspective. *Cognitive Science, 9*, 431–471.

Piaget, J., & Szeminska, A. (1952). *The child's conception of number*. New York: Norton.

Piaget, J. (1970). *Genetic epistemology*. New York: Columbia University Press.

Saxe, G. B. (1977). A developmental analysis of notational counting. *Child Development, 48*, 1512–1520.

Saxe, G. B. (1981). Body parts as numerals: A developmental analysis of numeration among a village population in Papua New Guinea. *Child Development, 52*, 306–316.

Saxe, G. B. (1982). Developing forms of arithmetic operations among the Oksapmin of Papua New Guinea. *Developmental Psychology, 18*(4), 583–594.

Saxe, G. B. (1985). The effects of schooling on arithmetical understandings: Studies with Oksapmin children in Papua New Guinea. *Journal of Educational Psychology, 77*(5), 503–513.

Saxe, G. B. (1988). The mathematics of child street vendors. *Child Development, 59*, 1415–1425.

Saxe, G. B. (1991). *Culture and cognitive development: Studies in mathematical understanding*. Hillsdale, NJ: Lawrence Erlbaum Associates.

Saxe, G. B. (1992). Studying children's learning in context: Problems and prospects. *Journal of the Learning Sciences, 2*(2), 215–234.

Saxe, G. B. (in press). From the field to the classroom: Studies in children's mathematics. In L. Steffe (Ed.), *Social constructivism in mathematics*. Hillsdale, NJ: Lawrence Erlbaum Associates.

Saxe, G. B., & Bermudez, T. (in press). Emergent mathematical environments in children's games. In L. Steff, P. Nesher, P. Cobb, G. Golding, & Greer (Eds.), *Theories of mathematical learning*. Hillsdale, NJ: Lawrence Erlbaum Associates.

Saxe, G. B., & Gearhart, M. (1990). The development of topological concepts in unschooled straw weavers. *British Journal of Developmental Psychology, 8*, 251–258.

Saxe, G. B., Gearhart, M., & Guberman, S. (1984). The social organization of early number development. In B. Rogoff & J. V. Wertsch (Eds.), *Children's learning in the zone of proximal development: New directions for child development* (No. 23, pp. 19–30). San Francisco: Jossey-Bass.

Saxe, G. B., Gearhart, M., Note, M., & Paduano, P. (1993). Peer interaction and the development of mathematical understandings: A new framework for research and educational practice. In H. Daniels (Ed.), *Charting the agenda: Vygotskian perspectives* (pp. 107–144). London: Routledge.

Saxe, G. B., & Guberman, S. R. (in press). Distributed problem solving in an educational game. In J. Greeno (Ed.), *Thinking practices*. Hillsdale, NJ: Lawrence Erlbaum Associates.

Saxe, G. B., Guberman, S. R., & Gearhart, M. (1987). Social processes in early number development. *Monographs of the Society for Research in Child Development, 52*(2).

Saxe, G. B., & Moylan, T. (1982). The development of measurement operations among the Oksapmin of Papua Guinea. *Child Development, 53*, 1242–1248.

Siegal, M. (1991). A clash of conversational worlds: Interpreting cognitive development through communication. In L. B. Resnick, J. M. Levine, & S. D. Teasley (Eds.), *Perspectives on socially shared cognition* (pp. 23–40). Washington, DC: American Psychological Association.

Siegler, R. S., & Jenkins, E. (1989). *How children discover new strategies*. Hillsdale, NJ: Lawrence Erlbaum Associates.

Vygotsky, L. (1978). In M. Cole, V. John-Steiner, S. Scribner, & E. Souberman (Eds.), *Mind in society*. Cambridge, MA: Harvard University Press.

Vygotsky, L. (1986). In A. Kozulin (Ed.), *Thought and language*. Cambridge, MA: MIT Press.

Werner, H., & Kaplan, B. (1962). *Symbol formation*. New York: Wiley.

6

▼▼▼▼▼▼▼

Biology, Culture, and Cross-National Differences in Mathematical Ability

David C. Geary
University of Missouri at Columbia

The primary goal of this chapter is to provide a principled consideration of the source of mathematical ability differences comparing children from East Asia and the United States (Husén, 1967; Stevenson, Chen, & Lee, 1993). Arguments for the source of these differences range from racial differences in intelligence (e.g., Lynn, 1982; Rushton, 1992) to cultural differences in the relative valuation of mathematical competencies (Stevenson & Stigler, 1992). In this chapter, cross-national differences in mathematical abilities are considered from an evolution-based framework that allows for biological as well as cultural influences on children's cognitive and academic development (Geary, 1995). Three general sections were required to achieve the primary goal of this chapter. In the first, a distinction is made between the architecture and developmental mechanisms associated with biologically based and culturally taught abilities, which are termed biologically primary and biologically secondary cognitive abilities, respectively. Next, this framework is applied to research on children's mathematical development, and finally, in the third section, to cross-national differences in the pattern of mathematical abilities.

EVOLUTION-BASED PERSPECTIVE ON COGNITIVE DEVELOPMENT[1]

At some level, all forms of cognition are supported by neurocognitive systems that have evolved to serve some function or functions related to reproduction

---

[1]This and the following section are adapted from Geary (1995).

or survival. These basic neurocognitive systems appear to be found in human beings throughout the world, and appear to support the emergence of species-typical cognitive domains, such as language (Pinker & Bloom, 1990; Witelson, 1987). However, some forms of cognitive ability, such as reading, emerge in some cultures and not others. The pattern of cross-cultural similarities and differences in the constellation of cognitive abilities suggests that the emergence of some domains of cognition is driven largely by biological influences, whereas other domains emerge only in specific cultural contexts. Therefore, when assessing the source of group or individual differences in cognitive abilities, it seems necessary to consider whether the ability in question is part of a species-typical, biologically primary cognitive domain, or whether the ability in question is culturally specific, and therefore biologically secondary.

Although biologically secondary abilities only emerge in specific cultural contexts, they must perforce be supported by neurocognitive systems that have evolved to support primary abilities. Indeed, these cultural-specific abilities might involve the co-optation of biologically primary neurocognitive systems or access to knowledge implicit in these systems for purposes other than the original evolution-based function (S. J. Gould & Vrba, 1982; Rozin, 1976; Rozin & Schull, 1988). The basic premise is that in terms of children's cognitive growth, the interface between culture and biology involves the co-optation of highly specialized neurocognitive systems to meet culturally relevant goals. In this section, a basic framework for distinguishing between primary and secondary abilities is presented, as is a consideration of the mechanisms that might support the acquisition of such abilities.

Biologically Primary and Biologically Secondary Abilities

Both biologically primary and biologically secondary forms of cognition can probably be hierarchically organized into domains, abilities, and neurocognitive systems. Domains, such as language or arithmetic, represent constellations of more specialized abilities, such as language comprehension or counting. Individual abilities, in turn, are supported by neurocognitive systems, and appear to consist of at least three types of competencies: goal structures, procedural skills, and conceptual knowledge (Gelman, 1993; Siegler & Crowley, 1994). The goal of counting, for instance, is to determine the number of items in a set of objects. Counting is achieved by means of procedures, such as the act of pointing to each object as it is counted. Pointing helps the child to keep track of which items have been counted and which items still need to be counted (Gelman & Gallistel, 1978). Counting behavior, in turn, is constrained by conceptual knowledge (or skeletal principles for the initial emergence of primary domains), so that, for instance, each object is pointed at or counted only once. Despite these similarities, there appear to be a number of important differences between primary and secondary abilities. In this section, basic features of the apparent architectures of primary and secondary abilities are outlined, followed by a consideration of developmental mechanisms.

Architecture. There appear to be three basic features associated with biologically primary cognitive domains. First, inherent in the neurocognitive systems that support primary abilities is a system of skeletal principles (Gelman, 1990). Skeletal principles provide the scaffolding on which goal structures and procedural and conceptual competencies emerge. For instance, one skeletal principle that appears to be associated with biologically primary counting abilities is "one–one correspondence" (Gelman & Gallistel, 1978). Here, as noted earlier, the counting behavior of human children and even the common chimpanzee (*Pan troglodytes*) is constrained by an implicit understanding that each item in an enumerated set must be tagged once and only once (Boysen & Berntson, 1989; Starkey, 1992). Second, it appears, at least initially, that the knowledge that is associated with primary domains is implicit. That is, the behavior of children appears to be constrained by skeletal principles, but children cannot articulate these principles. Third, it is likely that the systems that support primary abilities include an affective component. An affective component is likely to be necessary in order to motivate engagement in the activities that are needed to flesh out skeletal principles and to support the growth of the associated neurobiological systems (Geary, 1995; Greenough, Black, & Wallace, 1987).[2]

Although the initial structures for the cognitive competencies that might be associated with primary domains appears to be inherent, the goal structures and procedural and conceptual competencies for secondary abilities are likely to be induced or learned from other people (e.g., teachers) and emerge from primary abilities. For the latter, as mentioned earlier, there appear to be two possibilities. The first involves the co-optation of the neurocognitive systems that support primary abilities. Second, it appears that knowledge that is implicit in the skeletal principles of primary abilities can often be made explicit and used in ways unrelated to the evolution of these principles (Rozin, 1976).

For an example, consider the possibility that the development of geometry as a formal discipline involved, at least in part, the co-optation of the neurocognitive systems that have evolved to support navigation in the three-di-

---

[2]This position does not preclude self-motivated engagement in biologically secondary activities. For instance, I have argued elsewhere that reading is a biologically secondary cognitive domain, which involves, for phonetic-based languages, the co-optation of the neurocognitive systems that support language (Geary, 1995; Rozin, 1976). Nevertheless, many individuals are motivated to read. The motivation to read, however, is probably driven by the content of what is being read, rather than an inherent bias to enjoy the process of reading. In fact, the content of many stories and other secondary activities (e.g., video games, television) might reflect evolutionarily relevant themes that motivate engagement in these activities (e.g., social relationships; MacDonald, 1988).

mensional physical universe and access to the associated implicit knowledge. Arguably all terrestrial species, even invertebrates (e.g., insects), have cognitive systems that enable navigation in three-dimensional space (Gallistel, 1990; J. L. Gould, 1986; Landau, Gleitman, & Spelke, 1981; Shepard, 1994). Cheng and Gallistel (1984), for instance, showed that laboratory rats appear to develop a "Euclidean representation of space for navigational purposes" (p. 420), and, as a result, are sensitive to changes in basic representation, such as shape, and metric, such as angle. Implicit in the functioning of the associated neurocognitive systems is a basic understanding of geometric relationships amongst objects in the physical universe. So, for example, even the behavior of the common honey bee (*Apis mellifera*) reflects an implicit understanding that the fastest way to move from one location to another is to fly in a straight line (J. L. Gould, 1986).

Even though an implicit understanding of geometric relationships appears to be a feature of the neurocognitive systems that support habitat representation and navigation, this does not mean that individuals have an explicit understanding of the formal principles of Euclidean geometry. Rather, the development of geometry as a formal discipline might have been initially based on early geometers' access to the knowledge that is implicit in the systems that support habitat navigation. In keeping with this view, in the development of formal geometry, Euclid apparently "started with what he thought were self-evident truths and then proceeded to prove all the rest by logic" (West, Griesbach, Taylor, & Taylor, 1982, p. 220). Therefore, the implicit understanding, or "self-evident truth," that the fastest way to get from one place to another is to go "as the crow flies," was made explicit in the formal Euclidean postulate "a line can be drawn from any point to any point" (in Euclidean geometry, a line is a *straight* line; p. 221). The former represents implicit, biologically primary knowledge associated with the neurocognitive systems that support habitat navigation, whereas the latter represents the explicit formalization of this knowledge as part of a formal academic discipline.

Moreover, many spatial abilities, such as those assessed by traditional psychometric tests, likely reflect the operation of the neurocognitive systems that are associated with habitat navigation (Geary, 1996). Although these systems appear to have evolved in order to support movement in the physical universe (Shepard, 1994), they can also be used, or co-opted, for many other purposes. The problem-solving strategies of some preschool children, for instance, often involve the construction of three-dimensional representations of the task at hand (McGuinness, 1993). Johnson (1984) found that the solving of algebraic word problems was facilitated if important relationships in the problem were diagrammed (i.e., represented spatially). No doubt the evolution of spatial abilities was unrelated to algebraic problem solving, but, nevertheless, these systems can be co-opted during the solving of word problems (see Geary, 1996). More important, there appear to be differences in the ease with which these systems can be used for their evolution-based functions and co-opted tasks. The use of spatial systems for moving about in one's surroundings or developing cognitive maps of one's surroundings appears to occur automatically (Landau et al., 1981). However, most people need to be taught how to use spatial representations to solve, for instance, mathematical word problems (Lewis, 1989).

In summary, the neurocognitive systems that have more likely evolved to support movement in the three-dimensional physical universe (Shepard, 1994) can be adapted by human beings for purposes other than the original evolution-based function (Rozin, 1976). This adaptation, however, occurs in some cultures and not others and involves co-optation of primary neurocognitive systems or access to, or awareness and formalization of, implicit knowledge associated with these systems (Gelman, 1990; Rozin, 1976). An example of co-optation is the use of spatial representations of mathematical relationships to aid in the solving of word problems (a procedural competency), whereas Euclid's basic geometric postulates (conceptual competencies) appear to have involved an awareness of the knowledge implicit in the neurocognitive systems that support habitat navigation.

Developmental Mechanisms. The development of both primary and secondary abilities likely requires exposure to the associated content. For instance, even though there appears to be a biologically primary set of skeletal principles that guide the early counting activities of children, the mastery of counting requires considerable exposure to counting and number-related activities (Briars & Siegler, 1984; Fuson, 1988; Geary, 1995; Gelman & Gallistel, 1978). The issue is (a) whether the activities that promote the acquisition of primary abilities are sufficient for the acquisition of secondary abilities, and (b) the source of motivation for engaging in the associated activities.

Given that, by definition, biologically primary cognitive domains are found pan-culturally, it seems reasonable to assume that the types of activities that promote the acquisition of primary abilities are also pan-cultural. One activity that should be given serious consideration as a basic vehicle for the acquisition of primary abilities is children's play. The implicit goal of play, across mammalian species and across human cultures, appears to be the acquisition of functional adult-like abilities (Eibl-Eibesfeldt, 1989; Panksepp, Siviy, & Normansell, 1984; Rubin, Fein, & B. Vandenberg, 1983). In fact, it appears that children as young as 2 years of age engage in number-related games and activities throughout the world (e.g., Saxe, Guberman, & Gearhart, 1987; Zaslavsky, 1973). Moreover, engagement in early number-related activities and play is likely to flesh out the skeletal principles associated with the biologically primary mathematical abilities described in the next section (Gelman & Gallistel, 1978; Saxe et al., 1987). Therefore, biologically primary mathematical abilities (described later) include goal structures and skeletal principles that orient the child to numerical features of his or her environment, as well as procedures that can be used to achieve these goals. Moreover, a necessary aspect of primary systems is an inherent interest in, and at times enjoyment of, the activities that will facilitate the development of the associated neurocognitive systems.

The abilities that are associated with biologically secondary domains do not appear to have the initial advantage of skeletal principles or an inherent enjoyment of the activities which are likely to facilitate their acquisition (Geary, 1995; Siegler & Crowley, 1994). As a result, the acquisition of secondary abilities is typically slow, effortful, and occurs only with sustained deliberate practice that is specifically designed to facilitate their acquisition (Ericsson & Charness, 1994; Ericsson, Krampe, & Tesch-Römer, 1993; Gelman, 1993; Siegler & Crowley, 1994). The primary context within which children receive sustained exposure to secondary domains is school. Schools are essentially socio–cultural institutions that have emerged in socially and technically complex societies (Whiting & Whiting, 1975). The function of schools is to ensure that children acquire culturally relevant skills that would not emerge in more natural contexts or as a result of more natural activities (e.g., children's play and exploration). Therefore, it is not surprising that the abilities which are associated with most secondary domains only emerge for large segments of a given population in cultures with formal institutions, such as schools, that are explicitly designed to facilitate their acquisition (Ginsburg, Posner, & Russell, 1981).

One very important corollary of this view is that the motivation to acquire secondary abilities comes from the requirements of the wider culture and not the inherent interests of children. This is not to say that some individuals will not be motivated to engage in the activities that will facilitate the acquisition of secondary abilities (see Footnote 2, p. 147, this chapter, and Geary, 1995). Rather, the point is that the motivation to engage in the activities which will facilitate the acquisition of secondary cognitive abilities is not likely to be universal.

There are a number of important implications of this perspective. First, primary cognitive abilities should be found in all human cultures, should serve a plausible evolutionary function, and analogous abilities and functions should be found across related species (Pinker & Bloom, 1990). Secondary abilities, in contrast, are more likely to emerge in some cultures and not others. Cross-cultural differences in the emergence of secondary abilities are most likely to reflect cultural differences in goals and values associated with academic achievement and cognitive development, and any associated cultural differences in the development of formal institutions, in particular schools, to facilitate the acquisition of these academic and cognitive abilities in children (Geary, 1995). Cross-cultural variations in the extent to which secondary abilities are valued are important because the universal emergence of secondary abilities is only likely to occur in cultures with values that support and reward engagement in the associated activities. This is because the abilities associated with secondary domains are not likely to emerge from children's natural activities. This view contrasts, for instance, with the argument that cross-national differences in academic achievement largely reflect racial differences in intelligence (Lynn, 1982).

From this perspective, if cross-national differences in mathematical abilities have a biological basis, then these differences should be especially evident in biologically primary domains. On the other hand, if there are no cross-national differences in primary domains but consistent differences in secondary domains, then cross-national differences in schooling and attitudes toward mathematics become the primary candidates for the source of cross-national differences in mathematical abilities. Cross-national differences in secondary domains do not preclude biologically based differences in, for instance, the ease with which primary abilities can be coopted. Presumably, any such differences might be reflected on broader measures of cognitive ability, such as intelligence tests, which are predictive of academic achievement (Geary, 1996). Nevertheless, cultural attitudes toward academic achievement and especially schooling would be the primary candidates for the source of cross-national differences in secondary domains. These issues are addressed here, after a discussion of biologically primary and biologically secondary mathematical domains.

BIOLOGY AND MATHEMATICS

The gist of the earlier argument is that if the advantage of East Asian individuals over their American peers in mathematical abilities has a biological basis (e.g., an "Asian math gene"), then cross-national differences comparing individuals from East Asian nations to individuals from the United States should emerge for biologically primary mathematical domains. In contrast, if no cross-national differences are found for primary domains, but consistent differences emerge for secondary mathematical domains, then these differences are more likely to be due to cultural differences in schooling and attitudes toward mathematics, rather than to inherent differences in the ability to learn mathematics or to differences in intelligence (see Geary, Salthouse, Chen, & Fan, 1996). In order to make such comparisons, biologically primary and biologically secondary mathematical abilities need to be defined—a task that is addressed with the two following sections.

Biologically Primary Mathematical Abilities

I have argued elsewhere (Geary, 1995) that there is evidence for the pan-cultural existence of a biologically primary numerical domain which consists of at least four primary numerical abilities; numerosity (or subitizing), or-

TABLE 6.1
Potential Biologically Primary Mathematical Abilities

Numerosity or Subitizing
The ability to accurately determine the quantity of small sets of items, or events, without counting. In humans, accurate numerosity judgments are typically limited to sets of four or fewer items.

Ordinality
A basic understanding of more than and less than, and, later, an understanding of specific ordinal relationships. For example, understanding that $4 > 3$, $3 > 2$, and $2 > 1$. For humans, the limits of this system are not clear, but it is probably limited to quantities < 5.

Counting
Early in development there appears to be a preverbal counting system that can be used for the enumeration of sets up to three, perhaps four, items. With the advent of language and the learning of number words, there appears to be a pan-cultural understanding that serial-ordered number words can be used for counting, measurement, and simple arithmetic.

Simple arithmetic
Early in development there appears to be a sensitivity to increases (addition) and decreases (subtraction) in the quantity of small sets. This systems appears to be limited to the addition or subtraction of items within sets of three, perhaps four, items.

Geary (1995). © 1995 by the American Psychological Association. Reprinted with permission.

dinality, counting, and simple arithmetic. A brief description of these abilities is provided in Table 6.1.

Numerosity (or subitizing) represents the ability to quickly determine the quantity of a set of three to four items without the use of counting or estimating. The ability to quickly and accurately make numerosity judgments is evident in human infants in the first week of life, as well as in the laboratory rat, an African grey parrot (*Psittacus erithacus*), and the common chimpanzee (*Pan troglodytes*; Antell & Keating, 1983; Boysen & Berntson, 1989; Davis & Memmott, 1982; Pepperberg, 1987). Moreover, numerosity judgments appear to be based on an abstract representation of quantity rather than on modality-specific processes, as these judgments can be made by human infants for auditory and visual information (Starkey, Spelke, & Gelman, 1983, 1990). Supporting this view is the finding that certain cells in the parietal–occipital cortex of the cat are selectively responsive to small quantities, whether the quantities are presented in the visual, auditory, or tactile modalities (Thompson, Mayers, Robertson, & Patterson, 1970).

A sensitivity to ordinal relationships, for example, that three is more than two and two is more than one, is evident in 18-month-old infants (Cooper, 1984; Strauss & Curtis, 1984). Moreover, well-controlled studies have shown that nonhuman primates are able to make very precise ordinal judgments (Boysen, 1993; Washburn & Rumbaugh, 1991). For instance, after learning the quantity associated with specific Arabic numbers, a rhesus monkey (*Ma-*

caca mulatta) named Abel could correctly choose the larger of two Arabic numbers more than 88% of the time (Washburn & Rumbaugh, 1991). More important, Abel could choose the larger of two previously unpaired numbers more than 70% of the time.

Counting appears to be a pan-cultural human activity that is, at least initially, supported by a set of skeletal principles before children learn to use number words (Crump, 1990; Gelman & Gallistel, 1978; Ginsburg et al., 1981; Geary, 1994; Saxe, 1982; Starkey, 1992; Zaslavsky, 1973). As described earlier, one basic principle that appears to constrain counting is one–one correspondence (Gelman & Gallistel, 1978). Implicit knowledge of this skeletal principle is reflected in counting when each item is tagged (e.g., with a number word) or pointed to once and only once. Some human infants as young as 18 months of age are able to use some form of tag in order to determine the numerosity of sets of up to three items (Starkey, 1992), as can the common chimpanzee (Boysen, 1993; Rumbaugh & Washburn, 1993). In one study, a chimpanzee named Sheba was required to point to the Arabic number that corresponded to the number of food pellets on a food tray (Boysen, 1993). During this task, Sheba often pointed to the food pellets in succession and then pointed to the corresponding Arabic numerical.

Other research suggests that 5-month-old infants are aware of the effects that the addition and subtraction of one item has on the quantity of a small set of items (Wynn, 1992). Similar results have been reported for 18-month-olds (Starkey, 1992), and for the common chimpanzee (Boysen & Berntson, 1989). Moreover, these competencies in simple arithmetic appear to be qualitatively similar in the chimpanzee and human infants and young children (Gallistel & Gelman, 1992). Preschool children appear to be able to add quantities up to and including three items using some form of preverbal counting, whereas Sheba appears to be able to add items up to and including four items also by means of preverbal counting (Boysen & Berntson, 1989; Starkey, 1992).

Finally, psychometric and behavioral genetic studies support the argument that *some* numerical and arithmetical skills are biologically primary and cluster together. For 5-year-olds, tests that assess number knowledge and memory for numbers, as well as basic counting and arithmetic skills cluster together and define a Numerical Facility factor (Osborne & Lindsey, 1967). In fact, the Numerical Facility factor is one of the most stable factors ever identified through decades of psychometric research (e.g., Coombs, 1941; Thurstone, 1938; Thurstone & Thurstone, 1941), and has been found throughout the life span, as well as with studies of American, Chinese, and Filipino students (Geary, 1994; Guthrie, 1963; Vandenberg, 1959). Behavioral genetic studies of tests that define the Numerical Facility factor have yielded heritability estimates of about .5, suggesting that roughly ½ of the variability in some arithmetical abilities is due to genetic differences across people (Vandenberg, 1962, 1966).

Biologically Secondary Mathematical Abilities

The argument that certain features of counting, number, and arithmetic are biologically primary should *not* be taken to mean that all numerical and arithmetical abilities are biologically primary. In fact, there are many features of counting and arithmetic that are probably biologically secondary. These features include skills and knowledge taught by parents (e.g., the names of number words), concepts that are induced by children during the act of counting (e.g., that counted objects are usually tagged from left to right), and skills that are formally taught in school (e.g., the base-10 system, trading, fractions, multiplication, exponents, etc.; Briars & Siegler, 1984; Fuson, 1988; Geary, 1994; Ginsburg et al., 1981). Moreover, it is likely that most features of complex mathematical domains, such as algebra, geometry (except implicit knowledge of basic, nonanalytic, Euclidean geometry), and calculus, are biologically secondary given that the associated abilities only emerge with formal education.

One aspect of children's mathematical development that is the focus of much educational and cognitive science research is mathematical problem solving (Bransford & The Cognition and Technology Group at Vanderbilt, 1993; Schoenfeld, 1985). Mathematical problem-solving abilities are typically assessed by the solving of arithmetical and algebraic word problems. The solving of mathematical word problems requires the ability to spatially represent mathematical relations, the ability to translate word problems into appropriate equations, and an understanding of how and when to use mathematical equations, among other things (Geary, 1994; Mayer, 1985; Schoenfeld, 1985). More germane to the present discussion is the fact that word problems are an important aspect of cross-national comparisons of mathematical abilities (e.g., Husén, 1967; Lapointe, Mead, & Askew, 1992).

Psychometric studies suggest that mathematical problem solving, or mathematical reasoning (as psychometric researchers call it), is a biologically secondary cognitive domain. Although a Mathematical Reasoning factor has been identified in many psychometric studies (Dye & Very, 1968; Thurstone, 1938), a distinct Mathematical Reasoning factor does not emerge in all samples; not even in some samples of college students (e.g., Guthrie, 1963). In fact, a distinct Mathematical Reasoning factor is only found with groups of older adolescents (i.e., end of high school or early college) who have taken a lot of mathematics courses (e.g., Very, 1967). Therefore, unlike the Numerical Facility factor that has emerged in nearly all studies that have included arithmetic tests, and in samples of preschool children, a Mathematical Reasoning factor emerges only in samples with prolonged mathematical instruction. This pattern suggests that many individuals do not easily acquire the competencies that are associated with complex mathematical problem solving.

The fact that a Mathematical Reasoning factor does not emerge until adolescence does not of course preclude biological influences on the acquisition of the associated skills. Indeed, factor analytic studies suggest that mathematical reasoning abilities initially emerge from biologically primary mathematical abilities and general reasoning abilities, both of which are partly heritable (Vandenberg, 1966). However, by the end of high school, the abilities subsumed by the Numerical Facility and Mathematical Reasoning factors are largely independent (Geary, 1994). The point is that the abilities that are subsumed by the Mathematical Reasoning factor only appear to emerge with sustained mathematical instruction, and are therefore more likely to represent secondary abilities rather than primary abilities. In other words, it appears that instructional practices (e.g., teaching the use of diagrams to aid in the solving of mathematical word problems; Lewis, 1989) facilitate the co-optation of primary abilities and the eventual emergence of a coordinated system of secondary mathematical abilities.

Indeed, cognitive studies also suggest that mathematical problem solving is biologically secondary and involves the co-optation of more primary abilities. For instance, the work of Dark and Benbow (1991) suggests that superior performance on the SAT Mathematics test, which includes geometry problems and algebraic word problems, appears to involve, among other things, the co-optation of spatial abilities, and not necessarily an inherent understanding of mathematical problem solving. As noted earlier, spatial abilities appear to aid in the solving of algebraic word problems through, for example, the diagraming of important relationships in the problem (Geary, 1994, 1996; Johnson, 1984), but the solving of word problems is biologically secondary with respect to spatial abilities.

In sum, most of children's knowledge of complex arithmetic and complex mathematics emerges in formal school settings (Ginsburg et al., 1981) and only as a result of teaching practices that are explicitly designed to impart this knowledge. The conditions under which such biologically secondary mathematical abilities emerge are thus very different from the conditions that lead to the arguably pan-cultural emergence of biologically primary mathematical abilities. Because the conditions associated with the emergence of primary and secondary mathematical abilities differ (i.e., natural activities versus schooling), cross-national ability differences in primary and secondary mathematical domains should enable influences to be drawn regarding the source of any such differences. The development of primary and secondary mathematical abilities for East Asian and American children is described in the next section.

CROSS-NATIONAL DIFFERENCES
IN MATHEMATICAL ABILITIES

In this section, an overview of cross-national studies that have compared the mathematical abilities of U.S. children with children from East Asian nations (i.e., China, Korea, Japan, and Taiwan) in biologically primary and biologically secondary domains is presented. A more thorough review of this literature can be found in Geary (1994).

Biologically Primary Mathematical Domains

Although there have been no studies that were explicitly designed to compare East Asian and American children in biologically primary mathematical domains, there have been comparisons on numerical and arithmetical tasks that appear to largely assess primary abilities (e.g., Song & Ginsburg, 1987). In this section, comparisons of East Asian and American children on these tasks is presented.

In a large-scale comparison of the basic number and arithmetic skills of 4- to 8-year-old Korean and American children, Song and Ginsburg (1987) administered an array of tasks that appeared to assess both biologically primary and biologically secondary mathematical abilities, which were called informal and formal mathematical thinking, respectively, in this study. For the preschool children (i.e., 4-year-olds), the Americans outperformed their Korean peers on informal tasks that appear to have largely assessed biologically primary mathematical areas (e.g., basic counting and simple arithmetic). In keeping with the view that secondary abilities only emerge with formal schooling, at this age none of the children performed well on tasks that assessed biologically secondary abilities (e.g., base-10 knowledge). As a result, few national differences were found for these tasks. For 7- and 8-year-olds, there were few cross-national differences in biologically primary areas. Those differences that were found, now favored the Korean children. Song and Ginsburg argued that the American children's early advantage in informal mathematics (i.e., primary domains) likely resulted from the tendency of American parents to foster the development of the basic academic skills of their children during the preschool years. Korean parents, in contrast, tend "not to make active attempts to provide their children with intellectual stimulation during the preschool years" (p. 1293). Rather, parent–child interactions tend to focus on social and emotional development.

Kevin Miller and his colleagues have assessed the basic procedural and conceptual counting competencies of preschool children from mainland China and the United States (K. F. Miller, 1993; K. F. Miller, Smith, Zhu, & Zhang, 1995; K. F. Miller & Stigler, 1987). The results of these studies suggest that there are no differences in the biologically primary counting abilities of Chinese and American preschool children. Chinese and American preschool children are equally skilled (e.g., accurate) at counting small numbers of objects, and their counting behavior appears to be constrained by the same implicit knowledge, or skeletal principles, such as one–one correspondence. Any differences that are found at this age appear to be related to differences in English and Chinese number words. In Asian languages, the base-10 structure of Arabic numbers is reflected in the number words. For instance, "11, 12, 13," is counted "ten one, ten two, ten three." For most European-derived languages, in contrast, the structure of the base-10 system is not obvious in the number words. Most American children understand "twelve" as representing a set of 12 items, just as "eight" represents a set of 8 items. Asian children understand that "twelve" (i.e., "ten two") represents both tens and units values. This difference in the structure of Asian and English number words provides East Asian children with an advantage over their American peers in learning to count past 10, and in basic arithmetic (e.g., Fuson & Kwon, 1992). However, these advantages reflect differences in the surface structure of number words and do not reflect differences in biologically primary numerical competencies. Therefore, aside from the influence of language, the basic counting competencies of Chinese and American preschool children appear to be equivalent.

Stevenson and his colleagues assessed the basic mathematics skills of kindergarten children from the United States, Japan, and Taiwan (Stevenson, Lee, & Stigler, 1986). The test administered to the children appeared include items that assessed both biologically primary and biologically secondary mathematical abilities. Nevertheless, the finding of no overall difference in the performance of the Chinese and American kindergarten children suggests that there is no early Chinese advantage in basic mathematics, except for any advantage that might result from differences in Chinese and English number words (e.g., Geary, Bow-Thomas, Fan, & Siegler, 1993; K. F. Miller & Stigler, 1987). The finding that the Japanese children outperformed their peers from both the United States as well as Taiwan suggests that the early Japanese advantage is not related to broad racial categories, but rather to differences in exposure to mathematics in kindergarten.

Across studies, the most notable cross-national difference on tasks that appear to largely assess biologically primary mathematical abilities involved an advantage of young American children over their peers from Korea (Song & Ginsburg, 1987). This American advantage was eliminated, and for some measures reversed, by the end of first grade. The overall pattern in this study and related studies suggests that these differences reflect cultural differences in the level of early parental involvement in the acquisition of basic academic skills, and not a cross-national difference in biologically primary mathematical abilities. In fact, the research to date suggests that there are no systematic differences in the biologically primary mathematical abilities of preschool children in East Asian nations and the United States. When East Asian preschool children outperform American preschool children in basic counting and arithmetical areas, it is *only* after the onset of formal schooling or only on tasks that would be influenced by differences in the structure of number words (see K. F. Miller et al., 1995).

Biologically Secondary Mathematical Domains

In this section, a brief overview of multinational comparisons of the performance of American and East Asian children in biologically secondary mathematical domains is presented. Following the overview is a consideration of alternative explanations of the source of U.S. versus East Asian differences (described later) in the development of secondary mathematical abilities; that is, racial differences in intelligence, and schooling differences. Again, a more comprehensive review of this research is provided in Geary (1994).

The first large-scale multinational study of mathematics achievement was conducted in 1964 (Husén, 1967); the 12 participating nations were Australia, Belgium, England, Finland, France, Germany, Holland, Israel, Japan, Scotland, Sweden, and the United States. In this study, 13- and 17-year-olds were administered tests that assessed their basic skills in complex arithmetic, algebra, and geometry (these included arithmetical and algebraic word problems); the 17-year-olds were also assessed in trigonometry, calculus, probability, and logic. For the 13-year-old samples, the overall performance of the U.S. adolescents ranked 11th and 10th for two separate comparisons. The overall performance of the Japanese 13-year-olds was 1st and 2nd for these same two comparisons. For individual areas, the performance of the U.S. 13-year-olds was below (by $1/10$ to $1/2$ of a standard deviation) the international mean in all areas, whereas the performance of their Japanese peers was considerably above the international mean in all areas (as was the performance of students from Israel and Belgium). The performance of the U.S. 17-year-olds was even more abysmal than the performance of their 13-year-old peers, as they ranked 12th overall, and scored more than $1/2$ of a standard deviation below the international mean in most mathematical areas. Again, the overall performance of the Japanese students was among the best in this assessment and considerably higher than their U.S. cohorts.

A second multinational comparison of mathematical abilities conducted in the early 1980s yielded essentially the same results, although the addition of several third-world nations to this assessment resulted in lower overall international standards than the first multinational study (Crosswhite, Dossey, Swafford, McKnight, & Cooney, 1985). The overall mathematical abilities of U.S. 13- and 17-year-olds changed little from 1964 to 1981. For instance, about 60% of the U.S. students for whom mathematics was an integral part of their high school curriculum (the top 13%) scored substantially (≥ 1 standard deviation) below the international mean in algebra, geometry, and calculus (M. D. Miller & Linn, 1989). The United States' best students (the top 5%) were performing at about the ("watered down") international average for algebra, geometry, and calculus. The best Japanese adolescents, in contrast, outperformed the best students from all other nations, and scored between $1 1/2$ and 2 standard deviations above the international mean in algebra, geometry, and calculus.

A more recent comparison of the mathematical performance of 9- and 13-year-olds from 20 nations yielded the same pattern (Lapointe et al., 1992). The overall mathematical performance of the U.S. 13-year-olds ranked 13th out of 15 nations that included comparable samples. For this same comparison, students from Korea and Taiwan were ranked 1st and 2nd, respectively; Japan did not participate in this study. Students from mainland China were also assessed in this study, but were not included in the primary comparisons, because the researchers were not able to assess students from all areas of China. Those Chinese students who did participate in this study substantially outperformed the students from Korea and Taiwan. The overall performance of the U.S. 9-year-olds ranked 9th out of 10 nations, whereas the overall performance of 9-year-olds from Korea and Taiwan ranked 1st and 3rd, respectively; China did not participate in the assessment of 9-year-olds.

The research of Stevenson and his colleagues also shows that the mathematical development of U.S. children lags behind that of their peers from Japan, Taiwan, and China by first grade (Stevenson et al., 1993; Stevenson, Lee, Chen, Lummis, et al., 1990; Stevenson, Lee, Chen, Stigler, et al., 1990; Stevenson et al., 1986). Toward the end of first grade, there is a small to moderate difference in the mathematical skills of American children and their East Asian peers. This gap widens, however, by the time the children are in the fifth grade (Stevenson et al., 1986). Beginning in 1980, Stevenson et al. (1993) also conducted a longitudinal study of the performance of U.S., Chinese (i.e., Taiwan), and Japanese children. These children were assessed in the 1st, 5th, and 11th grades. Stevenson et al. also assessed new cohorts of 5th and 11th graders, to determine whether the magnitude of the East Asian versus American difference in mathematical performance changed from 1980 to 1990.

The cross-sectional comparisons indicated that from 1980 to 1990, the relative performance of American and Japanese fifth-grade children was unchanged, but "the difference between the performance of the Chinese and American children was greater in 1990 than in 1980" (Stevenson et al., 1993, p. 54). The mean test scores of American fifth graders improved slightly from 1980 to 1990, whereas the mean scores of their Chinese peers improved considerably (about 20%) during this 10-year span. The mean scores of the Japanese fifth graders was about the same in 1980 and 1990. The same general pattern was found for the comparisons of the 11th graders. The longitudinal component of the study indicated that "the achievement gap in mathematics increased between the 1st and 11th grades" (p. 55). Another study comparing first and fifth graders from the United States and mainland China yielded the same result: American children were behind their Chinese peers on nearly every dimension of mathematical competence in the first grade, and the gap widened by the fifth grade (Stevenson, Lee, Chen, Lummis, et al., 1990).

In all, the results of these and other studies (e.g., Fuson & Kwon, 1992; Geary, Fan, & Bow-Thomas, 1992) are clear: The mathematical development of American children in biologically secondary mathematical domains lags behind that of their peers in nearly all other industrialized, and some non-industrialized, nations. In contrast, the mathematical competencies of children and adolescents from East Asian nations in secondary domains are among the best in the world.

Summary

The pattern of cross-national ability differences for biologically primary and biologically secondary mathematical domains differs. Overall, there appear to be no systematic differences in the primary mathematical abilities of children from East Asia and the United States, but a clear and consistent advantage of East Asian children and adolescents over their same-age U.S. peers in nearly all, if not all, secondary mathematics domains. These differences between the secondary mathematical development of U.S. and East Asian children emerge from apparently no cross-national differences in biologically primary mathematical domains, or an occasional U.S. advantage (Song & Ginsburg, 1987). More important, the advantage of East Asian children in secondary mathematical domains is largely coincident with the advent of formal schooling, and increases with each successive year of formal schooling (e.g., Stevenson et al., 1993). The overall pattern of results across biologically primary and biologically secondary mathematical domains suggests that the advantage of East Asian children over U.S. children in mathematics is largely due to differences in schooling, broadly defined, and not to an inherent Asian advantage in mathematics.

Despite the finding that the East Asian versus U.S. performance differences in secondary mathematical domains only emerge with the advent of formal schooling, it does not necessarily follow that these performance differences are caused by schooling differences. First, it is possible that group differences in intelligence lead to differences in the facility of acquiring biologically secondary cognitive abilities (Rushton, 1995). Second, in the absence of group differences in intelligence, it must be shown that differences in the schooling of East Asian and U.S. children are sufficient to explain the just-described cross-national differences in the development of secondary mathematical abilities. These issues are addressed in the next section.

INTELLIGENCE, SCHOOLING, AND CROSS-NATIONAL DIFFERENCES IN MATHEMATICS

In this section, potential factors that might underlie the just-described advantage of East Asian children over their U.S. peers in biologically secondary mathematical domains are considered. In keeping with the earlier argument, the two most common explanations are racial differences in intelligence (e.g., Lynn, 1982; Rushton, 1995), and cross-national differences in schooling (e.g., Stevenson & Stigler, 1992). Evidence for both of these explanations is considered in turn.

Racial Differences in Intelligence

I argued at the beginning of this chapter that the acquisition of biologically secondary cognitive abilities likely involved, among other things, the co-optation of the neurocognitive systems that support primary cognitive abilities, an access to implicit knowledge associated with these systems, or both. There will also almost certainly be individual differences in the degree to which neurocognitive systems can be co-opted (i.e., individual differences in learning), as well as individual differences in access to knowledge implicit in primary systems (e.g., individual differences in "insightfulness"). Any such differences are likely to result in individual differences in the ease with which biologically secondary cognitive abilities are constructed. Because performance on intelligence tests is predictive of later achievement in secondary domains (e.g., Stevenson, Parker, Wilkinson, Hegion, & Fish, 1976), it is possible that IQ scores serve as a proxy for, among other things, the ease with which primary systems are co-opted and the ease with which implicit knowledge is made explicit. Either way, the possibility that the aforementioned differences in the mathematical development of East Asian and U.S. children result from racial differences in intelligence needs to be addressed.

Indeed, Lynn (1982) argued that the superior academic achievement of Japanese relative to U.S. children was due to higher mean IQs in Asian relative to Occidental peoples. In this study, Lynn compared the raw scores from the standardization samples for the Japanese and U.S. versions of the Wechsler intelligence tests (e.g., Wechsler, 1974). Basically, raw scores for the Japanese standardization samples were rescored using U.S. norms. On the basis of comparisons across 27 cohorts, Lynn argued that the mean IQ of Japanese children was 111, compared to a mean of 100 for U.S. and European children. Stevenson and Azuma (1983) argued that Lynn had overestimated the IQ scores of Japanese children, because the Japanese standardization samples included too many urban and higher SES (socioeconomic status) children relative to Japan as a whole. Statistically adjusting for these differences yielded a mean IQ of 104 for Japanese children (Lynn, 1983).

In contrast, the results of a large-scale study of the cognitive abilities of Japanese, Chinese (i.e., Taiwan and Hong Kong), and White U.S. elementary school children suggested no systematic cross-racial differences in intelligence (Stevenson et al., 1985). Here, groups of Japanese, Chinese, and White U.S. children were administered a battery of cognitive ability measures, including tests of auditory memory, verbal memory, memory for numbers, spatial skills, vocabulary, and general information, among others. All children were also administered achievement tests in reading and mathematics. If Asian children are more intelligent than White U.S. children, then the Asian children should have outperformed their U.S. peers on all, or nearly all, of the ability tests (Spearman, 1927). The overall results supported no such pattern: For some tests, such as spatial relations, the Japanese children outperformed the Chinese and U.S. children. On other tests, such as verbal memory, the U.S. children outperformed their Japanese and Chinese peers, while for still other tests, such as memory for numbers, the Chinese children outperformed their U.S. and Japanese peers. On the basis of these results, Stevenson et al. (1985) concluded, "This study offers no support for the argument that there are differences in the general cognitive functioning of Chinese, Japanese, or American children" (p. 733). Nevertheless, moderate to large cross-national differences were found for mathematics achievement, again favoring the Asian children.

This study and other studies (see Geary, 1994) suggest the following: First, even though IQ predicts later academic achievement, cross-national differences in academic achievement should not be used to make inferences about cross-national differences in IQ. Second, there do not appear to be large systematic differences in the intelligence of Asian and Occidental peoples; if any differences do exist they are rather small and not sufficient to account for the large differences in the mathematical development of Asian and U.S. children. Third, the superior spatial abilities of Japanese relative to U.S. children (Stevenson et al., 1985) might give them an advantage in certain mathematical areas, such as geometry, but probably not other areas, such as algebra (except maybe algebraic word problems; see Geary, 1996). However, this difference in spatial ability is not related to broad racial categories, because Stevenson et al. found no reliable differences in the spatial abilities of Chinese and U.S. children.

Schooling

Because the emergence of the advantage of East Asian children over U.S. children in biologically secondary mathematical domains is coincident with the advent of formal schooling, it seems reasonable to suspect that cross-national differences in schooling, broadly defined, govern cross-national differences in mathematical performance. The question is whether the schooling differences are likely to be sufficient to explain the mathematical ability differences. The two school-related factors that are the most likely source of cross-national differences in mathematical abilities are overall all exposure to mathematics (in school and at home; e.g., homework) and mathematics curricula, including teaching styles (Geary, 1994).

One outcome of the first multinational study of mathematics achievement was the finding that cross-national differences in the emphasis on mathematics instruction in the classroom were moderately to strongly related to cross-national differences in mathematics achievement (Husén, 1967). In nearly all mathematical domains, mathematics achievement levels varied directly with the relative degree of emphasis in the mathematics curriculum. Students with the best scores in algebra, for instance, came from nations where the mathematics curriculum emphasized algebra. The question here is whether the school curriculum in East Asian nations emphasizes mathematics to a greater degree than the school curriculum in the United States, and, if so, whether any such differences are likely to be sufficient to explain the differences in the mathematical development of East Asian and U.S. children.

The research of Stevenson and his colleagues suggests that there are, in fact, substantial differences in the extent to which East Asian and U.S. children are exposed to mathematics in school (Stevenson, Lee, Chen, Stigler, et al., 1990; Stevenson et al., 1986). For instance, extensive observations of the classroom activities of first- and fifth-grade children from Japan, Taiwan, and the United States suggest consistent differences in the activities of Asian versus U.S. students and teachers. Overall, during potential instruction time, U.S. first-grade children were engaged in academic activities about 70% of the time, compared to 85% and 79% of the time for their Chinese and Japanese peers, respectively. Fifth-grade U.S. children spent about 65% of their potential instruction time engaged in academic activities, relative to 87 to 92% of the time for their same-age Asian peers. Moreover, the typical first-grade teacher in the United States spent, on average, between 1½ and 2 hours less time per week on mathematics than their peers in Taiwan and Japan (Stevenson, Lee, Chen, Stigler, et al., 1990). Fifth-grade U.S. teachers spent between 4 and 8 hours less time per week, on average, on mathematics than did Asian teachers. Geary (1994) estimated that the net result of these instructional activity differences was that first-grade children in Taiwan would receive 63 more hours of mathematics instruction than first-grade children from the United States; this difference was estimated to be 346 hours in the fifth grade.

Asian children not only receive more exposure to mathematics in school, they also do more homework, in all areas, relative to their U.S. cohorts. For instance, Stevenson and his colleagues (Stevenson, Lee, Chen, Stigler, et al., 1990) found that across all areas, U.S. first-grade children did about 1 hour of homework per week, relative to 8 and 4 hours per week in Taiwan and Japan, respectively. In the fifth grade, U.S. children did about 4 hours of homework per week, as compared to 13 and 6 hours per week in Taiwan and Japan, respectively. An equally important finding is systematic differences in the relative difficulty of the mathematics curriculum in the United States and East Asian nations. In short, the mathematics curriculum in the United States is developmentally delayed in comparison to international standards (e.g., Fuson, Stigler, & Bartsch, 1988; Stigler, Lee, Lucker, & Stevenson, 1982). For instance, many topics in complex arithmetic (e.g., word problems) that are introduced in the second or third grade in East Asian, and other, nations are not introduced until the fifth or sixth grade in the United States.

Finally, these East Asian versus U.S. differences in mathematics instruction, homework, and the rigor of the mathematics curriculum reflect wider cultural values. "Asian culture emphasizes and gives priority to mathematical learning; high achievement in mathematics is taken by mature members of the culture to be an important goal for its less mature members" (Hatano, 1990, pp. 110–111). U.S. culture, in contrast, values achievement in sports more than achievement in mathematics (Eccles, Wigfield, Harold, & Blumenfeld, 1993). These differences in the cultural valuation of mathematics translate into differences in the investment of children, parents, and teachers in learning mathematics, and are likely to be the primary source of the mathematical ability differences comparing East Asian and U.S. children (Geary, 1994; Stevenson & Stigler, 1992).

Summary

Even though IQ scores are predictive of later academic achievement, and there are systematic mathematics achievement differences comparing East Asian and U.S. children, there do not appear to be large systematic differences in the intelligence of East Asian and U.S. children (see Geary, 1994): If there are small differences in IQ, these are not likely to be sufficient to explain the large gap in mathematical achievement. The Stevenson et al. (1985) finding of no systematic cognitive ability differences comparing East Asian and White U.S. children with simultaneous differences in mathematics achievement nicely illustrates this point. There are, however, substantial and systematic differences in the opportunity to learn mathematics in school, comparing East Asian and U.S. children. Relative to their U.S. peers, East Asian children receive considerably more mathematics instruction in school, do more mathematics homework, and are exposed to a much more rigorous mathematics curriculum. Although it cannot be stated with certainty, these and related (e.g., instructional styles; Geary, 1994) differences in schooling appear to be sufficient to explain the advantage of East Asian children over U.S. children in biologically secondary mathematical domains.

CONCLUSION

Examining children's cognitive and academic development from the perspective of human evolution provides a means by which biological and cultural influences on children's cognition might be disentangled (Geary, 1995, 1996). Evolutionary and biological influences on children's cognitive development are likely to be most evident and most direct for pan-cultural forms of cognition, which were termed biologically primary cognitive abilities. Cultural influences on children's cognition are most strongly reflected in the emergence of biologically secondary forms of cognition. Here, the motivation to acquire secondary abilities is provided by the values and goals of the wider culture, whereas the associated procedural and conceptual competencies appear to be constructed from bits and pieces taken from biologically primary cognitive domains.

One implication of this perspective is that the source of any group differences in cognitive abilities likely differs for biologically primary and biologically secondary cognitive domains (Geary, 1996). Group differences—for example, sex differences—in primary domains are likely to reflect differences in evolutionary selection pressures (e.g., sexual selection) and the operation of proximate biological mechanisms (e.g., sex hormones). Group differences in secondary cognitive domains, in contrast, are more likely to reflect differences in cultural values rather than the direct operation of biological mechanisms. Primary differences in other areas, such as spatial navigation, might of course lead to differences in secondary domains, such as geometry. For instance, Geary (1996) argued that the sex difference, favoring males, in geometric abilities reflects the greater elaboration of the neurocognitive systems that support habitat navigation in males than in females. As noted earlier, knowledge implicit in these systems appears to reflect the basic principles of Euclidean geometry, and thus might be one source of the male advantage in geometry. Nevertheless, the finding of no systematic difference in the spatial abilities of Asian and U.S. children (although there is a Japanese advantage) suggests that this is not the primary source of cross-national differences in mathematical abilities. Moreover, the sex difference in secondary mathematical domains is highly selective, whereas the East Asian versus U.S. difference in mathematical performance is found in nearly all secondary domains. The ubiquity of the cross-national differences in mathematical performance across secondary domains (e.g., geometry, algebra, probability) is consistent with the argument (once IQ differences are ruled out) that more general cultural factors, such as values and schooling, need to be seriously considered as the primary source of these mathematical ability differences. Again, cultural values are important because they provide the motivation to acquire cognitive abilities that would not emerge in more natural contexts and with more natural activities (e.g., children's play).

The use of this perspective to examine the mathematical development of East Asian and U.S. children provided the following conclusions: First, there appear to be no differences in the biologically primary mathematical abilities of East Asian and U.S. children—there is no "Asian math gene." Second, except for the influence of number words on early counting and arithmetic development, the clear and consistent advantage of East Asian children over their U.S. peers in secondary mathematical domains appears to be due to differences in schooling, broadly defined. Relative to U.S. children, East Asian children receive substantially more exposure to mathematics at school and at home (e.g., homework; for a discussion of specific instructional practices comparing classrooms from East Asia and the United States see Stevenson & Stigler, 1992, or Geary, 1994). Finally, these schooling differences reflect wider cultural differences in the relative valuation of achievement in mathematics. The bottom line is that U.S. children lag behind their international peers in the development of secondary mathematical abilities because U.S. culture does not value mathematical achievement. East Asian children, in contrast, are among the best in the world in secondary mathematical domains, because Asian culture values and rewards mathematical achievement.

Finally, perhaps the most important practical implication that arises from considering biological and cultural influences on mathematical development is understanding the source of motivation for acquiring secondary mathematical competencies. From this perspective, it should not be assumed that the acquisition of secondary skills, mathematical or otherwise, will necessarily be an inherently enjoyable or interesting process for children (Geary, 1995). In fact, it is likely to be the case that the attainment of mathematical expertise will require a sustained, often tedious and unenjoyable, investment in learning mathematics (Ericsson et al., 1993), contrary to current philosophical approaches to educational reform in the United States; in particular, constructivism (Geary, 1995). I have noted that "constructivism is largely a reflection of current American cultural beliefs and, as such, involves the development of instructional techniques that attempt to make the acquisition of complex mathematical skills an enjoyable social enterprise that will be pursued based on individual interest and choice" (p. 32). However, when we consider secondary mathematical domains from an evolutionary perspective, there is no reason to believe that the acquisition of the associated abilities will be inherently interesting or enjoyable for Asian or U.S. children. It is for this reason that the cultural valuation of mathematics, which is evident in Asian culture but not U.S. culture, is *essential* in motivating children to invest in mathematical learning.

ACKNOWLEDGMENTS

During the preparation of this chapter, the author was supported by Grant 1R01–HD27931 from the National Institute of Child Health and Human Development. I would like to thank Robert Sternberg and Talia Ben-Zeev for comments on an earlier draft.

REFERENCES

Antell, S. E., & Keating, D. P. (1983). Perception of numerical invariance in neonates. *Child Development, 54*, 695–701.
Boysen, S. T. (1993). Counting in chimpanzees: Nonhuman principles and emergent properties of number. In S. T. Boysen & E. J. Capaldi (Eds.), *The development of numerical competence: Animal and human models* (pp. 39–59). Hillsdale, NJ: Lawrence Erlbaum Associates.

Boysen, S. T., & Berntson, G. G. (1989). Numerical competence in a chimpanzee (*Pan troglodytes*). *Journal of Comparative Psychology, 103*, 23–31.

Bransford, J. D., & The Cognition and Technology Group at Vanderbilt (1993). The Jasper series: Theoretical foundations and data on problem solving and transfer. In L. A. Penner, G. M. Batsche, H. K. Knoff, & D. L. Nelson (Eds.), *The challenge in mathematics and science education: Psychology's response* (pp. 113–152). Washington, DC: American Psychological Association.

Briars, D., & Siegler, R. S. (1984). A featural analysis of preschoolers' counting knowledge. *Developmental Psychology, 20*, 607–618.

Cheng, K., & Gallistel, C. R. (1984). Testing the geometric power of an animal's spatial representation. In H. L. Roitblat, T. G. Bever, & H. S. Terrace (Eds.), *Animal cognition* (pp. 409–423). Hillsdale, NJ: Lawrence Erlbaum Associates.

Coombs, C. H. (1941). A factorial study of number ability. *Psychometrika, 6*, 161–189.

Cooper, R. G., Jr. (1984). Early number development: Discovering number space with addition and subtraction. In C. Sophian (Ed.), *Origins of cognitive skills: The eighteenth Carnegie symposium on cognition* (pp. 157–192). Hillsdale, NJ: Lawrence Erlbaum Associates.

Crosswhite, F. J., Dossey, J. A., Swafford, J. O., McKnight, C. C., & Cooney, T. J. (1985). *Second international mathematics study summary report for the United States.* Champaign, IL: Stipes.

Crump, T. (1990). *The anthropology of numbers.* New York: Cambridge University Press.

Dark, V. J., & Benbow, C. P. (1991). Differential enhancement of working memory with mathematical versus verbal precocity. *Journal of Educational Psychology, 83*, 48–60.

Davis, H., & Memmott, J. (1982). Counting behavior in animals: A critical evaluation. *Psychological Bulletin, 92*, 547–571.

Dye, N. W., & Very, P. S. (1968). Growth changes in factorial structure by age and sex. *Genetic Psychology Monographs, 78*, 55–88.

Eccles, J., Wigfield, A., Harold, R. D., & Blumenfeld, P. (1993). Age and gender differences in children's self- and task perceptions during elementary school. *Child Development, 64*, 830–847.

Eibl-Eibesfeldt, I. (1989). *Human ethology.* New York: deGruyter.

Ericsson, K. A., & Charness, N. (1994). Expert performance: Its structure and acquisition. *American Psychologist, 49*, 725–747.

Ericsson, K. A., Krampe, R. T., Tesch-Römer, C. (1993). The role of deliberate practice in the acquisition of expert performance. *Psychological Review, 100*, 363–406.

Fuson, K. C. (1988). *Children's counting and concepts of number.* New York: Springer-Verlag.

Fuson, K. C., & Kwon, Y. (1992). Korean children's understanding of multidigit addition and subtraction. *Child Development, 63*, 491–506.

Fuson, K. C., Stigler, J. W., & Bartsch, K. (1988). Grade placement of addition and subtraction problems in Japan, Mainland China, the Soviet Union, Taiwan, and the United States. *Journal for Research in Mathematics Education, 19*, 449–456.

Gallistel, C. R. (1990). *The organization of learning.* Cambridge, MA: MIT Press.

Gallistel, C. R., & Gelman, R. (1992). Preverbal and verbal counting and computation. *Cognition, 44*, 43–74.

Geary, D. C. (1994). *Children's mathematical development: Research and practical applications.* Washington, DC: American Psychological Association.

Geary, D. C. (1995). Reflections of evolution and culture in children's cognition: Implications for mathematical development and instruction. *American Psychologist, 50*, 24–37.

Geary, D. C. (1996). Sexual selection and sex differences in mathematical abilities. *Behavioral and Brain Sciences, 19*, xxx–xxx.

Geary, D. C., Bow-Thomas, C. C., Fan, L., & Siegler, R. S. (1993). Even before formal instruction, Chinese children outperform American children in mental addition. *Cognitive Development, 8*, 517–529.

Geary, D. C., Fan, L., & Bow-Thomas, C. C. (1992). Numerical cognition: Loci of ability differences comparing children from China and the United States. *Psychological Science, 3,* 180–185.

Geary, D. C., Salthouse, T. A., Chen, G. P., & Fan, L. (1996). Are East Asian versus American differences in arithmetical ability a recent phenomenon? *Developmentqal Psychology, 32,* 254–262.

Gelman, R. (1990). First principles organize attention to and learning about relevant data: Number and the animate–inanimate distinction as examples. *Cognitive Science, 14,* 79–106.

Gelman, R. (1993). A rational–constructivist account of early learning about numbers and objects. In D. L. Medin (Ed.), *The psychology of learning and motivation: Advances in research and theory* (Vol. 30, pp. 61–96). San Diego, CA: Academic Press.

Gelman, R., & Gallistel, C. R. (1978). *The child's understanding of number.* Cambridge, MA: Harvard University Press.

Ginsburg, H. P., Posner, J. K., & Russell, R. L. (1981). The development of mental addition as a function of schooling and culture. *Journal of Cross-Cultural Psychology, 12,* 163–178.

Gould, J. L. (1986). The locale map of honey bees: Do insects have cognitive maps? *Science, 232,* 861–863.

Gould, S. J., & Vrba, E. S. (1982). Exaptation—A missing term in the science of form. *Paleobiology, 8,* 4–15.

Greenough, W. T., Black, J. E., & Wallace, C. S. (1987). Experience and brain development. *Child Development, 58,* 539–559.

Guthrie, G. M. (1963). Structure of abilities in a non-Western culture. *Journal of Educational Psychology, 54,* 94–103.

Hatano, G. (1990). Toward the cultural psychology of mathematical cognition. Commentary on Stevenson, H. W., Lee, S. Y., Chen, C., Stigler, J. W., Hsu, C. C., & Kitamura, S. Contexts of achievement: A study of American, Chinese, and Japanese children. *Monographs of the Society for Research in Child Development, 55* (pp. 108–115, Serial No. 221).

Husén, T. (1967). *International study of achievement in mathematics: A comparison of twelve countries* (Vol. 1 & 2). New York: Wiley.

Johnson, E. S. (1984). Sex differences in problem solving. *Journal of Educational Psychology, 76,* 1359–1371.

Landau, B., Gleitman, H., & Spelke, E. (1981). Spatial knowledge and geometric representation in a child blind from birth. *Science, 213,* 1275–1278.

Lapointe, A. E., Mead, N. A., & Askew, J. M. (1992). *Learning mathematics.* Princeton, NJ: Educational Testing Service.

Lewis, A. B. (1989). Training students to represent arithmetic word problems. *Journal of Educational Psychology, 81,* 521–531.

Lynn, R. (1982). IQ in Japan and the United States shows a growing disparity. *Nature, 297,* 222–223.

Lynn, R. (1983). Reply to Stevenson and Azuma. *Nature, 306,* 292.

MacDonald, K. B. (1988). *Social and personality development: An evolutionary synthesis.* New York: Plenum.

Mayer, R. E. (1985). Mathematical ability. In R. J. Sternberg (Ed.), *Human abilities: An information-processing approach* (pp. 127–150). San Francisco, CA: Freeman.

McGuinness, D. (1993). Gender differences in cognitive style: Implications for mathematical performance and achievement. In L. A. Penner, G. M. Batsche, H. K. Knoff, & D. L. Nelson (Eds.), *The challenge in mathematics and science education: Psychology's response* (pp. 251–274). Washington, DC: American Psychological Association.

Miller, K. F. (1993, April). *U.S.–China differences in mathematical development: Preschool origins.* Presented at the annual meeting of the American Educational Research Association, New Orleans, LA.

Miller, K. F., Smith, C. M., Zhu, J., & Zhang, H. (1995). Preschool origins of cross-national differences in mathematical competence: The role of number naming systems. *Psychological Science, 6*, 56–60.

Miller, K. F., & Stigler, J. W. (1987). Counting in Chinese: Cultural variation in a basic cognitive skill. *Cognitive Development, 2*, 279–305.

Miller, M. D., & Linn, R. L. (1989). Cross-national achievement with differential retention rates. *Journal for Research in Mathematics Education, 20*, 28–40.

Osborne, R. T., & Lindsey, J. M. (1967). A longitudinal investigation of change in the factorial composition of intelligence with age in young school children. *Journal of Genetic Psychology, 110*, 49–58.

Panksepp, J., Siviy, S., & Normansell, L. (1984). The psychobiology of play: Theoretical and methodological perspectives. *Neuroscience and Biobehavioral Reviews, 8*, 465–492.

Pepperberg, I. M. (1987). Evidence for conceptual quantitative abilities in the African grey parrot: Labeling of cardinal sets. *Ethology, 75*, 37–61.

Pinker, S., & Bloom, P. (1990). Natural language and natural selection. *Behavioral and Brain Sciences, 13*, 707–784.

Rozin, P. (1976). The evolution of intelligence and access to the cognitive unconscious. In J. M. Sprague & A. N. Epstein (Eds.), *Progress in psychobiology and physiological psychology* (Vol. 6, pp. 245–280). New York: Academic Press.

Rozin, P., & Schull, J. (1988). The adaptive–evolutionary point of view in experimental psychology. In R. C. Atkinson, R. J. Herrnstein, G. Lindzey, & R. D. Luce (Eds.), *Steven's handbook of experimental psychology* (2nd ed.; Vol. 1, pp. 503–546). New York: Wiley.

Rubin, K. H., Fein, G. G., & Vandenberg, B. (1983). Play. In P. Mussen & E. M. Hetherington (Eds.), *Handbook of child psychology: Vol. 4. Socialization, personality, and social development* (pp. 693–774). New York: Wiley.

Rumbaugh, D. M., & Washburn, D. A. (1993). Counting by chimpanzees and ordinality judgments by macaques in video-formatted tasks. In S. T. Boysen & E. J. Capaldi (Eds.), *The development of numerical competence: Animal and human models* (pp. 87–106). Hillsdale, NJ: Lawrence Erlbaum Associates.

Rushton, J. P. (1992). Cranial capacity related to sex, rank, and race in a stratified random sample of 6,325 military personnel. *Intelligence, 16*, 401–413.

Rushton, J. P. (1995). *Race, evolution, and behavior: A life history perspective.* New Brunswick, NJ: Transaction Publishers.

Saxe, G. B. (1982). Culture and the development of numerical cognition: Studies among the Oksapmin of Papua New Guinea. In C. J. Brainerd (Ed.), *Children's logical and mathematical cognition: Progress in cognitive development research* (pp. 157–176). New York: Springer-Verlag.

Saxe, G. B., Guberman, S. R., & Gearhart, M. (1987). Social processes in early number development. *Monographs of the Society for Research in Child Development, 52* (No. 2, Serial No. 216).

Schoenfeld, A. H. (1985). *Mathematical problem solving.* San Diego, CA: Academic Press.

Shepard, R. N. (1994). Perceptual–cognitive universals as reflections of the world. *Psychonomic Bulletin & Review, 1*, 2–28.

Siegler, R. S., & Crowley, K. (1994). Constraints on learning in nonprivileged domains. *Cognitive Psychology, 27*, 194–226.

Song, M. J., & Ginsburg, H. P. (1987). The development of informal and formal mathematical thinking in Korean and U.S. children. *Child Development, 58*, 1286–1296.

Spearman, C. (1927). *The abilities of man.* London: MacMillan.

Starkey, P. (1992). The early development of numerical reasoning. *Cognition, 43*, 93–126.

Starkey, P., Spelke, E. S., & Gelman, R. (1983). Detection of intermodal numerical correspondences by human infants. *Science, 222*, 179–181.

Starkey, P., Spelke, E. S., & Gelman, R. (1990). Numerical abstraction by human infants. *Cognition, 36*, 97–127.

Stevenson, H. W., & Azuma, H. (1983). IQ in Japan and the United States. *Nature, 306*, 291–292.

Stevenson, H. W., Chen, C., & Lee, S. Y. (1993). Mathematics achievement of Chinese, Japanese, and American children: Ten years later. *Science, 259*, 53–58.

Stevenson, H. W., Lee, S. Y., Chen, C., Lummis, M., Stigler, J., Fan, L., & Ge, F. (1990). Mathematics achievement of children in China and the United States. *Child Development, 61*, 1053–1066.

Stevenson, H. W., Lee, S. Y., Chen, C., Stigler, J. W., Hsu, C. C., & Kitamura, S. (1990). Contexts of achievement: A study of American, Chinese, and Japanese children. *Monographs of the Society for Research in Child Development, 55*(Serial No. 221).

Stevenson, H. W., Lee, S. Y., & Stigler, J. W. (1986). Mathematics achievement of Chinese, Japanese, and American children. *Science, 231*, 693–699.

Stevenson, H. W., Parker, T., Wilkinson, A., Hegion, A., & Fish, E. (1976). Longitudinal study of individual differences in cognitive development and scholastic achievement. *Journal of Educational Psychology, 68*, 377–400.

Stevenson, H. W., & Stigler, J. W. (1992). *The learning gap: Why our schools are failing and what we can learn from Japanese and Chinese education.* New York: Summit.

Stevenson, H. W., Stigler, J. W., Lee, S. Y., Lucker, G. W., Kitamura, S., & Hsu, C. C. (1985). Cognitive performance and academic achievement of Japanese, Chinese, and American children. *Child Development, 56*, 718–734.

Stigler, J. W., Lee, S. Y., Lucker, G. W., & Stevenson, H. W. (1982). Curriculum and achievement in mathematics: A study of elementary school children in Japan, Taiwan, and the United States. *Journal of Educational Psychology, 74*, 315–322.

Strauss, M. S., & Curtis, L. E. (1984). Development of numerical concepts in infancy. In C. Sophian (Ed.), *Origins of cognitive skills: The eighteenth Carnegie Symposium on cognition* (pp. 131–155). Hillsdale, NJ: Lawrence Erlbaum Associates.

Thompson, R. F., Mayers, K. S., Robertson, R. T., & Patterson, C. J. (1970). Number coding in association cortex of the cat. *Science, 168*, 271–273.

Thurstone, L. L. (1938). Primary mental abilities. *Psychometric Monographs* (No. 1).

Thurstone, L. L., & Thurstone, T. G. (1941). Factorial studies of intelligence. *Psychometric Monographs* (No. 2).

Vandenberg, S. G. (1959). The primary mental abilities of Chinese students: A comparative study of the stability of a factor structure. *Annals of the New York Academy of Sciences, 79*, 257–304.

Vandenberg, S. G. (1962). The hereditary abilities study: Hereditary components in a psychological test battery. *American Journal of Human Genetics, 14*, 220–237.

Vandenberg, S. G. (1966). Contributions of twin research to psychology. *Psychological Bulletin, 66*, 327–352.

Very, P. S. (1967). Differential factor structures in mathematical ability. *Genetic Psychology Monographs, 75*, 169–207.

Washburn, D. A., & Rumbaugh, D. M. (1991). Ordinal judgments of numerical symbols by macaques (*Macaca mulatta*). *Psychological Science, 2*, 190–193.

Wechsler, D. (1974). *Manual for the Wechsler Intelligence Scale for Children–Revised.* New York: Psychological Corporation.

West, B. H., Griesbach, E. N., Taylor, J. D., & Taylor, L. T. (1982). *The Prentice-Hall encyclopedia of mathematics.* Englewood Cliffs, NJ: Prentice-Hall.

Whiting, B. B., & Whiting, J. W. M. (1975). *Children of six cultures: A psycho–cultural analysis.* Cambridge, MA: Harvard University Press.

Witelson, S. E. (1987). Neurobiological aspects of language in children. *Child Development, 58,* 653–688.

Wynn, K. (1992). Addition and subtraction by human infants. *Nature, 358,* 749–750.

Zaslavsky, C. (1973). *Africa counts: Number and pattern in African culture.* Boston, MA: Prindle, Weber, & Schmidt.

COGNITIVE/EDUCATIONAL
APPROACHES

7

▼▼▼▼▼▼▼

Toby's Math

Herbert P. Ginsburg
Teachers College, Columbia University

This chapter is a description and celebration of Toby's math, about 30 minutes of it, as captured in a clinical interview I conducted one day in her school. Toby was a first grader, 6 years old when I interviewed her, an unexceptional girl—which does not mean that she was unremarkable or uninteresting, but that she was typical of children her age. She was not considered extremely intelligent or an outstanding student. In my experience, she performed at about the same level as most first graders; she did not display remarkable insights or especially brilliant strategies; she did not make outrageous blunders. She could properly be called average. She was both White and middle class, but I mention this only to discount it: I believe that her basic approach to mathematical thinking, her experiences, her feelings about math all transcend boundaries of race and class. In key respects, poor African American or Hispanic children are basically no different from Toby. In describing and celebrating Toby's math, I aim to help you appreciate the minds and struggles of all children as they encounter the math taught in school.

THE STAGE AND ITS PLAYERS

My relationship with Toby was unusual. I had received permission from her school to make a series of videotaped interviews that day with children from the first through fourth grades. My plan was to use these interviews, if they turned out well, as material for a series of "video workshops" designed to

175

help teachers understand the nature of children's mathematical thinking (Ginsburg, Kaplan, & Baroody, 1992). Teachers would view the tapes, attempt to interpret them, and in the process learn something important about children. I was not Toby's teacher; I was not a psychologist attempting to help her; and I was not even assuming my usual role of a psychologist "studying" her. I was essentially trying to arrange a "performance" that would bring alive basic aspects of children's mathematical thinking. Acting as a kind of producer, I wanted Toby to act in ways that would fascinate teachers, that would reflect the basics of children's minds grappling with mathematics, that would illustrate the key phenomena of mathematical thinking as revealed by contemporary research.

My basic plan was to conduct an informal "clinical interview" that would explore the thinking behind Toby's school work and map out her underlying strategies and concepts. There were a few topics I knew that I would cover—like her strategies for mental addition, and her understanding of place value—but for the most part I was prepared to go with the flow, following up on whatever seemed interesting, and letting her responses determine the course of the interview.[1]

The room, normally the school's "resource center" in which children received extra help in reading, math, and the like, was set up for videotaping. Toby and I were to sit at a small round table. In front of us was a rather large video camera, operated by an assistant. Also present in the room, and clearly visible to Toby, was an associate who observed the interviews and occasionally made suggestions about topics I might cover or questions I might ask.[2] Announcements occasionally intruded over the loudspeaker system that no one in the school could avoid. A phone rang now and then.

Although we familiarized Toby with the video camera (after all, it is no longer very strange to many children) and, as you will see, tried to explain the purpose of the interview, from the child's point of view the whole situation was most unusual, and indeed must have been virtually unintelligible. Video cameras? Three adults in the resource room? Talking about math? What was this all about?

HELLO, TOBY

Before Toby entered the room, I had written on the board "Children's Math," which was to be the name of our imaginary television show. I began with a theatrical introduction including fanfare:

---

[1]This kind of control by the child is exactly the opposite of what occurs in standardized testing and is what defines the essence of the clinical interview.

[2]Rochelle Kaplan was my "director," and Takashi Yamamoto operated the camera.

Herbert Ginsburg (H): Let's start here . . . this is a show and it's on now? Let's have a little music, Toby. Da da da da—Welcome to Children's Math. [I point at "Children's Math" written on the board.] And Toby wrote her name on the board. [I then ask the camera operator whether he had got a picture of Toby's name, and then direct him to turn the camera back on us.] All right. Very good. Now we come over here and I say, "Hi, Toby, how old are you?"

Toby (T): Six.

H: Six years old. And what grade are you in?

T: First.

H: How do you like that? I already knew that already, didn't I?

Now this could easily be construed as bizarre. I won't elaborate on my reasons for doing it, except to say that this rather strange behavior was an attempt to put the child at ease, to set up a relaxed atmosphere.[3] In effect, I was saying to her, or trying to say to her, "This is a special, unusual event, different from school. You don't have to act here the way you do in school. We can laugh and have some fun."

What did Toby think of all this? Imagine the expectations with which she arrived at the interview. She must have thought that we would be doing something related to schoolwork and that as an adult I would act in a serious and task-oriented way. However, here I was making odd music, talking about television shows (which was actually the literal truth), and commenting on how I already knew the answer to the questions I had asked.[4] No doubt, the first seconds of introduction probably only served to violate her expectancies about what might and should happen in interaction with an adult in a school setting. Toby seemed bewildered, not knowing what to make of me.

I continued to put my foot in my mouth:

H: OK, and what we're going to do today is to do some fun math things. OK? And we'll start off real easy by asking you to count, as high as you can. Let's hear you count.

What did this mean to her? For many children the idea of "fun math things" is an oxymoron. Also, you can't *tell* children that something is going

---

[3]In my book *Entering the Child's Mind: The Cognitive Clinical Interview in Psychological Research and Practice* (in press), I describe the interaction with Toby from the point of view of what I was trying to accomplish as an interviewer, and the social psychology of the interview. Here we focus, however, on what it all meant to Toby.

[4]Actually, teachers frequently ask questions to which they already know the answers, as in "How much is two plus two?" However, teachers do not comment, semisarcastically, that they know the answer, thus implying that the question was improperly asked and that a command would have been more honest ("Tell me how much is two plus two. I already know. I want to see if you do.").

to be fun; you have to show them. Further, the statement that we would "start off real easy" might have unsettled her a bit. She might have interpreted it as saying, "You better do well at this; if you don't, I will think that you are a real dummy." Perhaps my (well-intentioned) remarks served only to put pressure on Toby. If she had then experienced difficulty with the counting task, she would have felt very badly and would probably have been terrified of the harder things that might be expected to follow.

Up to this point (which was less than a minute into the interview), Toby's overt response was very limited (mostly because she hadn't had much of a chance to say anything). In fact, Toby had said only two words, "Six" and "First" (both extremely important for an interview on mathematics), whereas I said approximately 111. This ratio of adult-to-child talk does not bode well for a situation in which the child is encouraged to reveal *her* thinking. What was going on in her mind? Perhaps, "What in the world is this person doing?"

Well, we were probably not off to a great start, and I do not offer this interaction as a primer on how to interview, but it does teach us important lessons. First, real contact between children and adults is very hard to achieve. It is not easy for an adult to enter the child's mind, to establish a relationship that allows and indeed encourages the child to reveal his or her genuine thinking. After all, I was not engaged in some rigid form of standard testing; experienced in interviewing, I was trying to engage her in an enjoyable way. But children are a world apart, and we adults—acting as psychologists or parents—should not think that we can easily enter and understand it.

Second, we should not underestimate the extent to which children have to put up with various forms of nonsense from adults, especially in schools. Adults run schools; children do not. Adults impose their points of view, their desires. If I think a television show needs to be made, then Toby must participate, even if she could not reasonably anticipate any benefit to her; it is just another thing adults tell her to do. Yet she continued to sit there, she was patient, she tried to help. So that is the first thing we celebrate: Toby's good will and tolerance.[5]

COUNTING GAMES

Asked to count "as high as you can," Toby shrugged her shoulders as if to indicate that she did indeed think the task would be easy. Beginning with "one," she counted deliberately, showing little emotion until she reached about "twelve," when she allowed herself a slight smile. Then she plodded

---

[5]Of course, the danger is that they can turn into mindless compliance. However, we are not talking of dangers here.

on, counting correctly, occasionally pausing and taking deep breaths, chugging along like the little engine that could, stoically exhibiting her competence. Perhaps she found the task a bit boring, but it allowed her to show what she could do. Eventually she reached "forty-four," whereupon I stopped her.

Learning to say the counting numbers (so far, her counting activities have nothing to do with objects; she is not counting *things* but saying *words*), can be seen as a linguistic game involving two separate goals. When the child first encounters counting, usually at the age of 2 years, the first goal is to memorize nonsense material. In all languages, the sequence of the initial counting numbers (usually about 10 of them) displays no rhyme or reason; it is quite arbitrary. In English, we say, "One, two, three . . ." There is no logical reason why the first number in English could not be "three" and second, "one," and the third "two."[6] Moreover, at first these counting numbers may have no meaning whatsoever, except that adults seem to like to say them, sing songs and make rhymes about them ("One, two, buckle my shoe"), and evidently want the child to learn them. For the young child, at 2 or 3 years of age, just learning to "speak math," the first task then is pure memorization of rote and meaningless material.[7]

Therefore, learning the counting words is not learning *math*. It is a kind of language game, like learning a song, which also must be rendered in a particular sequence (we do not sing "lamb Mary little a had"); it is a game of memorization in the absence of meaning.

Children around the world play this game. Almost every language of which we know uses counting words, and most often, as in English, the sequence of the first 10 or so counting words is completely arbitrary. Indeed, children in virtually every culture we know of learn the counting words early on. All normal children speak this kind of math; you can count on it. After all, humans are language learners, and the capacity to learn language may be considered a key aspect of our human biology.

---

[6]Of course, each individual word bears an arbitrary relation to its referent, as do most words: There is no inherent reason why the first three numbers in English should be "one, two, three," rather than "bik, mur, div," or "tres, deux, ein," in that order.

[7]Indeed, at the outset, the 2- or 3-year-old child may not even perceive each counting word as a separate, distinct entity different from the other counting words. In reality, when adults say the counting words, or utter any other kind of speech, the words normally blend into each other. They are not clearly segmented, and the adult is more likely to say, "Onetwothreefour . . ." than to place clear "space" between them. Under conditions like these, the counting "words" may be considered as a kind of song to be sung, much as the child parrots back "My country tizofthee" or sings other songs the meaning of which is obscure. The words gradually emerge from the undifferentiated mass (a kind of "blooming, buzzing confusion") only after considerable perceptual learning. The child needs to learn what the units (words) are, that each is separate from the others, and that all are different from one another. With practice, the child learns to detect the differences among words, just as one learns to taste the differences among wines previously indistinguishable.

Then the game changes. After about 10 or so, the counting sequence is no longer quite so arbitrary. Indeed, in some languages it becomes entirely orderly. In Chinese and other East Asian languages based on it, the sequence of the first 10 words is as nonsensical as in English. But then a regular pattern is introduced. The Chinese say the equivalent of "ten-one, ten-two, ten-three . . . ten-nine," up to our 20, for which they say the equivalent of "two-ten." Then they go on to say, "Two-ten-one, two-ten-two . . . two-ten-nine." After that comes, "Three-ten, three-ten-one, three-ten-two . . ." and so on, all the way up to "nine-ten-nine." What could be more orderly and systematic! The Chinese *talk base-10*; they say the numbers as if written in expanded notation: (1[10] + 1), (1[10] + 2), all the way up to (9[10] + 9).

In English, there is a pattern too, but it is not as elegant as the Chinese. In fact, it seems designed to confuse children at the outset. After the first 10 arbitrary numbers, English introduces two more—"eleven, twelve." They give little clue, if any, to the sequence, and so English speaking children have to memorize two more meaningless sounds to continue the sequence.[8] Next a sequence emerges, but it is strange: "thirteen" resembles "three-ten," "four-teen" is like "four-ten," "fifteen" like "five-ten," and so on very clearly until "nineteen" (aka "nine-ten"). It is as if English were speaking base-10 "back-wards." In expanded notation, the English "teens" words would be written (3 + 1[10]), (4 + 1[10]), up to (9 + 1[10]).[9]

From the point of view of an English-speaking child, the language game has shifted. After learning the meaningless song, "One, two . . . ten, eleven, twelve," the child must now try to learn a reverse base-10 pattern ("thirteen, fourteen . . . nineteen"). Of course children could try to memorize this too as a meaningless song, and some do. However, most children see quickly that there is a pattern and try to learn it. Why? Perhaps they see that it makes the task easier. After all, memorizing the rules underlying the pattern (say the "units" word first and then the "teen" word) requires less mental effort and "storage space" than memorizing all of the individual terms. (Think of it: you can count on indefinitely starting at "one million, five hundred forty-four" even though you have never memorized those particular counting words.) Or perhaps children pick up the pattern because they are pattern detectors; that is, human minds are so constituted as to make every effort to detect regularities in the environment, including the language environment.

---

[8]According to Webster's, "eleven" derives from an old Anglo-Saxon construction that meant literally "one left over (after ten)." Similarly, "twelve" derives from a word that meant "two left after ten." The base-10 idea was clear in the original construction of these words; over time, shortening and otherwise modifying the words obscured their meaning.

[9]German follows this "backwards" order: "ein-und-zwanzig," etc.

Now if English asked children to learn only the reverse base-10 pattern, I would not complain. There is nothing inherently wrong in saying "fourteen," writing it as 41, and in expanded notation as (4 + 1[10]). However, English is patently unfair in its inconsistency: As soon as children get up to "twenty," English reverses the pattern to something approximating the Chinese. (The main difference is that English decade words are not as transparent as their Chinese counterparts. Being circumspect, we Westerners say "fifty," whereas the Chinese don't beat around the bush, and come out with a bold "five-ten.")

So English-speaking children are faced really with several counting language tasks: memorize the initial arbitrary sequence, learn the pattern that follows, and then reverse it to get the next pattern. From the child's point of view, a crazy language world?[10]

BUGS

Recall that Toby had counted well up to 44 when I stopped her. At that point, I thought her counting was very smooth, and I figured that she might get bored if I simply let her count on and on. Therefore, I used my prerogative as a clinical interviewer (standard testers must deny themselves this flexibility) and skipped ahead to find out whether she would have trouble with some of the higher numbers:

H: OK, why don't you start now with 87. Just keep going from 87.
T: 87, 88, eighty niiiiiine—[Long pause.] A hundred?
H: OK, keep going.

On reaching 89, Toby clearly knew she was in trouble. She dragged out 89—"eighty niiiiiine"—as if she were buying time to figure out what came next and needed help. In saying, "A hundred?" she raised her voice as if asking a question. She went on successfully to 109, and again raised her voice as if asking me whether she was correct. Clearly, the transition was giving her trouble.

Toby had reached her counting limit and knew it. With a shrug and nervous laugh, she indicated that she had reached the end of the line (her whole number line, one might say):

---

[10]In a sense, all language is a little crazy in this way. All words bear an arbitrary relation to their referents (a "dog" could just as easily be called "cat" or "bear," although at first children do not seem to believe this). Although language contains many regularities ("I walked, I talked") which children pick up very easily, it also suffers from many irregularities (We say "I went" not "I goed").

T: That's all.

H: That's all. Oh, wow, you counted real high. OK?

She did not look too happy; however, I wanted to find out more about her counting. Recall that she first encountered difficulty when she was asked to count in the 80s—"87, 88, eighty niiiiiine. . . ." Research has shown that "decade transitions"—that is, going from 59 to the new decade, 60, or from 89 to 90—are especially difficult for children (Fuson, 1988). They learn quickly that once one has entered a new decade—whether 30 or 80—the correct procedure is to add on the "one, two, three . . ." that are already well known. The problem is to say the new decade. Once you figure out what comes after 39, you can easily go further. But what comes after 39?

Faced with this dilemma, children usually make a guess based on a sensible rule. After "thirty-nine" comes "thirty-ten." Why not? "Ten" normally comes right after "nine," and forty really is thirty-ten. Believing that Toby would be likely to make "errors" of this sort, I set out to test the hypothesis:

H: What if I tell you some numbers now and you tell me what comes next. OK. Like if I said, 1, 2 . . . you would say . . .

T: Three

H: OK. 57, 58. . . .

T: [jumps in quickly with]: 59

H: OK . . . ah . . . 68, 69 . . .

T: [hesitates a little]: 70.

H: Aaaahhh . . . 84, 85 . . .

T: 86.

H: . . . 87, 88 . . .

T: 89.

H: 89 . . .

T: Eighty-tennnn . . .

Almost all children do this, and it is a good thing that they do. It indicates that they are trying to make sense of the often strange (to them) world of numbers. Constantly on the alert for regularities, they use the patterns they find to deal with new problems. Toby knows that "ten" normally follows "nine." Faced with a situation in which counting on from a nine (the nine in 89) is the problem, she does the only thing sensible under the circumstances and given her limited knowledge: she "guesses"—or, better still, hypothe- sizes—that a "ten" must follow. Of course, it's the wrong answer, and we want her to learn the right one, but at least she is responding to a difficulty by making a reasonable hypothesis from the available data. She uses what she knows to make sense of the world of mathematics.

We say that Toby was using a "buggy" procedure; that is, a flawed strategy that systematically leads to error.[11] One of the clearest examples of such a bug is:

$$\begin{array}{r} 12 \\ -4 \\ \hline 12 \end{array}$$

How can you subtract 4 from 12 and get 12? Almost any first grader knows that if you start with 12 eggs and take 4 away you don't end up with 12! A child can get an answer like this because he or she is not trying to solve a real problem about removing eggs from a carton. Instead, the child is solving a *math* problem, and is using the buggy strategy—"always subtract the smaller number from the larger one." The child believes that because one cannot take away a larger number from a smaller, 2 must be subtracted from 4, which of course gives 2. Then take away nothing from 1, which of course gives 1, so that the answer must be 12. What could be more logical? You could say that the child is making sense out of a new kind of subtraction problem by assimilating it into what he or she already knows about math. Indeed, the teacher may have *said*, "Always subtract the smaller from the larger." The child's "knowledge" may well stem from a misinterpretation of the teacher's remarks, but the bug results from an attempt to make sense of new problems, given the (faulty) knowledge available.

Unfortunately, many teachers do not look below the surface of wrong answers, and simply accept them as such. Many teachers think that a wrong answer is simply a wrong answer. They do not realize that the child's wrong answer can be an intelligent answer, a sense-making effort. Indeed, we might even say that in a sense a wrong answer may be a correct answer to a different question. Suppose the question were, "What would follow 89 if 90 is not an option?" Then Toby's answer, basically 80 + 10, would be considered quite correct. Many teachers take wrong answers to indicate a lack of knowledge of mathematics or even stupidity. However, that may not be the case: Wrong answers of this type may well indicate an attempt at sensemaking, an effort

---

[11]The notion of "bugs" has a long and interesting history. Early in the 20th century, Buswell and John (1926) discussed children's "bad habits" in arithmetic, and in fact described many of the same "bugs" that can easily be observed today. Later, Erlwanger (1975) described "bugs" in the famous (at least in some circles) case of Benny, and I described them in the first edition of my book on children's mathematical thinking (Ginsburg, 1977). "Bugs" is a computer term that originated from the fact that real bugs (roaches, etc.) got into the innards of the vacuum tubes of old computers and caused systematic errors. Probably the most frequently cited example of work on bugs is that of Brown and VanLehn (1982).

at intelligent response. Of course, not all wrong answers are "intelligent" bugs like these. Some wrong answers result from wild guesses, and others from mere sloppiness; however, some errors result clearly from systematic strategies and principles, like Toby's "eighty-ten," or the answer 12 to the problem 12 − 4.

Therefore, counting has several interesting features. We have seen that at first counting is a rote activity, but then evolves into a search for patterns—a search made all the more difficult by the fact that the English language begins with one system for arranging numbers but then soon switches to the opposite. We also saw that Toby responded to a difficulty—the problem posed by the need to go from one decade to another—with a "bug," a wrong answer based on a systematically flawed strategy. Bugs like these can be interpreted as the child's attempt to make sense of the world of numbers.

RIGHT AND WRONG

When Toby claimed that 100 followed 89, I said, "OK, keep going," and when she did not know what comes after 109, I again did not criticize her, instead saying, "That's all. Oh, wow, you counted real high. OK?" Later, when Toby claimed that "eighty-ten" followed 89, I simply repeated "eighty-ten," as if it were correct, and asked for the next response. And at the very end of the counting sequence, I tried again to comfort her by using the same kind of remark made earlier: "Those are really big numbers, I mean that's very, very high." Although I never criticized Toby for getting the wrong answer, I never exactly told her that she was correct either.

I think Toby knew that she was wrong. She indicated her discomfort in various ways: She frowned, she shrugged her shoulders, she grimaced; she did not look too happy. Perhaps my failure to say, "That's right," led her to believe that she had made a mistake. Or perhaps something else, perhaps something in my tone of voice, caused her to feel uncertain of her response. In any event, she knew that she did not really know.

Children are overly sensitive to being wrong. To some extent, this stems from their psychology. As Piaget pointed out, the "egocentrism" of young children leads them to see the world in terms of black and white, yes and no, right and wrong. Subtleties are beyond them. In a similar vein, Freud attributed to young children a rigid, harsh superego: they see a trivial mistake as a sin, a transgression deserving of punishment.

In school, teachers often seem to reinforce this tendency. One of the first things they usually convey to children is that the world of mathematics can be divided into right and wrong answers, and that the essence of doing math is getting the right ones. In this view, math is learning that 3 comes after 2, and that the answer to 2 + 2 is 4. The focus on right and wrong is communicated in many ways. For one thing, a good deal of the curriculum during the early grades involves the grim exercise of learning—over and over again—the number facts for addition, subtraction, multiplication, and division. For another, the teacher ordinarily does not ask a question unless its purpose is to discover whether the child can produce a particular right answer. (The teacher almost never asks a math question because he or she does not know the answer!) All this serves to magnify children's natural egocentrism as it applies to mathematics, and to create a harsh mathematical superego. In this type of Manichean classroom of mathematical good and evil, a wrong answer can be devastating for the child: He or she should have known the answer or the teacher would not have asked for it in the first place.

If this is so, then Toby might have interpreted her inability to count beyond 109 as failure. She did not yet know—if she ever will—that the essence of mathematics is not producing correct answers, but thinking creatively. She did not yet know—although she would have the opportunity to learn it—that in the cognitive clinical interview, I would give her difficult and challenging problems, and would be more interested in her ways of attempting to solve them than in the correctness of the answers. And she also did not know that, according to the norms, her counting level was at least as good as that of other first graders.

FIGURING IT OUT

Now that I had established that Toby could count reasonably well—even though *she* may not have believed it and therefore felt badly about her performance—I decided to increase the level of difficulty and explore what she could do with simple series of numbers:

> *H:* Can you count by twos? 2, 4 [Toby nods], 6 . . . keep going.
> *T:* [As if reciting a song] 2, 4, 6, 8, 10, 12 [Hesitates at 12] . . .

It seemed as if Toby did not know what came next. I put her on the spot by saying nothing and letting her sit in silence. Her arm disappeared into her sleeve and there was a long pause:

> *H:* What do you think comes after 12? 10, 12 . . .

Again I paused and let her sit in silence. She could only shrug:

> *H:* 15?

I gave her this wrong answer to see if she would grasp at any straw. She nodded slowly, as if to indicate tentative agreement; but she was clearly not sure of herself. At this point it would have been easy and reasonable to conclude that she did not know anything about *constructing* sequences of 2. She could sing the "twos song" up to 12, but could not invent new lyrics after that.

It is important to put her failure into perspective. In math classes, children are seldom encouraged to think. In far too many schools, children learn that mathematics, as well as other subjects, do not make a great deal of sense, and that getting the "right answer" involves memory or the use of some arbitrary procedure. As I argued earlier, a good deal of the elementary mathematics curriculum is often devoted to the memorization of number facts. The child learns to respond quickly, correctly, and without thinking to number fact problems ("How much is 8 + 9?") presented on flash cards or the computer equivalent thereof (as 8 + 9 flashes on the screen, the child must type in the correct answer to prevent a rocket from blowing up some thing or other). Indeed, I believe it is no exaggeration to say that children may learn from repeated experiences like these the following lesson: Mathematics is that subject in which one is expected to obtain the correct answer quickly and without thought (which can be considered cheating).

With this in mind, I interpreted Toby's initial success ("2, 4, 6, 8, 10, 12") as rote memory, and her subsequent failure as indicating that she had never been expected to understand the logic of the series. Further, I expected that she might be able to solve the problem if she were encouraged to think about it.

I therefore introduced a new rule of the game: If you don't know the answer, try to figure it out:

H: Maybe. How could you figure it out? Suppose you do 10, 12 . . . how could you find out what comes next?

T: [She shrugs.]

H: You know like what comes . . . well after 12 is what? Is . . .

T: 13. [Quietly]

H: 13 . . . after 13 is . . .

T: 14.

H: OK . . . now how, if you're counting by twos, and you're at 12 . . .

T: 15 . . .

H: Yeah . . .

T: . . . 18 . . .

H: Uh-huh . . .

T: . . . 21 [Nods as she says this.] . . . 24 . . . 26 . . .

H: Uh-huh. . .

T: . . . 28 . . . 31 . . . 34 . . . [She nods as she says each number]

Now this was quite a surprise. Given the encouragement to "figure it out," Toby seemed to enter easily into the new form of discourse. And in doing so, she demonstrated a surprising degree of competence—more than she might have otherwise exhibited. Her "mistakes" (12, 15, 18, 21, 24) showed that she was capable of thinking; it is not easy for a first grader to produce a series increasing by threes. Indeed, her mistakes were more interesting and creative than her initial success, which was limited to the mere parroting of what was probably meaningless material (2, 4, 6 . . . 12).

It was now clear that Toby was thinking, but what was she up to? At first, her series involved threes, but then she seemed to shift to twos (24, 26, 28) before returning to threes (28, 31, 34). The flexibility of the clinical interview had allowed me to discover something, but I wasn't sure what it meant.

Consequently, I attempted to focus Toby's attention on how she "figured it out." I wanted her to introspect about her method and to report it to me:

> *H:* OK, now say you're at 31, and you say the next one is 34, how did you know that 34 comes next?
> *T:* 'Cause I was counting by [Holds up two fingers.] um . . . this . . . I was skipping two of them.

At this point, Toby was visibly excited. I interpreted this as indicating that she had succeeded in finding a sensible method for solving a problem, was happy that it worked (at least she thought it did), and was thrilled both that I was interested in her thinking and that she was competent at solving problems. Indeed, I think that this was the turning point of the interview. Now she knew what I meant about figuring out a problem in a sensible way that she created (as opposed to using a method which was imposed by the teacher and seemed to make no sense)—and she enjoyed solving problems in this way.

"I WAS LIKE TALKING TO MYSELF"

She was also able to "introspect"; that is, to examine her own thinking, and then to tell me something of how she had solved the problem. She had said, "'Cause I was counting by um . . . this . . . I was skipping two of them." This wasn't a bad description, but as part of the interview process, I wanted Toby to work on introspection and its expression. I persisted in encouraging Toby to express her thought as explicitly as possible:

> *H:* Tell me out loud how you do it. So, suppose you had, what was it, 31? [She nods] How would you do it? Tell me out loud how you would think to yourself.

T: [Jumps in quickly; looks straight ahead into space.] I was like, thinking like . . .

H: Yeah, like how?

T: . . . 31, 32, 33 . . . [Turns to the interviewer.] I was like talking to myself.

H: Ah-ha . . . so what did you say to yourself when you were talking to yourself?

T: I was saying . . . I was like skipping two, and then saying the next one, and then skipping two and saying the next one. [She gestures with her hands as she explains.]

H: Ooooo-K, so if you're at 31 you'd go . . .

T: 34 . . . [Nods]

H: 'Cause you skipped . . . thirty . . . thirty-two and thirty-three. [She nods slowly.]

At this point, she had said everything she was going to say about her solving the problem, but I made a mistake and for a while kept pressing her to say more. I will spare you the details. In retrospect I cannot imagine what else she could have said. In any event, she was so happy about what she was doing that the badgering did not upset her.

Research has shown that introspection and its expression are very difficult for young children.[12] It seems to be the case that young children seldom engage in spontaneous introspection, or at least they do not tell people about it. I wonder, however, whether they cannot easily learn to introspect and talk about it. I have observed that in the course of clinical interviews, which often last a half hour or so, many young children "catch on" to the introspection game and learn to talk, with various degrees of clarity, about their mental processes. Therefore, perhaps competence in introspection lies dormant in young children.

This possibility leads to a modest proposal. A major feature of mathematics education—and indeed education in general—should be introspection and its expression. Mathematics is a way of thinking. Learning mathematics should involve learning to think. Part of learning to think involves "metacognition"—the ability to reflect on one's thinking. The thinker should be able to access, examine, and describe his or her thought processes so as to improve on them. Therefore, from the very outset the mathematics curriculum should at least in part include training in introspection and its expression. First graders should learn not only how to add, but how to introspect about how they add and to describe the method to others. The discussion in the

---

[12]Piaget's (1964) earliest work proposed that the young child experiences difficulty at introspection, and his later research reinforces this finding (Piaget, 1976).

classroom should not revolve around "How much is 5 + 8?" but around "How did you figure out how much is 5 + 8?" Children should be schooled, among other things, in the language of introspection.[13] After all, the description of mental states is very tricky: What does "think" mean to you? In fact, one might almost say that the focus of the mathematics curriculum should not be *mathematics* (in the sense of a fixed body of knowledge), but *thinking and introspection about mathematics.*

The real mathematical mind is a thinking mind, an introspecting mind, and that is what schools should teach.

TOBY'S PROBLEM

At this point a little over 6 minutes had passed, and I knew that Toby could count reasonably well, could devise sensible strategies, and was excited about thinking about math and telling me about it. Next I wanted to investigate Toby's understanding of informal addition, a basic mathematical concept:

> *H:* Now, we're going to do something a little different, OK? [She nods.] We have two friends here that you looked at before . . . [Interviewer puts two small animal figures on the table.]
>
> *T:* Ohhh, they're so cute . . . [She is very excited about working with the animals.]
>
> *H:* OK what is this? [Points to one of the animals.]
>
> *T:* Rabbit.
>
> *H:* Uh-huh, rabbit and . . .
>
> *T:* A squirrel.
>
> *H:* A squirrel. OK. Now rabbit had five carrots. We're going to make believe rabbit has five carrots and squirrel has three carrots. OK? [She giggles.] What's so funny? A squirrel likes carrots?
>
> *T:* Nuts. [Giggles.]
>
> *H:* Yeah well, this squirrel likes carrots. OK? All right . . . so rabbit has how many carrots? [pause] Five, remember he had five, and squirrel has . . .
>
> *T:* Two.

I took care to remind Toby of the basic facts of the problem:

> *H:* Three, OK . . . so rabbit has five carrots, squirrel has three carrots, how many do they have all together?

---

[13]My colleagues and I have been working with teachers to implement this kind of classroom (Ginsburg, Jacobs, & Lopez, 1993).

T: Seven.

Following the basic rules of clinical interviewing, I accepted Toby's answer without comment, and inquired into her method of solution:

H: Seven! How did you know that?
T: I counted before you asked [very proud of herself]; I knew you were going to ask me that!

Note that Toby had learned very clearly that I was interested in her thinking and that I would ask her about it. And she was very pleased to engage in this kind of activity. I wonder if she thought of it as math:

H: You knew that! Ohhh . . . how did you count?
T: I counted like, there were seven . . .
H: No, five and three, tell me how you do it.

Again Toby got the terms of the problem wrong. She now wanted to transform it into seven and three:

T: Five and three. I counted seven, I counted three [uses hands to gesture towards each animal; looks at interviewer].

Again I wanted to bring her back to the "real" problem, five and three. So I reminded her again of the basic terms:

H: Five and three . . . can you do that out loud for me, how you get seven?
T: I thought, like, seven, I was thinking, seven plus three and I got ten . . .
H: You got ten! Seven plus. . . . How do you get ten if you do seven plus three . . . I mean do it out loud for me, count out loud for me.
T: I had seven . . .
H: Uh-huh, and then what do you do?
T: I have three, so that makes ten. [She gestures that she counts on her fingers.]
H: Oh you do it on your fingers? [She nods.] OK. Can you do five plus three for me now?
T: Eight.

Two aspects of this interaction are fundamental and deserve comment. One is that Toby added by using the method children this age usually use;

namely, counting. Some children do this "in their heads"; some do it on their fingers. Some children count on from the smaller number (in this case, "three . . . four, five, six, seven, eight, nine, ten") and some children, like Toby, do what is more efficient, namely counting on from the larger number ("seven . . . eight, nine, ten"). Children develop these strategies whether or not they attend school (Ginsburg, Posner, & Russell, 1981), and they gravitate toward the more efficient method (counting on) without the benefit of instruction (Groen & Resnick, 1977). Indeed, many teachers discourage the use of methods like these, especially adding on the fingers, on the grounds that they are a form of "cheating," or are immature, and prefer that instead children memorize the number facts (remember that mathematics is often seen as that subject in which one is expected to obtain the correct answer quickly and without thought, especially finger thought).

A second, and perhaps more interesting aspect of the observation, was that at the outset, Toby did not want to deal with *my* problem, five plus three. I do not know why, but she insisted in transforming my problem into something else. I resisted her. I insisted that she do five plus three, but she resisted too. Eventually, by sheer persistence, she transformed the problem into what she had in mind—namely, seven plus three—and got the right answer. Then, having done what she wanted to do, she allowed herself to consider my problem, five plus three, and easily solved it! If I had judged her ability by her initial performance on *my* problem, I would have concluded that she was not very competent. However, when *she* was allowed to choose the problem her competence was manifest.

It is a general rule of constructivism that children often do not deal with the interviewer's (or teacher's) problem. Instead, they construct and attempt to solve their own version of the problem. Moreover, they often believe that what they have in mind is what the adult had in mind!

EXPLANATION AND ACCURACY

Soon after this, I gave Toby a simple mental addition problem:

H: How much is three plus four?
T: Six.
H: Uh-huh, how did you know that?
T: I was like thinking and counting . . .
H: Thinking and counting at the same time? Can you do that out loud for me, how you do three plus four?
T: I had three in my head . . .
H: Uh-huh . . .

T: ... and I had four in my head ...

H: Uh-huh ...

T: ... so I had three plus four ... [she again uses her fingers to count] ... three, four, five, six, seven ... seven.

Note that Toby used the addition strategy of counting on from the *smaller* number (not the larger, as she had done before). Children's strategy use is often inconsistent (Siegler, 1988). Then she made an error, asserting that 3 + 4 is 6, but when asked to describe the method of solution, managed to get the right answer. This sort of thing happens frequently in the course of the clinical interview. Some initial errors seem to result from sloppiness. The child tries to retrieve a number fact too quickly or calculates an answer carelessly. However, explaining a strategy to another person forces the child to slow down and to consider carefully what he or she is doing. When this happens, the child easily corrects trivial mistakes. Therefore, in addition to their other benefits, introspection and its expression promote right answers.

THEY WANT TO MAKE SURE YOU KNOW YOUR MATH VERY WELL

After a while, Toby volunteered that in class the students work with a "robot book":

T: [W]e have this robot book, and that's how you do it, you see, you have all different math ... it has a robot and, um, there's math on it.

I thought I would explore what the robot book was all about. Was it the teacher's method for introducing drill and practice?

H: Can you show us what's in your robot book?

T: We like have high numbers up to ten—that's all we can go up to, like ...

H: Show me ...

T: Five plus four ... [she wrote the 4 under the 5] ... equals nine, but they don't have the line ... no line. [she is referring to the line that would conventionally be written under the 5 and 4.]

H: No line?

T: No, and they don't write this [meaning the answer], you have to solve it.

I concluded that the robot book was some kind of workbook, and for a while talked with Toby about the kind of problems it required her to do.

Although the details are of little interest, Toby's general views of schooling are worth noting:

> *H:* I don't understand what the robot is . . .
>
> *T:* OK, it's like a book . . .
>
> *H:* Yeah.
>
> *T:* . . . and it has math in it to help you with it. [She showed how she solved a robot book problem.] . . . See, that's how you do it . . . and if I made a mistake she would do this [she made a sad face], and if I didn't, if I was all correct, she would do this [she made a happy face].

Clearly, the teacher focused on the right and wrong answers. I then asked her why the problem was written in a certain way:

> *T:* They do it different ways . . . they do it any way they want.

I then suggested that the problem might be written in that form for a reason:

> *T:* It . . . no, they try to make it, um, tricky.
>
> *H:* Tricky . . . they try to trick you? [She nods.] How do you like that? [She smiles.] Why do they try to trick you?
>
> *T:* Because they want to make sure you know your math very well.

From experience in the classroom, Toby has acquired a view of mathematics education—*her* mathematics education—that might be paraphrased as follows. To help the child learn mathematics or to assess knowledge of mathematics ("they want to make sure you know your math very well"), the teacher (or the textbook) presents problems that are both arbitrary ("they do it any way they want") and deceptive ("they try to make it, um, tricky"). From the child's point of view, the teacher's role is to create obstacles, to present meaningless tasks, to trick, and then to reward the child's success with praise or punish failure with disapproval.[14]

Now, of course it is shocking that the child should come to believe that this is what the learning of mathematics (or anything else) is all about. It is even more shocking that a teacher (and I do not believe she is unique) would act in way that would lead Toby to believe this.

---

[14]Of course, a clinician might have another interpretation. The child might be implying that in general, adults are out to deceive her, to trick her. The statement about schooling might be a screen for something deeper. This level of analysis may indeed be useful in some cases, but does not seem useful in understanding that trusting soul, Toby.

OPENNESS

By this point in the process, the interview had demonstrated its power and sensitivity; it had helped Toby to achieve an openness that was striking. We had achieved a rapport so strong that she could share her perception of teaching as deceptive and learning as meaningless. The education game as Toby saw it was certainly different from the interview game!

Her openness extended to what might be considered personal ignorance, failure, or inadequacy. A short while later, we were discussing how she might solve a problem like 20 plus 100:

T: Twenty . . . plus . . . a hundred . . . [she writes "a hundred" as 00]. There's something like that and you have to figure it out . . . a hundred and twenty . . . so a hundred and twenty, so plus and you have to write the answers down here . . . I don't know . . .

H: You don't know how to do it?

T: I don't know how to do it.

H: Let me give you a couple like that, OK? Suppose that . . .

T: 'Cause I don't know the high numbers all that much.

Toby had learned that in the clinical interview she could freely reveal her thinking, including her ignorance. This of course is the first step toward real learning. However, such a strategy would not make a great deal of sense in a classroom in which the teacher's goal was to trick her.

WHAT DOES = MEAN?

Children throughout the world possess a relatively powerful informal mathematics including counting skills, notions of more and less, and strategies for addition and subtraction (Klein & Starkey, 1988). In most societies, these children, equipped as they are with functioning mathematical minds, enter school somewhere around the age of 5 or 6. Schools are artificially created social institutions designed to pass on to children the accumulated social wisdom—a cultural legacy—one aspect of which is formal mathematics. In contrast to children's informal system, formal mathematics is written, codified, a body of material conventionally defined and agreed on, organized and explicit. Formal mathematics is what Vygotsky (1986) called a "scientific" system—coherent, explicit, organized, logical. By contrast, children's informal mathematics is a "spontaneous" system—intuitive, emotional, implicit, and tied to everyday life. These are the intuitions from which formal mathematics has evolved.

What do children, who, as we have seen, operate with their own informal way of thinking, make of the symbols and conventions of the written mathematics introduced by schooling? This is what I wanted to learn when I explored with Toby the meaning of the + and = signs conventionally used in school arithmetic. In particular, I was first interested in whether Toby understood the = sign as equivalence.

The commonly accepted interpretation is that = is written to indicate that the terms on both sides of a number sentence (and later an algebraic equation) are equivalent. Therefore, when we write that 2 + 1 = 3, we mean that the quantity expressed as 2 + 1 is equivalent in value to the quantity 3. In this view, 2 + 1 is one way of "talking about" or "naming" the quantity "three"; the numeral 3 is but another. From this point of view, it is quite sensible and acceptable to write 3 = 2 + 1. If the terms on both sides are equivalent, then their physical position in the number statement is irrelevant: The quantity "three" is still "three" no matter where it is located. Ideas like these are especially important in algebra, where the rearrangement of terms on both sides of the = sign is basic to solving equations.

Accepting this line of reasoning, teachers and textbooks often introduce = as equivalence. But what does Toby make of it? I began by asking Toby to write a sentence using = in the typical manner:

> *H:* Can you write this for me: Three plus four equals seven. [She writes 3 + 4 = 7.] OK . . . can you write five equals two plus three?
>
> *T:* [She writes 5 = 2 + 3.] I hope . . . yeah, you could . . .
>
> *H:* You could?
>
> *T:* I think . . .
>
> *H:* Can you write it that way?

I meant, of course, "Is it proper to write it that way?", but Toby pounced on my imprecise formulation:

> *T:* Yeah . . . I just wrote it!
>
> *H:* You just . . . [I laugh and then she joins in]. You just wrote it . . . but is it *right* to do it that way? [She shakes her head.] It's not right. . . . What's wrong with it?
>
> *T:* Because this should be over here and this should be over here.

Toby seemed to mean that the order must be in the form a + b = c, with the = written on the right. Next I asked about the + sign:

> *H:* OK. Can you tell me, like in this one right over here, we have three plus four equals seven, what does plus mean?

T: I'm not sure.

H: Huh?

T: I don't know.

H: I mean, does plus tell you to do something . . . what is it all about?
     [A pause; she shrugs.] Not sure? What about equals? What does equals
     mean?

T: It tells you, um, I'm not sure about this . . .

H: Uh-huh . . .

T: I think . . . it tells you three plus four, three plus four, so it's telling
     you, that, um, I think, the, um, the end is coming up . . . The end.

H: The end is coming up. . . . What do you mean the end is coming up?

T: Like, if you have equals, and so you have seven, then. So if you do
     three plus four equals seven, that would be right.

H: That would be right, so equal means something is coming up . . . like
     the *answer*. [We both laughed.]

Toby has maintained the following views: She believes that addition sentences should be written in the form a + b = c. In her view, it is much more
desirable to write 3 + 4 = 7 than it is to write 7 = 3 + 4. She cannot say what
the + sign indicates, although it was evident that she in fact added in response
to +. Further, she stated that = means "the end is coming up."

Toby has an "action interpretation" of addition and subtraction. For her,
addition is an operation. Number sentences tell you what to do. When Toby
sees a + b = , she knows that adding is required. She cannot say what +
means, but clearly it sends her the message that she ought to add. Further,
she maintained that = means that "the end is coming up," and that is true:
= indicates that the next term in the expression is the result of the operation.
So if + shouts, "Add up those numbers," = screams, "Put the answer here."[15]

Why should we care about these trivial mistakes? For one thing, they
mean that in school, children may not learn what many teachers intend to
teach. For children, = means essentially "operate to get the answer," whereas
for teachers it means "both sides of the expression are equivalent." Moreover,
many teachers are mistaken in believing that children learn what is taught.

Why don't the children learn what teachers teach, here the approved version of = as equivalence? On a general level, the answer is that children do
not simply receive knowledge intact from adults; they must construct it or
reinvent it for themselves. On a more specific level, children interpret = as
an action to be completed mainly because their informal approach to addi-

---

[15]Again, Toby is not unique in her approach. Most children employ an action interpretation of +
and = at this age (Baroody & Ginsburg, 1983). Children say that = means "makes" (as in 5 + 3
makes 8) or that it means "get the answer."

tion involves acting on quantities in order to obtain a result. For years, children use such methods as counting on from the larger number to get an answer. From their point of view, the two individual numbers that comprise the problem need to be combined—transformed—into another number. The numbers are changed into something else. All this has nothing to do with equivalence in the sense teachers intend to convey and it leads quite naturally to the belief that + means add and = means "the end is coming up." Children assimilate the written + and = signs into their informal approach to addition.[16]

In brief, despite the official presentation of = as equivalence, children's informal knowledge leads them to conceptualize = as an indicator of activities to be performed. In this and in other areas, children do not simply learn what is taught, but construct their own interpretation of mathematics. Teachers teach one thing and children learn another!

ASCENDING TO THE CONCRETE

What can be done about this mismatch between teaching and learning? How should teachers react to a situation in which children construct ideas diverging from conventional mathematical notions? There are several ways to respond. One possibility is to "shout louder." The teacher can repeat the equivalence explanation more loudly than before, ignoring the child's spontaneous construction. Shouting louder includes the imposition of extensive practice and the use of textbooks that present the equivalence idea in an efficient and attractive manner. Shouting louder is the typical approach, but it is unlikely to succeed at any deep level. Although the children may repeat the teacher's words, they will no doubt continue to maintain their action interpretation, which persists into the study of algebra, even though teachers have by this time been shouting at a high volume for a number of years.

Another strategy is to understand the children's constructions and to use them in a productive fashion. We can begin with the assumption that the child adds by counting to combine sets, and we can relate the symbolism of addition—that is, the + and = signs—to the child's informal knowledge. This is what I did with Toby immediately after our discussion of + and =:

---

[16]Another reason for children's action interpretation of + and = is that the examples typically presented in class, in homework lessons, and in workbooks all stress addition as calculation. In the classroom, children's actual written work, or even their work with manipulatives, has little to do with addition as equivalence; the fact is that written problems of the sort $3 + 4 =$ (or similar problems involving manipulatives) mainly require children to calculate in order to get a result and do not involve consideration of the equivalence of the two sides of the statement. Indeed, Toby acknowledged that expressions of the form $c = a + b$ might be encountered "once in a while," but she was clearly uncomfortable with these aberrations.

H: Let's do a new one here. What if we do, ah, four plus two equals . . .
what should it be? [After a pause, she writes "6".] Six, OK. Now,
what does the plus mean in here?

T: The plus?

H: Yeah, what does plus mean there? [She shrugs.] OK, and the equals
means . . .

T: I think coming up.

So as before, she could not say what + meant, even though it clearly
caused her to add, and she believed that = means "coming up." I decided
then to find out whether she could understand the symbols in terms of her
informal notions of addition.

H: Something's coming up. Can you show me with these chips what this
means?

T: Four . . . [she counts out four chips.]

H: OK.

T: and two . . . [she counts out two chips.]

H: OK.

T: Lemme have these chips altogether, 'cause four: one, two, three, *four*,
and two, equals six . . . I would count it: one, two, three, four, five,
six, and I would get six altogether.

H: OK, so that's what that means, huh? OK, very good. You see when
. . . you were doing this . . . counting, you said "four," . . . and then
you said *"and* two" more. . . . The "and" is like the plus . . . right?

T: Oooohhhhh . . .

Toby lit up. A great revelation has just been made. She had a deep "ah-ha"
experience (or at least an "Oooohhhhh" experience), as if seeing for the first
time that her action of adding, of counting on so as to combine the two sets
of chips, was related to that little + on the paper. I would say that she made
a connection between the formal symbolism of mathematics and her informal
knowledge:

H: Yeah, it means you kind of put them all together, right? And then
the equals, what does the equals mean then?

T: Equal . . . mm . . . I think . . . I'm not sure about that.

H: Well, you're right, it says the answer's coming up, so you do four
and two . . . equals . . . the whole thing. [I gesture to the chips again.]

T: Six!

H: Right, OK, very good. OK.

What I did was relate the child's informal knowledge to the formalities of mathematics. I had "ascended to the concrete" (Luria, 1979). I essentially said to her, "You do adding this way, by means of counting the chips. These written symbols refer to aspects of what you are doing already, and that's OK."

But is it really? What happened to the concept of equivalence, which is usually seen as fundamental? From a mathematical point of view, an action interpretation of addition is quite legitimate. *One* acceptable way to conceptualize addition is in terms of an operation. For example, we can teach addition as movements on the number line. In this case, the + sign signifies the operation to be performed (a movement forward on the number line) and the = sign can be construed as indicating the result of the operation (the final resting place on the number line). Therefore, $3 + 4 = 7$ means that you start on position 3 on the number line, move ahead 4 spaces, and finally come to rest on position 7. All of this does not involve equivalence in the conventional sense. One approach, therefore, is to recognize that in this case the child's interpretation is indeed a legitimate mathematical view, which can then easily be related to compatible mathematical models like the number line.

TOBY'S FAREWELL

After some 37 minutes, the interview was at an end:

H: It was hard work, but you did very well. Did you enjoy it?

Toby nodded briefly and looked me straight in the eye:

T: Who are you?
H: Who am I? [Everyone laughs, and so does Toby.] At what level do you mean that, Toby?
T: Why do you want to know about different things that children know?
H: I see. You know why we study children? We try to find out how they learn math so that we can help them learn math if they have trouble.

Toby nodded and the interview was really over. The boldness of her question confirmed that we had accomplished something important.

WHAT HAVE WE LEARNED?

I hope that this account of Toby's work helps you to understand some basic features of children's mathematical thinking. It is not a unitary aptitude or skill or ability or strategy. It is not an achievement simply learned in school. Children's mathematical thinking is many things:

- It is in part a relationship with an adult. It is trying to do what teachers want. If the teacher assigns apparently senseless activities in a Robot book, the child will forge ahead. After all, "they want to make sure you know your math very well."
- It is a private activity that is only partly transparent to adults. The child defines and pursues her own problems; she uses strategies of which the adult is unaware; she does not necessarily learn what the adult believes is being taught.
- It is informal, employing intuitive ideas of more and less, using counting (sometimes with the fingers, sometimes "in the head") to carry out the tasks of calculation.
- It is trying to get right answers quickly without thinking (lest one be accused of cheating), and it is feeling miserable about getting wrong answers.
- It is a somewhat bizarre language game that first demands the memorization of meaningless material (the spoken numbers "one" through "twelve"), then involves the identification of a pattern ("thirteen" through "nineteen") which in English is merely a misleading and temporary distraction, and finally requires mastery of a sensible and even elegant system of counting rules (from "twenty" onwards).
- It is trying to make sense out of material that may not have been presented in a very sensible manner in the first place. Such efforts at sense-making may result in "bugs," which in turn produce answers that *seem* bizarre but are in fact quite "logical" in their own way.
- It is seeing math as an arbitrary set of activities and obstacles designed to deceive and trick.
- It is thinking about one's own thinking and taking great pride in describing it to another—and it is learning about one's own thinking, and even correcting it, in the course of describing it to another.

There is much to celebrate in Toby's work. I applaud her patience with me (and other adults), her valiant attempts at making sense of things that are sometimes not so sensible, her clever ways of coping, her informal intuitions and skills, her enthusiasm for trying to figure things out, her willingness to examine her own thinking and her openness in revealing it, and her perseverance in the face of many difficulties imposed on her by the system of formal education.

There is much also to celebrate in the "cognitive clinical interview," the "informal" and deliberately unstandardized mode of questioning that I used in an effort to enter Toby's world. The interview is based on several principles differentiating it from standardized testing: The interviewer is guided by an ethic of respect for the integrity of the child's mental life; the interviewer attempts to establish with the child a relationship of trust, such that the child is willing to reveal his or her most intimate mental processes; the interviewer engages in exploration, the goal of which is to discover how the child conceptualizes issues and solves problems, not simply how the child deals with the adult's problems and employs methods the adult believes to be important; and the interviewer employs nonstandardized questioning and tasks, tailored to the individual, and indeed often created on the spot in response to the idiosyncrasies of the child and the situation.

The "cognitive clinical interview" is hard to do, but the example of Toby demonstrates how this form of interaction can expose the child's strengths as well as her struggles, can illuminate her view of the world—not simply her reaction to the adult's—and indeed can help promote her cognitive development. Would standard tests have revealed to us the same Toby?

THE CENTRAL PROBLEM OF MATHEMATICS EDUCATION

In response to children like Toby, effective mathematics education should employ at least two useful strategies. One is to "ascend to the concrete"—to build on what the child knows or has constructed. Mathematics education should involve realizing that the child is competent in an informal addition which employs combining and counting to get a result, and that therefore addition should be taught as an action, not as a type of equivalence. Mathematics education should accept that the child's view of = as "the end is coming up" makes sense, and that instruction should flow from that insight. In particular, mathematics education should make serious attempts to relate the symbolism and formalities and mathematics as taught in school to the child's informal knowledge. Toby needs to see that the + sign is not mysterious and arbitrary, but that it refers to (at least in part) and gains meaning from what *she* does in the way of adding.

However, mathematics education should also accept the responsibility to help the child move beyond her intuitions. The child's constructions are not sufficient. Toby needs to learn, even if it is not her "natural" inclination, that = can also be interpreted in terms of equivalence. It is therefore the teacher's responsibility to guide the child's constructions, to help the child advance beyond his or her initial ideas. The teacher cannot leave the learning of mathematics entirely in the hands (or mind) of the child, and must instead intervene so as to lead the child to "reinvent" formal mathematics—to construct ideas and procedures that would not have arisen spontaneously in child's mind in the absence of adult help. That is what teachers are for.

How can teachers use and respect the child's constructions, but help the child to progress beyond them? That, I think, is the basic question of mathematics education (and of education generally), a question too immense to deal with here. Perhaps, however, I can interject a note on what to *avoid*.

The traditional approach of mathematics education, particularly at the more advanced levels, is to teach equivalence (and other mathematical topics) by defining it purely in terms of the formal system of written mathematics—by introducing explicit definitions, theorems, and the like. This may be how mathematicians eventually come to formulate equivalence, but it is not how they usually arrive at such notions and it is certainly not a good way to teach children. Except in the minds of the most advanced students, definitions in formal terms are usually mere words with little meaning.

Finally, math education should *not*, of course, involve propagating the beliefs that math is that subject in which one is required to get the right answer, quickly, without thinking, and that math must be tricky, deceptive, or arbitrary. That is no way to celebrate Toby.

REFERENCES

Baroody, A. J., & Ginsburg, H. P. (1983). The effects of instruction on children's understanding of the "equals" sign. *The Elementary School Journal, 84*(2), 199–212.

Brown, J. S., & VanLehn, K. (1982). Towards a generative theory of "bugs." In T. P. Carpenter, J. M. Moser, & T. A. Romberg (Eds.), *Addition and subtraction: A cognitive perspective* (pp. 117–135). Hillsdale, NJ: Lawrence Erlbaum Associates.

Buswell, G. T., & John, L. (1926). *Diagnostic studies in arithmetic* (Supplementary Educational Monographs No. 30). Chicago: University of Chicago Press.

Erlwanger, S. H. (1975). Case studies of children's conceptions of mathematics, Part I. *Journal of Children's Mathematical Behavior, 1,* 157–183.

Fuson, K. C. (1988). *Children's counting and concepts of number.* New York: Springer-Verlag.

Ginsburg, H. P. (1977). *Children's arithmetic: The learning process.* New York: Van Nostrand.

Ginsburg, H. P., Jacobs, S. F., & Lopez, L. S. (1993). Assessing mathematical thinking and learning potential. In R. B. Davis & C. S. Maher (Eds.), *Schools, mathematics, and the world of reality* (pp. 237–262). Boston: Allyn & Bacon.

Ginsburg, H. P., Kaplan, R. G., & Baroody, A. J. (1992). *Children's mathematical thinking: Videotape workshops for educators.* Evanston, IL: Everyday Learning Corporation.

Ginsburg, H. P., Posner, J. K., & Russell, R. L. (1981). The development of mental addition as a function of schooling and culture. *Journal of Cross-Cultural Psychology, 12,* 163–178.

Groen, G., & Resnick, L. B. (1977). Can preschool children invent addition algorithms? *Journal of Educational Psychology, 69,* 645–652.

Klein, A., & Starkey, P. (1988). Universals in the development of early arithmetic cognition. In G. Saxe & M. Gearhart (Eds.), *Children's mathematics* (pp. 5–26). San Francisco: Jossey-Bass.

Luria, A. R. (1979). *The making of mind: A personal account of Soviet psychology.* Cambridge, MA: Harvard University Press.

Piaget, J. (1964). *Judgment and reasoning in the child* (M. Warden, Trans.). Paterson, NJ: Littlefield, Adams.

Piaget, J. (1976). *The grasp of consciousness: Action and concept in the young child* (S. Wedgwood, Trans.). Cambridge, MA: Harvard University Press.

Siegler, R. S. (1988). Strategy choice procedures and the development of multiplication skill. *Journal of Experimental Psychology: General, 117,* 258–275.

Vygotsky, L. S. (1986). *Thought and language* (A. Kozulin, Trans.). Cambridge, MA: MIT Press.

8

▼▼▼▼▼▼▼

Fostering Mathematical Thinking in Middle School Students: Lessons From Research

John D. Bransford
Linda Zech
Daniel Schwartz
Brigid Barron
Nancy Vye
The Cognition and Technology Group at Vanderbilt
Peabody College at Vanderbilt University

In this chapter we discuss the issue of fostering mathematical thinking in middle school students (grades 5–8). Students of this age develop beliefs about whether they "are mathematical" and whether they like mathematics. Too often, they reach the conclusion that they are not good at mathematics (e.g., Cognition and Technology Group at Vanderbilt, 1994). However, their view of mathematical thinking is often restricted to the domain of mathematical computation and formula following. Our assumption is that different views of what counts as mathematical thinking can have strong effects on the length and quality of students' "mathematical careers."

Here we explore the challenges involved in fostering mathematical thinking by discussing changes in thinking about this issue that have occurred within our Learning Technology Center (LTC) during the past 7 years. These changes involve a shift in assumptions about what mathematical thinking looks like, and in assumptions about the challenges involved in promoting mathematical thinking in students.

Three major sets of events have influenced our assumptions about the nature of mathematical thinking and how to promote it. These involve opportunities to:

1. Interact with middle school students who were having difficulty in reading and mathematics and who had already decided that they were "not mathematical." Seeing their ideas of what counted as mathematical thinking taught us a great deal.

2. Work in classroom settings with teachers and, in the process, experience firsthand the classroom realities that influence actions and assumptions. A major struggle for teachers involves their own beliefs about mathematics—beliefs that were shaped by their school experiences. Many have not had the benefit of being exposed to new ideas about the nature of mathematics such as those discussed by the NCTM (1989). In addition, teachers' knowledge of mathematics is often taxed by the use of complex problem-solving environments such as the ones discussed here. It has become clear to us that teachers need ongoing support for creating professional communities that can continually discuss issues of mathematics. These dialogues support the development of teachers' mathematical thinking and their definitions of what mathematical thinking entails.

3. Merge the perspectives of researchers from two different communities: cognitive psychology and mathematics education. Both of these communities are currently represented within our LTC and on our national advisory boards.[1] However, when the LTC began, our projects were driven primarily from a cognitive perspective. DeCorte, Greer, and Verschaffel (in press) noted that these two communities have not always seen eye to eye. For example, they include the following from Kilpatrick (1992):

> Mathematics educators have often been wary of psychological researchers because of what they have seen as an indifference to or ignorance of the academic discipline of mathematics, but they have never hesitated to borrow ideas and techniques freely from psychology. (p. 5)

In retrospect, our LTC's early work on mathematics learning is well characterized by Kilpatrick's words. We were not *indifferent* to the academic discipline of mathematics, but we were *ignorant* of the idea that we should explore the nature of mathematics and its implications for instruction. After all, each of us had passed our middle school mathematics courses—what more was there to know?

In actuality, the LTC's initial foray into mathematics learning was more accidental than planned. As our work has progressed, it has increasingly reflected the benefits of strong collaboration between mathematics educators and cognitive psychologists in our community. Our experiences convince us that members of these two communities have a great deal to teach one another. We provide examples as our discussion proceeds.

Our discussion focuses on four phases of development that reflect our Center's thinking about the nature of mathematical thinking and how to

---

[1]Advisory Board Members include John Ahner, Jill Ashworth, Sallie Baliunas, David Bodnar, Raffaella Borasi, George Bright, Alma Clayton-Pedersen, Deborah Davies, Marcy Gabella, Rich Lehrer, Frank Lester, Henrietta Mann, Roy Pea, Nancy Ransom, John Wikswo, Horace Williams, David Wilson, and Chancellor Joe B. Wyatt. We are extremely appreciative of their creative insights and wise advice.

promote it. We begin by explaining how a group of cognitive psychologists found themselves grappling with issues of mathematics learning without ever intending to enter this domain.

PHASE I: THE ACCIDENTAL MATHEMATICIAN

When our Learning Technology Center began in 1984, we had no intention of venturing into the field of mathematics education. Our early research projects dealt with general issues of learning and instruction, not specific content areas such as mathematics, science, social studies, or history.

The Dynamic Assessment Project

One of the earliest projects undertaken by the LTC was the Vanderbilt dynamic assessment project, which focused on alternative assessments of children's potential (e.g., Bransford, Delclos, Vye, Burns, & Hasselbring, 1987; Vye, Burns, Delclos, & Bransford, 1987). The purpose of this project was to assess individuals' responsiveness to opportunities to learn (Campione & Brown, 1987; Feuerstein, Rand, & Hoffman, 1979; Lidz, 1987), to assess their "zone of sensitivity to instruction" (Vygotsky, 1978; Wood, 1980).

The methods of dynamic assessment were different from those used in standardized, "static" assessments, such as intelligence tests and achievement tests. In traditional assessments, instruction by the tester invalidates results. Test scores are supposed to reflect an individual's abilities to perform with no help from anyone. In contrast, the goal of dynamic assessment is to assess people's abilities to learn from new opportunities. Our version of dynamic assessment involved a systematic attempt to find effective learning conditions and assess children's responsiveness to these conditions (Vye et al., 1987). Because children may be more responsive to some learning conditions than others, the dynamic assessment project bought us face to face with issues of curriculum and instruction (e.g., Bransford et al., 1988).

Our initial work on dynamic assessment involved materials that were more like those found on intelligence tests than in classrooms. As our work progressed, we began to question the degree to which assessments involving general, intelligence-test-like items were most useful for helping students achieve school-relevant goals such as learning to read for meaning and learning to communicate. Evidence was mounting that the ability to think and learn could not be neatly separated from the nature and organization of the content knowledge available to individuals (e.g., Bransford, Sherwood, Vye, & Rieser, 1986; Bransford et al., 1987; Chi, Glaser, & Farr, 1991). Therefore, we included within the dynamic assessment project an emphasis on assessment in the context of tasks that had face validity with respect to school achievement. This generated a line of research that focused on dynamic assessments of students' potentials to solve verbally presented word problems. Word problems allowed us to look at issues of reading comprehension, and had the added advantage of assessing the degree to which students could quantify their thinking by using mathematics.

Early Work on Word Problems

Our work on word problems was conducted with fifth- and sixth-grade students who were having difficulties in school, especially in areas of reading and mathematics. Our goal was to understand why they were having difficulties, and to assess their responsiveness to new approaches to helping them learn.

We presented students with written versions of simple word problems such as the following:

1. Tony rides the bus to camp every summer. There are 8 other children who ride with him. The bus travels 9 miles an hour. It takes 4 hours to get there. How far away is the camp?

2. John is standing in front of a building. The building is 8 times as tall as John. John is 16 years old. John is 5 feet tall. How tall is the building?

Nearly every student with whom we worked used an approach to solving word problems that was mechanical rather than based on an attempt to understand the problem. For example, a typical answer for the first word problem noted here was $8 + 9 + 4 = 21$. The following explanation about solution strategies was quite typical:

Interviewer: Why did you decide to add the numbers?
Student: Because it said like, "How far away is the camp?" How is to add.

Interviews relevant to the second problem also involved a search for key words in the problems. For example:

Student: I saw the building is 8 *times* as tall as John so I know to multiply.
Interviewer: What did you multiply?
Student: Sixteen and 7 and 8.

Our experiments provided a picture of what "mathematical thinking" meant to these students. Mathematical thinking was the procedures used to solve numerical problems. The procedures involved a search for key words that specified the operations to perform on the numbers (i.e., add, subtract, multiply, or divide). The numbers to be operated on were rarely attached to meaningful elements of the problem context. For example, both of the problems noted earlier included numerical information that was clearly irrelevant (i.e., the fact that 8 other boys rode with Tony; that John is 16 years old). Despite this fact, students consistently attempted to use the irrelevant information in every problem we gave them. Basically, students demonstrated extremely poor comprehension of the problems they were being asked to solve.

As we searched the literature on word problems, we discovered that our findings were similar to those reported by other researchers. Several investigators showed that, instead of bringing real-world standards to their work, students seem to treat word problems mechanically and often failed to think about constraints imposed by real-world experiences (Charles & Silver, 1988; Silver, 1986). For example, Silver asked students to determine the number of buses needed to take a specific number of people on a field trip. Many of them divided the total number of students by the number that each bus would hold and came up with answers like $2\frac{1}{3}$. The students failed to consider the fact that one cannot have a functioning $\frac{1}{3}$ bus.

Studies by Reusser (1988) also provided dramatic evidence of many students' problem with word problems. He gave school children the following type of problem in the context of other mathematics problems:

There are 26 sheep and 10 goats on a ship. How old is the captain?

Approximately $\frac{3}{4}$ of the students in Reusser's study attempted to provide a numerical answer to the problem. Their overwhelming tendency was to ask themselves whether to add, subtract, multiply, or divide rather than ask whether the problem made sense.

Several authors questioned the generality of Reusser's findings and conducted their own version of his experiments:

Our reaction to Reusser's data was that this must have been a special group of students who had been taught poorly. We gave the problem to one of our own children who was in fifth grade. Much to our surprise, and dismay, the answer given was 36. When we asked why, we were told, "Well, you need to add or subtract or multiply in problems like this, and this one seemed to work best if I add." (Bransford & Stein, 1993, p. 196)

Support for Problem Comprehension

Our approach to working with students focused on efforts to improve their ability to understand the problems they were solving. We began to investigate the use of video-based scenarios that could help students generate mental models of situations (e.g., see McNamara, Miller, & Bransford, 1991). In several studies we used the first 12 minutes of the film *Raiders of the Lost Ark*, wherein Indiana Jones travels to South America to capture the golden idol (e.g., Barron, Bransford, Kulewicz, & Hasselbring, 1989; Bransford et al., 1988). We asked students to imagine that they wanted to return to the jungle to obtain some of the gold artifacts that Indiana left behind. If so, it could be important to know dimensions of obstacles such as the width of the pit one would have to jump, the height of the cave, the width of the river and its relationship to the size of the seaplane, and so forth.

The goal of learning about potential obstacles and events guided the selection of mathematically based problems that were derived from scenes from the movie segment. We decided to use known standards (e.g., Indiana Jones) to estimate sizes and distances that were important to know. For example, one problem asked students to estimate the width of the pit they would have to jump if they returned to the cave. This information could be estimated by finding a scene where Indiana used his bullwhip to swing over the pit. Through the use of freeze frame we were able to show a scene of Indiana swinging with his outstretched body extending halfway across the pit. Measurement on the screen (either by hand or through the use of computer graphics) allowed students to see that the pit was approximately two Indianas wide. Students were also encouraged to create visual and symbolic representations of problems, and they received individualized feedback about the strengths and weaknesses of their approach to each problem. All instruction was one-on-one.

Effects of learning in the video context were compared to the effects of learning in a control condition in which students received one-on-one instruction in solving and representing written problems without the use of the Indiana Jones context. The results indicated strong benefits of the context on students' abilities to solve analogous transfer problems that occurred both within and outside the context of Indiana Jones (see Bransford et al., 1988). Students in the video condition also showed marked improvements in their abilities to visually represent problems. Figure 8.1 shows pretest and posttest representations of an Indiana Jones problem that asked students to estimate the dimensions of various objects in the video.

Our findings with *Raiders of the Lost Ark* were encouraging to us, the students, and their teachers. Students enjoyed working on problems in the context of *Raiders* and most of them exhibited a major shift in their abilities to explain the nature of the problems they were trying to solve, represent these problems visually, and explain their work. They also showed evidence of transfer to real-life settings. For example, students began to use known heights (e.g., of one another) to estimate the height of trees, flagpoles, and other objects in their environment.

Pretest

Indiana Jones is lying across the pontoon. The pontoon is 3 times as long as Indiana Jones. The plane has 2 pontoons. If Indiana Jones is 6 feet tall, how long is the pontoon?

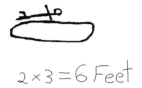

$2 \times 3 = 6$ Feet

Posttest

Indiana Jones is lying across the pontoon. The pontoon is 4 times as long as Indiana Jones. The plane has 2 pontoons. If Indiana Jones is 6 feet tall, how long is the pontoon?

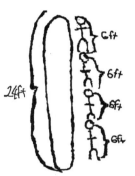

FIG. 8.1. Pre- and posttest visual representations of an Indiana Jones problem.

Needs for New Problem Contexts

We began to worry about a limitation of our work with *Raiders*; namely, that the problems we were able to devise were too restricted. The primary problem type involved simple measurement problems given a standard. In particular, we helped students see that there was some object (e.g., the width of the cave, the length of the pontoon on the plane) that was important to measure and that was X number of Indiana Joneses long. If Indiana Jones were Y feet tall how long was the object? We worried that students could learn to do well on this type of problem yet still lack a deep understanding of what they were doing. In particular, we were worried about what Duncker (1945) called the *functional fixedness* problem. Given a change in problem type so that new solution strategies must be generated, people often remain "functionally fixed" and attempt to apply familiar solution strategies even though they are no longer relevant. Working with only a single problem type is almost a sure way to get people functionally fixed.

The manner in which *Raiders* was edited precluded us from generating additional problem types in that context. For example, we would have liked to develop problems that involved dynamic rather than static approaches to measurement. An example involves efforts to estimate the width of the forest in *Raiders* given that it took Indiana Jones X seconds to run through it going at a speed of Y miles per hour. A similar problem could be written for the width of the large field that separated the forest from the river where the airplane was parked.

Unfortunately, the movie did not let us see continuous sequences of Indiana Jones running so that students could time them. Instead, the movie showed Indiana Jones going into the forest, then halfway through it, then going into the clearing, and suddenly leaving the clearing and getting to the river. The kinds of edits that appeared in the movie did not support the scenes we needed to help students begin to think about rate. (Movie directors and editors know that continuous scenes shot from a single perspective tend to be boring visually.)

The River Adventure.   The limitations on creating additional problem types in the *Raiders* context prompted us to think about creating our own videos that included the kinds of scenes and data needed in an educational context. We eventually designed and produced our own prototype videodisc—*The River Adventure.* In this adventure viewers are told that they have won a 1-week trip on a houseboat and must do all the planning for food, gas, water, docking the boat, and so forth. Data concerning the boat (e.g., its length, width, height), cruising speed, fuel consumption and capacity, the route, marinas along the route, and so forth were all embedded in the video. The students watching the video had to determine when and why to use various sets of data to help them achieve particular goals. For example, one important consideration in planning for the houseboat trip was to reserve a dock at a certain marina that was the appropriate size for the boat. The houseboat's dimensions were not explicitly given in the video; instead, students saw scenes of a 6-foot person on the boat and could use them to estimate its length, width, and height (analogous to using Indiana Jones as a standard in our earlier work).

The adventure also required students to call the dock (via marine radio) and provide their estimated time of arrival. This meant that students had to use scenes to estimate the speed of the boat (e.g., the number of minutes to travel between mile markers on the river) and then use the boat speed to determine how long it would take to travel the distance to the dock (the distance was discoverable by exploring the map included on the videodisc). The adventure included additional data such as fill times for the water tank in order to estimate its capacity, estimates of amount of water needed for various tasks, and so forth. Overall, the adventure included all the embedded data needed to plan for the trip.

As we have discussed elsewhere (e.g., CTGV, 1994), we used the same type of instructional approach described for *Raiders* (see earlier discussion) to help students learn to understand, represent, and solve problems in the *River Adventure* context. However, we worked with multiple problems so that functional fixedness was less of a threat. Results were highly encouraging: Students liked the challenge and were able to transfer to posttest problems. Examples of pre- and posttest representations of problems are illustrated in Fig. 8.2.

PHASE II: BEYOND WELL-DEFINED WORD PROBLEMS

As we thought more about our assumptions of mathematical thinking, we began to question the fact that our approach to using *Raiders* and *River Adventure* still involved a traditional word-problem format. All we had added was video support. As students watched the video, we stopped it in order to present word problems to them. By doing so, we explicitly defined the problems to be solved rather than helping students learn to generate and pose their own problems. The latter seemed important for developing the kind of mathematical thinking necessary to solve complex problems in the real world (e.g., Brown & Walters, 1993).

Historical accounts of great mathematical thinkers (e.g., Turnbull, 1993) provide ample evidence of the importance of identifying and posing problems rather than simply solving problems that others presented to them. For example, Eratosthenes made ingenious use of simple principles of geometry to accurately estimate the circumference of the earth. Similarly, Thales estimated the height of a pyramid by using simple geometric principles based on shadows. (The trick was to determine the length of the pyramid's shadow given that part of it was covered up by the pyramid.) In both cases, the thinkers essentially generated their own word problems rather than solved well-defined problems provided by someone else.

At a less complex level of mathematical sophistication, the need to generate problems and subproblems arises frequently in everyday life. As a simple example, imagine the task of going from one's house to a breakfast meeting at 8:30 in a new restaurant across town. First, one needs to identify the existence of a problem to be solved; namely, the need to determine the time one should leave in order to make the breakfast meeting. To solve this general problem one has to generate subproblems such as "How far away is the meeting?", "How fast will I be able to drive?", and so on. The ability

Pretest

Students view a still frame of a boy lying across the bow of the houseboat. The announcer notes that the boy is 6 feet tall. One can see perceptually that the boat is twice as wide as the boy. The interviewer asks, "Can you think of a way to figure out how wide the boat is?" The students replies, "Multiply?" When the interviewer doesn't answer right away, the student says, "Divide?" He eventually draws the following:

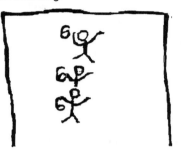

Posttest

A student views a still frame of a garbage can sitting on the bow of the houseboat. The announcer notes that the can is two feet tall. One can see perceptually that the top of the boat is about 6 cans high. The interviewer asks, "Can you think of a way to figure out how tall the boat is?" The student draws the following and explains the math:

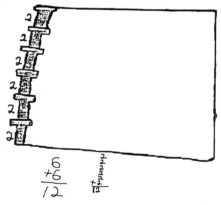

FIG. 8.2. Pre- and posttest representations of problems for the River Adventure.

to identify the general problem and generate the subproblems to be solved is crucial for real-world problem solving. We considered it to be an important component of mathematical thinking and believed that typical uses of applications problems did not develop such generative problem-finding and problem-formulation skills (Bransford & Stein, 1984; Brown & Walters, 1993; Charles & Silver, 1988; Sternberg, 1986).

Research on Problem Generation

We used *The River Adventure* to study problem generation by collecting baseline data on people's abilities to engage in the types of mathematical thinking necessary to plan for the houseboat trip. Members of our research team worked with three groups of individuals: college undergraduates, academically successful fifth graders, and fifth graders who exhibited delays in their mathematics development and were receiving special services. After watching the video, students were given a structured interview consisting of several levels of questions. The initial questions were general and open-ended and were designed to assess students' abilities to articulate and elaborate important categories to consider in planning the trip (e.g., fuel, estimated time of arrival, food, water, etc.). Subsequent questions were designed to tap students' abilities to collect relevant data and formulate mathematical solutions for specific aspects of the plan (e.g., "How might you estimate the dimensions of the houseboat?").

The results of the planning questions suggested that most college students were relatively good at identifying and elaborating the important categories to consider to adequately plan for the trip (this was not surprising, because the categories were mentioned at the beginning of the video). In contrast, fifth-grade students, whether academically successful or mathematics delayed, were much less likely to mention key categories. When a category was mentioned, the responses of the students tended to be quite general (e.g., "You need to bring enough water."). Students' responses almost never involved quantitative thinking such as systematic attempts to estimate how much water would be needed for a 1-week trip. In addition, nearly all of the fifth graders had a difficult time identifying the relevant mathematical data that would be needed for solving the problems associated with their plans, such as determining the boat's dimensions or estimating arrival time. Not surprisingly, mathematics delayed students had even greater difficulty in these areas than their academically more successful peers (Furman et al., 1989; Montavon, Furman, Barron, Bransford, & Hasselbring, 1989).

We also found that the more structure we provided in our questioning, the better our participants responded. (These findings have been replicated in the context of our Jasper series; see CTGV, 1993a.) By the time we reached our third level of questioning, we were essentially presenting participants with simple, well-defined word problems (e.g., If this boat is twice as wide as this boy lying on the deck, and this boy is 6 feet tall, how wide is the boat?). The fact that everyone did much better at level 3 questioning than level 1 (with 1 being the most general level) shows that they had the potential to answer many of the questions but were unable to do so initially because they had difficulty formulating relevant subproblems. The fact that these results were found even for students who scored very high on standardized tests of mathematics achievement suggested that the process of problem formulation was a part of mathematical thinking that was worth targeting in our instruction.

Instruction to Facilitate Problem Formulation

As we began to develop instructional procedures for using *The River Adventure* to teach problem formulation as well as problem solving, we had the opportunity to work with a number of experienced mathematics educators and mathematics teachers who provided information that changed the trajectory of our research project. Three members of the LTC (Elizabeth Goldman, Linda Barron, and Bob Sherwood) received a National Science Foundation grant in mathematics teacher preparation that brought them in contact with experienced middle school mathematics teachers in our area. These teachers proved to be extremely helpful to our work. For example, when we asked them to discuss problems in the curriculum that they wanted to improve, a major concern centered around word problems. The teachers were enthusiastic about the possibility of videodisc-based problems like our *River Adventure*. However, they were not at all enthusiastic about the production values of our prototype. They helped us see that, as researchers, we could get by with such a prototype because we were a special event that got children out of their scheduled classes. When something was introduced as regular instruction, however, the teachers wanted it to be compelling to the students. Because we needed the teachers to help us study the effects of different types of instruction, we paid close attention to their concerns. Our collaboration with the teachers eventually led to the development of the Jasper Woodbury Problem Solving Series, and in that context to attempts to better define the nature of mathematical thinking. These developments are discussed in the next section.

PHASE III: MATHEMATICAL THINKING IN THE CONTEXT OF THE JASPER WOODBURY PROBLEM SOLVING SERIES

Our assumptions about mathematical thinking continued to evolve as we went through a series of develop, test, and redesign cycles in the context of the Jasper *Woodbury Problem Solving Series*. Jasper is a series of 12 videodisc-based adventures (plus video-based analogs, extensions, teaching tools and teaching tips) that are designed to improve the mathematical thinking of students from grade 5 and up (see Fig. 8.3). Each videodisc contains a short (approximately 17-minute) video adventure that ends in a complex challenge. The adventures are designed like good detective novels where all the data

The Adventures of Jasper Woodbury

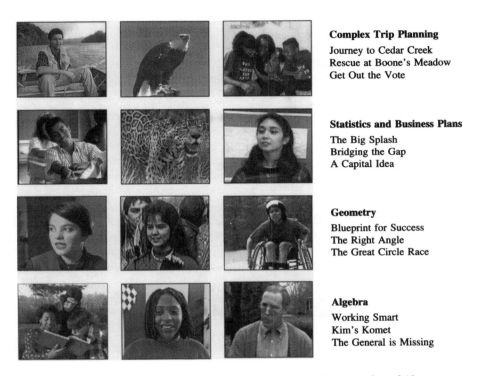

Complex Trip Planning
Journey to Cedar Creek
Rescue at Boone's Meadow
Get Out the Vote

Statistics and Business Plans
The Big Splash
Bridging the Gap
A Capital Idea

Geometry
Blueprint for Success
The Right Angle
The Great Circle Race

Algebra
Working Smart
Kim's Komet
The General is Missing

FIG. 8.3. Overview of the Jasper Series. The Jasper Series consists of 12 videodisc based adventures (plus video based analogs and teaching tips) that focus on mathematical problem finding and problem solving. The 12 adventures are illustrated here. Each adventure is also designed to provide links to other subjects such as science, social studies, and literature.

necessary to solve the adventure (plus additional data that are not relevant to the solution) are embedded in the story. Models of effective mathematical thinking are also frequently provided in the videos.

Each Jasper adventure is designed from the perspective of the standards recommended by the National Council of Teachers' of Mathematics (1989). In particular, Jasper adventures provide multiple opportunities for problem solving, reasoning, communication, and making connections to other areas such as science, social studies, literature, and history.

The Jasper Series that currently exists did not arise full-blown from the research and thinking discussed earlier in this chapter. Instead, its design has evolved over a 6-year period that involves extensive testing with hundreds of teachers and thousands of students.

Our experiences with Jasper have helped us rethink the idea of enhancing mathematical thinking in middle school students. One of the lessons learned is that the cognitive psychologists among us had to deepen their own thinking about mathematics—not just pedagogy. Our research team also discovered the need to help teachers understand mathematics in ways that they had not been taught when they attended school. Discussion of these and other issues relevant to the goal of promoting mathematical thinking follow.

From Problem-Driven to Mathematics-Driven Adventures

The opportunity to develop the Jasper series resulted in increased interactions among the cognitive psychologists and mathematics educators in the LTC. Many of the cognitive experts on our team had done well at mathematics in school but had never had the opportunity to explore the subject matter deeply. A number of them adopted the role of "intelligent novices" who helped make sure that the ideas from the mathematicians were meaningful to "regular people." At the same time, the mathematics educators kept emphasizing the importance of finding "big ideas" in mathematics that were useful in a wide variety of contexts. Ongoing dialogue between the "experts" and the "intelligent novices" helped the Jasper series evolve along a number of dimensions. These interactions have been so fruitful that the idea of linking content area experts with "intelligent novices" has become a basic principle of all our Center's design teams.

Early Jasper Adventures. The first Jasper adventure, *Journey to Cedar Creek*, was modeled after the original *River Adventure*. It featured an old cruiser that had no running lights and a temporary gas tank; Jasper wanted to buy it to fix it up. After he traveled up river to buy it, students had to decide if the old cruiser could make it home before sunset and whether Jasper had enough fuel for the trip and enough cash to purchase fuel.

The second Jasper adventure, *Rescue at Boone's Meadow (RBM)*, was designed to reintroduce the distance–rate–time considerations from the first Jasper, plus add a new twist; namely, that there were many more possible solution paths. RBM featured a wounded eagle and an ultralight airplane that could be used to rescue it. Students were asked to find the fastest way to rescue the eagle and state how long it would take. They had to consider issues of fuel and its effects on the payload limits of the ultralight, issues about which pilot to choose (they weighed different amounts and hence affected the payload), and issues about when to use vehicles of different speeds.

The first two Jaspers allowed us to replicate many of the effects found with *Raiders* and *The River Adventure*. For example, we found that even the highest achieving sixth graders (on standardized tests of math achievement) had a very difficult time formulating subproblems that they needed to solve in order to solve the adventures. When these subproblems were explicitly defined for them, they were much better able to solve the problems they faced (e.g., CTGV, 1993a).

We also found that instruction in the context of Jasper had powerful effects on students' abilities to formulate and solve subsequent complex problems. In contrast, students whose instruction consisted solely of one- and two-step word problems that included the same mathematical content as the overall Jasper problem showed very poor abilities to transfer to new complex problems (e.g., CTGV, 1993a; Van Haneghan et al., 1992).

As our work progressed, we began to realize that our implicit design strategy had been to begin with "authentic" adventures (either ones such as *Raiders* that were already available or ones we were able to film) and add the mathematics later. We developed a new strategy of beginning with mathematics concepts and deriving our adventures from them. The NCTM (1989) standards, plus a highly talented national advisory board, were invaluable for thinking about the types of mathematical concepts that seemed particularly important for middle school. We eventually decided to focus on the areas of introductory statistics, geometry, and algebra (including pre-algebra). Next, the types of mathematical thinking that we hoped to promote in these areas are discussed.

Statistics in the Context of Creating Business Plans. The third and fourth Jasper adventures that we produced were *The Big Splash* and *A Capital Idea*. Both were organized around the idea of developing a business plan that used a random sample of peoples' responses to questionnaires to make inferences about the characteristics of a population of individuals. The adventure *Bridging the Gap* was added later. It focuses on sampling in the context of creating a grant proposal to save endangered species.

Pilot data collected prior to developing *The Big Splash* suggested a clear need to introduce middle school students to key concepts about statistics. We interviewed a number of sixth-grade students who had scored very high on standardized tests of mathematics achievement. The interviews centered around issues of taking samples of peoples' opinions in order to arrive at predictions about the beliefs of a larger population. For example, one of our interview problems involved the goal of sampling people in a neighborhood to determine their interest in having their car washed the next weekend. How might one take a fair sample? How might the sample be used to estimate the response rate of people in the entire neighborhood?

We found that no students spontaneously generated the idea of taking samples and using them to make predictions about the people's interest in having their cars washed. Students viewed attempts to talk with people in the neighborhood as attempts to advertise the car wash rather than gather data. Our interviews convinced us that appropriately designed contexts could help students appreciate the value of taking samples and making predictions. Given the large number of opinion polls used on the news and elsewhere, this idea appeared to be an important aspect of mathematical thinking that was very useful to introduce in the middle grades.

The Jasper adventure *The Big Splash* illustrates how we attempted to help students understand important concepts involving the use of statistics. The adventure features a student, Chris, who wants to have a dunking booth at the schools' fun fair. The principal explains that she needs to have a plan which shows sufficient student interest to generate revenue equal to at least twice the amount of the loan needed to rent the equipment. Chris takes a random sample of students in his school and students watching the video see the results of his sample. Their job is to help Chris create a business plan that predicts the amount of revenue (based on extrapolating from the sample to the population) and expenses. Calculation of expenses involves numerous issues such as whether students will have to pay for water to fill the dunking booth's pool and, if so, how much water they will need.

Data indicate that students learn important information about sampling and business plans after solving *The Big Splash* (e.g., Barron et al., 1995; CTGV, 1994; Schwartz, Goldman, Vye, Barron, & CTGV, in press). They also learn to communicate their ideas. We also find that students' understanding is deepened by the opportunity to engage in additional extension activities that follow the solution of *The Big Splash*. For example, students who solve the challenge have a sense of the randomization procedure used in the video (Chris sampled every sixth student in the cafeteria line at school). Nevertheless, most lack a deep understanding of the characteristics that make samples representative of the larger population. Specially designed Jasper extension problems help develop this understanding.

Extension problems for *The Big Splash* also include several "hucksters" who make claims and back them with "data." The students' job is to learn to evaluate these claims. With practice, students learn to spot erroneous arguments such as ones that involve data based on biased sampling techniques, or on incorrect procedures for extrapolating from samples to the general population. The ability to critically evaluate data-based arguments is an aspect of mathematical thinking that seems especially important for students to acquire.

From Problems to Projects. After solving a Jasper adventure and its extensions, we encourage teachers to carry the thinking over into class *projects* that are tailored to the interests and resources of students and their community. For example, students who have solved *The Big Splash* have then proceeded to collect data in their own schools in order to demonstrate the feasibility of plans for their own fun fair. Plans that are well communicated and appropriately justified have actually been implemented (e.g., Barron et al., 1995).

The Jasper adventures *Bridging the Gap* and A *Capital Idea* build on the statistics concepts introduced in *The Big Splash*. For example, students learn about differences between conducting a census and taking a sample, and are introduced to multiple methods of sampling and multiple methods for representing data. In *A Capital Idea*, students also learn about differences between making inferences from people's actual *behavior* (e.g., with respect to recycling) versus from statements about their behavior (e.g., whether they will agree to recycle and how much material they think they will collect each week).

Geometry. It was not an easy matter for us to create contexts that made geometry meaningful to students. Most of the people on our research team had learned geometry only as a formal set of principles devoid of interesting applications. They held frequent conversations with mathematics experts in an attempt to understand the purpose of geometry. Many mathematics experts explained that geometry was "the mathematical study of shapes and space." The nonmathematicians kept asking, "But what does that mean?"

In one case a mathematics educator suggested that we help students understand the geometric proof that three points always lie on a plane. The nonmathematicians kept asking, "Who cares? Why is this relevant to anything?" After a great deal of discussion, the mathematics expert finally said, "Well, for example it proves that a 3-legged stool will always balance." This was the kind of insight for which our nonmathematicians were looking. We eventually decided not to focus primarily on proof in the Jasper geometry adventures. Nevertheless, the experience gave our team a clear example of an application of geometry that was exciting to everyone.

It took over one year of conversations among novices and experts to develop the ideas behind the geometry adventure *The Right Angle*. We then developed *The Great Circle Race* and, finally, *Blueprint for Success*. Our experiences in classrooms suggest that *Blueprint* provides the easiest introduction to geometry followed by *The Right Angle* and then *The Great Circle Race*.

The goals of the three Jasper geometry adventures are consistent with ideas about geometry suggested by Geddes (1992):

> Students' experiences in learning geometry should make them perceive geometry as having a dynamically important role in their environment and not as merely learning vocabulary, memorizing definitions and formulas, and stating properties of shapes. . . . The middle school geometry curriculum affords many opportunities for students to explore their environment and to learn and enjoy many new, exciting and fascinating aspects and applications of mathematics in their world. (pp. 2, 7)

All three Jasper geometry adventures are designed to help students understand that geometry originated as a study of the measure and relationship of elements of the world. The word *geometry* literally means "earth measure."

We want to help students see the value of discovering invariant mathematical properties of simple shapes such as triangles and circles and using them as models to measure the world. The concept of scale models is important as well.

Interviews with Students and Teachers.   Interviews with students convinced us that the majority of middle school students were being taught geometry like most members of our research team had learned it. Students we interviewed had memorized definitions of geometric concepts, but had little idea of anything more. The following interview with a fifth-grade student is very representative of what we found:

> *Interviewer (I):* Do you know anything about geometry?
> *Student (S):*   Sure. We study it in school.
> *I:*   What do you do in geometry?
> *S:*   Measure angles. We use a protractor.
> *I:*   Why do people measure angles?
> *S:*   To find out if they are obtuse or acute and stuff.
> *I:*   Why is it useful to know that?
> *S:*   To pass the fifth grade. (Zech et al., 1994)

Zech and colleagues reported data from a survey of 308 students from sixth, seventh and eighth grades that included questions about the usefulness of geometry. Sixty-six percent of the students were unable to state any reasons why geometry was useful in the real world. The remaining 34% listed only simple ideas such as "to find the area of something." Surveys conducted with college freshman at Peabody College at Vanderbilt, and with middle school teachers of mathematics, yielded similar results. Zech and colleagues noted that, of 25 teachers surveyed, only 3 were able to list uses of geometry that went beyond the calculation of area and volume. Five of the teachers were unable to list any ideas about geometry's usefulness in the real world.

Blueprint for Success.   The adventure *Blueprint For Success* provides students with an opportunity to learn about measurement concepts such as scale drawings, perimeter, area, volume, and the optimization of area. It features two students, Christina and Marcus, who visit an architectural firm during career day. While there, they encounter information about blueprints and design. They overhear a newscast about a young boy in their neighborhood who has been hit by a car while playing in the street—the fourth such accident in the last month. They wish something could be done.

A member of the community visits the architectural firm and announces that his company is donating a sizable piece of land to the community. Marcus and Christina suggest the idea of building a playground there and ask if they can help design it. The challenge for students watching the video is to help Marcus and Christina design a swingset, slide, sandbox, and item of their choice, determine how to best utilize the 280 feet of fence that has been donated, and specify the amount of pea gravel needed to achieve playground safety standards. Students solving the challenge are asked to provide a front view, side view, and top view of everything on the playground as if they were giving the blueprint to a builder. All of the measurements must be specified.

In order to solve the challenge, students must generate the subproblems they must consider in order to design the playground (e.g., What is a realistic height for a swingset? What angle should a slide make with the ground? What are the dimensions of a sandbox that holds 32 cubic feet of sand? How do I draw to scale?). Students have been extremely motivated to design playgrounds. Many teachers also have children build models to see if their designs work.

As with all Jasper adventures, *Blueprint for Success* also contains analog and extension problems. One asks students to explore a problem that Christina confronted in the story: What figure has the greatest area given a fixed perimeter? Using graph paper and string as Christina did in the story, students are encouraged to explore the problem and identify the variables and how they are related. The goal is to help students engage in systematic mathematical inquiry, including how to record their findings so that they can review them later. Eventually, students generate a summary of their investigations and learn how to represent their discoveries symbolically. Extensions also exist that help students understand proofs of various principles; for example, a proof of why a square of any perimeter encompasses more area than any rectangle with the same perimeter.

The Right Angle and The Great Circle Race. The adventures *The Right Angle* and *The Great Circle Race* build on the geometric concepts introduced in *Blueprint for Success*. In *The Right Angle*, one of the characters, Ryan, learns about isosceles right triangles. His initial understanding involves a set of facts such as "isosceles right triangles have one 90 degree angle and two 45 degree angles, and they have legs of equal lengths." This level of understanding allows Ryan to label isosceles right triangles and differentiate them from other kinds of triangles, but it does little else (see Fig. 8.4).

Later in the movie, embedded teaching scenes provide glimpses of the power of isosceles right triangles for measurement. The grandfather of another character featured in the movie, Paige, used this type of triangle to measure the height of objects such as tall trees or mountain peaks (see Fig. 8.4). The grandfather adjusted his distance from the base of the object until the angle of elevation to its top reached 45 degrees. Because isosceles right triangles have legs of equal length, the grandfather knew that the height of the object was equal to his distance from its base (see Fig. 8.5).

FIG. 8.4. Ryan's introduction to isosceles right triangles.

FIG. 8.5. Paige's grandfather estimates the height of a tree.

In the challenge for *The Right Angle*, students use a topo map and follow the grandfathers' directions to find a cave where someone has traveled and needs help. In order to do so, they must make a number of different measurements. Some allow them to use the principle of "isosceles right triangles." Others require more elaborate uses of geometry such as the use of graph paper to draw angles and objects to scale. As students in the classroom work to solve the challenge, they receive multiple opportunities to appreciate the power of geometry as a tool for practical problem solving rather than simply as a set of facts to be memorized.

The Great Circle Race extends the concept of measurement to geometric properties involved in orienteering methods like triangulation. Students also learn the invariant properties of circles (e.g., the constant ratio of circumference to diameter in circles of any size) and use this information to make estimates and measurements.

Data reported by Zech et al. (1994; in press) indicate that students who use *The Right Angle* and *The Great Circle Race* developed a much better understanding of possible uses of geometry, and were excited by the adventures. Teachers of these students also increased their understanding of the uses of geometry for measuring the world. Data reported by Barron et al. (1995) show highly significant gains in understanding for students who solved *Blueprint for Success*.

From Problems to Projects.   After solving a geometry adventure and its extensions, we encourage teachers to carry their thinking over into class projects. In several classes in Nashville, students solved *Blueprint For Success* and then constructed blueprints for playhouses that were built by volunteers and donated to kindergarten classes in their schools. An eighth-grade class drew a map of their school campus after they had solved *The Right Angle*. In completing this project students determined the measurements that they needed to make, made the required measurements by taking bearings and measuring lengths, and correctly represented this information by creating a map.

Algebra.   The three algebra adventures in the Jasper series are designed to be used as early as fifth grade and to prepare students for the formal study of algebra by helping them understand concepts such as variable and function. As we developed the algebra series, we discovered some new approaches to fostering mathematical thinking that have implications for the entire Jasper series. We explore these ideas in the next section, where we discuss the fourth phase of the LTC's thinking about mathematical thinking and how to promote it. Prior to this discussion we consider some additional lessons about mathematical thinking that we learned in Phase III.

Understanding Learning in Classrooms

We noted earlier that a major reason for creating professional quality materials such as Jasper involved the opportunities these presented for collaborating with teachers. Our original work with *Raiders* and *The River Adventure* had involved "pull-out" experiments conducted by members of our research team. With Jasper, we were able to find a large number of teachers who invited us to observe and conduct research as they taught with Jasper. These opportunities taught us a great deal about the nature of mathematical discussions in classrooms and how they might be supported and enriched.

Multiple Approaches to Instruction. A number of lessons learned from our opportunities to observe Jasper being taught in classrooms have been discussed elsewhere (e.g., CTGV, 1992b; 1992c; 1994). For present purposes we summarize only some of these here. Probably the most important lesson is that problem-based curricula such as Jasper can be used in a variety of ways that promote different types of mathematical thinking. In one of our articles (CTGV, 1992c) we discussed approaches to teaching with Jasper that range from computation-based (with a heavy emphasis on developing computation skills), to "worksheet-based" (where the problem solving is broken down into steps on worksheets), to more "student-generated" (where students are given primary responsibility for generating goals and subproblems and scaffolding is provided as needed). An important lesson learned from observing Jasper being taught in multiple settings is that problem-based curricula can make it easier to foster the kinds of mathematical thinking that we hoped to see in classrooms, but they certainly do not guarantee the existence of this kind of thinking.

A related lesson learned involves the critical importance of the pedagogical and mathematical norms operating in the classrooms (e.g., Cobb, 1994; CTGV, 1993b). These are influenced by the teachers' beliefs and knowledge about the nature of teaching and learning in general, and about mathematics learning in particular. In addition, the climate of the classroom is affected by the teachers' knowledge of the mathematics content domain (e.g., Shulman, 1986, 1987).

The Importance of Role Models. Our classroom observations also made clear the importance of characters in Jasper who could serve as positive role models for students from a wide variety of backgrounds. We realized that we could not provide a wide range of role models in any particular adventure; however, across the series we have been able to include a diverse set of heroes and heroines.

The Jasper series is named after Jasper Woodbury, who attempts to solve the problem in the first Jasper adventure (*Journey to Cedar Creek*). However,

Jasper is not the primary problem solver in the remaining adventures. Emily Johnson (an African American female) is the heroine in *Rescue at Boone's Meadow*; Julie Carillo (a Hispanic female) is the primary problem solver in *A Capital Idea*; Chris (an African American male) is the hero in *The Big Splash*; Paige Littlefield (an American Indian) is a heroine in *The Right Angle*; Donna (a wheelchair-bound African American female) is the heroine in *The Great Circle Race* (she uses her intricate knowledge of the importance of slope for navigation, plus her ability to read topographical maps, to pick the best route for the race); and so forth.

It is gratifying that our attempts to portray positive role models have not gone unnoticed. In her review of the Jasper Series for *Technology and Learning*, Eiser stated, "Of the products we have looked at, the one that most fully incorporates the ideas expressed in the NCTM standards—including mathematical sophistication, stress on group work, and real-world relevance, is . . . the Adventures of Jasper Woodbury" (p. 58). Later in her review, Eiser stated:

> The quality of the video is particularly noteworthy, with characters carefully portrayed as rough hewn and realistic. Without making an issue out of race, religion, gender or appearance, the videos are remarkably free of stereotypes. It is only in looking back that you notice the woman gas jockey, the black principal, the Native American and Hispanic heroines.

Challenges.   Our observations of classrooms illustrate some of the challenges involved in promoting effective mathematical thinking. One involves the fact that some teachers had difficulty managing classrooms that involved collaborative group learning. Appropriate approaches to management are necessary, but not sufficient for promoting high-quality mathematical discussions. An excellent program for teaching management that we have used is COMP by Evertson and her colleagues (Evertson & Harris, 1994).

Even with appropriate management of group learning, some Jasper classrooms focused almost exclusively on discussions of computation. Therefore, when asked to explain how and why they came up with their particular plan for solving a Jasper, the teachers had their students focus on showing that their computations were correct. There was very little emphasis on assumptions underlying proposed solutions, or on discussions of alternative approaches that one might consider. It became clear to us that the idea of what it meant to have a mathematical discussion in the context of Jasper needed to be clarified.

Our classroom observations also drove home another lesson that we saw again and again: Student-generated questions about Jasper adventures and its extensions frequently taxed teachers' knowledge of mathematics. They often taxed the knowledge of our research team as well. For example, in *The Big Splash* Chris uses a sample size of 60. When students extend their

Jasper experience by developing business plans relevant to their own schools, they encounter issues of sample size. If their school population size is twice as large as the one in the Jasper adventure (Chris's population size was 360), should the sample size be 120? Remain at 60? What principles of statistics help one decide?

We also discovered that it was difficult to come up with on-the-spot ways to help students understand difficult concepts. How could students be helped to *conceptualize* rate problems such as the time to fill the pool rather than simply compute an answer based on a formula? How could they be helped to understand the mathematics involved in translating from minutes to hours rather than to simply consult a look-up table? How could they be helped to understand how to draw a top view of a swingset or slide for their blueprints and why a top view was necessary? These and many additional issues made it clear that teachers needed help in supporting the kinds of mathematical discussions that we hoped would take place.

Overall, our experiences in classrooms helped us realize how much we as a research team rely on our own "learning community" as a source of information to help us make sense of new or complex situations (Barron et al., 1995). We could not rely solely on teachers manuals for professional development, nor could we rely on one-shot workshops that prepared teachers for every contingency when they taught Jasper. Instead, teachers needed ongoing access to their own learning community so that they could continue to question and learn for themselves.

Tools for Teachers and Students.   One strategy that we have developed for supporting teacher learning communities involves the development of video-based teaching tools that teachers can use to help students (and sometimes themselves) understand difficult concepts. Some of these tools are made available on the Jasper videodisc and can be viewed first by teachers and then shown to the class when the need arises. Many illustrate ways to help students and teachers think visually about mathematical concepts rather than only computationally. For example, a visual "proportional reasoning" tool helps students understand proportions visually and then helps them translate this understanding to symbolic representations. A dynamic visual of a clock helps students translate minutes into hours.

Other tools for students and teachers are embedded in the Jasper adventures and referred to as *embedded teaching*. These involve the equivalent of "worked-out examples" (Chi, Bassok, Lewis, & Glaser, 1989; Chi, deLeeuw, Chiu, & LaVancher, 1994) that are part of the story line leading to the challenge. For example, a character in the video might show how to use graph paper to avoid the need for trigonometry in solving a geometry problem; how to use a compass to triangulate; how to create a graph paper ruler to measure the length of diagonals. We do not expect viewers to fully understand the embedded teaching the first time through the Jasper story; instead, they can return to these scenes and engage in "just-in-time learning" while attempting to solve the Jasper challenge. The embedded teaching examples in Jasper never directly provide answers for the Jasper challenges; instead, they model solution strategies that have to be adapted to the challenges in order to work.

SMART Challenges That Are Anchored Around Jasper Videos. Our classroom observations also helped us see the need to break the isolation of classrooms by having teachers and their students become part of a larger community that was jointly working on selected Jasper challenges and projects based on these challenges. We developed the idea of SMART Challenges as a way to achieve this goal (CTGV, 1994).

SMART stands for "Special Multimedia Arenas for Refining Thinking." These arenas use telecommunications and television technology (and eventually the Internet) to provide students and teachers with feedback about the thoughts of other groups who are attempting to solve a particular Jasper adventure. Students can look at others' work and decide whether they want to revise their own. For example, students working on *Blueprint for Success* may see data from 60 other students about relationships between the length of the legs for their A-frame swingsets and the desired height of their swingsets (see Fig. 8.6). Students also see visual representations of various types of designs. Figure 8.7 shows a design for an A-frame swingset where the length of the legs equals the desired height of the swingset. This design is one that is commonly suggested by many students. The visual model helps students see that this design does not work.

SMART Challenges also include the introduction of "just-in-time tools" that help students conceptualize the subproblems on which they are working in the Jasper adventure. For example, Fig. 8.8 shows a static representation of a dynamic scene that lets students see the top view of a swingset, slide,

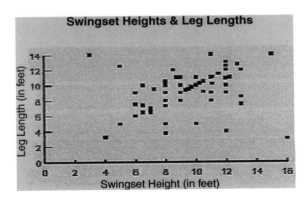

FIG. 8.6.   Data on swingset heights and leg lengths.

Swingset Heights & Leg Lengths

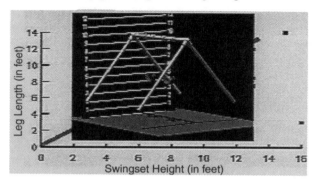

FIG. 8.7.   Visual illustration of a problematic design.

and sandbox. The specification of top views is necessary for accurate architectural drawings. Without visual models, many students have a difficult time imagining appropriate top views.

SMART Challenges also include models of students discussing their proposed solutions to various parts of the Jasper adventure. These are designed to provide models of discussions that emphasize mathematical understanding rather than just computation. Students learn to critique these models and improve on them.

SMART Challenges have been explicitly studied in the context of *Rescue at Boone's Meadow, The Big Splash,* and *Blueprint for Success.* (Barron et al., 1995; CTGV, 1994). The addition of SMART Challenges to the Jasper series has been shown to have a value-added affect on achievement relative to Jasper alone. Students in SMART learn more relevant content and are

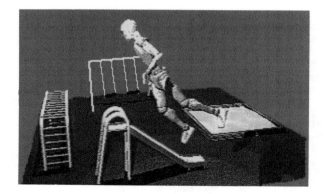

FIG. 8.8.   Scene from a dynamic tool to show the top views of the playground equipment.

able provide better explanations of their thinking than students who have not had the benefit of SMART (Barron et al., 1995).

PHASE 4: INCREASED EMPHASIS ON POWERFUL MATHEMATICAL IDEAS

Within the past year, our LTC has reached a new phase of thinking about mathematical thinking by placing increased emphasis on the goal of helping students and teachers understand powerful mathematical ideas that transcend particular Jasper adventures (including their analogs and extensions). Examples include concepts such as rates, proportions, and functions. We have also developed a way to make these abstract concepts interesting and meaningful to students by encouraging them to make mathematical models of situations and create "SMART Tools" that can be used to solve a large number of problems with great efficiency. The idea of creating SMART Tools has been exciting for students.

The emphasis on building mathematical models and SMART Tools arose in the context of developing the Jasper pre-algebra and algebra adventures. We wanted to avoid approaches to algebra that simply introduce students to the syntax of symbol manipulation but provide no understanding of the concepts underlying the manipulations. In accordance with recommendations from the NCTM (1989), the concept of function was one that we particularly wanted students to understand.

Observations and interviews with students indicated that problems encountered by students when learning algebra were similar to those encountered in geometry. Like the geometry students discussed previously, algebra students often spent their time manipulating strings of symbols and learning how to make graphs from function tables, yet had very little idea of what they were doing and why.

We wanted to help students realize that, in defining functions, they are constructing mathematical models of situations that are potentially very powerful. Furthermore, when these models are tailored to fit particular contexts, they can function as SMART Tools for making problem solving highly efficient. Simply trying to explain this to students, however, did little good. The first Jasper adventure in the algebra series that we completed, *Working SMART*, was designed to help students develop an insight into the power of building mathematical models and creating SMART Tools. It is illustrated in Fig. 8.9.

In order to solve *Working SMART*, students must re-explore the video to find the four problem types featured in the game show. They then must determine reasonable constraints on the problems; for example, constraints on the types of speed limits in the area, on the fuel capacity and fuel efficiency

Set in 1968, Working Smart is a story about three teenagers - Jasper, Emily, and Larry. Jasper and Larry start a business building and delivering birdhouses. To help them determine a fair price to charge for delivery, Grandpa shows them a Smart Tool that he used when he had a similar business. The Smart Tool is a graph showing delivery times and distances for 3 different modes of transportation.

Emily arrives with exciting news. There is going to be a contest at a local travel agency. All student teams who do well in the contest will receive an all expense paid trip anywhere in the country. Jasper suggests that the three of them study geography in order to have an edge in the contest. Grandpa suggests that they should create some Smart Tools like his to help them answer questions about travel time.

Ignoring Grandpa's advice the three friends diligently study geography to prepare for the contest. But when they arrive at the travel agency for the preliminary round, they discover that none of the questions are about geography. They are about travel time (including overtake problems), cost of renting vehicles, and fuel consumption. As a result, Jasper, Emily, and Larry do not do as well as they had hoped in the preliminary round. Disappointed and discouraged, the three leave the travel agency to ponder what to do next.

As they are discussing their options for the next round of the contest, Grandpa returns from delivering birdhouses. He mentions that his Smart Tool is still helpful in determining the time it will take to deliver a birdhouse. Emily realizes that Grandpa's Smart Tool would be helpful in answering questions for the contest at the travel agency, and she convinces Jasper and Larry that they should create Smart Tools.

Challenge: Create Smart Tools to help Larry, Jasper, and Emily pass the final interview.

FIG. 8.9. Synopsis of "Working Smart."

of the types of cars rented by the travel agency, on the range of distances people usually drive, and so forth. These constraints allow students to create SMART Tools that fit the needs of the situation. More information about the construction of these tools is provided in the following discussion.

Working SMART in the Classroom

The Jasper Algebra adventures are new, therefore we have limited experience using them in classrooms. Nevertheless, we have had opportunities to conduct several pilot experiments that have been extremely informative. One involved seventh graders whose mathematics skills were quite low. (These were not students who had previously worked with Jasper adventures.) For example, on a pretest the students scored less than 20% correct on simple problems such as the following:

1. How long does it take Emily and her mother to drive 165 miles at 55 mph?
2. Emily and her family took a trip. They traveled for 2½ hours at a speed of 55 mph. How far did they travel?

The students' reactions to these problems reminded us of our early research on word problems that led to the development of Jasper (see our earlier discussion). There was a great deal of anxiety expressed by students as they attempted to solve the problems on the pretest.

After asking students to calculate answers to problems, we supplied them with graphs that they could use to solve the problems. For example, a graph relevant to problem 1, which was just presented, appears in Fig. 8.10. Data indicated that few students knew how to use the graphs to solve problems. Their scores on the pretest were only 30% correct.

Following the pretest, students watched *Working SMART* and then started on the challenge. They were initially asked to develop a SMART Tool to help with one of the four problem categories in the travel agency quiz—the "Are We There Yet?" category.

Students' initial reaction to the challenge was revealing. They wanted to know what the problem was that they would be asked to solve. Without specific information, they felt that they could not do anything to prepare a tool to help them.

Using an Existing Tool. One approach to helping students develop an understanding of SMART Tools is to use Grandpa's SMART Tool that was shown in the video (an example of embedded teaching). Students need to understand how it allowed him to solve a *whole class* of distance–rate–time problems (see Fig. 8.11). For example, consider problems such as the following:

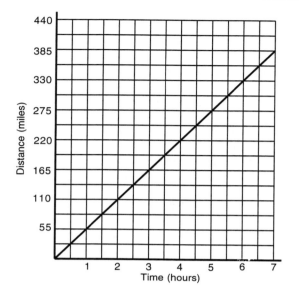

FIG. 8.10. Smart Tool to determine travel times and distances for speed of 55 mph.

1. Grandpa agrees to deliver a birdhouse to someone who lives 5 miles away. He takes his bicycle and rides at an average speed of 15 miles per hour. How long will it take Grandpa to deliver the birdhouse?

2. Grandpa has been walking for 2 hours at a speed of 3 mph. How far has he traveled?

3. Grandpa has traveled 30 miles in 2 hours. What method of transportation is he using?

4. Grandpa is traveling at a speed of 15 miles per hour. How long will he have traveled after ½ hour?

5. Grandpa can take his truck or his bicycle to deliver a birdhouse that is 10 miles away. How much sooner will he arrive at the house if he takes his truck?

Grandpa's SMART Tool (Fig. 8.11) allows students to answer these questions and many more. A useful exercise is to have students generate additional problems that can be answered by using Grandpa's SMART Tool.

Adapting an Existing Tool. Grandpa's SMART Tool needs to be adapted in order to help young Emily, Larry and Jasper win the travel agency contest. Students must re-explore the video in order to learn about the constraints that are relevant for constructing SMART Tools that fit the context.

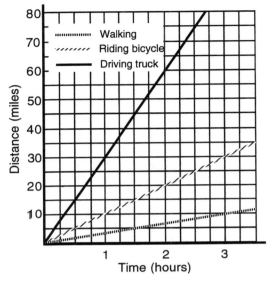

FIG. 8.11. Grandpa's Smart Tool.

As an illustration, consider creating a SMART Tool for the problem category "Are We There Yet." This involves simple distance–rate–time problems that people who rent cars from the travel agency are likely to ask. A search of the video reveals that relevant constraints on distances and rates are contained in the map used during the Travel Agency quiz (e.g., the primary speed limits to worry about are 30, 45, and 60 mph; the range of driving distances are from 1 to about 500 miles). Using these constraints on distances and speed limits, students must prepare a SMART Tool that fits the constraints.

Students who participated in our pilot study were asked to prepare their tools for the "Are We There Yet" category. They were given a copy of the map shown in the game show and then received a set of problems that allowed them to test their tools' mettle. For example:

1. How long should it take me to get to Sue City by car?
2. I have been driving for 2 hours at 60 mph and I am in the country. Can you tell me the nearest town.
3. If I drive 45 mph rather than 60 mph, how much longer will it take me to get to Hanford (which is 260 miles away)?

Opportunities to test the mettle of their tools are very important for students. Until they create tools and test them, many fail to appreciate the power of the SMART Tool concept. In addition, creating and testing tools gives students a better sense of what it means to think about the kinds of constraints they should consider (e.g., with respect to distances and speeds) when building their tools.

In our pilot studies, students have been allowed to revise their tools for the "Are We There Yet" category and test their mettle once again. All groups created better SMART Tools the second time around. An example of an effective SMART Tool for the problem category "Are We There Yet" is illustrated in Fig. 8.12.

In our pilot studies, students then had opportunities to create SMART Tools for two additional categories in *Working SMART*: "Burning Backs" and "Catch 'Em If You Can." (We did not do all possible categories due to time constraints.) This time the students had a much better understanding of their goals and constraints. A posttest provided students with graphs that they could use as SMART Tools to solve the original problems presented during the pretest. Students averaged over 75% correct on the posttest (compared to a score of 30% on the pretest). In addition, every student showed a clear gain in scores from pretest to posttest.

Overall, our experiences with helping students create SMART Tools show that it helps them begin to make the transition from thinking about mathematics as "using numbers to get answers to a problem" to thinking about it as a way to build models that are applicable to a wide range of situations, and to build special purpose SMART tools that are consistent with these models. For example, thinking of average speeds in terms of functions is quite different

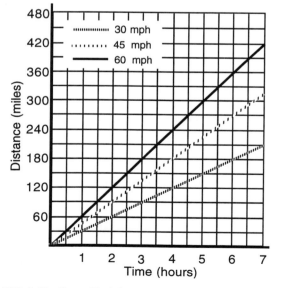

FIG. 8.12. Smart Tool for category "Are We There Yet?"

from thinking of them in terms of single numerical values (e.g., 3 mph, 15 mph, and 30 mph). Information about functions can also become an efficient SMART Tool in a way that a value such as 30 mph cannot.

The experience of learning to think visually about problems was empowering to students—they were very excited to discover an approach to mathematics that was different from the computation-based approach that had so frequently caused them problems. This is a reaction to SMART Tools that we have found repeatedly—both during the formative work that led to the Jasper algebra adventures and in subsequent pilot studies as well.

Extension Problems. Extension problems to *Working SMART* are being designed to help students deepen their understanding of mathematical modeling and, in the process, to begin to appreciate the power of thinking in terms of abstract concepts such as rates, proportions, and functions. (We design extension problems and teaching tools after having the opportunity to work with Jasper adventures on multiple classroom contexts.) In addition, the two additional Jasper algebra adventures are being designed to help students further develop an understanding of the power of algebraic thinking. We describe these additional adventures after discussing our plans for extensions to *Working SMART*.

Modeling By Defining Functions. Extensions to *Working SMART* will help students deal with models that represent nonlinear as well as linear functions. For example, imagine modeling Grandpa's speed while walking, riding a bike, and driving in his old truck under conditions where the total distance to be traveled is 20 miles and the speed limit is 30 mph for the first 10 miles and 20 mph for the second 10 miles. Assuming that Grandpa always obeys speed limits (which he does), the change from a speed limit of 30 mph to 20 mph will affect his rate in the truck, hence changing it from a linear to a piecewise-defined function. In addition, the fact that humans tire out when walking or riding long distances means that a model of Grandpa using these two modes of transportation must also be nonlinear (e.g., they may include rest times with 0 speed or gradually decreasing rates of speed as fatigue sets in).

With additional information about how Grandpa plans to handle fatigue, students can create a SMART Tool that allows them to estimate (a) how far Grandpa would have traveled given a particular mode of transportation and particular length of time, and (b) how much time Grandpa must have been traveling given that he used a particular mode of transportation to travel a given number of miles (e.g., "Grandpa is walking and has traveled 3 miles. Approximately how long has he walked?").

Other kinds of extension problems will involve additional nonlinear functions such as power functions. We eventually want to help students realize that there are properties of different kinds of functions that are very useful to understand.

We emphasize the idea of *creating* mathematical models and SMART Tools because this seems to represent one of the essential characteristics of effective mathematical thinking. Of particular importance is the idea of creating mathematical models of real life situations (e.g., a model of Grandpa's truck driving at 30). This is very different from being given a function table and asked to create the appropriate graph. (The latter task can easily become a purely procedural exercise with no connection to insights about the power of "modeling the world.")

Revisiting Other Adventures. Additional extensions to *Working SMART* will revisit many of the earlier Jasper adventures and give students practice at generating models that can serve as SMART Tools for further problem solving. For example, in *Rescue at Boone's Meadow*, Larry's ultralight is used to rescue a wounded eagle. How might one model the flying time of the ultralight given particular conditions of headwinds and tailwinds? In addition, how might one model flying time given the range (fuel capacity and consumption) of the plane? In *The Big Splash*, how might one model the rate of filling the pool with the school hose given particular values about flow rate of the water from the hose and volume of the pool?

Eventually, we want to help students understand that a general model for rate can apply to a variety of different situations. The model can be transformed into useful SMART Tools when it is calibrated for particular contextual conditions (e.g., when it takes into account the appropriate values for range and speed that fit Larry's ultralight, or the flow rate for the school hose and volume for the pool in *The Big Splash*).

Additional "Big Ideas." Extensions to *Working SMART* will also emphasize other "big ideas" in mathematics. The idea of creating scale models that preserve proportions is another powerful idea which we want students to understand. One extension for *Working SMART* will show scale models of vehicles from the 1960s (the time period of this episode): vehicles such as a Volkswagen bus, a classic Schwin bicycle, and a classic Corvette. Students will be shown how information about a particular scale (e.g., 1:18) can be used to predict the actual size of a real vehicle from the model, and vice versa.

The challenge to be posed to students is to create a SMART Tool that allows easy conversations from information about scale models to real objects and vice versa. For example, if one wants to make a model of a VW bus that is 1:12 scale, what should be the height and length of the model bus and its doors and windows, the diameter of its wheels, and so forth. What should these be if the scale is 1:18? SMART Tools that involve proportions can also be created for adventures such as *Blueprint for Success,* which involve the creation of blueprints and models of playgrounds that are accurate with respect to scale.

Figure 8.13 provides an illustration of a SMART Tool for working with models of particular proportions. As long as we are dealing with length, width, and height, the functions are linear. However, as soon as we ask about relationships such as area and volume (e.g., the area of the back door on the van, the volume of the interior of the van), the relationships are no longer linear. Exercises such as this help students think about linear versus nonlinear functions, and linear and nonlinear aspects of creating scale models. It also sensitizes them to the importance of knowing the conditions under which to use a SMART Tool.

Figure 8.14 illustrates a commercial version of a wheel-based Proportions Tool for illustrators and designers. It is an ingenious device that is based on a model of proportions that is invisible to most students. By helping students create their own wheel-based proportions tools and compare them to their graphs, the mathematical model underlying the SMART Tool can be appreciated and understood.

The idea of models that preserve essential ingredients of "the real thing" can also be extended to the Jasper statistics adventures. These adventures feature the use of techniques of randomly sampling to make estimates about important characteristics of larger populations. In essence, the sample serves as a model for the population. Extrapolating to a population involves proportional reasoning as well. Therefore, if 20 out of 40 people in a randomly

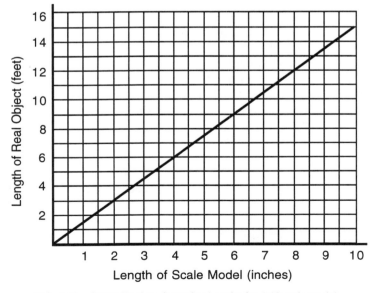

FIG. 8.13.   Smart Tool to determine lengths for 1:18 scale model.

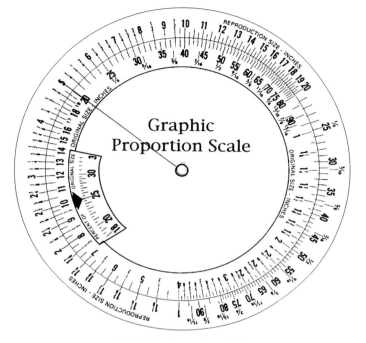

FIG. 8.14. Proportion wheel.

drawn sample answer "yes" to a question, the best estimate is that 50 people will say "yes" if one's population size is 100. Students can build SMART Tools for converting from sample to population data that look very much like the proportion tools discussed earlier.

Clearly, the principles underlying a model based on probability theory is different from the principles underlying models for creating scale models such as model cars or models of buildings. Helping students understand the similarities underlying these uses of models should set the stage for appreciating their differences as well.

The General is Missing

A follow-on adventure to *Working SMART* is designed to reinforce the idea of creating models and SMART Tools, plus help students understand the value of symbolizing their models and using algebra as a tool for communication. Called *The General Is Missing*, this adventure also features young Larry, Jasper, and Emily, plus Larry's Grandpa. Early in the adventure Grandpa introduces students to a code used in the revolutionary war and, in the process, does some "embedded teaching" about algebra. He has Emily, Larry, and Jasper plot two functions, cut out the space in the middle of them, and use the cutout as a stencil to place over a message he has written. The stencil reveals a secret message that he wants them to see.

Young Larry, Jasper, and Emily eventually leave Grandpa's workshop and three shady characters enter. They want Grandpa's secret invention and demand that he come with them. The movie shows scenes of Grandpa being blindfolded and occasionally peeking out of his blindfold to record relevant data (e.g., speed limits and how long they traveled at these speeds; time of day relative to sounds such as an air raid siren; etc.).

When the shady characters get to their hideout, Grandpa convinces them that he must continue to communicate with the children or they will become suspicious. He needs to send a set of algebra problems for them to work on the next day. Grandpa disguises his messages as algebra homework and attempts to tell the children where he is. However, one of the characters has taken his notebook and he cannot remember all the data. He decides to send a general message that helps the children create SMART Tools.

The challenge for students in the classroom is to construct SMART Tools from Grandpa's algebra messages. Examples of the information they receive is shown in Fig. 8.15. Students learn that Grandpa will send additional data later. When he does, they need to use their SMART Tools to determine as quickly as possible where Grandpa is on the map.

The solution to this adventure again requires students to create SMART Tools in order to respond quickly to final data to be sent by Grandpa. However, in this case students must begin to understand algebraic notation in order to construct their SMART Tools. Extensions to this adventure will continue to help students model events in terms of functions and represent them symbolically as well as visually. Pilot data suggest that the adventure helps students develop the idea of algebra as a language for communicating important mathematical ideas.

We are just beginning to create the third Jasper adventure in the algebra series. It will probably become the middle one in the series because we have found that students need help in understanding the concept of rate. Our ultimate goal for the three Jasper algebra adventures is to provide a foundation for the formal study of algebra that enables students to understand what they are doing and why.

OVERALL SUMMARY AND CONCLUSIONS

The focus of our discussion has been on the goal of facilitating mathematical thinking in middle school students. We approached this topic by discussing important changes in our LTC's thinking about the nature of mathematical thinking, and we organized our discussion into four temporally ordered phases.

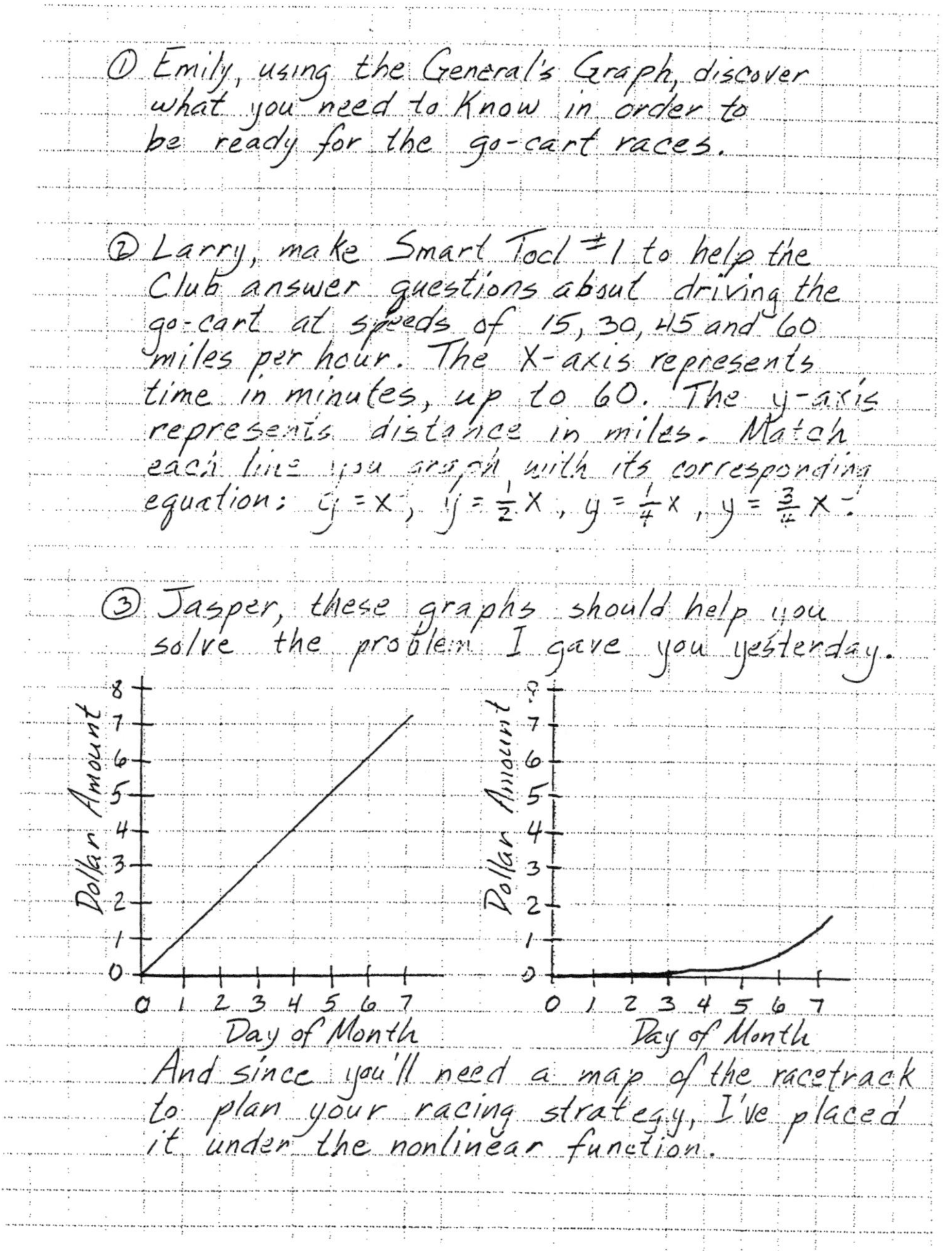

① Emily, using the General's Graph, discover what you need to Know in order to be ready for the go-cart races.

② Larry, make Smart Tool #1 to help the Club answer questions about driving the go-cart at speeds of 15, 30, 45 and 60 miles per hour. The X-axis represents time in minutes, up to 60. The y-axis represents distance in miles. Match each line you graph with its corresponding equation: $y = x$, $y = \frac{1}{2}x$, $y = \frac{1}{4}x$, $y = \frac{3}{4}x$.

③ Jasper, these graphs should help you solve the problem I gave you yesterday.

And since you'll need a map of the racetrack to plan your racing strategy, I've placed it under the nonlinear function.

FIG. 8.15. *(Continued)*

240

④ Emily, some racetracks are circular. Make Smart Tool #2 to help the Club determine the distance of each lap if you only know the diameter of the track in miles. Measuring several circular objects in the workshop might help. Check your work.

Which of the following graphs more closely approximates your Smart Tool?

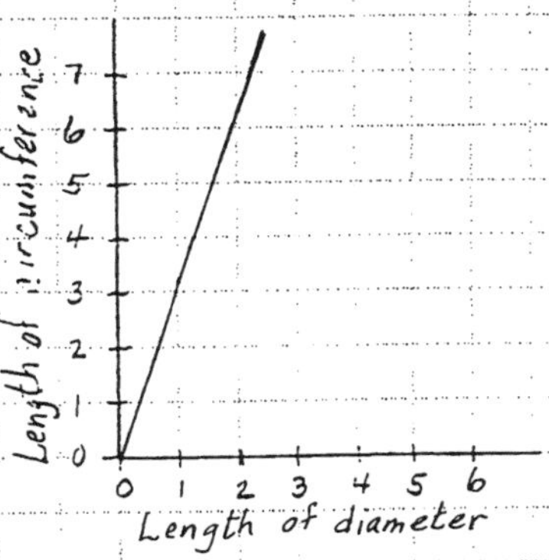

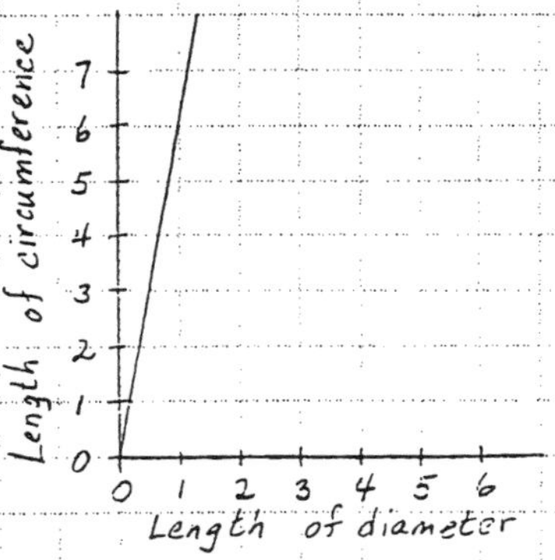

Which of the following symbolic expressions describes the correct graph: $y = 6.28x$, $y = 3.14x^2$, or $y = 3.14x$?

⑤ Larry, in a road rally race, you often have to drive up hills. It's helpful to determine their elevations based on the horizontal distance you travel. Make Smart Tool #3 for these equations: $y = \frac{3}{100}x + 200$, $y = \frac{4}{100}x + 200$, $y = \frac{5}{100}x + 200$, and $y = \frac{6}{100}x + 200$. The horizontal distance you drive (up to 10,000 feet) should be represented on the bottom axis.

⑥ Jasper, create Smart Tool #4 to help you determine how far sound will travel in x seconds. Make sure your graph shows the distance (in miles) sound travels as a function of time (in seconds). Remember that sound travels at 760 miles per hour.

FIG. 8.15. Grandpa's directions.

Phase 1. Making Word Problems Meaningful

We found that students were failing to comprehend even simple word problems and, instead, were simply looking for key words that would tell them whether to add, subtract, multiply, or divide the numbers provided in the problem. They used all the numbers in problems, even those that were clearly irrelevant. Our approach to this problem was to provide visual support for understanding word problems; for example, we taught problem solving in the context of relevant scenes from *Raiders of the Lost Ark* (Bransford et al., 1988). The findings were very promising, but we needed to extend the range of problems to be considered. Therefore, we expanded our work to *The River Adventure* prototype and, eventually, to the Jasper Series.

Phase 2. Helping Students Identify and Define
Their Own Word Problems Rather Than Always Rely
on Others to Define Them For Them

We worried that typical approaches to presenting students with well-defined word problems would not help them learn to take complex, real-world situations and generate their own problems. Because this was an aspect of mathematical thinking that seemed particularly important to us, we designed our *River Adventure* prototype, and our subsequent Jasper adventures, so that students would be given an overall goal but had to define for themselves the necessary subgoals, plus find the data relevant to each subgoal. Our pretest data on problem generation indicated that even students who scored very well on traditional tests of mathematics achievement had a very difficult time generating appropriate subgoals for themselves. However, after experience with complex problems such as those used in the Jasper series, students exhibited a very promising ability to transfer to additional, complex problems (e.g., CTGV, 1992d, 1994).

Phase 3. Focusing More Directly on Mathematical
Concepts, Reasoning, and Communication

This phase of our work involved the opportunity to develop the Jasper Woodbury Series. The mathematics educators and cognitive psychologists in our center began to work much more closely with one another. The NCTM (1989) standards provided extremely useful guidelines for (a) choosing the mathematical content to be taught, and (b) providing a vision of the kinds of mathematical thinking we wanted to see in the students. We especially focused on the NCTM goals of problem solving, reasoning, communication, and making connections to a variety for disciplines.

Development of the first two Jasper adventures was modeled after the earlier work conducted with *Raiders* and *The River Adventure*—these had essentially involved the creation of interesting adventures with the mathematics tacked on afterward. Subsequent Jaspers were developed by first considering the mathematical content to be understood and then creating contexts for making this information meaningful. Domains that were covered include introductions to statistics, geometry, and eventually pre-algebra and algebra.

The development of Jasper provided numerous opportunities for us to collaborate with classroom teachers who used various adventures with their students. They suggested innovative ways to use Jasper, including using it as a context for parents and others to try their hand at problem solving while being guided by the experts—the students. We were also able to conduct a number of studies on the effects of Jasper on students' attitudes toward mathematics as well as their ability to solve problems and communicate their ideas (e.g., CTGV, 1992b; 1992d; 1994).

Opportunities to collaborate with classroom teachers also helped us understand the challenges of working with open-ended materials such as Jasper. Students' questions frequently took all of us—our research team and the teachers—to the edge of our knowledge of mathematics. This prompted us to create a number of supports for teaching, including teaching manuals to accompany each adventure, an interactive disc showing ways to teach Jasper in the classroom, and video-based tools that help make important mathematical concepts understandable both to teachers and students. We also developed our SMART programs, which represent ways to break the isolation of classrooms by inviting teachers and students to tune into programs designed to help them reflect on their own work, and revise when necessary, as they solve various Jasper adventures (CTGV, 1994). Data indicated clear advantages for using Jasper adventures by themselves, but noted that they were even more valuable when used in the context of SMART (Barron et al., 1995).

Phase 4. Taking Jasper to a New Level by Focusing on Powerful Mathematical Ideas

The fourth phase of thinking about mathematical thinking is one that we entered only within the past year, and find extremely exciting. It involves attempts to move the thinking of students, teachers, and many members of our research team to a new level of mathematical competence and understanding. The goal is to help students understand mathematics at levels of abstraction that are well-known to mathematicians. Ideas at this level are populated by concepts such as rates, proportions, and functions.

A major challenge for our research team has been to find ways to help students acquire abstract mathematical knowledge in a manner that is meaningful. The Jasper pre-algebra and algebra adventures are designed to help students develop the idea of creating mathematical models of situations (e.g., by thinking in terms of functions) and then contextualizing these models to create SMART Tools that make problem solving efficient. As particular models and SMART Tools are adapted to a variety of situations involving the same concept (e.g., rates, proportions), we hope to help develop an appreciation of the power of these concepts. The goal is to help students, teachers, and ourselves develop the habits of mind of mathematizing the world by thinking in terms of models and the creation of SMART Tools. Students move from visually based tools to computer tools that are symbol-based.

THREE MAJOR THEMES

The opportunity to reflect on our Center's path of development during the past 7 years suggests three major themes that are relevant to thinking about mathematical thinking.

Variable Views About Mathematical Thinking

First, what is meant by mathematical thinking varies greatly among individuals. To many students, the definition of mathematical thinking is restricted to the use of numbers and formulas to find answers to specific problems, and to the memorization of mathematical terms. There is little emphasis on inquiry, creativity, problem finding and pattern finding. There is little emphasis on the fact that, by mathematizing aspects of the world, one can discover systematicity across a wide variety of seemingly different situations. There is little opportunity to experience the excitement that accompanies discovery of the usefulness of powerful mathematical ideas.

In our early work described in the first section of this chapter, we noted that many students simply looked for key words (e.g., "times") in word problems and used these to select a mathematical operation to use on all the numbers in a problem. Similarly limited views of mathematical thinking were discovered when we worked with students in the context of developing the Jasper triplets for statistics, geometry, and algebra. Our interviews on statistics suggested that middle school students had little idea of the process of taking a systematic sample of cases in order to make estimates about a larger population; instead, they kept viewing efforts to contact individuals about their opinions as efforts to advertise. Similarly, in our work on geometry we found that most students had memorized definitions of geometric terms (e.g., the definitions of a line, a point, or acute and obtuse angles) but had little or no idea of what geometry was used for. In our work on algebra we saw an emphasis on symbol manipulation, but almost no understanding of what these symbols represented and how they could function as powerful conceptual tools. Throughout all our work, we saw a great deal of anxiety with respect to mathematics. This anxiety is also evident in a large number of the nonmathematics majors we see at the college level. It is unfortunate, and it is unnecessary.

In many cases students' limited views of mathematics were quite similar to their teachers' views. Many middle school teachers have not had the opportunity to explore mathematics from the perspective suggested by groups such as the NCTM (1989). Their views are derived primarily from their experiences as students in mathematics classes. As noted earlier, many of the nonmathematicians in our center were in a position similar to the middle school teachers. Our views of mathematical thinking were restricted because that is the way we learned mathematics in school.

Helping People Change their Views
About Mathematical Thinking

A second major theme that emerges from our experiences is that the task of changing people's understanding of mathematical thinking is a daunting challenge. We know this from our own personal experiences as well as from our research. The nonmathematicians on our team (the "intelligent novices") have repeatedly expressed appreciation for the opportunity to work closely with mathematics educators and observe firsthand their approaches to problems. Similarly, the mathematics educators report having benefited from the opportunity to interact with "intelligent novices" and see what it takes to make mathematical concepts meaningful to "outsiders." Changes in thinking about mathematical thinking have occurred for members of both groups.

Although it is hard to believe we were so naive, in our early days with Jasper we tended to assume that the adventures alone would be sufficient to change students' views of the nature of mathematical thinking. Indeed, we have evidence that students who used Jasper across the course of a school year increased their appreciation of mathematics and their willingness to tackle complex problems (CTGV, 1992d). Furthermore, we have added to Jasper a number of scaffolds for students and teachers such as "embedded teaching," "video-based teaching tools," and SMART programs that are wrapped around Jasper adventures. Each of these additions to Jasper has helped the teaching and learning that takes place in classrooms. Nevertheless, we still see that environments such as Jasper can be used very differently depending on the beliefs of the teachers (CTGV, 1992c, 1994). Without changing teachers' beliefs in ways that impact the classroom norms that are created (e.g., Cobb, 1994), innovative curriculum materials fail to achieve their potential.

We have also learned that the idea of "belief" is more complicated than appears at first glance. Many teachers seem willing to believe in the idea of expanding students' views of mathematical thinking so that it includes ideas such as problem solving, reasoning, communication, and making connections to other disciplines (NCTM, 1989). The "intelligent novices" on our research team began with similar beliefs. Nevertheless, humans have a strong tendency to *assimilate* information to their existing knowledge or schemata rather than change their schemas to accommodate to new knowledge (e.g., Anderson, Osborn, & Tierney, 1984; Bransford, 1984). Therefore, it is easy to think one is following recommendations such as those in the NCTM standards and yet, in reality, be far away from the intent of the authors of those standards. *We believed we were being consistent with the NCTM standards during each of the four phases of thinking about mathematical thinking that we described in this chapter*—and it seems clear that our thinking about mathematical thinking still needs to (and hopefully will) evolve.

We know from other literatures (e.g., Bruer, 1993) that the process of conceptual change is not easy and rarely (if ever) instantaneous. Our experiences in working with teachers, and our personal experiences of change as we have worked on Jasper, testify to this fact. Conceptual change requires ongoing opportunities to interact with members of a broader community and reflect on those interactions. The establishment of professional "learning communities" is something that we now view as "necessary and not just nice" (e.g., Barron et al., 1995; CTGV, 1994).

We believe we have been successful in making some "intermediate" level changes in thinking about mathematical thinking, and in helping teachers and students also make these changes. Our work in geometry represents a case in point. Our data indicate that students and teachers have a much greater appreciation of uses of geometry after working with the Jasper Geometry adventures (Zech et al., 1994, in press). Instead of simply memorizing facts and performing procedures such as measuring angles, students and teachers have begun to understand how to use geometry for "measuring the world." Similar insights have occurred with respect to uses of statistics in everyday life (e.g., Barron et al., 1995; Schwartz et al., in press).

Our work in the area of algebra represents a change in thinking about mathematical thought that has implications for the way we view the entire Jasper series. The idea of focusing on the importance of creating mathematical models, and SMART Tools based on these models, can be used in each of the Jasper adventures and beyond. It represents a change in thinking both by the mathematics educators in our group as well as by the "intelligent novices."

Our Concept of Mathematical Thinking Is Still Evolving

The third theme that emerges from opportunities to reflect on the development of our center's thinking is that our efforts to define and promote mathematical thinking are still evolving. Our current emphasis on SMART Tools is helping us focus on making abstract mathematical concepts meaningful and useful to students. We are not exactly sure where this level of thinking will lead us; nevertheless, it seems to be an avenue that is valuable to pursue. We also believe that the availability of new technologies (e.g., CTGV, in press) presents exciting opportunities for changing the nature of how students think mathematically. For example, a host of mathematical concepts such as rate and proportion can now be represented *dynamically* rather than statically, hence making them easier to understand. Similarly, computer tools make it easier to link symbolic with dynamic visual representations, and to provide simulations of complex mathematical models of situations (e.g., CTGV, in press; Zech & Bransford, in press).

Overall, our experiences with changes in our own thinking make us aware that we still have a great deal to learn. Like the students and teachers with whom we work, we need the advantages of ongoing conversations about mathematical thinking and how to enhance it. Toward that end, we are posing a World Wide Web site (http://peabody.vanderbilt.edu/projects/funded/jasper/Jasperhome.html). The site provides more information about Jasper and will ultimately become a place to discuss issues such as creating mathematical tools, SMART Tools, and problems for testing the mettle of those tools. We are hopeful that this site can help generate conversations that will allow our group, and others, to move beyond the "intermediate-level" changes in mathematical thinking that we have experienced. As a community, we have the chance to introduce students to a concept of mathematical thinking that is much more exciting and appealing than the ones that many of them, and many of us, have encountered in school.

ACKNOWLEDGMENTS

The research reported in this chapter was supported, in part, by grants from McDonnell Foundation No. JSMF91–6 and the National Science Foundation, Nos. ESI9252990, ESI9252900, and MDR9050191. The ideas expressed in this chapter are those of the authors, not the granting agencies.

The Cognition and Technology Group at Vanderbilt (CTGV) refers to an interdisciplinary group of individuals at the Learning Technology Center, Peabody College at Vanderbilt University. Members of the CTGV contributing to the work discussed in this chapter are the following (in alphabetical order): Linda Barron, Thad Crews, Laura Goin, Elizabeth Goldman, Susan Goldman, Rachelle Hackett, Ted S. Hasselbring, Daniel Hickey, Cindy Hmelo, Ronald Kantor, Xiaodong Lin, Cynthia Mayfield-Stewart, Joyce Moore, Mitchell Nathan, James W. Pellegrino, Faapio Poe, Anthony Petrosino, Teresa Secules, Robert Sherwood, Carolyn Stalcup, Laura Till, Sashank Varma, and Susan Williams.

REFERENCES

Anderson, R. C., Osborn, J., & Tierney, R. (Eds.). (1984). *Learning to read in American schools: Basal readers and content texts*. Hillsdale, NJ: Lawrence Erlbaum Associates.

Barron, B. J., Bransford, J. D., Kulewicz, S., & Hasselbring, T. S. (1989, April). *Uses of macrocontexts to facilitate mathematical thinking*. Paper presented at the meeting of the American Educational Research Association meeting, San Francisco, CA.

Barron, B., Vye, N. J., Zech, L., Schwartz, D., Bransford, J. D., Goldman, S. R., Pellegrino, J., Morris, J., Garrison, S., & Kantor, R. (1995). Creating contexts for community-based problem solving: The Jasper challenge series. In C. N. Hedley, P. Antonacci, & M. Rabinowitz (Eds.), *Thinking and literacy: The mind at work* (pp. 47–71). Hillsdale, NJ: Lawrence Erlbaum Associates.

Bransford, J. D. (1984). Schema activation versus schema acquisition. In R. C. Anderson, J. Osborn, & R. Tierney (Eds.), *Learning to read in American schools: Basal readers and content texts* (pp. 259–272). Hillsdale, NJ: Lawrence Erlbaum Associates.

Bransford, J. D., Delclos, V., Vye, N., Burns, S., & Hasselbring, T. (1987). Approaches to dynamic assessment: Issues, data and future directions. In C. Lidz (Ed.), *Dynamic assessment: An interactional approach to evaluating learning potentials* (pp. 479–495). New York: Guilford.

Bransford, J. D., Hasselbring, T., Barron, B., Kulewicz, S., Littlefield, J., & Goin, L. (1988). Uses of macro-contexts to facilitate mathematical thinking. In R. I. Charles & E. A. Silver (Eds.), *The teaching and assessing of mathematical problem solving* (pp. 125–147). Hillsdale, NJ: Lawrence Erlbaum Associates & National Council of Teachers of Mathematics.

Bransford, J. D., Sherwood, R., Vye, N., & Rieser, J. (1986). Teaching thinking and problem solving: Research Foundations. *American Psychologist, 41*, 1078–1089.

Bransford, J. D., & Stein, B. S. (1984). *The IDEAL problem solver*. New York: Freeman.

Bransford, J. D., & Stein, B. S. (1993). *The IDEAL problem solver* (2nd ed.). New York: Freeman.

Brown, S. I., & Walters, M. I. (1993). *The art of problem posing* (2nd ed.). Hillsdale, NJ: Lawrence Erlbaum Associates.

Bruer, J. T. (1993). *Schools for thought*. Cambridge, MA: MIT Press.

Campione, J. C., & Brown, A. L. (1987). Linking dynamic assessment with school achievement. In C. S. Lidz (Ed.), *Dynamic assessment: An interactional approach to evaluating learning potential* (pp. 82–114). NY: Guilford.

Charles R., & Silver, E. A. (Eds.). (1988). *The teaching and assessing of mathematical problem solving*. Hillsdale, NJ: Lawrence Erlbaum Associates & National Council for Teachers of Mathematics.

Chi, M. T., Bassok, M., Lewis, P. J., & Glaser, R. (1989). Self-explanations: How students study and use examples in learning to solve problems. *Cognitive Science, 13*, 145–182.

Chi, M. T. H, deLeeuw, N., Chiu, M., & LaVancher, C. (1994). Eliciting self-explanations improves understanding. *Cognitive Science, 18*, 439–477.

Chi, M. T. H., Glaser, R., & Farr, M. (1991). *The nature of expertise*. Hillsdale, NJ: Lawrence Erlbaum Associates.

Cobb, P. (1994). Where is the mind? Constructivist and sociocultural perspectives on mathematical development. *Educational Researcher, 23*(7), 13–20.

Cognition and Technology Group at Vanderbilt. (1992a). The Jasper experiment: An exploration of issues in learning and instructional design. *Educational Technology Research and Development, 40*, 65–80.

Cognition and Technology Group at Vanderbilt. (1992b). The Jasper series: A generative approach to mathematical thinking. In K. Sheingold, L. G. Roberts, & S. M. Malcolm (Eds.), *This Year in Science Series 1991: Technology for teaching and learning* (pp. 108–140). Washington, DC: American Association for the Advancement of Science.

Cognition and Technology Group at Vanderbilt. (1992c). The Jasper experiment: An exploration of issues in learning and instructional design. *Educational Technology Research and Development, 40,* 65–80.

Cognition and Technology Group at Vanderbilt. (1992d). The Jasper series as an example of anchored instruction: Theory, program description, and assessment data. *Educational Psychologist, 27,* 291–315.

Cognition and Technology Group at Vanderbilt. (1993a). The Jasper series: Theoretical foundations and data on problem solving and transfer. In L. A. Penner, G. M. Batsche, H. M. Knoff, & D. L. Nelson (Eds.), *The challenges in mathematics and science education: Psychology's response* (pp. 113–152). Washington, DC: American Psychological Association.

Cognition and Technology Group at Vanderbilt. (1993b, March). Anchored instruction and situated cognition revisited. *Educational Technology, 33,* 52–70.

Cognition and Technology Group at Vanderbilt. (1994). From visual word problems to learning communities: Changing conceptions of cognitive research. In K. McGilly (Ed.), *Classroom lessons: Integrating cognitive theory and classroom practice* (pp. 157–200). Cambridge, MA: MIT Press.

Cognition and Technology Group at Vanderbilt. (in press). Looking at technology in context: A framework for understanding technology and education research. In D. C. Berliner & R. C. Calfee (Eds.), *The Handbook of Educational Psychology.* New York: Macmillan.

DeCorte, E., Greer, B., & Verschaffel, L. (in press). Center for instructional psychology and technology. In D. Berliner & R. Calfee (Eds.), *Handbook of Educational Psychology.* New York: Macmillan.

Duncker, K. (1945). Experiments demonstrating functional fixedness were conducted on problem solving. *Psychological Monographs, 58*(5).

Evertson, C., & Harris, A. (1994). *COMP: Classroom organization and management program.* (Workshop manual for elementary teacher, 4th Ed.). Nashville, TN: Peabody College at Vanderbilt University.

Feuerstein, R., Rand, Y., & Hoffman, M. (1979). *The dynamic assessment of retarded performers: The learning potential assessment device, theory, instruments, and techniques.* Baltimore, MD: University Park Press.

Furman, L., Barron, B., Montavon, E., Vye, N. J., Bransford, J. D., & Shah, P. (1989, April). *The effects of problem formulation training and type of feedback on math handicapped students' problem solving abilities.* Paper presented at the meeting of the American Educational Research Association meeting, San Francisco, CA.

Kilpatrick, J. (1992). Problem formulating: Where do good problems come from? In A. H. Schoenfeld (Ed.), *Cognitive science and mathematics education* (pp. 3–38). New York: Macmillan.

Lidz, C. (Ed.). (1987). *Dynamic assessment: An interactional approach to evaluating learning potentials.* New York: Guilford.

McNamara, T. P., Miller, D. L., & Bransford, J. D. (1991). Mental models and reading comprehension. In R. Barr, M. Kamil, P. Mosenthal, & T. D. Pearson (Eds.), *Handbook of Reading Research* (Vol 2, pp. 490–511). New York: Longman.

Montavon, E., Furman, L., Barron, B., Bransford, J. D., & Hasselbring, T. S. (1989, April). *The effects of varied context training and irrelevant information training on the transfer of math problem solving skills.* Paper presented at the meeting of the American Educational Research Association meeting, San Francisco, CA.

National Council of Teachers of Mathematics (1989). *Curriculum and evaluation standards for school mathematics.* Reston, VA: Author.

Reusser, K. (1988). Problem solving beyond the logic of things: Contextual effects on understanding and solving word problems. *Instructional Science, 17,* 309–338.

Schwartz, D., Goldman, S. R., Vye, N. J., Barron, B. J., & Cognition and Technology Group at Vanderbilt (in press). Using anchored instruction to align everyday and mathematical reasoning: The case of sampling assumptions. In S. Lajoie (Ed.), *Reflections on statistics: Agendas for learning, teaching, and assessment in K–12*. Hillsdale, NJ: Lawrence Erlbaum Associates.

Shulman, L. (1986). Those who understand: Knowledge growth in teaching. *Educational Researcher, 15*(2), 4–14.

Shulman, L. (1987). Knowledge and teaching: Foundations of the new reform. *Harvard Educational Review, 57*, 1–22.

Silver, E. A. (1986). Using conceptual and procedural knowledge: A focus on relationships. In J. Hiebert (Ed.), *Conceptual and procedural knowledge: The case of mathematics* (pp. 181–189). Hillsdale, NJ: Lawrence Erlbaum Associates.

Sternberg, R. J. (1986). *Intelligence applied*. San Diego, CA: Harcourt Brace Jovanovich.

Turnbull, H. W. (1993). *The great mathematicians*. New York: Barnes & Noble.

Van Haneghan, J. P., Barron, L., Young, M. F., Williams, S. M., Vye, N. J., & Bransford, J. D. (1992). The Jasper series: An experiment with new ways to enhance mathematical thinking. In D. F. Halpern (Ed.), *Enhancing thinking skills in the sciences and mathematics* (pp. 15–38). Hillsdale, NJ: Lawrence Erlbaum Associates.

Vye, N. J., Burns, M. S., Delclos, V. R., & Bransford, J. D. (1987). A comprehensive approach to assessing intellectually handicapped children. In C. S. Lidz (Ed.), *Dynamic assessment: An interactional approach to evaluating learning potential* (pp. 327–359). New York: Guilford.

Vygotsky, L. S. (1978). *Mind in society: The development of higher psychological processes*. Cambridge, MA: Harvard University Press.

Wood, D. (1980). Teaching the young child: Some relationships between social interaction, language and thought. In D. Olson (Ed.), *The social foundations of language and thought* (pp. 280–296). New York: Norton.

Zech, L., & Bransford, J. D. (in press). Cognition, technology and mathematics education: Issues and opportunities. *NCSM Newsletter of the National Council of Teachers of Mathematics*.

Zech, L., Vye, N. J., Bransford, J. D., Swink, J., Mayfield-Stewart, C., Goldman, S. R., & Cognition and Technology Group at Vanderbilt (1994). Bringing the world of geometry into the classroom with videodisc technology. *Mathematics Teaching in the Middle School, 1*(3), 228–233.

Zech, L., Vye, N. J., Bransford, J. D., Goldman, S. R., Barron, B. J., Schwartz, D. L., Kisst-Hackett, R., Mayfield-Stewart, C., & Cognition and Technology Group at Vanderbilt. (in press). An introduction to geometry through anchored instruction. In R. Lehrer & D. Chazan (Eds.), *New directions for teaching and learning geometry*. Hillsdale, NJ: Lawrence Erlbaum Associates.

MATHEMATICAL
APPROACHES

9

On Different Facets of Mathematical Thinking

Tommy Dreyfus
Center for Technological Education
Holon, Israel

Theodore Eisenberg
Ben-Gurion University
Beer Sheva, Israel

AESTHETICS

What is "Mathematics"? Is it the science of patterns that is motivated through observations of nature, or is it the body of knowledge derived from pure axiomatic logic, aspects of which have applications in nature? Is it manmade or are individuals simply uncovering the work of a higher deity? Is mathematics intuitively driven or is it logically driven? Is abstraction an inherent part of it or is it simply the medium of its communication? Are proofs of theorems time dependent or do they stand as absolute truths? Does it stand on a base of Aristotelian logic or can mathematical statements have a variety of meanings and degrees of truth? Are the demarcation lines as to what is mathematics as opposed to physics, economics, linguistics, or even astronomy defined clearly enough so that one could classify selected pages of textbooks from those disciplines as belonging to those disciplines? Questions like these soon lead us to the unsettling conclusion that there is no definitive answer as to "what is mathematics and what is not." When asking "what is mathematical thought," however, the situation gets a little better, and a little worse.

For most individuals the nature of mathematics is formed from the impressions of its facets studied in the school curriculum, and through one's interactions with the teachers who tried to unlock their mysteries and explain their interconnections. Those facets consist of arithmetic, algebra, geometry, trigonometry, and calculus. For school mathematics it is irrelevant if mathe-

TABLE 9.1
Two Solutions to the Same Problem

A	B
512 matches were played in the first round, 256 were played in round two, 128 in round three. . . . So the number of matches played to determine the winner must be: 512 + 256 + 128 + 64 + 32 + 16 + 8 + 4 + 2 + 1 = 1023	1024 players were enrolled in the tournament. There was only one winner, so there were 1023 losers. Each loser lost exactly one match, so there had to be 1023 matches to determine the winner.

matics is discovered or uncovered, if it is based on Aristotelian logic, or is based on some other type of logic. The curriculum consists of mastering certain notions and different types of problems, and many of them are not easy. One can "do" mathematics without being able to define what "is" mathematics. Mathematical thought is therefore simply the type of thinking process used in doing mathematics. Thus, on the surface things seem to be a little better—mathematical thought has been defined on a notion that is ill-defined. Delving deeper, things get muddled pretty quickly, for some thought patterns seem to be more mathematical than others. For example, suppose there are 1024 tennis players in a single elimination tournament. How many matches must be played to determine the winner? Suppose A and B reason as in Table 9.1.

In another example, assume that there are four numbers among which you are to find out the largest on the basis of the following information: When the numbers are summed up in threes, they add up to the results 10, 11, 13, and 14 respectively. Person A would presumably set up a system of four equations in four unknowns and use one of several well-known algorithms to solve that system. However, B might reason that when we sum all four results each of the original numbers occurs three times in this sum; dividing it by three, we will thus get the sum of the four original numbers (16 in our numerical example). Now subtract the smallest of the four results (the one from which the largest number is missing) to get the largest number – 6 in our example.

The same solution is reached by two different routes of thought, but the reasoning of B seems to be much more elegant than that of A. The method used by A is a pedestrian route, but the simplicity of the argument used by B has a touch of class about it, a certain aesthetic appeal—and for many professional mathematicians, that is the essence of mathematical thinking. Henri Poincaré put it this way:

> Mathematicians attach great importance to the elegance of their methods and their results. This is not pure dilettantism. What is it indeed that gives us the feeling of elegance in a solution, in a demonstration? It is the harmony of the diverse parts, their symmetry, their happy balance; in a word it is all that introduces order, all that gives unity, that permits us to see clearly and to

comprehend at once both the ensemble and the details. But this is exactly what yields great results. (cited in Moritz, 1914, p. 97)

G. H. Hardy (1940) put it much more succinctly: "The mathematician's patterns, like the painter's or the poet's must be beautiful" (p. 25).

There seem to be two schools of thought: To one school, mathematical reasoning deals with much more than the thought patterns needed to solve particular problems. It deals with a way of thinking that can be assessed by the subjective metric of aesthetics. The minute aesthetics enters into the picture, however, assessing mathematical thought gets complicated, for a mathematical structure or solution must not only "do the job," it must do it elegantly. The four color problem (any planar map can be colored with exactly four colors in such a way that adjacent countries have different colors) was solved with the aid of a computer by analyzing a huge number of configurations. However, this method of proof caused an uproar in the mathematics community, for it did the job but it did it in a crude, inelegant, brute-force sort of way. This method of proof shook mathematics to its very foundations, but the role of aesthetics as being at its core has survived in spite of it:

> I am much less likely now, after their work, to go looking for a counter-example to the four color conjecture than I was before. To that extent, what has happened convinced me that the four color theorem is true. I have a religious belief that some day soon, maybe 6 months from now, maybe 60 years from now, somebody will write a proof of the four color problem that will take up 60 pages in the Pacific Journal of Mathematics. Soon after that, perhaps 6 months or 60 years later, somebody will write a four page proof, based on the concepts that in the meantime we have developed and structured and understood. The result will belong to the grand glorious architectural structure of mathematics. (Halmos cited in Albers, 1982, pp. 239–240)

Mathematical thought, therefore, is much more than the abilities utilized in absorbing some piece of mathematics or in solving some mathematical problem; it is closely associated with an assessment of elegance. For those in this school, mathematical thinking "reflects . . . the desire for aesthetic perfection" (Courant & Robbins, 1941, p. xv), and its hallmarks are "simplicity, intricacy and above all, logical analysis" (Halmos, 1968, p. 30).

Some teachers believe they know how to instill in students the necessary criteria against which elegance can be measured. For example, there is a compendium of school-level problems with several solution paths, one of which is considered to be much more elegant than the others. Juxtaposing the solution paths and comparing and contrasting them is a classic method for developing an appreciation for the aesthetics and power of mathematical thought. Proofs of the irrationality of $\sqrt{2}$ (Harris, 1971) and the infinitude of primes (Davis & Hersh, 1981) are two of the more popular exercises used to introduce students to the aesthetics of thought. Members in the second school of thought agree that there are such classic proofs and exercises to instill in students a sense of aesthetics and the power of mathematical thought, but submit that it is irresponsible to even attempt to teach such things to students because most students seem to be completely ignorant of even the most basic problem-solving skills.

Members of the second school readily admit that their teaching and the curriculum have failed miserably to instill even a modicum of mathematical thinking in the overwhelming public majority. Lists of "simple" problems that no one seems to be able to do are becoming so long that it is embarrassing to continue the practice of making them. Forget aesthetics, forget elegance and juxtaposed solutions paths—so many students are deficient in so many simple skills that we are in the midst of an epidemic of ignorance running wild. Orton (1992) has bemoaned the fact that there are high school students in the U.K. who write the number four hundred and twenty-seven as 40027, and they have no idea why their answers are incorrect; Gillman (1994) has bemoaned the finding that 97% of the more than a quarter of a million U.S. high school students queried could not correctly answer the following question:

> Under a proposed income tax, you pay nothing on income up to $10,000, then 6% on any excess over $10,000. The effective tax rate is the percent of the income that you pay in tax. Can this be 5%? Can it be 6%?

Mason, Burton, and Stacey (1982) have complained that students don't know how to determine what to do first: take a 20% discount on an item and then pay a 15% tax, or pay the tax first and then take the discount. Selden, Selden, and Mason (1994) have lamented our failures at the collegiate level with their finding that *even good calculus students cannot do nonroutine problems.*

The lists enumerating our failure to get students to solve problems in even pedestrian ways seems to be never ending. Perhaps the highest level of mathematical thought does deal with elegance and aesthetics, but should we be concerned with aesthetics where there is the mountain of data detailing our miserable performance in getting students to solve even the simplest of problems and which society has legitimized by making it "socially acceptable" to claim that "I was never very good in math" and "Math is not for me"?

In the following discussion, problems from different areas of mathematics are discussed and used for illustrating particular facets of mathematical thinking. These problems are collected in Table 9.2 not only for convenience, but also to give readers a chance to analyze their own mathematical thinking before reading on.

In this chapter we identify several facets of thought that are common to both characterizations of mathematical thinking. At the base of our discussion is the premise that within each characterization most everyone can be

TABLE 9.2
Some Mathematical Problems

1. Into how many regions, at most, can five planes split E_3 (the ordinary, three-dimensional Euclidean space)?

2. Given the numbers 1, 7, 13, 29, 31, 43, 57, 59 and 61, is it possible to choose five of them which sum to 188?

3. What is the probability that an arbitrarily picked integer is divisible by three, five or seven?

4. Prove that $\dfrac{(a^2 + 1)(b^2 + 1)(c^2 + 1)}{abc} \geq 8$.

5. Given a line and two points A, B on the same side of the line, find the shortest path from point A to B via a (any) point on the line.

6. Tom went for two runs, one of 3 and one of 5 miles. For the 3-mile run he needed 17 minutes. How long did he need for the 5-mile run, if he ran slower than on the 3-mile run by half a minute per mile?

7. Given two intersecting lines in the plane, find the geometric locus of all points the sum of whose distances from the two lines equals a given length.

8. In a parking lot there are only bicycles and cars; if there are a total of 20 tires in the lot, how many bicycles and how many cars are there?

---

trained to think in a mathematical way, and that the best way to achieve this is through problem solving. Specifically, we illustrate the facets of mathematical thinking that deal with analogy, structure, representation, visualization, and reversibility of thought. We also comment on the role self-confidence plays in mathematical thinking and on several schools of thought as to how mathematical thinking should be developed. As is so often the case, however, the whole is greater than the sum of its parts, and thus we attempt to show in the concluding section that these facets add up and combine to increase the flexibility of one's mathematical thinking patterns.

SELF-CONFIDENCE

Self-confidence built on success is the most important objective of the mathematics curriculum.
—"Everybody Counts," 1989

The pursuit of good feeling in education is a dead end. The way to true self-esteem is through real achievement and real learning.
—Krauthammer, 1990

These quotes reflect our firm belief that everyone, to a large extent, can be taught to think mathematically and that the way to do this is through problem solving. There are at least two successful schools of thought on how mathematical thinking can be developed. One advocates intense competition—this is the heart of the Moore Method; the other uses Cooperative Learning as its main teaching technique. The two approaches may at first seem to be diametrically opposite but they are, in fact, related.

The Moore Method

There are many ways of teaching mathematics. The "chalk-and-talk" method is probably best known, but it forces students into a receptive and passive role: Students take notes from a learned professor and digest the content in them. They absorb knowledge and often apply it through well-designed problem sets, but they seldom create knowledge themselves. Essentially, students become receptive validators of information created by others. Students certainly do internalize the concepts, but it is a digestive process rather than a creative one. The Moore method of teaching mathematics is built from a different premise.

R. L. Moore (1882–1980) was a professor of mathematics at the University of Texas. His style of teaching was unique and very, very successful as evidenced by the cadre of individuals he developed who surged to the forefront of 20th-century mathematics. His technique was to pit one student against another in a competitive situation. He would present to students the definitions and the hypotheses of theorems, and they themselves would construct appropriate conclusions and proofs of the statements. In other words, the students under his tutelage built mathematical structures day by day, year after year. Moore had his students promise that they would never look anything up in textbooks or in journals, and that they would address all of their questions on the material to him, and to him alone. His thesis was that progress and creative abilities are nurtured through competition—not friendly competition—but cut-throat competition. The easiest way to get a person to solve a problem is to tell him that an (unnamed) dunce (of another class) solved it! During class Moore would call on student X to present a particular problem. If others in the room had not yet solved the problem themselves, and they did not wish to see the solution, they could leave the class and return when student X had finished his presentation. Moore's premise was that mathematical progress is a result of intense competition, and that confidence in one's ability is a result of one's mathematical progress. In other words, there is a symbiotic relationship between progress and confidence. Strange as this might sound, the system really worked—at least for Moore's students. For example, Mary Ellen Rudin, by her own admission, was an average student. However, she fell under Moore's tutelage and went on to become one of the leading topologists in the United States. In an interview, she stated:

> He built up your ego and your competitiveness. . . . I had my confidence built, and my confidence was plenty strong. . . . He built your confidence that you

could do anything. No matter what mathematical problem you were faced with you could do it. I have that total confidence to this day. (Albers & Reid, 1988, p. 122)

The Moore method is built on the Chinese proverb "I hear, I forget; I see, I remember; I do, I understand." Moore simply had his students construct mathematics—something that most teachers do not even try to get their students to do. For most of us, we are content if students can understand the mathematics, but many of us believe that to have them construct mathematics is out of the realm of their ability. This, as we see later, is nonsense. One reason we hold these views is that few of us have created mathematics ourselves, and another reason is technical: Moore dealt with highly motivated graduate students—we see unmotivated undergraduates or high school students with deeply ingrained inferiority complexes with respect to their mathematics ability. As we see here, both of these can be overcome.

Humanizing Moore: Cooperative Learning

Moore was successful in producing research mathematicians, but his method of pitting one student against another is rather repugnant, at least to many in the education field. Therefore, several intense efforts were made to humanize him. One of the more successful of these approaches was initiated by Neil Davidson (1986) of the University of Maryland—and this turned into a new international educational movement called "cooperative learning." Davidson developed a teaching method over a 25-year period that is built on Moore's principles, but which factors out the competitive element of the Moore method. Davidson divides classes into groups of four, poses definitions and theorems to the groups, and then stands back to let the students develop the solutions themselves. The role of the instructor is drastically changed, from being the presenter of information to that of acting solely as a resource individual. Davidson has a long list of guidelines to aid the instructor in deciding when he can join in with discussions of the students and when he should remain quiet, but the idea is that students construct their own mathematics. Davidson is interested in the mathematics as well as the social dynamics of the working sessions, but a serendipitous outcome of his teaching style is that students have their self-confidence bolstered. Indeed, they often create novel proofs of theorems. One of us personally observed a group of average students in Davidson's class construct the proof that the limit of the product of two functions is equal to the product of the limit of the functions (assuming that the individual limits exist). This is a very difficult theorem and to think that these students did this with only the barest of mathematical machinery attests to the power of his methods.

This idea of cooperative learning is relatively new in mathematics, but it seems to work. Treisman (1992), for example, noticed that many Asian students would do their mathematics together in small groups, whereas Black American students would attempt to do all of their work alone. For the Asian students, the mathematics was an extension of their social life; for the Black Americans it seemed to be separate from their social life. Treisman developed a program that encourages Black American students to talk mathematics, to bring mathematics into their social milieu. His method has been so successful that it is being adopted throughout the United States (Jackson, 1988).

REASONING BY ANALOGY

An extremely important key in developing mathematical thinking ability is to train oneself to look for analogies. "Problem X looks like problem Y and Y was solved by concentrating on property Z; therefore, perhaps there is an analogy to property Z in Problem X which acts like Z such that . . ." is a heuristic of problem solving that is cumulatively unique to each individual and develops over time. However, one must be trained to look for such analogies and there are general kinds of questions one can be taught to ask oneself when faced with a new problem or situation.

A tremendous literature exists on the heuristics of problem solving but George Polya (1887–1987) is considered the modern day father of it all. He was born in Budapest and was an eminent mathematician, first at the Swiss Federal Institute in Zurich (from 1914 to 1940) and then at Stanford until his death. He was a classical mathematician working in the areas complex variables and combinatorial analysis. However, throughout his career he was always interested in how mathematics is done, how discoveries are made, and how problems are solved. His reflections on this and his deep interest in teaching gave birth, in 1945, to the book *How to Solve It*. This is very much a "how-to" book that starts off with a set of heuristics in the form of questions and commands. *What is the unknown? Do you know a related problem? Find the connection between the data and the unknown. Draw a figure. . . .* This book has become a classic in the mathematics education literature, and to those interested in the role of analogy, models, and metaphors in science and mathematics. "How to Solve It," however, disavows an overall systematic theory for solving problems; to Polya, problem solving is an art, and what he did was to lay down general hints as to how to develop it.

Over the years Polya wrote six books on the heuristics of problem solving, each extending the tone set in *How to Solve It* and laying bare the thinking processes and the tangential themes considered and abandoned in effecting solutions to problems. Collectively these books are case studies in how to attack a mathematical problem, but they do not present an overall theory for problem solving—to Polya, problem-solving abilities should be nurtured in the same way that skills in any other art form are nurtured. As such, Polya's books introduce one to the art of self-questioning, which is exemplified by taking the student through various types of exercises; introducing one to tangential paths, some taken and others abandoned, in effecting a solution and always, as his last step in the process, looking back and assessing what was done. Throughout his books there are gems of wit that made wide impact on teachers: "Work in letters, not numbers" (1945, p. 58). "If you can't construct a figure, construct one geometrically similar" (1965, p. 9). "Check only 'touchy' parts of an argument" (1945, p. 17). "Two proofs are better than one" (p. 60). "Good problems, like mushrooms, grow in clusters" (p. 64). "An idea that can be used only once is a trick. If one can use it more than once it becomes a method" (Polya & Szegö, 1972, p. viii).

Polya was a master at exhibiting thinking in terms of analogies. If the givens of the problems are too restrictive, relax them, solve the simpler problem, and then reason inductively to the more complex case. Problems in 3-space often have counterparts in 2-space; and problems in the plane often have counterparts on the line; solve these simple cases first. By using this method of thinking on problem after problem, students seemed to learn the heuristic of looking for analogies. We illustrate his method by discussing the Problem 1 of Table 9.2: Into how many regions, at most, can five planes split E_3 (the ordinary, three-dimensional Euclidean space).

The solution is that a single plane cuts space into two pieces; two planes can cut space into a maximum of four pieces and three planes into a maximum of eight pieces. Visualizing four planes and counting we might be able to see that they can cut space into a maximum of 15 separate pieces—but visualizing five planes is much more difficult and six or even more planes seems to be beyond the realm of visualization of most people. In the spirit of Polya, let us look for analogies in the plane and on the line.

A point separates a line into 2 distinct pieces. Two points separate a line into three distinct pieces; four points will separate it into five pieces and n points will separate it into $(n + 1)$ pieces.

Now let us look at lines in a plane. One line will separate a plane into two distinct pieces. Two lines will separate it into a maximum of four pieces because the second line can be positioned so as to cut through both parts generated by the first line. Of course, the third line cannot be positioned so as to cut through all four parts but only through three; thus, three lines will separate the plane into a maximum of seven pieces; similarly, the fourth line can be positioned so as to cut through four parts, thus four straight lines cut the plane into a maximum of 11 pieces. Continuing in like manner, a pattern arises; one easy way to detect this pattern is by organizing our findings into Table 9.3 listing the maximal number of regions as it depends on the dimension d of the space to be cut and the number n of points/lines/planes/hyperplanes that cut d-dimensional space.

In the second column of this table—the column giving the number of regions into which a plane is cut—every entry equals the sum of the entry

TABLE 9.3
Into How Many Parts Do n Hyperplanes Divide d-Dimensional Space?

d	1	2	3	4	5	...
n						
0	1	1	1	1	1	...
1	2	2	2	2	2	...
2	3	4	4	4	4	...
3	4	7	8	8	8	...
4	5	11	A_{34}	16	16	...
5	6	16	A_{35}	A_{45}	...	
...						
n	$n+1$	A_{2n}	A_{3n}	...		

above it and the number n of the line in which it occurs: $7 = 4 + 3$, $11 = 7 + 4$, $16 = 11 + 5$. This pattern allows one to easily continue column 2 ad infinitum; it is, however, one characteristic of mathematical thinking to put closure on such infinite processes by expressing them in a general manner. This can be done and leads to $A_{2n} = 1 + \frac{n(n+1)}{2}$ for the maximal number of regions into which n lines cut the plane. (The proof of the formula for A_{2n} is not difficult, but would serve no purpose here.)

Studying Table 9.3 more closely, we might now also be able to discover the recursive pattern according to which all entries of the table can be obtained. Namely, each entry equals the sum of the entry directly above it and the one to the left of that entry; that is, $A_{d,n} = A_{d,n-1} + A_{d-1,n-1}$. Therefore, $A_{34} = 8 + 7 = 15$, $A_{35} = 15 + 11 = 26$ (this, we note, provides the answer to the original problem), and $A_{45} = 15 + 16 = 31$. More generally, one can obtain formulas such as $A_{3n} = 1 + \frac{n(n^2+5)}{6}$. It is interesting to note here another crucial aspect of mathematical thinking that has played a central role in the solution process for this problem: generalization. Generalization and simplification are two aspects of analogy. Establishing analogies has led us here to attack a far more general problem than we originally intended; namely, into how many parts, at most, n hyperplanes cut d-dimensional space. We have also found some statements that are true but not easily visualized such as "five three-dimensional spaces cut the four-dimensional Euclidean space into at most 31 regions."

Finally, it is important to the mathematician to be very clear about what has been established rigorously, and what has not. It should be clear that we have not proved the solution we gave to this problem, but we most certainly have a better feel for it than before—and we obtained this feeling through the heuristic of analogy. It is satisfactory to note that a proof of the recursive relation $A_{d,n} = A_{d,n-1} + A_{d-1,n-1}$ can be built directly from the recursive relation itself by analyzing what happens when the nth hyperplane is added to the d-dimensional space with $n - 1$ hyperplanes. The analogous reasoning in the special case of E_3 is: Imagine $n - 1$ planes are given in E_3 cutting it into $A_{3,n-1}$ regions; now add an nth plane; look at this new plane as a two dimensional space E_2; the number of regions $A_{2,n-1}$ into which this E_2 is cut by the intersections with the $n - 1$ existing planes equals the number of newly generated regions in E_3, because these regions are exactly the newly introduced separations.

Polya maintained that by exposing students to many such problems, the heuristic of looking for analogies will be internalized by the student and exploited as needed. Whether or not it is sufficient to "expose" students may be doubted, and in the following sections some techniques are pointed out that may help students to more actively impose a structure on problems and observe analogous structures between problems. However, there is no doubt that analogies are a powerful tool in problem solving. Moreover, psychologists have shown that often new knowledge is also acquired through analogical reasoning, be it through overt analogies or subtle ones (e.g., Gick & Holyoak, 1983).

Indeed, we try to accommodate anything new into existing knowledge, and this is often done by making analogies. Although the demarcation lines between analogical reasoning and other educational constructs that are used to interpret "how" new knowledge is internalized by an individual are not well defined, analogical reasoning also seems to play a major role in concept formation, not just in problem solving. Statistics for continuous probability distributions are a case in point.

To start with a simple example, take the median. Given a random variable V, the median can be defined as a value m such that V falls with equal probability above and below m. If V is a discrete variable whose frequency distribution is known, m can be found by simply counting frequencies from both extremes on the distribution until one gets to the middle. But how to find the median of a continuous probability density? For this we need to understand what it means to "count" frequencies in the continuous case; and it is here that establishing an analogy can help the student in building the necessary generalization. This can be done by choosing to represent discrete and continuous distributions in the setting in which they are most alike; namely, the graphical setting. Depending on the background of the students, the analogy can then be carried out in more or less detail; in any case, the analogy should help students understand that the frequency, which in a discrete probability distribution is represented graphically by an area in the histogram, should be represented by a corresponding area under the curve giving the probability density. From there to the median it is only a small step.

If the students have previously understood how the Riemann integral is constructed as a limit of sums, the continuous probability density can be constructed, in the process of establishing the analogy, as a limiting case of a sequence of ever finer, ever more detailed discrete probability distributions. This may help stress the difference between the value of the probability density (which, as its name says, is a density) and the value of the discrete distribution, which represents a frequency or, graphically, an area of a rectangle (of width one—and that is where the confusion originates, because for such a rectangle the area numerically equals the height). By the way, we note that a second analogy has surreptitiously crept into our argument; namely, the one between Riemann integrals and probability densities.

It is also worth noting that although we started from the simple case of the median, the analogy we have proposed reaches the very ground of the connection between the discrete and the continuous case, and can therefore be used as a basis for establishing many more notions in the continuous case, including percentiles, means, variances, and standard deviations. On the other hand, it should also be realized that students' use of these concepts in the continuous case may rest on a rather superficial understanding unless the analogy has been established and understood in sufficient detail. Such detailed understanding can not be expected in view of the superficial treatment of the analogy in most general statistics books. In fact, more often than not, the analogy is not dealt with explicitly at all but appears in examples. Under such conditions, students cannot be expected to learn more than to mechanically go through the motions in the continuous case as well, and confusions such as the one between probability density and probability distribution are likely to occur.

Descriptive statistics has been used here as an example only. Analogies are as ubiquitous in concept formation as in problem solving. The transition from the area of a rectangle to more general areas and to the notion of integral (Dreyfus, 1987) is an example; so is the extension of the number system from the natural numbers to the integers, rationals, reals, and complex numbers (conservation of the properties of the operations), or the transition from numerical to algebraic thinking; in effect, any generalization or abstraction necessarily uses underlying analogies. A deep understanding of these analogies is apt help students make transitions in either direction: from the more general case to the simpler one, for example, when simplifying assumptions are needed in a problem-solving situation, or from the specific case to the general one in order to get a more encompassing result. In both cases, the use of analogies adds flexibility to the students' thinking processes.

STRUCTURE

Structure is one of the main characteristics of mathematics, one that by its pervasiveness in mathematics, and by its importance in mathematical thinking, sets mathematics apart from other sciences. In mathematics, facts are less important than in other domains; on the other hand, relationships between facts, relationships between relationships, and thus structure, are more important than in other domains.

It is a fact that $3 + 5 = 8$. It is a relationship between sets of numbers that the sum of two odd numbers is even. This relationship, as elementary as it is, helps one to come to grips with problems such as Problem 2 of Table 9.2; namely, given the numbers 1, 7, 13, 29, 31, 43, 57, 59, and 61, is it possible to choose five of them that sum to 188? In fact, if we also use the additional relationship that the sum of an even and an odd number is odd, it becomes clear that any sum of seven odd numbers must be odd, and thus the problem has no solution.

These relationships impose some structure on the integers; for example, even and odd numbers alternate, and this is true not only in those regions with which we are fairly familiar (between $-1,000,000$ and $+1,000,000$, say) but in any region of the integers; indeed, using the relationships for an arbitrary integer N and 1: if N is even, $N + 1$ is odd, and vice versa. (A similar argument, using -1 instead of 1, works in the opposite direction, down to minus infinity.) This structure can be further exploited: Pick any set of consecutive integers; in this set there are as many even numbers as there are odd ones, or one more or one less. In other words, the number N_e of even numbers differs from the number N_o of odd numbers by one, at most. Therefore, if $N_e + N_o$ is even, they must be equal.

A slight generalization of this result allows us to make progress towards solving far more general problems, such as Problem 3 in Table 9.2: What is the probability that an arbitrarily picked integer is divisible by 3, 5, or 7? The generalization structures the set of integers even more. Look at any set of consecutive integers—every second integer in this set is even; that is, divisible by 2, every third one is divisible by 3, every eleventh one by 11, and every Nth one by N. For the moment, let us assume that our set starts with 1 (or, more generally, with $105 \cdot k + 1 = 3 \cdot 5 \cdot 7 \cdot k + 1$ for an arbitrary k; for other starting numbers, slight corrections will be needed that are of no interest here). Then a third of the numbers in our set are divisible by 3; a fifth are divisible by 5 and a seventh by 7. We might think that we have solved the problem and that $\frac{1}{3} + \frac{1}{5} + \frac{1}{7}$ of all numbers in our set are divisible by 3 or by 5 or by 7. That is not quite correct, however, because numbers such as 15 and 21 play tricks on us (we counted them twice); but we have certainly made some progress—we have found an approximate solution to the problem.

Note that we have so far exhibited and used only a small fraction of the structure that can be imposed on the set of integers; for example, we have not looked closely at the multiplicative structure. We have not related to the fact that the integers form a group, a ring, a vector space, and so forth. These are some of the most important and most frequent structures occurring in mathematics. Groups, for example, are of central importance for the description of symmetry. In fact, symmetry may be defined using groups.

Suppose we are given a symmetric object; for simplicity, let us think about a geometric object, such as a regular pyramid (tetrahedron). The statement that the object is symmetric means that there are certain motions (rigid transformations: rotations and reflections) of the object that leave the object in a state which cannot be distinguished from the original state. For our pyramid, one such motion is to rotate the pyramid by 120° around an axis that contains one vertex of the pyramid and is perpendicular to the plane containing the other three vertices. There are other such motions—altogether 24 of them for the pyramid (12 of which are rotations). Each of these motions has an inverse motion that cancels its effect; carrying out any two motions in a row is equivalent to carrying out a different motion—one says that the set of all motions is closed. Closedness and the existence of an inverse are the two crucial properties of a group. Therefore, the motions of a tetrahedron form a group.

Similarly, the integers form a group if we consider addition of integers as the relevant group operation: Each integer has an inverse; namely, its negative. Indeed, adding the negative of a number cancels the effect of adding the number; also, the integers are closed. Adding a number and then adding another number is equivalent to adding their sum. Other groups are the (set of) permutations of n objects, and the rational numbers (with multiplication as the group operation, whereby the number 0 has to be omitted from the set).

Therefore, the symmetry of an object can be expressed economically, elegantly, and efficiently by means of the mathematical structure of a group. Vice versa, a group always points to some inherent structure of the object described by that group. For example, crystals have symmetry properties that point to their internal structure and to the manner in which the atoms are arranged within the crystal.

Identifying symmetries in a mathematical situation, describing the situation by means of symmetries, and exploiting the symmetries is a useful problem-solving heuristic. For example, in order to prove that $\frac{(a^2+1)(b^2+1)(c^2+1)}{abc} \geq 8$ (Problem 4 in Table 9.2) it helps to observe that the inequality is symmetric in a, b, and c (i.e., a and b can be exchanged without changing the inequality); in fact, based on this observation, it is sufficient to show that $\frac{(a^2+1)}{a} \geq 2$ because from that implies that also $\frac{(b^2+1)}{b} \geq 2$ and $\frac{(c^2+1)}{c} \geq 2$, and thus the product is greater than 8. Problem 5 in Table 9.2 is even better known: Given a line and two points A, B on the same side of the line, find the shortest path from a point A to B via a (any) point on the line. An intuitive and convincing solution to this problem reduces the problem to the much easier problem of finding the shortest path from A to B′ where B′ is symmetric to B with respect to the given line; namely, the straight line from A to B′. In fact, any path from A to B (via the line) has a corresponding path from A to B′ (the corresponding path is identical from A to the line and symmetric with respect to the line after that). Because the shortest way from A to B′ is the straight one, the shortest path from A to B is identical with the straight line from A to B′ until the line, and is its reflection after that.

Another class of symmetry transformations that are efficient in solving problems are function transformations (Eisenberg & Dreyfus, 1994)—that set of procedures which allows one to generate from a graph given in a Cartesian coordinate system, its translated and reflected images. Being conscious of these transformations often helps one extend the range of problems we are able to solve by several orders of magnitude. A frequent situation is the need to associate a formula with a given graph; suppose we know how to do that for a parabola whose vertex is at the origin, namely to associate with it a formula of the form $y = ax^2$. Using only the aforementioned transformations, we can then immediately associate the correct formula with any parabola. Similarly, if we know that the Laplace transform of a given function $F(t)$ is the function $f(s)$, we can find the Laplace transforms of the entire family of functions $F_a(t) = e^{-at}F(t)$ (for any number a)—it is simply the translate $f(s-a)$ of $f(s)$. (For more examples of the use of symmetry in mathematical problem solving, see Dreyfus & Eisenberg, 1990.)

In summary, being able to determine structure, of which symmetry is often an integral part, is central to mathematical thinking. What is structured are typically mathematical concepts. Structure comes from the concepts and thus naturally imposes itself on any problem or situation that concerns an instance of this concept. The structure tells one what actions one may or may not carry out. The structure develops one's appreciation, feeling for what could be done to solve a problem. Recognizing structure in a given problem, imposing structure on a situation, and exploiting this structure enormously increases one's mathematical power and flexibility. Identifying the same structure in different situations helps one to solve problems by analogy.

Finally, structure helps memory. We recall structured knowledge far better than unstructured knowledge; the prime example of this phenomenon is linear algebra, which is a very structured topic. As a consequence, there is a central core of concepts and relationships that, once grasped and integrated, allow one to organize the entire topic and conceive its unity. It can be observed that once a student gets to this stage, the amount of knowledge involved seems to collapse; examples that were completely disjoint now turn out to be essentially identical. Learning becomes a matter of adding minor additions to a well-structured body of knowledge, and problem solving becomes a matter of fitting the problem at hand into this structure (Harel & Kaput, 1991).

REPRESENTATION

In order to express any mathematical statement, concept, or problem, a representation must necessarily be used. Such a representation can be formal or informal, visual or verbal, explicit or implicit. Any representation will express some but not all of the information, stress some aspects and hide others. Some representations will be more adapted to express the mathematical structure in a problem or situation, others less. For example, Thompson (1990) proposed a theoretical framework that allows one to structure any word problem by means of a diagrammatic representations; we illustrate this by means of Problem 6 of Table 9.2:

> Tom went for two runs, one of 3 and one of 5 miles. For the 3-mile run he needed 17 minutes. How long did he need for the 5-mile run, if he ran slower than on the 3-mile run by half a minute per mile?

To the experienced solver, this problem is hardly more difficult than the following simple proportion problem:

> Tom ran 3 miles in 17 minutes. How long would it take him to run five miles?

To the student, however, even to the student who can handle proportions, the difference between the problems may be decisive; and the reason for this is the failure to recognize the structural analogy between them. The information in the verbal statement is fairly concise but not structured—certainly not structured in a manner that could support a learner to progress with the solution of the problem. The hint to look at a similar but simpler problem (Polya, 1945), although certainly correct, can only help those students who recognize the structural analogy; the hint does not provide any tools to find a simpler problem. An appropriate representation may provide such tools.

Thompson proposed the more structured representation of the problem situation given in Fig. 9.1. This figure expresses the inherent structure much more explicitly than the verbal statement, and it does this by using several conventions, some of which are easily understood by common sense, whereas others are specific agreements; one such convention is to list (or graph or sketch) all quantities that either occur among the givens, or occur in the question, as well as any related quantities that can be obtained from the

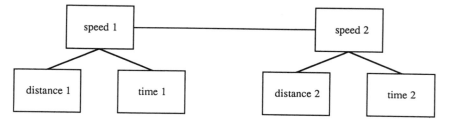

FIG. 9.1. Structured problem representation. Adapted from Thompson (1990). Reprinted with permission.

givens or might lead to the answer. The key word in the previous sentence is "related"! In fact, these quantities are listed not independently of each other, but with connecting lines that express links between the quantities. Further conventions could be to give different types of quantities (intensive, extensive, . . .) and different types of links (equality, multiplicative, additive, . . .) different graphical appearance, but this goes beyond the scope of the present discussion.

Although the general principles of this diagrammatic representation for word problems—represent "all" quantities, connect related quantities, and so on—are applicable to any word problem, the specific geometrical arrangement the specific connections in Fig. 9.1 have been chosen to stress the analogy between the two problems; indeed, the only difference between them, in this representation, is the type of link between speed 1 and speed 2; this link is an equality in the direct proportion problem, but a comparison in the more complex problem. Once one grasps that structural similarity, one problem is only slightly more difficult than the other one.

As Thompson (1990) pointed out, other geometrical arrangements and other links can be chosen to conceptualize and structure the simple proportion problem. Each of these other ways are more or less appropriate for various different views and generalizations of the proportion problem. Therefore, the general tool of diagrammatically representing word problems are effective problem-solving tools only to a student who has learned to use them flexibly, playing with different possible arrangements during the problem-solving process. As Thompson pointed out further, an (appropriately programmed) computer is an ideal learning environment for such problem solving because boxes can be moved around, connected and disconnected again in a flexible manner. (See Thompson, 1990, for a description of Word Problem Assistant—an appropriate computer environment.)

For many problems, representations may be and often are generated ad hoc; for many concepts, there is a standard representation and other ad hoc representations may be generated when necessary or useful; for other concepts, however, several different standard representations are commonly being used in conjunction. The paradigm for this is the function concept with its algebraic, graphical, tabular, and possibly other representations. Function is an abstract concept, and we cannot talk about a particular function without using at least one type of representation, such as the graphical one and specifying a particular representative; for example, the one given in Fig. 9.2.

This representative is partial: It shows, at best, the part of the graph of the function for which $-2 \leq x \leq 2$; and even this part is shown with rather limited accuracy. Another graphical representative of the same function, such as the one for $2 \leq x \leq 4$, would look very different. Although it is true that accuracy can be improved and other domains can be chosen, each graph will have some limitation of domain and of accuracy.

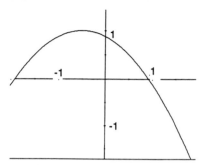

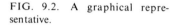

FIG. 9.2. A graphical representative.

Similarly, other representation have each their own limitations; different algebraic representatives of the same function like $f(x) = 4 \frac{(2-x-x^2)}{9}$ or $f(x) = 1 - \frac{4}{9} (x + \frac{1}{2})^2$ each give (and hide) very different information from each other and from the graphical representatives. Therefore, a function cannot be fully described in practice because this would require all its possible representatives. A student should thus become acquainted with several representations and learn how to generate representatives with specific properties. The use of functions in solving problems makes further demands: Just as in the word problem situation described earlier, a functional problem may be given in one representation but require another one, or even several other ones to be solved. Therefore, flexible use of the function concept in problem solving necessitates not only acquaintance with various representations but the establishment of strong and detailed links between these representations and the ability to translate and switch between them. Typical function problems where such switching is necessary and an investigation of how students learn to do this in a computerized learning environment have been reported elsewhere (Schwarz & Dreyfus, 1995; Schwarz, Dreyfus, & Bruckheimer, 1990). We therefore limit ourselves here to a general description.

The complexity of the structure of the function concept makes learning to switch representations difficult; think, for example, of a trigonometric function, which already has the properties of periodicity, frequency, amplitude, and phase. Now consider the algebraic formula for this function, a graph with a particular window showing, for instance, a little more than two periods, and a table listing the value of the function at special points including extrema and zeros. Moreover, establish links between these three representations, such as clarify to yourself where some of the points in the table appear on the graph or how changing the amplitude would influence the shape, position, or both of the graph. This is already a lot of information to be dealt with, especially for students who lack appropriate mental structures. However, all of this information may only be the background needed to solve a problem connected to, say, the behavior of the graph of a given trigonometric function under a change of frequency or of phase. As a consequence, students often limit themselves to working in a single representation; for example, even when they are required to draw a sketch, such as before integrating an absolute value function, they often ignore their own sketch and thus fail to solve the problem correctly.

It may be worthwhile to note that the one and same structural aspect may be expressed in very different ways in different representations. To illustrate this, let us consider a symmetry property of functions; namely, evenness. As teachers and writers, we would now like to say what evenness is and then describe it in the graphical as well as in the algebraic representation; this, however, is an impossible undertaking, precisely because of the abstractness of mathematical concepts and the nature of representation. All we can say in general terms is that evenness is a symmetry property; as soon as we want to characterize this symmetry property more precisely, say what the symmetry is, we need to use (at least) one representation. In the graphical representation, evenness appears as symmetry of the functional graph with respect to the axis of the function's values (usually the vertical axis, often denoted by y). Therefore, a graph is the graph of an even function if together with any point in the right half-plane, the corresponding point in the left half-plane belongs to the graph, and vice versa.

In the algebraic representation, evenness appears as symmetry of the formula that is used to compute the functional values with respect to a sign change of the independent variable (often denoted by x). Both these descriptions are efficient, correct, and complete; but in spite of this, they do not, by themselves, provide a fully satisfactory description of evenness. In fact, one's conception of evenness is powerful only if one can call up and use in a problem-solving process the particular form, the particular representation, which is useful in that same situation; and for that purpose, one's conception needs to include not only an understanding of evenness in either representation but also the link between them. This link may be established, for example, as follows: If $f(x)$ stands for the formula in the algebraic representation of the function, then the graph contains exactly the points $(x, f(x))$. Starting now from the graphical representation, evenness means that together with this point, also the point $(-x, f(x))$ is on the graph; it follows that $f(-x)$, the value of the function at $-x$, is equal to $f(x)$; that is, it is not sensitive to a sign change in the independent variable x. With a similar argument, the link can be started from the algebraic side and pulled through to the graphical side.

In summary, any one representation rarely fulfills all requirements needed to deal with a problem or situation. Usually, several representations need to be used. Mathematical thinking is more powerful when it uses more than one representation in parallel, and establishes links between them. This provides flexibility and thus the links become overwhelmingly important. It is in those properties that are representation independent, and in the relationships between the representations that the mathematical power resides. Representation-independent properties are at the core of the formation of abstract concepts (Dreyfus, 1991).

VISUAL REASONING

Visualization is frequently used and accorded increasing value in mathematics, including research in mathematics. The reason that this is not well known is due to the fact that, with very few exceptions, mathematicians do not publish the (often visual) reasonings that led to their results but the (propositional) proofs that they constructed for these results. The sociological reasons for this are complex but attitudes toward visualization in mathematics are starting to change. Van der Waerden is a case in point: In 1954, he published a paper describing how he found a proof almost 30 years earlier. Indeed, although the 1954 paper describes how visual reasoning was used to obtain the result, the 1927 proof does not show any hint or trace of this visual reasoning.

The recent publication of an entire volume on visualization in mathematics and mathematics teaching (Zimmermann & Cunningham, 1991) by the MAA is a more substantial sign for the added importance of this change in attitude. Visualization is helpful in gestalting, in generating and managing the global picture of a problem situation. As it has been shown in an earlier sections of this chapter, imposing, analyzing, and exploiting structure is intimately connected to such gestalting; and indeed, structure can frequently be visualized. For example, the aspects of the structure of the integers have their visual representation on the number line. Similarly, symmetry as a structural element has its equivalent in symmetry as a geometric property. Finally, function transformations are by their very nature visual, and using a visual approach to understand them has been the topic of a recent paper by the authors (Eisenberg & Dreyfus, 1994).

Visualization and imagery have played a role in several of the examples dealt with in earlier sections. For example, Thompson's (1990) method for representing the structure of word problems is based in an essential manner on diagrammatically represented relationships between quantities, and the diagrammatic representation of links between quantities is expected to lead students to generate corresponding links in the (mental) imagery they associate with the problem. In this case, the diagrammatic, visual representation of a problem situation can safely be expected to support students' problem-solving efforts. The analogy between the discrete and the continuous case for the notion of median has been specifically built in the visual representation because that is where the analogy is most easily accessible. On the other hand, the five planes problem discussed in the section on analogies is from the outset a geometric problem with a natural visual representation. In trying to solve the problem using this visual representation, even most experienced mathematicians get stopped by the complexity of the geometric situation; and it was the reorganization of the numerical and algebraic data in a table (which, to some extent, also has a visual aspect) that allowed us to find the answer to the problem by numerical and algebraic means. Interestingly, the proof of the correctness of this solution, which was only hinted at in our description, is crucially based on an interplay between the different representations, and the links between them.

It thus seems that although visualization can serve as a versatile tool of mathematical reasoning for students, it may also impose limitations on our ability to progress beyond certain limits imposed precisely by the visual representation of a problem situation. Research results are consistent with this observation: Visualization may help some of the weaker students to successful problem solving. Bondesan and Ferrari (1991), for example, reported that even poor problem solvers adapt or invent new strategies in a geometric setting, but not in an algebraic one. On the other hand, concrete, pictorial, visual representations of the problem situation itself are often of limited value; indeed, Presmeg (1986) has found that although children have little difficulty in generating visual images, their imagery is predominantly concrete pictorial, with far less pattern imagery, and hardly any dynamic one. Because pattern and dynamic imagery is more apt to be coupled with rigorous analytical thought processes, this means that students are likely to generate visual images, but are unlikely to use them for analytical reasoning. In other words, they need to be trained to use visually based analytical thought processes or, for short, visual reasoning.

To make the idea of visual reasoning more concrete, consider an example taken from a unit on geometric loci, designed specifically for developing visual reasoning patterns (Hershkowitz, Friedlander, & Dreyfus, 1991). Suppose you have to deal with Problem 7 of Table 9.2: Given two intersecting lines in the plane, find the geometric locus of all points the sum of whose distances from the two lines equals a given length. This problem can be approached from many angles and in many ways. One global way of starting out would be to argue that the locus must be contained in a bounded region of the plane because any point that is very far away must be far from at least one of the lines. A more local way of starting would be to ask whether any points of the locus are going to lie on the given lines, and to start searching along these lines. This search may be approached dynamically by starting at the point of intersection and moving out along one of the two lines. As one does so, the distance from the other line grows from zero without bound; therefore, one must at a certain stage pass a point that belongs to the locus. Because of symmetry reasons, this yields four points. The locus turns out to be the rectangle whose corners are these four points, as shown in Fig. 9.3. This again is not trivial but needs a detailed analytical argument, which may be based on appropriate ratios in suitably chosen similar triangles. Every part of this argument is considered to be visual reasoning because it makes essential use of visual information. Visual reasoning used in this kind of argument may be global or local, dynamic or static, but it is never purely

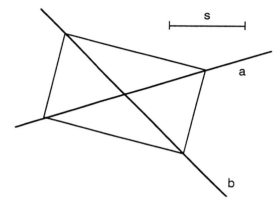

FIG. 9.3. A problem for visual reasoning.

perceptual: It includes valid analytical argumentation leading from step to step.

Visual reasoning is by no means limited to geometric situations. Many problems in elementary mathematics can be solved in both an analytical and visual way. For example, the inequality $\frac{3x}{x^2-1} > 2$ can be solved by determining when $\frac{(2x+1)(x-2)}{(x+1)(x-1)} < 0$. This can be done by checking cases of the form:

$\left(\begin{smallmatrix}++\\+-\end{smallmatrix}\right), \left(\begin{smallmatrix}++\\-+\end{smallmatrix}\right), \left(\begin{smallmatrix}+-\\++\end{smallmatrix}\right), \left(\begin{smallmatrix}-+\\++\end{smallmatrix}\right), \left(\begin{smallmatrix}+-\\--\end{smallmatrix}\right), \left(\begin{smallmatrix}-+\\--\end{smallmatrix}\right), \left(\begin{smallmatrix}--\\+-\end{smallmatrix}\right), \left(\begin{smallmatrix}--\\-+\end{smallmatrix}\right)$ to find those values of x for which nu-

merator and denominator are of opposite sign. Although some of the cases give an empty solution set, the idea is to exhaust all possibilities of the factors. Another way to solve this problem is to graph the snake representing the polynomial $(x + 1)(x - 1)(2x + 1)(x - 2)$, as in Fig. 9.4, and then to read off those values of x for which polynomial is greater than zero.

As with many of the aspects of mathematical thinking dealt with in previous sections, the value of visualization as a tool for mathematical thinking resides less in the tool itself that in the flexibility with which it is used: When is it appropriate to generate a visual representation, and when not? Should a visual representation be abandoned because of the limitations it imposes? Can a diagram be used to exhibit only, or mainly, those features of the problem situation that are relevant at present?

REVERSAL OF THINKING

Often times when faced with a mathematical problem it is wise to ask, "Where could this have come from?" and "Why should this occur?" Such questions often provide a motivating incentive in science also—"Why does X happen?"—and they often start one thinking from the result, to the source or

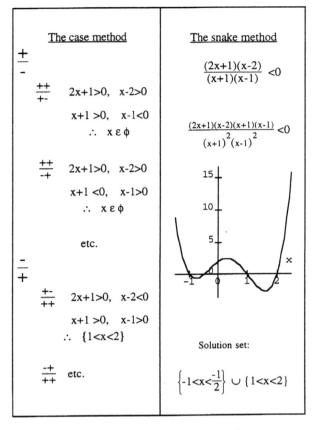

FIG. 9.4. Two different ways to solve $\dfrac{3x}{x^2 - 1} > 2$.

sources causing the result. Feynman (1989) illustrated this sort of reasoning beautifully; as a youth he was once faced with fixing a radio that made tremendous amounts of noise when first turned on, but which subsided after the radio warmed up:

> I start walking back and forth, thinking, and I realize that the one way it can happen is that the tubes are heating up in the wrong order—that is, the amplifier's all hot, the tubes are ready to go, and there's nothing feeding in, or there's some back circuit feeding in. . . . Then I said to myself, "All right, take the tubes out, and reverse the order completely in the set." So I changed the tubes around, stepped to the front of the radio, turned the thing on, and it's quiet as a lamb: it waits until it heats up, and then plays perfectly—no noise.
>
> Radio circuits were much easier to understand in those days because everything was out in the open. After you took the set apart (it was a big

problem to find the right screws), you could see this was a resistor, that's a condenser.... So it wasn't hard for me to fix a radio by understanding what was going on inside noticing that something wasn't working right and fixing it.

Feynman then went on to discuss other radio sets he fixed as a kid and the aura that developed around him because of this. The last sentence—"It wasn't hard for me to fix a radio by understanding what was going on"—tells it all (p. 8).

On the surface it seems as though Feynman simply thought in a reversed way; the radio made noise, the source of the noise could have been X, Y, or Z; if it was X, then a, b, or c would happen; if it was Y then d, e, or f would occur, and so on. Focusing in on his exact words, however, we see that he had a really deep understanding of the problem.

Feynman had a global gestalt understanding of the workings of the radio, having built in his mind a superstructure of the interconnectedness of its component parts. When faced with pinpointing the trouble, he rephrased the problem and thought about it in the more general abstract setting, not in the content-specific setting.

Such global gestalting is rarely an object of consideration in school mathematics, where the stress is usually on a compilation of skills and facts that are associated with various subtopics. The curriculum certainly lends itself to such an interpretation for the typical sequence of study is linearly ordered with algebra being followed by geometry and then trigonometry, analytic geometry, and calculus. Even within its various subtopics the curriculum is linearly ordered, and parceled down into little bits and pieces (The process by which mathematics is so prepared for school has been called *didactic transposition*; Chevallard, 1985.) This leads to compartmentalization rather than a global view in the minds of the students. It is often the case that students can do the mechanics of a problem, but miss the bigger picture of how it all fits together.

Good problem solvers seem to have the ability of seeing paths of development of particular issues in larger contexts, which often provides for them an "abstract working space" to reason from the result, to the source or sources causing the result. Poorer problem solvers seem to collect in their minds only the results, rather than the paths and superstructure encompassing them. They have less trouble seeing these superstructures once they are pointed out, but seldom are they able to build them. Therefore, ideas associated with notions around the start of a line of thought appear unconnected to those associated with its end.

Examples illustrating this disconnectedness abound in elementary mathematics. Elementary school teachers have found that children often do not have a clue as to how to approach problems such as Problem 8 in Table 9.2: In a parking lot there are only bicycles and cars; if there are a total of 20 tires in the lot, how many bicycles and how many cars are there? However, these same children have no trouble with the standard question of computing the number of tires in the lot if the number of bicycles and cars is known. Admittedly, the problem required of them is much more difficult than the standard question, for there is no unique solution to it. However, the difficulty seems to be that the solution requires them to see the problem in a more general abstract setting. Few students seem to have the depth of understanding in order to solve this reversal of the standard problem.

Similarly, the slope of a line is a measure associated with its steepness. It is often defined as rise over run; that is, the slope of the line segment connecting two points with coordinates (a,b) and (c,d) is, by definition, $\frac{d-b}{c-a}$. If this number is positive, the line segment is moving upward as one moves along the x-axis in a positive direction, if it is negative the line segment is moving downward, if it is zero the line segment is parallel to the x-axis, and if it is undefined then the line segment is parallel to the y-axis (see Fig. 9.5). Typical school problems present the student with the coordinates of two points in the plane and then ask them to develop the equation of the line segment connecting the points. Most students have little trouble with such problems because their solution, in effect, mimics the development that was done in class and has been practiced over and over again. The procedures of finding the equation of the straight line through two given points, or through a given point with a given slope, are well known to most students. However, trouble often enters when the problem is stated in a reversed way, such as by presenting students with Fig. 9.6, which shows a set of *n* uncoordinatized points in the plane two of which have been circled, and asking them which of the other *n*-2 points satisfy the equation of the line through the two circled points. Such problems are troublesome because the students often have only a partial understanding of the Cartesian connection (Schoenfeld, Smith, & Arcavi, 1993); namely, that all points on the graph of an equation satisfy the equation, and if a point is not on the graph then its coordinates do not satisfy the equation. Again, the solution to the reversed question requires a deeper understanding of underlying concepts than the solution to the standard question.

Composition of functions offers still another set of exercises employing the same heuristics: an approach from an angle that reverses the underlying notion's developmental path. Standard textbooks generally introduce the notion of composition of functions by first defining a function f mapping A into B and a function g mapping B into C, and then guides the students

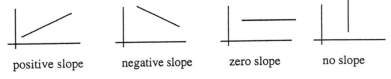

positive slope   negative slope   zero slope   no slope

FIG. 9.5. Slopes.

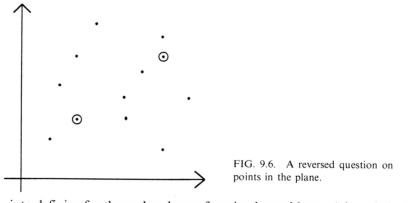

FIG. 9.6. A reversed question on points in the plane.

into defining for themselves how a function h would map A into C (by briefly going through B). Typical exercises include defining f and g and asking the student to build $h(x) = g(f(x))$. The domain and range of function h is often discussed and students seem to immediately grasp the notion that function h can be defined only if the range of f is contained in the domain of g as illustrated in Fig. 9.7. However, if the students are given $g(f(x))$ and $f(x)$ and then they are asked to construct $g(x)$, they often seem to be at a loss as to what to do, because the typical solution again involves having an abstract understanding of the developmental procedure.

Even in collegiate mathematics, this sort of thinking pattern causes trouble. The concept image (Tall & Vinner, 1981) of the derivative of a function which most students hold is that for any point on the graph of the function, the derivative function gives the slope of the tangent line to the graph at that point. As such, students have no trouble in graphing the derivative of a function, which is represented by its graph as in Fig. 9.8. To give them the graph of the derivative and ask them to sketch a graph (from the family of functions) which has this derivative, however, is another matter. In this situation, going from the graph of the derivative to that of the function seems to be far harder than to go from the graph of the function to that of the derivative.

A similar situation exists with respect to integration. The integral $\int_0^1 x^2 dx$ can be thought of in terms of area and setting up the appropriate limiting sums is often an exercise in beginning calculus. Students seem to grasp the

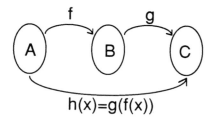

FIG. 9.7. Composition of functions.

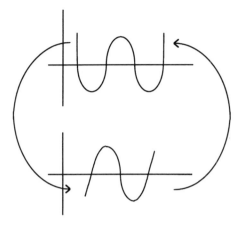

FIG. 9.8. Passage between the graphs of a function and its derivative in both directions.

this idea very quickly and have little trouble setting up the limiting sums for other functions. However, going in the other direction is again another story completely. Very few calculus course graduates can correctly identify the limiting sum with its integral. Seventy percent of the more than 10,000 calculus course graduates queried (Educational Testing Service, 1988) could not identify the integral representing the $\lim_{n \to \infty} \frac{1}{n}[(\frac{1}{n})^2 + (\frac{2}{n})^2 + (\frac{3}{n})^2 + \ldots . (\frac{3n}{n})^2]$, yet most of these students could go in the other direction.

Thinking about *the path of thought leading to X* is extremely difficult for many individuals because it places an equal emphasis on the line of thought as on its result. Moreover, the process involved in the line of thought is extra baggage the concept must carry. Many notions in mathematics have such a structure associated with them. Addition and subtraction can be thought of as being inverse operations of each other, as can multiplication and division, exponentiation and root extraction, and integration and differentiation. Good mathematical thinking seems to entail having the flexibility of thought to see applications of reversing paths of thought. It is a skill that can only be developed with practice. Many textbooks, heretofore, have not emphasized this type of thinking; test makers however, have.

CONCLUSION: FLEXIBILITY OF THOUGHT

In this final section, we attempt to show how the different aspects of mathematical thought discussed in the preceeding sections of this chapter contribute to the flexibility of thought required from expert mathematical problem solvers. The history of mathematics is rich with stories of how inflexible thought patterns and beliefs have hindered its development. "Euclides ab omni naevo vindicatus" ("Euclid Freed of Every Flaw") was the title of a text by Saccheri, who is known in history as the man who should have discovered non-Euclidean geometry, but did not (Eves, 1964, p. 124). He missed the call to fame because he could not tear himself away from Euclidean notion of parallel lines which says that given a line L and a point P not on L, there is exactly one line parallel to L through P. This is true in the plane and our thinking tends to be strongly limited by our experience; in this case, the planar experience—and that is what happened to Saccheri. He could simply not imagine other geometries in which there may be more than one line through P, which is parallel to L, or no line at all, such as, for example, on a sphere. Therefore, instead of being heralded as the "father of the most notable discovery of [his] century" (Hilbert, cited in Moritz, 1914, p. 353), Saccheri is remembered as one of the greatest could-have-beens in the history of mathematics.

It takes extreme flexibility to rid one's thinking of commonly made assumptions on the way to great mathematical discoveries. Einstein obviously comes to mind. The discovery of the negative, the irrational, the complex numbers, and the extension of the complex numbers to what is known as quaternions provide further examples. In each case, a property previously considered as self-evident and used without any need for justification had to be dropped, and our thinking seems to resist such breaking of habits, even when we consciously search for the new and unexplored. It took Hamilton (see Bell, 1937), for example, 15 years of labor before it dawned on him how to define a multiplication of the quaternions, the final bug in their development. Indeed, he also had to drop the requirement of commutativity—a property that had been true for all previously known multiplications.

Many people have tried to understand how mathematical insights take place; most notable among them is Hadamard's (1945) work on the psychology of mathematical invention, but throughout each of the case histories studied to understand how the discovery was made is the crystal-clear observation that great discoveries are made by being able to think in a flexible way. No one knows exactly how this flexibility of thought and the ability to make insights occur. Feynman's (1989) autobiographies seem to imply that some of the potential for great discoveries is inborn; although this may be true for the Einsteins and the Feynmans, hard work certainly plays a part even for top scientists. The old adage that genius is 10% inspiration and 90% perspiration is true. Moreover, we contend that to a large degree, at least at the level needed by teachers and students of mathematics, flexibility of thought can be trained and acquired.

Therefore, having a good mathematical mind involves the ability to think in a flexible way. Versatile thinking can be learned and didactic approaches have been specifically been designed for this (e.g., Tall & Thomas, 1991). If one path does not work, perhaps another one will; if one way of organizing the givens does not lead to progress, another one probably does; if one representation does not provide illumination, another one might be more likely to do so; if starting from the givens does not lead anywhere, maybe beginning at the end and thinking in reverse direction could work. Flexible thinking involves the ability to be "inside" the problem and to be able to see it from many different aspects. Exposure to various sorts of problem situations on many occasions and in many different settings, in and outside of classrooms, is likely to help one develop such ability. In this regard, problems from recreational mathematics are a boon to developing flexible thinking skills.

The mathematical puzzles that are sometimes printed on placemats in restaurants illustrate this sort of problem situation and often require the flexibility of thought good problem solvers have trained themselves to use. Some such problems are presented in Table 9.4.

Because different facets of mathematical thinking can be enhanced through such "recreational" problems, there is good reason to use them systematically as challenges in schools and extracurricular activities. Although the flexibility required in many of these puzzles is extreme, many students seem to be attracted to them.

On the other hand, flexibility also plays an important role in all aspects of the processes of concept formation and of the problem-solving activities typical for mathematical thinking that have been analyzed in the earlier sections of this chapter. It has been pointed out that recognizing structure in a given problem, imposing structure on a situation, and exploiting this structure enormously increases one's mathematical power and flexibility. Identifying the same structure in different situations helps one to solve problems by analogy. We have also shown that a deep understanding of analogies is apt help students make transitions from a more general case to a simpler one, or from a specific case to a more general one in order to get a more encompassing result. In both cases, the use of analogies adds flexibility to the students' thinking processes.

Further, we have stressed that acquaintance with various representations related to a set of concepts, the establishment of strong and detailed links between these representations, and the ability to translate and switch between them is equivalent to a deep understanding of these concepts and enables their

TABLE 9.4

Placemat Problems

1. With six toothpicks build four equilateral triangles.
2. Is it possible to cut a pancake into 8 parts with exactly three straight line cuts with a knife?
3. What is the largest number of spots that can be painted on a basketball in such a way that every spot is exactly the same distance from every other spot?
4. Three men named Lewis, Miller, and Nelson fill the positions of accountant, cashier, and clerk in the leading department store in Centerburg. If Nelson is the cashier, Miller is the clerk. If Nelson is the clerk, Miller is the accountant. If Miller is not the cashier, Lewis is the clerk. If Lewis is the accountant, Nelson is the clerk. What is each man's job?

flexible use in problem-solving situations. Mathematical thinking is more powerful, when it uses more than one representation in parallel, and establishes links between them. This provides flexibility and thus the links become overwhelmingly important. It is in the representation independent properties, and in the relationships between the representations, that the mathematical power resides.

Similarly, the value of visualization as a tool for mathematical thinking resides less in the tool itself that in the flexibility with which it is used: This flexibility includes knowing when it is appropriate to generate a visual representation, and when not; whether a visual representation should be abandoned because of the limitations it imposes; and whether a diagram can be used to exhibit the relevant features of a problem situation. Finally, it has been shown here earlier that the flexibility to reverse the direction of thinking can often considerably simplify a problem solution.

Mathematical thinking ability can only be enhanced by working at it—it does not come by itself, and it is a dangerous myth to think that you either have it or you do not (Usiskin, 1990). In this chapter, we have systematically analyzed some of the crucial patterns of mathematical thinking and their relationship to concept formation and flexibility in problem solving. We have discussed how flexible mathematical thinking patterns appear in gestalting and structuring ideas and problems situations, how analogies contribute to flexibility, how flexible choice and linkage between representations is part of mathematical understanding, how visualization is related to flexible problem solving, and how reversing thinking paths may contribute to flexibility. To a large extent, these thinking patterns can be learned; and on the basis of our analysis of thinking patterns, we have pointed out some ways to enhance flexible thinking in students of mathematics. However, as stated earlier, mathematics thinking as a whole is greater than the sum of its facets.

REFERENCES

Albers, D. J. (1982). Paul Halmos: Maverick mathologist. *College Mathematics Journal, 13,* 226–242.

Albers, D. J., & Reid, C. (1988). An interview with Mary Ellen Rudin. *College Mathematics Journal, 19,* 115–137.

Bell, E. T. (1937). *Men of mathematics.* New York: Simon & Schuster.

Bondesan, M. G., & Ferrari, P. L. (1991). The active comparison of strategies in problem-solving: An exploratory study. In F. Furinghetti (Ed.), *Proceedings of the 15th International Conference on the Psychology of Mathematics Education* (Vol. I, pp. 168–175). Genova, Italy: U Press.

Chevallard, Y. (1985). *The didactic transposition from the scientific knowledge to the knowledge being taught.* Grenoble, France: La pensée sauvage.

Courant, R., & Robbins, H. (1941). *What is mathematics?* London: Oxford University Press.

Davidson, N. (1986). *Cooperative learning in mathematics.* London: Addison-Wesley.

Davis, P. J., & Hersh, R. (1981). The mathematical experience. Boston: Birkhäuser.

Dreyfus, T. (1987). Approximation of area under a curve: A conceptual approach. *Mathematics Teacher, 80*(7), 538–543.

Dreyfus, T. (1991). Advanced mathematical thinking processes. In D. Tall (Ed.), *Advanced mathematical thinking* (pp. 25–41). Dordrecht, The Netherlands: Kluwer.

Dreyfus, T., & Eisenberg, T. (1990). Symmetry in mathematics learning. *Zentralblatt für Didaktik der Mathematik, 22*(2), 53–59.

Educational Testing Service. (1988). *Report on the Advanced Placement Examinations.* Princeton, NJ: Author.

Eisenberg, T., & Dreyfus, T. (1994). On understanding how students learn to visualize function transformations. *Research on Collegiate Mathematics Education, 1,* 45–68.

Everybody Counts. (1989). *A Report to the Nation on the Future of Mathematics Education.* Washington, DC: National Academy Press.

Eves, H. (1964). *An introduction to the history of mathematics* (rev. ed.). New York: Holt, Rinehart & Winston.

Feynman, R. (1989). *Surely you're joking Mr. Feynman.* New York: Bantam.

Gick, M. L., & Holyoak, K. J. (1983). Schema induction and analogical transfer. *Cognitive Psychology, 15,* 1–38.

Gillman, L. (1994). Can students solve math problems? *Focus, the Newsletter of the MAA, 14*(3), 12–13.

Hadamard, J. (1945). *The psychology of invention in the mathematical field.* Princeton, NJ: Princeton University Press.

Halmos, P. (1968). Mathematics as a creative art. *American Scientist, 56,* 375–389.

Hardy, G. H. (1940). *A mathematician's apology.* Cambridge, UK: Cambridge University Press.

Harel, G., & Kaput, J. (1991). The role of conceptual entities and their symbols in building advanced mathematical concepts. In D. Tall (Ed.), *Advanced mathematical thinking* (pp. 82–94). Dordrecht, The Netherlands: Kluwer.

Harris, C. (1971). On proofs of the irrationality of $\sqrt{2}$. *Mathematics Teacher, 64*(1), 19–21.

Hershkowitz, R., Friedlander, A., & Dreyfus, T. (1991). Loci and visual thinking. In F. Furinghetti (Ed.), *Proceedings of the 15th International Conference on the Psychology of Mathematics Education* (Vol. II, pp. 181–188). Genova, Italy: U Press.

Jackson, A. (1988). Research mathematicians in mathematics education: The national scene. *Notices of the American Mathematical Society, 35*(8), 1123–1131.

Krauthammer, C. (1990, Feb. 5). Education: Doing bad and feeling good. *Time Magazine,* p. 78.

Mason, J., Burton, L., & Stacey, K. (1982). *Thinking mathematically.* London: Addison-Wesley.

Moritz, R. E. (1914). *Memorabilia mathematica.* Washington, DC: Mathematical Association of America.

Orton, A. (1992). *Learning mathematics: Issues, theory and classroom practice.* London: Cassell.

Polya, G. (1945). *How to solve it.* Princeton, NJ: Princeton University Press.

Polya, G. (1965). *Mathematical discovery* (Vol. 2). New York: Wiley.

Polya, G., & Szegö, G. (1972). *Problems and theorems in analysis* (Translation and expansion of *Aufgaben und Lehrsätze aus der Analysis,* published 1924). New York: Springer.

Presmeg, N. (1986). Visualization in high-school mathematics. *For the Learning of Mathematics, 6,* 42–46.

Schoenfeld, A., Smith, J., & Arcavi, A. (1993). Learning: The microgenetic analysis of one student's evolving understanding of a complex subject matter domain. In R. Glaser (Ed.), *Advances in instructional psychology* (Vol. 4, 55–177). Hillsdale, NJ: Lawrence Erlbaum Associates.

Schwarz, B., & Dreyfus, T. (1995). New actions on old objects: A new ontological perspective on functions. *Educational Studies in Mathematics, 29*(3), 259–291.

Schwarz, B., Dreyfus, T., & Bruckheimer, M. (1990). A model of the function concept in a three-fold representation. *Computers and Education, 14*(3), 249–262.

Selden, A., Selden, J., & Mason, A. (1994). Even good calculus students can't solve nonroutine problems. In J. Kaput & E. Dubinsky (Eds.), *Research issues in undergraduate mathematics learning* (MAA Notes Series Vol. 33, pp. 19–26). Washington, DC: Mathematical Association of America.

Tall, D., & Thomas, M. (1991). Encouraging versatile thinking in algebra using the computer. *Educational Studies in Mathematics, 22*(2), 125–147.

Tall, D., & Vinner, S. (1981). Concept image and concept definition with particular reference to limits and continuity. *Educational Studies in Mathematics, 12*(2), 151–169.

Thompson, P. W. (1990). *A theoretical model of quantity based reasoning in arithmetic and algebra* (Tech. Rep. No. 101). Normal: Illinois State University.

Treisman, U. (1992). *New approaches to the mathematical education of minorities in the United States.* In C. Gaulin, B. R. Hodgson, D. H. Wheeler, & J. C. Egsgard (Eds.), *Proceedings of the 7th International Congress on Mathematical Education* (p. 376). Québec, Canada: Les presses de l'université Laval.

Usiskin, Z. (1990). If everybody counts, why do so few survive? *University of Chicago School Mathematics Project Newsletter, 6*, 5–11.

Van der Waerden, B. L. (1927). Beweis einer Baudetschen Vermutung. *Nieuw Archief voor Wiskunde, 15*, 212–216.

Van der Waerden, B. L. (1954). *Einfall und Überlegung: Drei kleine Beiträge zur Psychologie des mathematischen Denkens.* Basel, Switzerland: Birkhäuser.

Zimmermann, W., & Cunningham, S. (Eds.). (1991). *Visualization in teaching and learning mathematics* (MAA Notes Series, Vol. 19). Providence, RI: Mathematical Association of America.

10

Structuralism and Mathematical Thinking

Charles Rickart
Yale University

Mathematical thinking is only one aspect of thinking in general. Therefore, questions concerning mathematical thinking raise questions concerning all thinking. Although mathematical thought is in many ways very special, it admits of a straightforward analysis that throws light on all thinking and suggests a powerful general approach to studying the latter. The basis of our analysis of mathematical thinking involves the abstract concept of structures. Furthermore, structures play the same essential role in all thinking as they do in mathematics, whether or not the thinker is aware of their presence.

A general point of view firmly based on structure is developed in some detail in a recent book by the author entitled *Structuralism and Structure* (Rickart, 1995). A main objective of the book is to build for the reader a solid notion of abstract structure as well as an understanding of how structures are involved in the study of any serious field of information. Because the book is strongly influenced (at least indirectly) by mathematics, much of this material is obviously relevant to the material presented throughout this chapter and is referred to as needed.

The general assumption behind all of the following is that information is coded and stored in the brain in the form of structures, and that the brain is especially "designed" for recording and processing these structures. This is true despite the fact that an individual is seldom aware of what is going on. Although our ultimate objective is to explain why this point of view on thinking is both valid and useful, it is desirable for obvious reasons first to take a careful look at structures for their own sake. This provides basic concepts and the necessary language for dealing with a serious structural approach to any subject. (In this connection, a reader might also find useful the discussion of structures and examples that appear in various sections of Rickart, 1995, especially in the introductory chapters 1 through 3.)

Structures are present everywhere, either explicitly or implicitly, and provide an approach by which any situation or mass of data might be made intelligible. In fact, the general discipline that is known as "structuralism" and is devoted to discovering and studying the structural content of a field is called "The Art of the Intelligible" by Caws (1988) in his book entitled *Structuralism*. In other words, the structural content represents the contained information that is ultimately recorded in one's understanding. What all of this means becomes clearer as we proceed.

The subject of structures, for which we are about to offer a formal introduction, is rather different from most subjects. This is because virtually everyone already has a fairly clear notion of what a structure is without the benefit of a definition. In other words, they are able to decide offhand which of many familiar objects in their surroundings may legitimately be called a structure. Up to a point this may be an advantage, but few people understand what it is that these familiar objects actually have in common. In other words, they lack the general notion of structure, something exceedingly helpful in a serious structural approach to any subject of substance.

The next section contains some of the basic material required for dealing systematically with structures. The perceptive reader will note the similarity of this situation with a common mathematical case in which one can be familiar with certain mathematical concepts at, say, a notational level, without being able to think of them in the same way that a mathematician might. The difference here is between concreteness and abstraction. In other words, does the concept exist in terms of the "material world," or is it independent of the latter? Note that an abstraction, at least for purposes of communication, usually requires a formal language to deal with it.

STRUCTURE DEFINITIONS AND PROPERTIES

A *structure*, by definition, consists of a set of *objects* along with certain *relations* among those objects. The set of objects is also said to *have structure*. A subset of the objects along with some of the relations restricted to the subset is called a *substructure* of the given structure. A substructure is obviously a structure in its own right, and properties of a given structure are often expressed in terms of its substructures.

Two structures are said to be *isomorphic* if there exists a one-to-one correspondence between their objects that preserves relations (in the sense that objects in one structure are related if and only if their associates in the other structure are also related). Isomorphic structures are said to have the *same structure*, and what is common to them is an *abstract structure*.

We regard abstract structures as having an independent existence. They are also regarded as consisting of abstract objects and relations. Within an abstract structure, an object has only those properties that it gains by being a member of the structure, including, for example, the property of being related to certain other objects in the structure. A similar remark applies to properties of relations. In fact, a relation may be thought of as being determined by the (possibly ordered) sets of objects that it relates.

A concrete structure consists of concrete objects, and may be thought of as isomorphic to the abstract structure that defines it as a structure. It may also be regarded as a *representation of*, or as *represented by*, the associated abstract structure. Observe that the objects and relations in a concrete structure may have *intrinsic* properties that are quite irrelevant to their properties derived from belonging to the given concrete structure.

With these definitions and conventions, it is possible to state precisely what it is that familiar objects recognized as structures have in common: Each one is a concrete structure according to the aforementioned definition of structure.

It is worth noting at this point that the term "system" often appears in common usage as a synonym for "structure." We prefer, however, to use the term to mean *any collection of interrelated objects along with all of the "potential" structures that might be identified within it*. This turns out to be a useful concept that includes many mathematical examples, of which we mention only one—"a number system." It is instructive with respect to both structures and systems to spell out some of the details of this example. Recall that a number system, which consists of the numbers themselves as objects, also admits operations of addition and multiplication. The operations determine two "ternary" relations defined as follows: The numbers in an ordered triple (x,y,z) are defined to be *addition*-related provided $x + y = z$, or *multiplication-related* provided $xy = z$. This identifies two structures in the number system. A complete description would, of course, require precisely stated axioms giving definitions along with individual and joint structure properties.

Although the general structure definitions enable us to concentrate on basic structure concepts, they do not bring out explicitly the fact that structures may also be dynamic in character (a subject discussed briefly in chapter 3 of Rickart, 1995). As might be expected, the analysis of almost any dynamic structure is likely to present special problems. One example of such a structure is a typical machine in operation, and it may be represented as an "ordinary" structure existing in four-dimensional "space time." Another kind of dynamic structure is the classical model of an atom. The latter admits a very different, but especially effective, representation of a dynamic structure in which the orbit of a moving electron around the nucleus of the atom is suggested by simply drawing the orbit.

The general structure definitions outlined here may be a bit misleading because they represent structures as more or less isolated entities. In actual practice, nothing could be farther from the truth. For example, most structures that we encounter are embedded (as substructures) in larger structures that may or may not be relevant to whatever interest that we might have in the initial structure. At the very least, our attention to a structure automatically embeds a representation of it in our ever-present system of mental structures. Furthermore, our perception of a structure is not a passive experience, but is shaped by previous experience that will determine much of what we see in the presented structure.

One further comment on our approach is that the emphasis on abstract structures is obviously a partial commitment to an idealistic point of view. Although most mathematicians do not appear to be very strongly committed to any particular philosophical position, most of them seem to think and talk of mathematical structures as being abstract. In fact, it is a bit awkward to do otherwise.

A STRUCTURAL ANALYSIS OF THINKING

It is time now to discuss in more detail the structure basis for thinking in general. As we have already noted, information is obviously recorded in some manner or other in the mind–brain system. Although "nerve cell" details are relatively sparse as to how such material is actually recorded, it is reasonable to assume that the information is somehow coded into a structure which is in turn represented by a nerve structure. The mind–brain construct is often referred to as a *mental structure*. The term can mean either the associated concrete nerve structure or the abstract structure that represents it. Observe that the second point of view focuses more attention on the structure concept. For this reason, we usually think of a mental structure as an abstract entity.

As was already mentioned, our assumption is that the thinking process is one of the special functions of the general structure processing activity of the human brain, and the material of thought consists of information recorded as structures in one's mind–brain system. This material consists of ideas and concepts; either structures extracted from current sense data, or retrieved from previously recorded information.

Despite the difficulties of determining just how structures are generally recorded or coded in the brain, a very important and better known intermediate device involves the use of language in any form. In this case, a structure is represented by a language structure that involves time. In other words, the structure is presented piecewise and strung out in time. This form of representation is of special importance because it provides a mechanism for *communicating* the content of a structure from one person to another (de

Saussure, 1966; see Rickart, 1995, chapter 5). From our point of view, use of language is only one among many special ways that structures may be manipulated. In other words, thinking is a remarkable tool for dealing with mental structures but is generally independent of language, although the possibility of communication provided by language is of an unquestioned special importance.

Thinking, with or without language, involves ideas or concepts directly in terms of their basic intrinsic relationships. They are somehow represented so that they can evolve and interact, largely independently of the outside world. The system may, of course, use material out of memory banks and even occasional inputs from the outside. In this context, language becomes just another method of manipulating structures. Although thinking is normally independent of language, it may shift into the communication mode, if needed.

Language can play a very important positive role in thinking, but it can also play a seriously negative role. For example, it is possible for language to function quite independently of the underlying ideas for which it was ostensibly created. It is, of course, by virtue of its structure that language is able to represent a system of ideas. At the same time, the language structure may exist independently of the idea structures that it usually organizes. When this separation occurs, the underlying substance ideas may be lost and we are left with the empty language itself. Everyday examples of this are found, for example, in the use of clichés. We see it in mathematics when the formalism is used without the underlying mathematical ideas. In other words, the structure of the formalism is adopted for its own sake. This comes up again later, when we examine, for example, some of the problems associated with the teaching of elementary algebra.

Despite our insistence that thinking is not dependent on language, there are some who maintain that all thinking is actually self-communication, and thus is dependent on language in some form or another. Although this point is obviously dependent on ones definition of thinking, the language restriction would exclude many instances of mental activity that, in my opinion, should be classified as genuine thinking. Included, for example, are certain mental experiences of any creative mathematician. I offer specific examples later.

Thinking is generally regarded as taking place in the conscious part of the mind. However, again because of some rather vivid mathematical experiences, plus certain other ordinary phenomena, it appears that there does not exist a sharp distinction between the conscious and unconscious thinking. The process can evidently take place in either the conscious or unconscious mind and even shift back and forth between the two. What is missing when the unconscious is involved is the monitoring or censoring of the whole process by the conscious. The unconscious setting, despite a lack of discipline, may allow a freedom of mental activity that can be far more creative than when restricted by the conscious. Illustrative examples are presented later.

At this point it is important to make a distinction between the *general unconscious*, which we have in mind here when we refer to the unconscious, and the Freudian unconsciousness. There is not a sharp line dividing the general unconscious and the conscious mind. Although there are regions in the general unconscious that are not easy to access, much of it is very close to the conscious so that passage between the two is not difficult. This is not the case with the Freudian unconscious, which is difficult to access and is normally widely separated from the conscious. Any influence that it has on mathematical thinking is probably limited to familiar Freudian phenomena, which are not easily related to the highly rational mental phenomena characteristically associated with mathematical thought.

SPECIAL ASPECTS OF MATHEMATICAL THINKING

Although mathematical thinking is just one form of ordinary thinking, it does exhibit special features that set it apart from most other thinking. One thing that stands out here is the fact that its subject matter is unambiguously abstract, consisting of pure mathematical structures. Whether the content is ordinary arithmetic, elementary algebra, or a very advanced topic, it is necessarily abstract when correctly understood. Anyone whose understanding falls short of this is to that degree handicapped in the use of mathematics.

Another special feature of mathematics is its language. As far as ordinary thinking is concerned, the language used when needed is ordinary language that already exists, whereas in the case of mathematics, the language is usually very special and needs to be learned along with the subject matter. It is ordinarily quite formal and also very close to the underlying mathematical content; so close, in fact, that the formalism is sometimes naively confused with the mathematics itself. As in ordinary thinking, mathematical thinking may involve only the content or it may also involve the formal language. Involvement of only the language, which amounts to either ignoring content or identifying it with the language structure, is usually not good in either case. There are exceptions, however, that are mentioned in the next section. The *naive* confusion of content and formalism is, in most cases, a low-level weakness that stands in the way of a correct understanding of mathematics. This is a special problem in the case of elementary topics such as elementary algebra. Restriction to content is not so common and usually involves more experienced mathematicians.

Some of the important special differences between mathematical thinking and ordinary thinking can be brought out by examining how children learn the most elementary material. A good place to start is with the case of language. It is obvious that children have an instinctive drive to learn the language, as attested by the spontaneous way they become involved in the learning process. It is also clear that one cannot separate the learning of new material and the learning of the language in terms of which the material is described. In other words, the learning process mixes the two. Furthermore, if anyone bothers to pay attention, they will be impressed by the way virtually every adult who comes in contact with the child automatically assumes the role of a teacher. They will adjust their voice and repeat phrases to make it easier for the child to learn the correct use of the language.

A closer observation will suggest that children are also equipped to learn numbers, along with their structure, just as they can learn a language. Learning about a number system is, of course, very different on the surface from learning about a language system. In the first place, few are able to recognize the process and the result does not compare in importance with language. The development of an understanding of a number system could be encouraged along with learning a language, but few parents, skilled or not in elementary mathematics, think to encourage and help the child grow in this way. The difference is in sponteneity, which dominates the learning of ordinary language but is ignored in learning numbers. The result is an individual that will have to struggle later with the problem of elementary mathematics on an entirely different level. We mention the problem here because it is important and also demands a very different treatment later. This is crucial in both the teaching of arithmetic and elementary algebra.

I digress briefly at this point to cite a rather different example, a personal one that involved my youngest son when he was an early preschooler. One day I showed him an ordinary fork and asked him first how many prongs the fork had and then how many "spaces" it had. The answer here was 4 and 3, both of which were very easy, so I asked how many spaces there were when the fork had various other (reasonable) numbers of prongs. These answers were also very easy, although I am sure that he had never seen a fork with more than 4 prongs. The point is that he could visualize without any effort something he had never seen and also understand immediately that it would have to possess a specific structural feature. This is the kind of intuitive understanding that I regard as fundamentally significant and closely related to other mathematical understanding. Incidentally, I did not understand the event then as well as I do now, or I would have pursued it further.

We turn now to the question of how we learn and come to understand elementary mathematics at the level of elementary arithmetic and algebra. Although the general problems here are superficially much the same as the problems associated with learning elementary material of any kind, the mathematics is different in the details.

Virtually all students in elementary school have long since passed the stage of being able spontaneously to learn about the structure of the ordinary number system. Therefore, these things need to be addressed in a different way. Ideally, the number system should be introduced and its structure somehow communicated to the student so that the basic *idea* predominates apart from a word description of it. At the elementary level, it is not practical to do this in a formal way. The message can ordinarily only be implicit in the way arithmetic is taught, so much of the picture has to be communicated in the attitude and expressions of a teacher who understands what is going on. This is a very delicate matter and is often flawed. Therefore, it is not unusual for many students to wind up with either an empty or a seriously defective notion of the arithmetic number system. It becomes very difficult to help students when such handicaps become established, even if a teacher understands the nature of the problem—something that may not be common. Students who avoid this problem often are able to do so because they retain some of their instinctive ability to make sense out of numerical material.

This brings us to the stage of trying to teach students about elementary algebra. The ideal situation is to deal with students who have derived from their experience with arithmetic a correct intuitive picture of the ordinary number system. Unfortunately, such students are probably somewhat rare. Too often, success with students is a hit-or-miss matter with many who never are able to understand the true nature of a number system apart from a list of rules. It should be admitted here that a similar situation can exist in the learning of anything new of substance. The problem is especially difficult in mathemtics, however, because students may have a very wrong, but very solidly established, picture of the elementary number system because of their bad experiences with arithmetic.

Even with students who have a correct notion of the elementary number system, there remains a problem with the learning of algebra. Although the algebra system may be motivated by the earlier understanding of the elementary number system, the fact remains that the algebra system is more inclusive. It includes in addition, for example, the much larger system formed by all polynomials. The number system obviously has special properties that are not held by the algebra system. This is not unusual, of course, because a structure need not address all of the properties of a concrete structure that represents it. In any case, an appropriate representation of the algebra system will not be isomorphic with a full representation of the number system. The transition between the number system and the algebra system is obviously not a minor step in understanding.

For practical purposes, to this point I have restricted attention to ordinary arithmetic and elementary algebra. As far as the level of mathematics is concerned, however, geometry should also be included, but it is actually rather different from the others. For example, the subject matter of elementary geometry consists of familiar figures, such as straight lines, triangles, and circles plus, perhaps, some three-dimensional objects. These are acquired very early and painlessly. They also have a different relationship to the language. In fact, up to a point, the associated language is close to ordinary language.

This is probably one reason many students report that elementary geometry was easy, whereas elementary algebra was impossibly difficult. In other words, elementary geometry is learned much like anything else is learned, so can be dealt with in a relatively routine manner. Ultimately, of course, it is necessary in geometry to face questions similar to the ones that ultimately underlie any serious mathematical field.

FORM VERSUS CONTENT

The problem of teaching elementary algebra is similar to the problem of teaching (or learning) any new piece of mathematics. There are two questions that must be addressed. The first involves the degree of understanding of the background subject matter leading up to the immediate subject of interest, and the second involves the formalism associated with the subject. The latter item is very special in mathematics, making it different from learning other material. It refers very explicitly to the *structural content* of the subject.

Notice that there is an ambiguity here because a mathematician may react to the material in two different ways. There are times when the content is of vital importance, which means that the emphasis is almost wholly on the mathematical nature of the system described by the formal language. At other times, the user's attention may be absorbed by a related mathematical system and the given operations are reduced to little more than pure formalism. What is important, however, is the fact that the mathematician's attention can be shifted immediately to the content behind the given formalism when needed. I also mention in passing that there are a few formalists who *equate* mathematics to its formalism. This, however, is a sophisticated philosophical position having nothing in common with the views of elementary students.

One of the problems in the routine teaching of elementary algebra is that it sometimes reduces to nothing more than teaching the formalism. This can be a very serious problem when a student's understanding of the underlying arithmetic structure is inadequate, and therefore the only recourse is to fall back on the formalism. It is not uncommon for many tests to be constructed to measure mastery of the algebra formalization rather than the mathematical content behind it. For this reason, it is not uncommon to find students who have a pretty good record as far as grades are concerned, so are fairly adept at the formalization of elementary algebra, but do not *understand* elementary algebra well enough to deal with its application to calculus. Needless to say, such students are almost beyond salvaging. The farther they have gone in this direction, the more difficult it is to supply the missing understanding so necessary for many applications of elementary algebra.

It is only fair to point out that most courses in elementary algebra do not address directly the problem of understanding. Nevertheless, some of the students automatically fill in a correct understanding. This is a late manifestation of an ability that small children tend to show automatically if they are allowed or encouraged to do so. It is also an example of a drive to complete, in one way or other, an "unfinished" structure. Such students repair, at least partially, some of the deficiences in their previous training. The tendency of many teachers, however, to avoid the problem of understanding tends to blunt the self-correction that may save a student. The teacher's objective in algebra should include a constant awareness of the desirability of helping the student to supply or develop the basic understanding of an *algebra system*.

The student who masters the formal algebra operations without being able to associate with them the concept of an algebra *system* has somehow replaced the desired algebra concept with the relatively superficial structure of the associated formal language. We call this *form without content* (or structure). It is a special case of substituting the structure of the language for the structure of the material that the language is supposed to describe. This can actually occur at a level much higher than algebra, as shown by the following personal example.

A number of years ago I was invited to give an hour-long talk before a meeting of The American Mathematical Society. This was an important assignment, so I devoted considerable effort to the preparation of my talk. In fact, I prepared it much too well! As a result, when I gave the talk I found myself standing before the audience and listening to, rather than thinking about, my lecture. In other words it reduced to a clear case of form without content. The content of the lecture was reduced to the language rather than to ideas, and instead of enjoying a flow of ideas, I experienced only a flow of words. Needless to say, this was a very unusual and unpleasant experience for me and I can only hope that the audience did not notice what was happening. Incidentally, this is probably why mathematicians seldom give lectures by "reading" a manuscript to the audience. At the same time I am mystified by the fact that distinguished representatives of nonscientific fields often deliver a lecture by reading a prepared manuscript.

CREATIVE MATHEMATICAL EXPERIENCES

It is exceedingly difficult for a mathematician to convey to any nonmathematician some idea of the nature of a creative experience in mathematics. Much of the problem is due to the fact that some of the richest experience with mathematical thinking involves nontrivial mathematics that cannot be adequately described without use of highly technical mathematical language. Despite this problem, a very distinguished mathematician, Henri Poincaré, published an essay, *Mathematical Creation* (Poincaré, 1913, pp. 383–394).

The essay contains an account of his personal experience in discovering some definitely nontrivial mathematics. A fairly detailed discussion of Poincaré's essay is given in Rickart (1995, section 44), where the emphasis tends to be more in the way that mathematics fits into a general structuralism approach. All of my references to Poincaré are to the essay.

Needless to say, the Poincaré essay does not provide a technical analysis of the mathematics on which his remarks are based, but rather is devoted to a discussion of the way his mind dealt with the ideas. Although there is a mystery as to what actually happened with the mathematics, one can appreciate to a degree how the ideas were manipulated. An interesting fact is that a significant part of the experience took place in Poincaré's unconscious. Although all approaches to this subject have much in common, it is important to understand that the Poincaré account describes only one of many possible variations on experiences of this kind. It is also important to understand that what occurs is not uniquely determined by the fact that it concerns mathematics. Experiences of this kind can occur in any subject and at any level of understanding. What is unique about mathematics is the relative ease with which events can be isolated and studied.

Poincaré emphasizes that the creative experience was preceded by a lot of hard mathematical work on the problem, which did not yield a solution. This was followed by relaxation or preoccupation with something totaly unrelated to the unsolved problem. Although Poincaré's conscious mind thus ceased to deal with the problem, his unconscious ("subliminal self") continued to work on the problem and eventually came up with a solution. He thinks of the solution as a "good combination" of known mathematical entities and suggested that the result has an aesthetic value that brings it into consciousness. He also attributed the aesthetic value to a character of beauty and elegance. Such entities "are those whose elements are harmoniously disposed so that the mind without effort can embrace their totality without realizing the details." These are the most useful and beautiful because they lead to a mathematical law. It is their beauty and usefulness that distinguishes them from the ordinary combinations and brings them to consciousness before the many others.

Poincaré emphasized the importance of the preliminary conscious work that provides the unconscious with an enormous supply of combinations, most of which are useless. He figured that "the future elements of our combinations are something like the hooked atoms of Epicurus," normally motionless and "hooked to the wall." Under certain nonrandom circumstances (perhaps resulting from the preliminary conscious work), certain atoms are detached from the wall and move about "like the molecules of gas in the kinematic theory of gases," so new combinations are produced by their mutual impacts. The point is that the ultimately *selected* combinations tend to be good combinations.

It is possible to give a more structural description of what may occur in the Poincaré picture. The following account, based on the brain structure, is a sketch of a more detailed discussion given in Rickart (1995). It views the brain structure as a massive electrical network, despite the fact that it is considerably more complex than that. In this picture, all of our mental structures appear as electrical networks, each of which is a substructure of the all-inclusive brain structure.

A brain network is inactive (or may not even exist as a structure) until it can become an element in the general structure processing. We may therefore think of the "active" structures as being "highlighted" and therefore candidates for general processing. The process relevant to mathematical creation is an *extension* process. This means the creation of a larger (mathematical) structure that includes the given one as a substructure. The extension may be either a new structure or a structural joining of the given structure to another previously existing structure. Either case may be regarded as growth of the given or known structure and the result normally a new mathematical structure. The question now is, "How can the Poincaré experience be described in terms of such a structure extension?"

We may think of a given structure as a potential for growth through the existence of sensitive connector points on the "surface" of the structure. These are points with the potential of entering into an electrical nerve connection with material outside the given structure, possibly with another structure. Mathematical creativity consists in replacing a given familiar mathematical structure with a larger one that is a previously unknown *good* mathematical structure. Just as for Poincaré, the extensions are unplanned aside from things learned in the preliminary work on the problem, and good extensions are the beautiful ones, which are forced into consciousness by their beauty. Needless to say, just what constitutes the beauty, aside from usefulness, is rather difficult to detail. In any case, to the experienced mathematician the beauty is often quite apparent, although perhaps difficult to explain.

It is worthwhile to describe another far more ordinary example of a creative experience that has something in common with the earlier discussion. This is another personal experience and would probably not rate mentioning in another context. (It is also discussed, along with another example, in Rickart, 1995.)

The example involves the proofs of a paper that I had written to be published in a standard research journal. Everything was quite routine because the corrections were only trivial ones, so normal practice would consist of returning the sheets in the mail. For some reason unknown at the time, I put the sheets aside and postponed returning them to the journal. In the meantime, I noticed that I was automatically reviewing the proof of one of the lemmas in the paper. This occurred at odd times even when the paper was not in my thoughts. The experience, however, was not unpleasant, because the lemma was an important one and I was generally pleased with it. In fact, remembering the proof was analogous to reviewing mechanically a melody from a favorite piece of music. The only difference here was that I recalled the proof at odd or inconvenient times and there was a certain compulsiveness about the whole thing. Under a growing anxiety, I finally forced myself to sit down and review the proof of the lemma. The problem, of course, was that the proof of the lemma contained an error. Fortunately, the error was not a bad one, so was rather easy to correct, enabling me to return the proofs without further delay.

Notice that the aforementioned experience was an unconscious one and suggests that the unconscious is not only uninhibited as a creator, but is also a subtle critic as well. At the same time, one can ask why the unconscious did not give an answer along with the warning of an error. Although it is not completely clear why this is so, perhaps the unconscious can deal with an exploration or development of structure, but does not have the facility to make references about a structure. Therefore, it can "exhibit" a structure defect but cannot account for it. In fact, the exhibition of a structure defect may be nothing more than an immediate result of running into the defect while exploring the structure. Poincaré also pointed out the fact that the unconscious never seems to present one with the details of a solution. The conscious is apparently always required in the filling out of confirmation details, or in supplying communication of any kind.

The reader will find additional discussion of mathematical creativity by Hadamard (1954). One of the troubles with these frequently cited accounts of creativity is that they suggest that creativity is an experience reserved for the great minds. This is simply not the case, because similar experiences are common with ordinary persons when they experience something as commonplace as face recognition. The problem is that these experiences occur so frequently and so casually that they are not recognized as genuinely creative. A simple analysis of many experiences of this kind will reveal their creative qualities.

QUALIFYING REMARKS

I include here some remarks on our earlier use of brain nerve structures. The reader is probably aware of the fact that my appeal to nerve structures is not rigorous and functions only as a convenient way of visualizing what is going on. To determine how structures are actually represented in the nerve structure is actually a very difficult problem, so it is perhaps not surprising that not very much is known about the matter. Regardless of the difficulty, however, the symbolic use of nerve structure representations is convenient up to a point. At the same time, certain mathematical objects suggest that nerve structures are not what is ultimately needed.

Consider, for example, the concept of a triangle. Note that this is something rather precise and we might expect the concept to be recorded more or less as a sharp picture of a triangle. It is difficult to understand, however, how the clean figure of a triangle can be represented in a chaotic mass of nerve fibers. Everything becomes even more difficult when it is realized that the concept of a triangle must cover a wide variety of triangles; including, for example, triangles that are equilateral, right angled, acute or obtuse angled, and so on. Perhaps the brain structure is being considered at the wrong level. The following, very different kind of example, is suggestive.

Consider a drawing of a (mathematical) figure on a piece of paper. This structure can be very sharp and may contain a great deal of information. Furthermore, the paper that carries the drawn structure is also a complex structure whose objects are molecules of various kinds. Although the paper plays a vital role in the representation of the mathematical figure, its structure, at least at the molecular level, appears to be totally irrevalant. Is it possible that the underlying nerve structure of the brain is just as irrelevant for the representation of the structures that interest us? Is there a level at which the brain may be seen as a structure that may serve a role analagous to that served by the gross structure of the piece of paper in the case of a drawn figure? Needless to say, I cannot answer this question and do not know which structural level might be more relevant.

ON MATHEMATICAL ABILITY

It is obvious that individuals vary greatly in thir ability to understand mathematics—an ability that varies greatly with age. Some children may have difficulty from the very beginning, whereas others are good at mathematics up to the point where suddenly it becomes impossible. A sudden difficulty with mathematics can occur at almost any stage. Finally, there are some who are very talented with mathematics and seem to be unlimited in their ability to develop in the subject. What are the differences here? Are they genetic or do they result from certain combinations of experiences? Are there some who, for some reason, simply cannot think mathematically beyond a certain point? Differences in ability in any subject are difficult to analyze, but it may be easier to deal with mathematics than with other fields because of the clearer involvement of structure in the latter.

We have already seen some of the difficulties that arise with children who are faced with the problem of learning mathematics. Some of these go back to the very first experiences with numbers that occur at the same level as learning the language. It is obvious that difficulties at this level will increase the difficulty of developing a proper notion of the number system in the course of learning about numbers in elementary arithmetic. We have also seen that trouble with the ordinary number system automatically creates difficulties when it comes to learning about an algebra system in the course of studying elementary algebra. Unfortunately, these problems pile up and the problem of correcting them becomes increasingly difficult. Observe that in all of these cases the problem is not built in but results from gaps or errors in teaching or learning. In other words, the difficulties could have been avoided by correct handling of the problem, so it is not something that an individual is stuck with because of heredity.

It is obvious that anyone who has had misconceptions about number or algebra systems corrected will be better able to deal with the more advanced mathematics. At the same time, it is important to point out that there can be a lasting defect left over from such an experience. The mind is not like a computer: When something is corrected it is not wiped clean, but is simply "flagged" and then followed by the correction. The flagged item is always there and may not normally arise to consciousness, but it still exists and may inadvertently force its way into attention. Therefore, despite the correction, the error is never completely erased and may slow down one's use of the concepts involved. I believe that most mathematicians can dredge up mathematical experiences to support these remarks, but it will probably be better instead to cite an everyday experience, which I now do.

Some years ago we planted a small peach tree in our back yard. It surprised us the very first season by producing some unusually large peaches. My first unthinking reaction to the event was to be amazed that such a small tree produced such large peaches. I had known for a long time, of course, that the size of peaches had nothing to do with the size of the tree, but sometime before I learned that fact I must have associated the size of fruit with the size of tree. That piece of misinformation, unless it is sharply monitored, can still force its way into my consciousness. Items may vary greatly, of course, in their tendency to be recalled. It is not surprising that a piece of mathematical misinformation can appear in the same way. An occurrence in consciousness may be rare, but it is easy to see that it might still frequently slow one's thinking about the subject of interest.

Although we have emphasized elementary mathematical items in this chapter, the same phenomena can occur with more advanced material. Therefore, an uncorrected piece of mathematical information at any level might terminate a career in the subject. In other words, mathematical type ideas are so vital to an understanding of many things that it would be surprising if limitation on mathematical learning was limited to inborn qualities. An exception to this conjecture may be in order for the very rare, extremely gifted mathematicians. Admittedly, their ability may be based on something that is even absent in many very successful mathematicians.

REFERENCES

Caws, P. (1988). *Structuralism: The art of the intelligible. Contemporary studies in philosophy and the human sciences.* Atlantic Highlands, NJ: Humanities Press International.

de Saussure, F. (1966). *Course in general linguistics.* New York: McGraw-Hill.

Hadamard, J. (1954). *The psychology of invention in the mathematical field.* New York: Dover.

Poincaré, H. (1913). *The foundations of science* (G. H. Halstead, Trans.). New York: The Science Press.

Rickart, C. E. (1995). *Structuralism and structures: A mathematical perspective.* Singapore: World Scientific.

VI

CONCLUSIONS

What Is Mathematical Thinking?

Robert J. Sternberg
Yale University

What is mathematical thinking? Although the chapters in this volume address a number of questions, certainly this question is the most fundamental. We can look at how to teach or assess mathematical thinking, at how mathematical thinking develops, or at how mathematical thinking differs across cultures, but in order to look at any of these things, first we have to understand what mathematical thinking is.

In reading through the chapters of this volume, it becomes clear that there is no consensus on what mathematical thinking is, nor even on the abilities or predispositions that underlie it. If one were to start the volume with little conception of the definition of mathematical thinking, one might end the volume with many conceptions whose relations to each other are not completely clear. In this chapter, I discuss what I see as some of the relations among these conceptions.

To the extent that one's goal is to understand *mathematical thinking* in terms of a set of clearly defining features that are individually necessary and jointly sufficient for understanding the construct, one is going to be disappointed. Indeed, it is difficult to find any common features that pervade all of the various kinds of mathematical thinking discussed in this volume. For example, the abilities needed to learn to count seem quite different from those needed to prove a difficult theorem in topology; the abilities needed to compute the correct answer to a subtraction problem with borrowing seem quite different from those needed to understand the role of base rates in probabilistic inference. The point is that the classical theory of meaning in semantic theory (Katz, 1972; Katz & Fodor, 1963) just does not seem to apply to mathematical thinking, any more than it seems to apply to the notion of what a game is (Wittgenstein, 1953). In other words, *mathematical thinking*, like *game*, does not seem to be a classically defined concept with a set of defining features that are necessary and sufficient.

MATHEMATICAL THINKING AS A SET OF PROTOTYPES

A better model for understanding mathematical thinking seems to be the prototypical model that has been proposed by Rosch (1973, 1978) and elaborated on by others (e.g., Medin & Smith, 1984). The idea in this model is that there are typically no defining features at all, but rather only characteristic features that are typical of the construct. For example, manipulation of numerical symbols, as in computation, might be a characteristic feature of mathematical thinking, but it is certainly not necessary. One could use mathematical thinking to solve a word problem, but do all of the symbol processing on a calculator so as to avoid doing any mental computation. Multiple operators and verbal equivalents for numerical symbols would be other aspects of the prototype. The complete set of possible attributes in the prototype would be difficult or impossible to specify, and might well differ from one numeration system to another (e.g., some languages have unique symbols for numbers; others do not).

It is not clear that there is a single prototype for mathematical thinking. There might be multiple prototypes, as there probably are, say, for what constitutes "good teaching" (Sternberg & Horvath, 1995). For example, what would constitute outstanding mathematical thinking might be different in algebra versus geometry, or statistics versus calculus. The existence of multiple prototypes seems likely, if only because the people who seem to be the best statisticians are not necessarily the same as those who are best at calculus, and vice versa.

In order to understand fully one or more prototypes of mathematical thinking, one would probably have to combine multiple approaches to the understanding of mathematical thinking. As in the case of intelligence, there are multiple models or metaphors that can be applied to the understanding of mathematical thinking (see Sternberg, 1990), each of which complements the others in elucidating the construct. The multiple metaphors, such as the psychometric and information-processing ones, are complementary rather than contradictory, helping us to understand a single construct from multiple points of view.

The chapters in this volume self-consciously take different approaches to the understanding of mathematical thinking. If we were to try to figure out, as well as we can, characteristic features of one or more prototypes, what might these features be, combining elements of the different approaches?

CHARACTERISTIC FEATURES OF PROTOTYPICAL MATHEMATICAL THINKING

The Psychometric Approach

The psychometric or "geographical" approach to understanding mathematical thinking views the mind as a map with multiple regions varying in size and location. Some of these regions may be more central (i.e., characteristic of the prototype), others more peripheral. In chapter 1, Carroll takes a psychometric approach to understanding prototypical features of mathematical thinking.

At the most general level is general ability, or g, which seems to be relevant to many different types of thinking, including but in no way limited to mathematical thinking. Psychometric approaches have never been at their best in specifying the information-processing characteristics of the entities they define, although g has been suggested to be the ability to apprehend information, induce relations, and apply those relations (Spearman, 1923), as well as the amount of conscious mental manipulation required by complex tasks (Jensen, 1980; Marshalek, Lohman, & Snow, 1983). Other abilities involved in mathematical thinking, according to Carroll, include fluid intelligence (which may or may not even differ from g—Gustafson, 1988; Undheim & Gustafsson, 1987, and which seems to be closely related to the ability to reason inductively), and involves quality of sequential reasoning as well as speed of reasoning; crystallized intelligence, which involves knowledge and may comprise language skills, including reading comprehension; general memory ability; general visual perception, including visualization, spatial relations, mechanical knowledge, perceptual speed, closure speed, and closure flexibility; and speed of information processing.

The psychometric metaphor effectively shows why it is better to think of mathematical thinking in terms of multiple prototypes rather than in terms of a single classical semantic entity. An ability such as spatial visualization will be heavily involved in many kinds of geometric and topological problems, but will almost certainly be less involved in most statistical problems. Speed of information processing will be important in many testing situations, such as when students' mathematical thinking is assessed via the SAT or a similar test, but is likely to be far less involved when a mathematician spends months or even years trying to work out a proof. In sum, the different abilities seem more or less central to the extent that they pervade more versus fewer kinds of mathematical thinking. Someone who is relatively weaker spatially may never become a world-class topologist, but may have at least a shot at becoming a world-class statistician.

Even within a given kind of mathematics, there are probably alternative routes to success, as there are in any field. For example, factor analysis can be approached either algebraically, geometrically, or both, as can many different multivariate techniques. One could understand multivariate data analysis well via either an algebraic or a geometric conceptual framework. Probably those who understand multivariate analysis best would be able to use both frameworks. In my own experience teaching multivariate analysis, different students understand the material in different ways (e.g., algebraically or geometrically), and teaching the material in different ways helps more students comprehend the material of the course.

The Computational Approach

The computational approach loosely embraces work that seeks to elucidate the information processing required in mathematical or other kinds of thinking. For example, Mayer and Hegarty's (chapter 2, this volume) theory of mathematical understanding is based on this approach.

Mayer and Hegarty suggest a number of information-processing bases of mathematical thinking. One is quantitative reasoning, used in what they refer to as a direct-translation strategy of problem solving, and another is qualitative reasoning, used in what they refer to as a problem-model strategy. In the former strategy, one selects some of the apparent key numbers in a problem, and tries to fit them into arithmetical formulas. The authors refer to it as a "compute first and think later" kind of strategy. In the latter, one constructs a qualitative understanding of a problem, constructs an internal representation that unifies, to the extent that it is possible, the statements of the problem, and only then computes a solution to the problem.

The direct-translation strategy can be quite fast, but it is also likely to be incorrect if what seem to be salient numbers in the problem are red herrings. For example, when we are given the socks problem—"Blue and black socks are mixed together in a drawer in a ratio of 4:5; how many socks do we need to take out of the drawer in order to be assured of having a pair of the same color?"—the direct-translation strategy primes the numbers 4 and 5, and is thereby likely to lead to an error as the problem solver tries to use the 4:5 ratio as a basis for solving a problem in which the ratio is irrelevant.

Mayer and Hegarty's model shows the extent to which multiple kinds of representations and processes can be involved in mathematical thinking. For example, to comprehend a mathematical problem, the problem solver first has to translate the statements into a mathematical representation, then construct a problem representation, and then construct a plan for solution. One can see how crystallized abilities, as discussed by Carroll, would be relevant in decoding the words of the problem and seeking past formulas that one has stored in order to solve the problem; but one can also see how fluid abilities would be important in overriding stereotyped uses of formulas that may not apply in a given instance, and in going beyond past mental models in order to construct a new mental model that applies appropriately to a given, unique problem.

Ben-Zeev's analysis in chapter 3 further specifies information-processing attributes of mathematical thinking. She suggests the importance of analogical thinking in mathematics, as when one forms a mapping between past problems one has solved and the present problem one is seeking to solve, and also when one seeks to see the relations among a set of problems one needs to solve in the present. Of course, good analogical thinking involves seeing points of disanalogy as well as of analogy—how the present problem is different from as well as similar to past problems. Again, in psychometric terms, we can see the roles of both crystallized abilities (development of past knowledge base) and fluid abilities (flexibly using but also departing from past knowledge base) in the solution of mathematical problems. Translation and construction of a plan for solution, in Mayer and Hegarty's terms, will certainly be facilitated by proper drawing of analogies, and inhibited by the perception of false analogies. These aspects of mathematical problem solving will also involve what Ben-Zeev calls "schematic thinking," in that, presumably, past mathematical information is represented in part in terms of mental schemas.

Much of the information-processing work that has been done on human abilities has concentrated on the decomposition of response times, assuming correct responses (see, e.g., chapters in Sternberg, 1984). In studies of mathematical thinking, of course, the role of errors has been seen as more important, because the principal issue has usually been seen as producing correct answers rather than quick answers (although the measurement of the number factor in tests based on Thurstone's, 1938, theory of mental abilities often involves numerical speed at least as much as accuracy). Ben-Zeev's work emphasizes errors, but in an interesting twist, focuses on a sense in which errors may be "correct"; that is, reasoning that is logical, but that starts from incorrect premises, and hence leads to wrong conclusions.

Mathematical ability, in this view, involves not only developed reasoning processes for solving problems, but developed processes of inferring or otherwise generating correct premises to serve as the bases for solving problems. One is reminded of the problems children face when they are first learning language, and overgeneralize their use of words (Clark, 1973; Nelson, 1973). Nelson's work is particularly interesting in this regard, in that Nelson suggested that overgeneralizations are functional. When problem solvers overgeneralize the use of mathematical formulas, they, too, seem to be trying to use the formulas for functions to which the formulas do not truly generalize.

The Anthropological Approach

I have referred to the anthropological approach as encompassing models of abilities that view a given construct as, at least in part, a cultural invention (Sternberg, 1990). Mathematical thinking might seem like anything but a cultural invention. However, it almost certainly has highly culturally bound aspects to it as it is actually done. For example, cultures, such as the Chinese one, that make use of the abacus in mathematical learning and problem solving might end up rewarding abilities different from those rewarded by a culture that relies on paper-and-pencil computational skills. In turn, a culture that relies heavily on the use of calculators and computers may reward still different abilities.

The anthropological approach shows how the nature of a construct may vary across time as well as space. When I grew up in the 1950s and took college admissions tests in the 1960s, we needed to be facile in arithmetical computation skills. Today, children use calculators in school and even for college admissions tests, obviating the need for many of those computational skills. Similarly, the use of slide rules has essentially disappeared from courses on mathematics and engineering. The skills leading to adept use of this device, therefore, have simply become irrelevant to observable mathematical abilities, whereas they were quite relevant 40 years ago.

In chapter 4, Miller and Paredes show that how numbers are expressed in a language can make an important difference to how easily various aspects of mathematics are learned and internally represented in that language. On this view, Chinese children have an advantage over English or American children because of the greater regularity in their system of verbal expression of numbers. These fascinating results cast a new view on cultural differences in mathematical performance, showing that one needs not only take into account differences in schooling, but differences in the way the numbers that are taught in schools are represented in the first place.

In chapter 5, Saxe, Dawson, Fall, and Howard suggest, along similar culturally based lines, that individuals structure and work toward mathematical goals that are interwoven with cultural artifacts, social interactions, activity structures, and individuals' prior knowledge. Therefore, mathematics cannot be truly separated from everyday life.

Saxe and his colleagues, like Mayer and Hegarty and like Ben-Zeev, view mathematical thinking in cognitive terms, but as filtered through the lens of culture. They argue that goal formation in mathematics depends on four parameters—activity structures, social interactions, sign forms and cultural artifacts, and prior understandings.

The activity structure of a practice consists of a routine organization of participation in the practice. For example, when we go to a supermarket, there is a fixed sequence of events involving mathematics. We compare products to see which are better buys than are others. We choose our entire set of products to make sure that they fit within the total amount of money we have or can spend on our shopping. We may check to make sure that the addition is correct. Increasing computerization at the supermarket, as well as of cash registers in general, has changed the abilities needed to function properly with a cash register. As a child, I watched my grandmother at the cash register computing change, and taking into account people who gave her extra bits of money so as not to end up with a lot of change. Today's computers make such computations unnecessary.

Some people have taken the increasing computerization of checkouts in the supermarket to suggest that the checking of the clerk's work is no longer necessary. Errors, however, remain—they are just of a different type. Now they are more likely to take the form of a product being charged twice, for example, or being charged at a price different from that marked on the supermarket shelf. Both have happened to me. People who pay attention to the products that are spit out of computers—and not everyone does—quickly realize that errors do not go away, but merely change in kind. They also change in persistence: Try getting a computerized bill that is in error corrected! A recent error with a microchip that had been installed into many computers showed just how susceptible to error even computers can be.

Social interactions are also important in mathematical thinking as it occurs in the real world. For example, a banker may help a client figure out how much of a mortgage he or she can afford. A stock broker may help a client compute the cost of a stock purchase. Some people, of course, are inclined to leave the computations to the professionals—the bankers or the stock brokers. It usually only takes getting burned once, however, for these people to realize that placing the whole responsibility on someone else can be an extremely risky strategy. Customers may find that they are stuck with a mortgage they cannot afford because of false assumptions made by the banker, or may find that they are even turned down for the mortgage because in allowing the banker to do everything, the customers forgot to provide crucial information that later turned out to be relevant in the bank's decision not to offer the mortgage. Ironically, the increasing availability of resources for performing computations—machine or human—has increased the responsibility we need to take for making sure that the resources have the information they need, presented in the correct form, for the computations to take place correctly.

Students and others often consider a computer output not to need checking, because how could the computer make mistakes? In my experience, computer outputs contain errors quite frequently, not because of errors in computation by the computer, but because the information was not presented correctly to the computer, or because the assumptions under which the computations were done were erroneous, or because the mathematical model did not fit the data in the first place. Computerization, if anything, has increased the importance of higher order thinking in performing mathematical computations.

Artifacts and conventions include use of body parts, such as fingers, in counting, or the use of slide rules and computers. As noted earlier, these artifacts are quite important not only because they are used in computing answers to mathematical problems, but because they help define who will be perceived as having more, and who as having less, mathematical-thinking ability. It is important to realize that new artifacts, in reducing the role of certain factors in contributing to individual differences, increase the role of others. Computational ability may matter less today to individual differences in mathematical ability in Western countries. However, the ability quickly and correctly to use a calculator matters more. In the case of complex calculators, the ability to program them may become important. In my children's high school, for example, students are allowed to use programmable calculators, and those students who can program their calculators to cut down on their work are at a big advantage over those who cannot. Indeed, social interactional abilities are even relevant here—in being able to convince better programmers to share their programs.

Particularly interesting in the framework of Saxe and his colleagues is the emphasis on the interplay between developments across contexts and practices. This emphasis is reminiscent of the work of Carraher, Carraher, and Schliemann (1985), which has demonstrated that the same Brazilian children who are successfully able to do street mathematics in order to run a business may be totally unable to do formally isomorphic mathematics in the context of the school; and of the work of Lave, Murtaugh, and de la Roche (1984) and Murtaugh (1985) showing that the same individuals who may be able to do comparison shopping in the context of a supermarket may not be able to do isomorphic abstract arithmetical operations in the context of a paper-and-pencil test administered in a classroom. Findings such as these suggest that there may be quite a gap between the abilities required for pure mathematics and those required for everyday mathematics, much as there is between academic and practical intelligence (Sternberg, 1985; Sternberg, Wagner, Williams, & Horvath, 1995).

It is nontrivial to bridge the gap between work such as that of Saxe and his colleagues and work such as that of Mayer or Ben-Zeev. All are talking about mathematical thinking, but from different points of view. The work of Geary in chapter 6 helps bridge the gap. In distinguishing between primary and secondary abilities, Geary shows how it may make sense biologically as well as culturally to distinguish between abilities that are universal and that will apply to mathematics no matter where it is used, and abilities that are culturally specific, and that will be closely tied to the uses of mathematics and the conventions surrounding these uses.

For example, Geary suggests that abilities such as those of counting and simple arithmetic are universal, whereas abilities such as mathematical problem solving are secondary and culturally specific. On this view, we might see some abilities as interacting with cultural contexts, and others as not so interacting.

In that counting appears to be universal, at least as far as we know, and the study of real analysis is not, Geary's distinction may well make sense. I am not sure the distinction is quite as simple as Geary states, however.

First, one might argue that the thinking required for mathematics of all kinds is universal; what differs is whether a given culture at a given time exercises it. The laws of mathematics—the commutative property of addition, for example—is culture independent, as is the Pythagorean theorem. Whether a culture has developed mathematics that takes advantage of it may be particular, but in this case, we need to consider whether we want to make a distinction between the mental ability for mathematics—which is perhaps universal—and the particular set of mental abilities on which the culture draws—which may not be. The higher order question is whether the list of abilities or kinds of thinking should depend on what the culture requires, or on mental capacities that exist, whether or not they are called for in a given culture. For example, I would argue that the universe of mental abilities is constant across cultures, but that the abilities that constitute intelligence may vary across cultures as a function of what is adaptive in the various cultures (Sternberg, 1985). Therefore, it may not be mathematical abilities or thinking, per se, that differ across space and time, but those aspects of it that are exploited at a given place or time.

Second, the culture may not know about the Pythagorean theorem, but the same mental abilities used to understand or exercise it may be used as well in other mathematical pursuits. Because we do not yet have a good mapping between tasks and abilities, we need to be careful about specifying which abilities are used, based on analysis of the tasks in which the culture engages. The fact that a culture has not discovered the Pythagorean theorem does not mean that the abilities needed to use it are not used in other aspects of mathematics that are used in the culture.

Third, even universal or primary abilities may manifest themselves differently in different cultures. For example, the words for numbers are simpler and more logically generated in some cultures than in others. As noted by Miller and Paredes in chapter 4, this very fact appears to be partially responsible for some of the difference we observe in mathematical performance across cultures (see also Miller, Smith, Zhu, & Zhang, 1995). The children of the cultures with the simpler or more logical words may thus appear to have higher mathematical abilities—and in fact they do better on mathematical tests—but not because of any underlying capacity difference, but rather because of a Whorfian sort of linguistic advantage.

The Pedagogical Approach

One way to learn about mental processes is to attempt to teach them, and then draw inferences back to the mental processes as a result of what is more and less easily taught (e.g., Brown, 1974, 1975; Brown & Barclay, 1976). In this volume, two chapters use this kind of backward inferencing process in order to understand mathematical thinking. They let us make inferences about cognitive and other processing on the basis of what is taught more or less easily.

An interesting result of the pedagogical approach is that it almost immediately expands the prototype for mathematical thinking to include variables that go beyond the narrowly cognitive. Attitudes, relationships, and social constraints quickly become part and parcel of the prototype taken as a whole. For example, Ginsburg's analysis in chapter 7 points out how sometimes mathematical thinking for children involves trying to get right answers as quickly as possible without thinking, as, for example, when children are timed on how quickly they can write down answers to problems that test their knowledge of addition, subtraction, multiplication, or division facts. As Ginsburg also points out, and as discussed earlier, the game of mathematics differs from one culture to another, partly as a function of language: For example, the word "eighty" may be processed in a way that is different from the way "quatre-vingts" (80 in French, and which means literally "four twenties") is processed.

Purist cognitive psychologists might be inclined to view attitudes as the province of social rather than cognitive psychology, and as interacting with but not as being part of mathematical thinking. Such a position would be hard to defend in view of work as old as that of Janis and Frick (1943) or as recent as that of Cosmides (1989) and Johnson-Laird and Byrne (1991) showing major effects of content and attitude toward material on thinking about it. In a task such as the Wason selection task—which requires people to recognize information needed in order to draw valid conditional inferences—you cannot abstract the difficulty of the problem from the content via which the task is presented. The task has no meaningful difficulty independent of its content and people's attitudes toward that content. The work of Lave with California shoppers and of Carraher and coll. agues with Brazilian street children suggests that the same is true for mathematical as for logical problems (see also Ceci & Roazzi, 1994). Indeed, in his theory of multiple intelligences, Gardner (1983) posited that logical and mathematical abilities combine in a single intelligence.

The work of Bransford and his colleagues in chapter 8 further shows that mathematical thinking and learning are highly context dependent. Children learn mathematics far better when word problems are meaningful to them, when students are helped to identify and define their own word problems rather than always relying on others to define the problems for them, and when teachers focus on communication of mathematical concepts and not just on the concepts themselves. Bransford and his colleagues were most successful in teaching mathematical thinking with highly contextualized problems that look virtually nothing like those that constitute the material in American mathematics texts, past and present. To the extent that we have not had much success in teaching mathematical thinking, we perhaps have ourselves to blame for developing instructional methods that seem to depart so greatly from the ideal, or anything even resembling it.

The Mathematical Approach

It is worth observing that the most mathematically oriented of the chapter authors are those who probably depart the most from purely cognitive models of mathematical thinking based wholly or largely on cognitive information-processing considerations. Although the model of mathematical thinking proposed by Dreyfus and Eisenberg in chapter 9 includes some of the same cognitive elements found in the work of Mayer and Hegarty and of Ben Zeev—for example, reasoning by analogy, considerations of structure and representation, and visual reasoning—Dreyfus and Eisenberg also emphasize the importance of the affective. They discuss right up front, for example, and in some detail, the Moore approach, which emphasizes self-confidence, and the Davidson "humanization" of Moore's approach, which involves a more cooperative and less competitive approach to teaching mathematics.

In chapter 10, Rickart, the mathematician, places more emphasis on mathematical creativity than do any of the other contributors to the volume. Perhaps because of my own interest in creativity (Sternberg & Lubart, 1995), I found the relatively scarce consideration of mathematical creativity in the volume to be somewhat surprising. A comment I have heard a number of times from mathematicians is that performance in mathematics courses, up to the college and even early graduate levels, often does not effectively predict who will succeed as a mathematician. The prediction failure is due to the fact that in math, as in most other fields, one can get away with good analytic but weak creative thinking until one reaches the highest levels of education— in this case, the later years of graduate training. However, it is creative mathematical thinking that is most important for the development of mathematics as a discipline. Without such creativity, the mathematical curriculum of today would be no different from that of hundreds and perhaps even thousands of years ago. For mathematical thinking to develop as a discipline and not just as an individual skill, creative mathematical thinking is of supreme importance. Similarly, for individuals to use mathematics in ways that go well beyond what they are taught, creative mathematical thinking is key.

Creative thinking in mathematics is not important only in higher math. Any data analyst, economist, accountant, investor, or even citizen filling out tax forms can attest to the need to be creative with numbers. In data analysis, for example, one often finds that the results of planned analyses do not work out as had been hoped. However, there may be a structure in the data that the initial analyses are not showing. The creative data analyst figures out a way to elucidate this structure; the uncreative one may never even discover the structure that was in the data waiting all along to be discovered.

A TRIARCHIC APPROACH TO MATHEMATICAL THINKING

The approaches described previously have in common the fact that they attempt to abstract from the universe of possible elements of thought those that apply to mathematics. Thus, the psychometrician asks what factorially defined abilities are relevant to mathematical thinking. The cognitive psychologist asks what mental processes and representations are relevant. The cognitive–cultural psychologist seeks to determine what elements of thought interact with what elements of culture. The cognitive–educational psychologist seeks to abstract principles of instruction that are relevant for mathematical instruction as well as learning. The mathematician may ask what aspects of thought and, as it turns out, affect are important. As noted earlier, there is no one "right" way to approach mathematical thinking. Each approach contributes different elements to the prototype.

The triarchic theory of human intelligence (Sternberg, 1985, 1988) would look at mathematical thinking, or any other kind of thinking, for that matter, in a somewhat different way. Here, in fact, the elements of the theory that would be applied to mathematical thinking would not differ substantially from the elements that would be applied, for example, to verbal thinking.

Roughly speaking, the triarchic theory posits that analytic, creative, and practical thinking are all relevant and crucially important to intelligence. In particular, they are relevant to mathematical thinking as well. As we have seen in reviewing the chapters, all three of these kinds of thinking are important, and they seem to be relatively distinct. The people who are good everyday mathematicians are not necessarily good pure mathematicians, and the people who may be the best at analyzing existing problems are not necessarily those who prove to be adept at creative mathematical thinking that goes beyond the existing state of knowledge—however, let us get more specific.

The first of three subtheories of the triarchic theory—the componential subtheory—specifies three kinds of processes relevant to intelligent thought: metacomponents, performance components, and knowledge-acquisition components. Metacomponents—such as recognizing the existence of a problem, defining the problem, representing information about the problem, and monitoring solution of the problem—are the kinds of elements described in this volume under the cognitive approach to mathematical thinking—but they are also crucial higher order processes in verbal thinking, such as in reading for meaning or writing a play, for that matter. In writing, for example, one needs to decide what one wants to write about, figure out an approach to writing about it, decide how to describe the elements about which one writes, and check one's writing as one writes to make sure it is accomplishing what it is supposed to.

Performance components, such as those involved in analogical thinking—encoding elements of a problem, inferring relations, and applying these relations—are crucial, according to Spearman (1923), to general ability, as well as to verbal and mathematical thinking. Knowledge-acquisition components, such as selectively encoding relevant elements of a problem, selectively combining these elements to come up with a meaningful representation, and selective comparison in order to determine what ones knows from the past that is relevant to the present, are also as relevant in reading a book or writing a play as they are in solving a mathematics problem.

The second subtheory of the triarchic theory, the experiential subtheory, posits the importance of coping with novelty and of automatization in intelligence. Again, these aspects of intelligence are relevant in mathematical thinking—from dealing with new numeration systems or formulating new proofs for coping with novelty, to remembering and spitting back addition facts for automatization. However, both are also relevant to reading (from a new novel to rapidly recognizing familiar lexical elements) and to writing (from coming up with creative ideas to knowing how to put together a sentence without consciously thinking about its structural elements).

The third subtheory, the contextual subtheory, suggests that intelligence involves adaptation to, as well as shaping and selection of, environments. We teach mathematics in school because of its importance in adaptation. It is hard to live in today's world without being able to balance a checkbook, compute change, understand something about mortgage or rent payments, understand discounts, and the like. Mathematical thinking is important to all of us because we need it to survive, or at least to survive well.

What, then, according to the triarchic theory, is unique about mathematical thinking? What distinguishes it, say, from verbal thinking? According to this theory, the distinctions are largely in (a) the mental representations of information on which components operate and in (b) the "group" and "specific" performance components that operate on these representations. Some of the more specific mental operations of mathematics, such as multiplication, are not in fact used in reading or writing. Of course, the mental representation of numbers is different from that of words, because the symbol system is different. It is the difference in symbol systems and the rules under which each operates that lead to the differences in the operations on them. Indeed, we have found in our own research (Sternberg & Clinkenbeard, 1995;

Sternberg & Gardner, 1983), as have others, that the mental representation of information often has a greater effect on consistent patterns of individual differences than do the mental processes that act on these representations.

Affective factors will also be important. For example, Bandura (1977) has shown that views of one's own self-efficacy can have a substantial effect on one's performance in a given domain. People who believe they cannot do mathematics often end up not being able to do it, in large part because they have convinced themselves that they cannot. That is the basis of the Moore technique cited by Dreyfus and Eisenberg: By giving people self-confidence, the people often come to realize that the mathematics they had thought was impossible for them really is not.

To conclude, therefore, I believe that future work needs especially to focus on the effects of various mental representations on efficacy in a given field, and also that it needs to help us understand differences among the analytic, creative, and practical aspects of mathematics, which appear to be roughly as distinct as these aspects are in other domains. We also need a much better understanding of how affective components affect our attitudes toward mathematics and toward our ability to do mathematics (as in self-efficacy). We have made a great deal of progress in understanding mathematical thinking, as the chapters in this volume have shown. We will make a great deal more, I believe, as we turn our focus specifically toward these issues.

ACKNOWLEDGMENTS

Preparation of this chapter was supported under the Javits Act Program as administered by the Office of Educational Research and Improvement, U.S. Department of Education (Grant No. R206R50001). Grantees undertaking such projects are encouraged to express freely their professional judgment. This chapter, therefore, does not necessarily represent the positions or policies of the Government, and no official endorsement should be inferred.

REFERENCES

Bandura, A. (1977). Self-efficacy: Toward a unifying theory of behavioral change. *Psychological Review, 84,* 181–215.

Brown, A. L. (1974). The role of strategic behavior in retardate memory. In N. R. Ellis (Ed.), *International review of research in mental retardation* (Vol. 7, pp. 55–111). New York: Academic Press.

Brown, A. L. (1975). The development of memory: Knowing, knowing about knowing, and knowing how to know. In H. W. Reese (Ed.), *Advances in child development and behavior* (Vol. 10, pp. 103–152). New York: Academic Press.

Brown, A. L., & Barclay, C. R. (1976). The effects of training specific mnemonics on the metamnemonic efficiency of retarded children. *Child Development, 47,* 71–80.

Carraher, T. N., Carraher, D., & Schliemann, A. D. (1985). Mathematics in the streets and in the schools. *British Journal of Developmental Psychology, 3*, 21–29.

Ceci, S. J., & Roazzi, A. (1994). The effects of context of cognition: Postcards from Brazil. In R. J. Sternberg & R. K. Wagner (Eds.), *Mind in context* (pp. 74–102). New York: Cambridge University Press.

Clark, E. V. (1973). What's in a word? On the child's acquisition of semantics in his first language. In T. E. Moore (Ed.), *Cognitive development and the acquisition of language* (pp. 65–110). New York: Academic Press.

Cosmides, L. (1989). The logic of social exchange: Has natural selection shaped how humans reason? *Cognition, 31*, 187–276.

Gardner, H. (1983). *Frames of mind: The theory of multiple intelligences.* New York: Basic Books.

Gustafsson, J.-E. (1988). Hierarchical models of individual differences in cognitive abilities. In R. J. Sternberg (Ed.), *Advances in the psychology of human intelligence* (Vol. 4, pp. 35–71). Hillsdale, NJ: Lawrence Erlbaum Associates.

Janis, I. L., & Frick, F. (1943). The relationship between attitudes toward conclusions and errors in judging logical validity of syllogisms. *Journal of Experimental Psychology, 33*, 73–77.

Jensen, A. R. (1980). *Bias in mental testing.* New York: The Free Press.

Johnson-Laird, P. N., & Byrne, R. M. J. (1991). *Deduction.* Hillsdale, NJ: Lawrence Erlbaum Associates.

Katz, J. J. (1972). *Semantic theory.* New York: Harper & Row.

Katz, J. J., & Fodor, J. A. (1963). The structure of a semantic theory. *Language, 39*, 170–210.

Lave, J., Murtaugh, M., & de la Roche, O. (1984). The dialectic of arithmetic in grocery shopping. In B. Rogoff & J. Lave (Eds.), *Everyday cognition: Its development in social context* (pp. 67–94). Cambridge, MA: Harvard University Press.

Marshalek, B., Lohman, D. F., & Snow, R. E. (1983). The complexity continuum in the radex and hierarchical models of intelligence. *Intelligence, 7*, 107–127.

Medin, D. L., & Smith, E. E. (1984). Concepts and concept formation. In M. R. Rosenzweig & L. W. Porter (Eds.), *Annual Review of Psychology, 35*, 113–138.

Miller, K. F., Smith, C. M., Zhu, J., & Zhang, H. (1995). Preschool origins of cross-national differences in mathematical competence: The role of number naming systems. *Psychological Science, 6*, 56–60.

Murtaugh, M. (1985, Fall). The practice of arithmetic by American grocery shoppers. *Anthropology and Education Quarterly.*

Nelson, K. (1973). Structure and strategy in learning to talk. *Monographs of the Society for Child Development, 38*(149).

Rosch, E. (1973). On the internal structure of perceptual and semantic categories. In T. E. Moore (Ed.), *Cognitive development and the acquisition of language* (pp. 111–144). New York: Academic Press.

Rosch, E. (1978). Principles of categorization. In E. Rosch & B. Lloyd (Eds.), *Cognition and categorization* (pp. 27–48). Hillsdale, NJ: Lawrence Erlbaum Associates.

Spearman, C. (1923). *The abilities of man.* New York: Macmillan.

Sternberg, R. J. (Ed.). (1984). *Human abilities: An information-processing approach.* New York: Freeman.

Sternberg, R. J. (1985). *Beyond IQ.* New York: Cambridge University Press.

Sternberg, R. J. (1988). *The triarchic mind.* New York: Viking.

Sternberg, R. J. (1990). *Metaphors of mind.* New York: Cambridge University Press.

Sternberg, R. J., & Clinkenbeard, P. (1995). A triarchic view of identifying, teaching, and assessing gifted children. *Roeper Review, 17*(4), 255–260.

Sternberg, R. J., & Gardner, M. K. (1983). Unities in inductive reasoning. *Journal of Experimental Psychology: General, 112*, 80–116.

Sternberg, R. J., & Horvath, J. (1995). A prototype view of expert teaching. *Educational Researcher, 24*(6), 9–17.

Sternberg, R. J., & Lubart, T. I. (1995). *Defying the crowd: Cultivating creativity in a culture of conformity.* New York: The Free Press.

Sternberg, R. J., Wagner, R. K., Williams, W. M., & Horvath, J. (1995). Testing common sense. *American Psychologist, 50*(11), 912–927.

Thurstone, L. L. (1938). *Primary mental abilities.* Chicago: University of Chicago Press.

Undheim, J. O., & Gustafsson, J.-E. (1987). The hierarchical organization of cognitive abilities: Restoring general intelligence through the use of linear structural relations (LISREL). *Multivariate Behavioral Research, 22*, 149–171.

Wittgenstein, L. (1953). *Philosophical investigations.* Oxford, England: Blackwell.

Author Index

Subject Index

A

Abacus, 95, 96
  computational skills and, 105, 107
  conceptual consequences of, 107, 110
  Japanese-style, 96
Abacus skill, effect of, 107, 110, 109, 110
Ability(ies)
  biologically primary/secondary, 146, 151
  definition of, 4
  as entirely neutral, 6
  mathematical, 298, 299
  relevant to mathematical thinking
    auditory perception, 20
    broad cognitive speediness, 20
    broad retrieval ability, 20
    crystallized intelligence, 15, 17
    fluid intelligence, 12, 15, 13
    general factor, 9, 11, 11
    general memory ability, 17, 18
    general visual perception, 18, 20, 19
    information processing speed, 20
    second-stratum abilities, 11, 20
Abstract structures, definition of, 287
Accidental mathematician
  assessment project, 205, 206
  problem comprehension, 207, 208, 209
  problem contexts, 208, 209, 211

The River Adventure, 210, 211, 212
  word problems, 206, 207
Accuracy, in Toby's math, 191, 192
Acquisition effects, of number name structure, 96, 99, 101, 102
Activity structure
  in Oksapmin case, 130, 131
  of practice, 124
Addition
  children's, format effects in, 102, 105, 103, 104, 105, 106
  in NewAbacus system, 75, 76
Aesthetics of mathematical thinking, 253, 257, 254, 257,
Algebra, in Jasper *Woodbury Problem Solving Series*, 223
Algebra system, 294
Analogical thinking, 60, 63
  characteristics of, 62, 63
  rational errors and, 61, 62
  See also Inductive thinking
Analogy, reasoning by, 260–264, 262
Anthropological approach to understanding mathematical thinking, 308–311
"Are We There Yet", SMART Tool for, 233, 234
Arithmetic
  development of, 126–128
  sociogenesis of, 122–129

F

Factor analysis
confirmatory, 67
exploratory, 6
in studies, 7, 8
Factor-analytically derived cognitive abilities,
21–23
Failures
at inductive level, 71–72
at monitoring level, 69–71
Flexibility of thought, 279–282
Fluid intelligence, 12–15
Format effects in children's addition, 102–105,
106
Form-function relations, microgenetic analysis
of, 134–136
Form-function shifts
in cognitive development, 125–128
in development of arithmetic, 126–128
in Oksapmin case, 132–138
Form versus content, 293, 294
Form without content, 294
Fractions, clinical interviews on, 129, 130
activity structure in, 130, 131
artifacts/conventions in, 131
emergent goals in, 130–132, 133
form/functions in
form-function shifts, 132–138
forms with prior functions, 138
functions with prior forms, 138, 139
microgenetic analysis of, 134–137
interplay in
between development across practices,
138–141
between form and function, 139–141
John's efforts in
after fractions unit, 136, 137
before fractions unit, 134–136, 135
longitudinal shifts across, 137–138
microgenesis in, 132–134
prior understandings in, 132
social interactions in, 131
Frames, in schema-based thinking, 65
Function
composition of, 277, 278
definition of, 126
Functional fixedness problem, 209, 210

G

General factor g, 9–11
The General Is Missing, SMART Tools for, 238,
239, 240, 241
General memory ability, 17, 18

General unconscious mind, 290
General visual perception, 18–20
Geographical approach to understanding mathe-
matical thinking, 305, 306
Geometry, in Jasper *Woodbury Problem Solving
Series*, 219, 220
German counting sequence, 180
Global enumeration strategy, 127
Grandpa's directions for *The General Is Miss-
ing*, 240, 241
Grandpa's SMART Tool, 231, 232, 233
adaptation of, 232–234
The Great Circle Race, 221–223

H

Hindu-Arabic numerals, 94
Hindu-Arabic system, ascendancy of, 95

I

Imagery, *See* Visual reasoning
Indiana Jones problem, 208–210
visual representations of, 209
Induction hypothesis, analysis of, 59
Inductive level, failures at, 71, 72
Inductive thinking
rational errors and, 58–60
See also Analogical thinking
Information Processing Speed, 20
Initial acquisition, symbolic structure and, 85
Instruction, multiple approaches to, 224
Integration and planning phase, definition of, 42
Intelligence
crystallized, 15–17
fluid, 12–15
mathematical abilities and, 161–162
mathematical thinking and, 9–11
Interactions, social
between participants in practices, 124
mathematical thinking and, 309
in Oksapmin case, 131
Internal critic, role of, 69–71
Interpretation
of = and + signs, 194–197
Interviews
with students/teachers, 220
See also Clinical interviews on fractions
Introduction to Toby, 176–178
Introspection, in Toby's math, 187–189
IQ, mathematical thinking and, 9–11
IRT, *See* Item response theory
Isomorphic structures, definition of, 286–287
Item response curves, 5
Item response theory (IRT), 4–6